P
R
that
HE
& AC
L

JOHN

Most CHARISMA
quantity discoun
fund-raising, and
Book Group, 600
(407) 333-0600.

PRAYERS THAT B
   by John Eckha
Published by Cha
Charisma Media/
600 Rinehart Roa
Lake Mary, Florid
www.charismaho

Book 1

Prayers that Bring Healing

John Eckhardt

CONTENTS

INTRODUCTION

EXPECT TO BE HEALED

And, behold, a woman, which was diseased with an
issue of blood twelve years, came behind him, and
touched the hem of his garment.

—Matthew 9:20, KJV

RECENTLY, THE LORD has impressed me to share with
God's people the importance of putting a demand on the
anointing. The word *demand* means "a seeking or state of being
sought after." It means pressing forward despite obstacles to get
to a place where the anointing is and expecting it to fall on you.
The woman with the issue of blood put a demand on the healing
anointing and received her miracle. She expected that once she
pushed through that crowd, pushed past the disappointment
of years of failed treatments, and pushed against the stigma of
being unclean, she would be healed.

Too often God's people do not receive miracles and healing
because they do not place a demand on the anointing. They don't
push forward because they don't expect that something miraculous will happen.

Sometimes believers let themselves get discouraged. Let me
tell you this: Don't let the devil talk you out of your healing.

1

Put your mind on God. You have to press through discouragement and frustration so that you don't miss your miracle. Don't let anyone stop you. You have to press through—press through traffic, press through the parking lot, press through people coming in the door—but don't get upset. Just stay in the Spirit and get to the place where the anointing is and reach up and get your miracle. Just like the woman who pressed, reached, and was healed by touching Jesus's garment, you too can press, reach up, and grab your healing.

GOD'S HEALING IS AVAILABLE TO ALL!

Healing is available to *all* during the kingdom age. It is amazing that some Christians still believe that God puts sickness on His people. Some may ask, "God, why do You allow this sickness to come upon my body?" They feel, or may have been told by a church leader, that it is the will of God for them to suffer sickness and not be healed. However, that is not biblical. God does not put sickness on *His* people. Jesus died so that we might be healed. I do believe that there may be times when God allows sickness, especially for rebellion or disobedience. But for God's people, we can expect to live in health and to be healed of all our diseases because of what Jesus did on the cross.

When Jesus came, He announced the coming of the kingdom of God. In the kingdom of God, where His presence and glory dwell, no sin or sickness can coexist. We are in the kingdom of God now, but it is not fully manifested. However, it can be established in your life and in your heart. Wherever Jesus preached the message of the kingdom, He healed people. Healing accompanies the kingdom message. This is the kingdom age where you don't have to be sick, broke, or run over by the devil. That is GOOD NEWS! You don't have to be sick, broke, poor, or confused any longer. Sickness and disease are works of the devil, and Jesus came and "disarmed principalities and powers, He made a public spectacle of them, triumphing over them" (Col. 2:15).

Healing comes with the territory. When you are in Christ, you can expect to be healed. Mark 16:17–18 says, "And these signs will follow those who believe: In My name they will cast out demons; they will speak with new tongues; they will take up serpents; and if they drink anything deadly, it will by no means hurt them; they will lay hands on the sick, and they will recover." So not only should you expect to be healed, but you should also know that you are to pass that healing on to all those around you. That is true kingdom living.

JESUS HEALS ALL MANNER OF SICKNESS

Sickness and disease are the worst things that can happen to an individual. Jesus cares about people. He cares about the things that make the abundant life He paid for miserable and unbearable. That is why He had no problem breaking man-made religious laws and stale traditions to see to it that people were healed. He had great compassion on the people who came to Him to be healed. In Matthew 9:36, the Bible says that "when [Jesus] saw the multitudes, He was moved with compassion for them, because they were weary and scattered, like sheep having no shepherd." Jesus cares very deeply that you are hurting and suffering. He doesn't want that for you. That is why He made a way for every sickness, ailment, illness, dysfunction, and disease to be healed and for you to be made whole.

When Jesus walked the earth, there was nothing that Jesus didn't heal. When He left, He sent the Holy Spirit, who works in us to have the full extent of salvation that Jesus paid for on the cross. So just know that what was good for the people then is good for us now, because Jesus is the same yesterday, today, and forever (Heb. 13:8). God does not change (Mal. 3:6). There is no shadow of turning with Him (James 1:17). Because of God's faithfulness we can trust that if He healed then, He will heal today.

Matthew 4:23 says, "Jesus went about all Galilee, teaching in their synagogues, preaching the gospel of the kingdom, and healing *all kinds of sickness* and *all kinds of disease* among the people" (emphasis added). Jesus healed every disease or sickness people came to Him with—no exceptions. There was nothing too hard for Him. So don't let the devil or the doctor tell you that you have something that's incurable. It might be incurable to the doctor, but it's not incurable to Jesus Christ.

> When evening had come, they brought to Him many who were demon-possessed. And He cast out the spirits with a word, and healed all who were sick.
> —Matthew 8:16

From the verse above, it doesn't appear that Jesus told people it wasn't the will of God for them to be healed or that God wanted them to suffer. He never said, "God wants you to carry this for a while to teach you something."

The prophet Isaiah says that Jesus bore our griefs and sorrows

4

(Isa. 53:4). In Matthew 8:17, it says He took our infirmities and sickness. What causes so much grief and so much sorrow? Sickness and disease. When you're not healthy, you can't enjoy the blessings and the fullness of God.

Isaiah 53 is the redemptive chapter. Verse 5 talks about being healed by the stripes of Jesus. The Bible says that Jesus took thirty-nine lashes on His back and body. There are thirty-nine major categories of sickness and disease. Every stripe that Jesus endured took care of a different sickness and disease.

Young's Literal Translation puts Isaiah 53:4 this way: "Surely our sicknesses he hath borne, and our pains—he hath carried them." God doesn't even want people to be in pain. Millions of dollars are spent on pain relief. Toothaches, headaches, neck pain, earaches, joint pain, back pain—Jesus delivers you from pain. Pain is not the will of God for you. Jesus died so you could be healed from both sickness *and* pain.

HOW YOU CAN BE HEALED

God has a lot of ways to heal us based on the redemptive work of Christ. It is something Jesus paid for—something He suffered for. His desire for you to be healed and walk in divine health is the reason He went through so much pain and suffering. He was taking upon Himself the pain and suffering of humanity. Therefore, He has made healing available to you through many avenues. They are:

1. Healing through the laying on of hands (Luke 4:40)

He didn't tell them it wasn't God's will for them to be healed. Everyone who came to Jesus got healed. No exceptions.

2. Healing through deliverance (Matt 8:16)

Demons can be the reason why people are sick in their bodies. They may have a spirit of infirmity. See also Luke 8:2.

3. Healing through breaking curses (Gal. 3:13)

People are plagued with generational demons of infirmity such as diabetes, high blood pressure, certain heart conditions, and more. If there is a generational curse that is activating sickness in your body, know that because Jesus was made a curse for us, you can tell the devil that he will not put this sickness in your body. Tell him, "I don't care if my mother, grandmother, or great-grandmother had this disease; the curse stops here. I break it in the name of Jesus." Begin to rise up and use your authority! Say, "I am not cursed. I am blessed. My body is blessed with healing, in Jesus's name."

4. Healing through anointing oil (Mark 6:13)

Anointing oil represents the Spirit of God and the anointing. The anointing is what drives sickness and disease out of our bodies. The anointing oil breaks yokes of bondage (Isa. 10:27), and sickness is a form of bondage.

5. Healing through faith (Mark 11:23)

For some people, sickness is a mountain. It's always in their way. It seems like something they can't overcome. But Mark

11:23 says that when you have faith and don't doubt, you will speak to a mountain and it will move. So speak to that mountain of sickness; don't climb it! You have to talk to mountains: "Lupus, be removed and cast in the sea!" "Cancer, be removed and cast in the sea!" But don't doubt in your heart. This is why you have to be careful to guard your heart. Don't hang around people who doubt. Keep your heart free from doubt and unbelief. There is going to come a time when you will have to speak to some things. Every time a mountain gets in your way, instead of turning around and running, you need to stand face-to-face and say, "Be thou removed!" Grow up in faith. Open your mouth and talk to sickness. Say, "I command this sickness to leave my body in the name of Jesus." Mark 11:23 says, "…those things which he saith" (kjv). This is not even about prayer. This is just speaking. Some stuff you have to just speak to! "He shall have whatsoever he saith" (kjv).

6. Healing through virtue or touch (Mark 5:29–30)

Jesus's virtue can be in you if you pray and fast. Luke 6:19 says, "The whole multitude sought to touch Him, for power went out from Him and healed them all." Worship is a way to reach out and touch the heart of God. True worshipers know how to get in God's presence. As you reach up in pure worship, you will be like the multitudes in Jesus's day, for "as many as touched it were made perfectly well" (Matt. 14:36). "But the hour cometh, and now is, when the true worshippers shall worship the Father in spirit and in truth: for the Father seeketh such to worship him" (John 4:23, kjv). Is this your hour?

7

7. Healing through the presence of God (Luke 5:17)

"The power of the Lord was present to heal them." Praise and worship is there to invite God's presence in so that people will get healed. It is not a warm-up to the message.

8. Healing through prayer (Matt. 21:22)

"All things" (KJV) includes healing. James 5:16 says that we must confess our faults and pray for one another that we may be healed. Sometimes healing doesn't come until you confess your faults and let somebody pray for you. Sometimes the key is humility.

9. Healing through the gift of healing (1 Cor. 12:9, 28)

When Jesus left the earth, He said that we would do greater works than He did. He also said that He would send a helper to instruct us and guide us in these greater works. The Holy Spirit came among men to indwell us, giving us supernatural ability to carry out the works of Christ. He accomplishes this by endowing us with various gifts that all work together to bring people into relationship with God. One of these gifts is the gift of healing.

> But the manifestation of the Spirit is given to each one for the profit of all: for to one is given the word of wisdom through the Spirit, to another the word of knowledge through the same Spirit, to another faith by the same Spirit, to another gifts of healings by the same Spirit, to another the working of miracles, to another prophecy, to another discerning of spirits, to another different kinds of tongues, to another the

interpretation of tongues. But one and the same Spirit works all these things, distributing to each one individually as He wills.... And God has appointed these in the church: first apostles, second prophets, third teachers, after that miracles, then gifts of healings, helps, administrations, varieties of tongues.

—1 Corinthians 12:7–11, 28

10. Healing through fasting (Isa. 58:8)

When you fast in the way that God leads you, He says that "your light shall break forth like the morning, your healing shall spring forth speedily, and your righteousness shall go before you; the glory of the LORD shall be your rear guard." According to this verse, you will be healed when you fast, but better yet, fasting can serve as preventative medicine. It says, "The LORD shall be your rear guard." In other words, sickness can't sneak up on you. God's got your back. While everyone else is getting swine flu, you're healthy. While there's no cure for the common cold, you sail through cold season with not so much as one symptom, sniffle, or cough.

Then there are just those times when nothing else will do except a sacrifice of going without food, a time to surrender your flesh to the Spirit of God that brings life. Jesus talks about this in Matthew 17:21: "This kind does not go out except by prayer and fasting."

11. Healing through the word (Ps. 107:20)

The Bible says that God "sent His word and healed them, and delivered them from their destructions" (Ps. 107:20). We also know that God's word does not return to Him void. It accomplishes everything for which it was sent (Isa. 55:11). If He spoke healing to you, then you are healed. Jesus said that man would not live by bread alone but by every word that proceeds out of the mouth of God. That is why learning and meditating on the Word of God is so important for your healing. Declare that by the Word of God you "shall not die, but live, and declare the works the LORD" (Ps. 118:17). Read the Word. Confess the Word. Get healing scriptures. Trust God because His word will accomplish in you all that He intends.

12. Healing through cloths/clothing (Acts 19:12)

The healing anointing is transferable. It can be in clothing. It is tangible. We pray over prayer cloths at my church, and people have been healed. Years ago while preaching in Ethiopia, I took my shirt off after ministering and cut it up into small pieces of cloth. We passed them out to all the people there, and we heard so many testimonies of healings. One person set a cloth on fire in his sick mother's home, and the smoke from the cloth healed her. She had been bedridden for years, and she got up out of her bed healed. In other countries they don't have doctors and hospitals as we do in America. They have to believe God. They are desperate for healing. They don't have all the prescription medicines, health insurance, Medicaid, and Medicare. So they come to services believing that if they don't get their healing there, they are not going to make it. They have high expectancy and high faith. God honors faith.

And when the men of that place recognized Him, they sent out into all that surrounding region, brought to Him all who were sick, and begged Him that they might only touch the hem of His garment. And as many as touched it were made perfectly well.

—Matthew 14:35–36

Now God worked unusual miracles by the hands of Paul, so that even handkerchiefs or aprons were brought from his body to the sick, and the diseases left them and the evil spirits went out of them.

—Acts 19:11–12

HEALING DECLARATIONS

By the stripes of Jesus I am healed. He took my sickness; He carried my pain. I believe it is the will of God for me to be healed.

In the name of Jesus, I break every curse of infirmity, sickness, and premature death off of my body.

In the name of Jesus, I break every curse of witchcraft and destruction over my body from both sides of my family.

In the name of Jesus, I speak to every sickness in my body and I command it to leave.

In the name of Jesus, I speak to diabetes, high blood pressure, cancer, heart attack, stroke, and multiple sclerosis. Be removed and cast into the sea.

I speak to heart, kidney, back, lung, and liver problems. Be removed and cast into the sea.

I speak to blood, skeletal, and bone conditions. Be removed and cast into the sea.

I speak to lupus and every other disease. I command you to leave my body.

Every hidden sickness and every hidden disease, I command you to leave my body in the name of Jesus.

Arthritis, pain, and rheumatism, you must go in the name of Jesus.

I command all pain to leave my body in the name of Jesus.

I come against skin conditions in the name of Jesus.

I speak to infections to come out of my body in the name of Jesus.

I speak to breathing conditions, asthma, hay fever, sinusitis, chest congestion, and pneumonia to come out of my body in the name of Jesus.

Joint conditions and pain must go in the name of Jesus.

I come against any conditions and infirmities that affect me as a woman—lupus, fibroid cysts, and tumors in the female organs.

I command those tumors to die! I loose the fire of God to burn them out in the name of Jesus.

I come against nervous conditions, insomnia, and acid reflux. God has not given me the spirit of fear, but of love, power, and a sound mind.

Heart and circulatory conditions, irregular heartbeat, angina, and stroke must leave my body. I am the temple of the Holy Spirit. Be gone in the name of Jesus.

I speak to digestive disorders and allergies to certain food. You have no place in my body. You must go in the name of Jesus.

I break any and all addictions to pain pills in the name of Jesus.

Corroded disks; slipped disks; spine, back, and neck problems—be realigned and put back in place in the name of Jesus.

I release miracles of healing in my body in the name of Jesus.

I believe God for miracles of healing in my life and in my family wherever I go in Jesus's name.

Thank You, Lord, for healing me and delivering me from all sickness and all pain in Jesus's name.

I speak to every condition: you must obey.

I speak to miracles, healings, signs, and wonders. Be released into me in Jesus's name.

I thank You, Lord, that health and healing are coming now.

CASTING OUT AND RENOUNCING THE SPIRIT OF INFIRMITY*

Forgive me, Lord, for allowing any fear, guilt, self-rejection, self-hatred, unforgiveness, bitterness, sin, pride, or rebellion to open the door to any sickness or infirmity. I renounce these things in the name of Jesus.

Jesus carried my sickness and infirmities (Matt. 8:17).

I break, rebuke, and cast out any spirit of cancer that would attempt to establish itself in my lungs, bones, breast, throat, back, spine, liver, kidneys, pancreas, skin, or stomach in the name of Jesus.

I rebuke and cast out all spirits causing diabetes, high blood pressure, low blood pressure, heart attack, stroke, kidney failure, leukemia, blood disease, breathing problems, arthritis, lupus, Alzheimer's, or insomnia in the name of Jesus.

I cast out any spirit of infirmity that came into my life through pride in the name of Jesus.

---

* This section is taken from John Eckhardt, *Prayers That Rout Demons* (Lake Mary, FL: Charisma House, 2008), 91–95.

I cast out any spirit of infirmity that came into my life through trauma or accidents in the name of Jesus.

I cast out any spirit of infirmity that came into my life through rejection in the name of Jesus.

I cast out any spirit of infirmity that came into my life through witchcraft in the name of Jesus.

I rebuke any sickness that would come to eat up my flesh in the name of Jesus (Ps. 27:2).

I break all curses of sickness and disease, and I command all hereditary spirits of sickness to come out (Gal. 3:13).

No sickness or plague will come near my dwelling (Ps. 91:10).

I command every germ or sickness that touches my body to die in the name of Jesus.

I am redeemed from sickness and disease (Gal. 3:13).

I loose myself from every infirmity (Luke 13:12).

CHAPTER 1

HOW MUCH IS IT WORTH?

> And when the unclean spirit had convulsed him
> and cried out with a loud voice, he came out
> of him.... And immediately His fame spread
> throughout all the region around Galilee.... Now
> at evening, when the sun had set, they brought to
> Him all who were sick and those who were demon-
> possessed. *And the whole city was gathered together
> at the door.* Then He healed many who were sick
> with various diseases, and *cast out many demons.*
> —Mark 1:26, 28, 32–34, EMPHASIS ADDED

WHEN PEOPLE GOT word that Jesus was coming to their region, they made way to meet Him. Some traveled far on foot or donkey. Some tarried with Him for days on end with no food. Some who were crippled or maimed were carried into town by friends and family. One person's friends tore up some-body's roof and lowered him into the house Jesus was visiting. Multitudes of people pressed and prodded against each other at the risk of being trampled just to get close to Jesus. Their healing, deliverance, and hunger for the Word were so valuable to them that they put their lives on hold and safety at risk. They knew that if they could just get into Jesus's presence, all their worries would be subsided and their needs met.

How much is your healing worth to you? Are you willing to travel long distances, go without food, brave large crowds, and do whatever it takes to get to the place where the anointing is active and effective?

People came to hear Jesus because He created a demand by setting people free. When people hear of miracles, they will gather to hear the Word of God. They will come with expectancy and faith and draw from the anointing of the servant of God. *There is no substitute for miracles.* They will cause a hunger to come into the hearts of people. Hungry hearts will always gather and put a demand on the anointing.

If we want hungry people, we must have miracles. Some churches wonder why their people are so unconcerned and apathetic about serving God. People drag to service. Some pastors will try all kinds of programs to raise the excitement of the people, but there is no substitute for doing it God's way. Where there are miracles, there will be people gathered. Miracles increase the authenticity of our salvation, and people come to value the presence of God more and more. Faith levels rise when miracles happen.

> And straightway many were gathered together, insomuch that there was no room to receive them, no, not so much as about the door: and he preached the word unto them.
>
> —Mark 2:2, KJV

As people gathered to hear the Word, there was not enough room. This was the result of "His fame spread abroad throughout all the region around Galilee." I like ministering in packed houses. When a church is filled up, there is a higher level of expectancy and faith among the people. It shows how much the people in that area value the anointing and how much they desire to be healed. When a church is half empty, it seems to be harder to minister. We need the anointing to build churches—but we also need the anointing to fill them. I have been to churches that seated a thousand and only a hundred showed up.

Some only show up because the pastor tells them to, or they are just in the habit of going to church. Miracles, prophecies, and healing will not flow out of the servant of God to the extent that they will where there is a demand. Of course, a minister can stir up the gifts of God and minister by faith. However, when the faith of the people is high, it is much easier to minister. The giving and receiving of the anointing is a give-and-take relationship. The more you want to receive and the more value it has for you, the more you will demand it and draw from it, and the more the Holy Spirit will flood the minister with the anointing so that all who are touched will be healed.

Jesus could, in His own hometown, do no *mighty* work because of their unbelief. Unbelief hinders the flow of the anointing. Faith releases the flow. Unbelievers will not put a demand on the anointing, but believers will.

The more people hear and are taught about the anointing, the greater will be their capacity to put a demand on it. As a pastor of a local church, I teach the members about different gifts and anointings. When I teach about the gift of healing, this builds their faith for healing. When ministers come to minister at our church, I tell the members about the anointing on the person's life. They then have the responsibility to draw from and put a demand on that anointing by their faith.

You will find that most of the people who received miracles from Jesus either came or were brought to Him. Many beseeched Him.

> And it came to pass, that the father of Publius lay sick of a fever and of a bloody flux: to whom Paul entered in, and prayed, and laid his hands on him, and healed him. So when this was done, others also, which had diseases in the island, came, and were healed: who also honoured us with many honours; and when we departed, they laded us with such things as were necessary.
>
> —Acts 28:8–10, KJV

After the father of Publius was healed, the whole island of Melita came to be healed. That one miracle increased the value of Paul's anointing. It caused the people to do whatever they could to get some of what Paul had. Notice, they honored Paul with many honors. Honoring the servant of God is a key to receiving from the anointing in his or her life. We will talk more about honor in a later chapter. The scripture states that the people came. They came with the sick, expecting to be healed. They put action on their faith and came.

Passive, apathetic saints do not receive from the anointing.

We cannot be passive and expect to receive from these gifts. We must be active with our faith. People have to have a hunger and thirst for the things of the Spirit. Hungry souls will always draw from the anointing.

How much is your healing worth to you? How far will you follow the leading of God to capitalize on all He has for you?

PRAYERS THAT INCREASE HUNGER FOR THE HEALING ANOINTING

O God, let me see You face-to-face so that my life will be preserved (Gen. 32:30–31).

I will follow the instructions of the man of God, so that my body is restored like that of a little child and I will be clean (2 Kings 5:14).

I declare that it is well with my family and me, no matter what it looks like to my natural eyes. I will go and seek out the man of God that he may stretch his anointing over the dead places in our health. He will breathe into us, and we will rise up to new life (2 Kings 4:8–37).

I will follow You, Lord Jesus. I cry out to You, "Son of David, have mercy on me!" I believe that You are able to heal me and restore me. Touch me and let it be to me according to my faith (Matt. 9:27–30).

Son of David, have mercy on me and do not send me away. I have come from a far region crying out to You for healing.

I worship You, O Lord. Help me! I am hungry for even the crumbs that fall from Your table. Let my healing come to me as I desire (Matt. 15:22–28).

Jesus, I come to You in the midst of the multitude. I am hungrier for Your healing than for food. I feel Your compassion for me and know that You will heal me (Matt. 15:30–33).

I will fast according to Your leading. Then I know that my healing will break forth like the morning. My healing will spring forth speedily (Isa. 58:6–8).

I have walked before You, O Lord, in truth and with a loyal heart. I have done what is good in Your sight. I weep bitterly before You. I know You have heard my prayer and have seen my tears. Surely You will heal me (2 Kings 20:3–5).

I humble myself before You, O God. I pray and seek Your face. I turn from my wicked ways. Then I know You will hear from heaven. You will forgive my sin and heal me (2 Chron. 7:14).

Have mercy on me, O Lord, for I am weak. Heal me, for my bones are troubled (Ps. 6:2).

Lord, be merciful to me and heal my soul (Ps. 41:4).

I declare that this is my time to be healed (Eccles. 3:3).

You have seen my ways and will heal me. You will also lead me and restore comforts to my mourners and to me (Isa. 57:18).

Words of praise are on my lips. May peace be unto me, for the Lord will heal me (Isa. 57:19).

Heal me, O Lord, and I will be healed. Save me and I will be saved. You are my praise (Jer. 17:14).

You will restore health to me and heal me of all my wounds (Jer. 30:17).

You will bring health and healing to me. You will heal me and reveal to me the abundance of peace and truth (Jer. 33:6).

You have said, "I will come and heal him" (Matt. 8:7).

The power of the Lord is present to heal me (Luke 5:17).

Let news of Your healing power, O Lord, be like a ripple effect, causing all those near and far to come so that they will be healed (Acts 28:8–10).

Let many gather together so that there be no more room to receive them, that they may hear the preaching of the Word and be healed (Mark 2:2).

I will press against the crowds, fight my way through traffic, and let no one stop me until I get into Your presence. If only I can touch the hem of Your garment, I know I will be made whole (Mark 5:27–28).

I hunger and thirst for Your righteousness, and I know I will be filled (Matt. 5:6).

HEALING by PUTTING AWAY ANGER, BITTERNESS, and UNFORGIVENESS

ANGER

I will cease from anger and put away wrath to stay connected to God. If I wait on Him, I will inherit the earth (Ps. 37:8–9).

My whole body is sick, and my health is broken because of my sins. But I confess my sins and am deeply sorry for what I have done. Do not abandon me, O Lord. Come quickly to help me, O Lord my Savior (Ps. 38:3, 18, 22, NLT).

I will speak soft words, kind words, and words of life to turn wrath and anger away from me. I will not grieve anyone with my words (Prov. 15:1).

I will appease the strife against my health and my family by being slow to anger (Prov. 15:18).

I am better than the mighty because I control my anger. There is more gain in ruling my spirit than conquering a city (Prov. 16:32).

I use discretion to defer my anger; I earn esteem by overlooking wrongs (Prov. 19:11).

I will not sin against my own soul by provoking the King to anger (Prov. 20:2).

I will silence anger with a secret gift (Prov. 21:14).

I declare that anger's reign in my life will come to an end (Prov. 22:8).

I cast out the cruelty and destruction of wrath and anger. They will not flood my emotions any longer (Prov. 27:4).

I will be slow to anger and will keep its clutches from resting in my bosom (Eccles. 7:9).

Let all wrath and anger be put away from me (Eph. 4:31).

I am a new person, having been renewed after the image of Him who created me; therefore, I put off anger (Col. 3:8–10).

I will not discourage my children by provoking them to anger (Col. 3:21).

BITTERNESS

Lord, I give the bitterness of my soul to You. Please look upon my affliction and remember me. I will go in peace because You have granted my petition (1 Sam. 1:10–11, 17).

I will speak openly to You, O Lord, and release all of my bitterness to You (Job 7:11).

I will speak to You, God, in the bitterness of my soul. I will find the root of why my spirit contends with Yours (Job 10:1–2).

I declare that I will not die in the bitterness of my soul, and I will eat with pleasure (Job 21:25).

My heart knows its own bitterness (Prov. 14:10); I release it to You.

I will raise wise children who will cause me no grief or bitterness (Prov. 17:25).

I had great bitterness, but in love You delivered me from the pit of corruption. For You have put all my sins behind Your back (Isa. 38:17).

I was in bitterness and in the heat of my spirit, but the hand of the Lord is strong upon me (Ezek. 3:14).

I repent of my wickedness and pray to God that the thoughts of my heart be forgiven, for I am bound by bitterness and iniquity (Acts 8:21–23).

My mouth is full of cursing and bitterness, but You have shown me a better way and I have been made right in Your sight (Rom. 3:14, 21–22).

I diligently look within myself so that I will not be defiled by any root of bitterness that may spring up (Heb. 12:15).

FORGIVENESS

I will go to my brother and ask that he forgive me of my trespasses against him (Gen. 50:17).

I pray that my brother will forgive me so that when I go before God, He will take this death away from me (Exod. 10:17).

Like Moses, I come to You asking Your forgiveness on behalf of Your people and myself. Thank You, God, that You forgive all those who sin against You, for You have blotted them out of Your book (Exod. 32:32–33).

God, I thank You that when You hear our prayers You also forgive us (1 Kings 8:30).

You have heard from heaven, forgiven my sin, and have delivered me into the land You promised my fathers (1 Kings 8:34).

You have heard from heaven, forgiven my sin, and have taught me the good way in which I should walk (1 Kings 8:36).

You have heard from heaven, forgiven my sin, and will do and give me according to my ways because You know my heart (1 Kings 8:39).

Forgive me of my sins, and have compassion upon me (1 Kings 8:50).

I am called by Your name and have humbled myself before You. I pray and seek Your face and have turned from my wicked ways. Now You will hear from heaven and forgive my sin and heal me (2 Chron. 7:14).

Look upon my affliction and my pain, and forgive all my sins (Ps. 25:18).

You, O Lord, are good and ready to forgive. Your mercy is plentiful to all those who call on You (Ps. 86:5).

The Lord declares that He will forgive my iniquity and remember my sin no more (Jer. 31:34).

O Lord, hear. O Lord, forgive. O Lord, listen and do! For I am called by Your name (Dan. 9:19).

As I forgive others, Lord, I pray that You will forgive me (Matt. 6:12).

I will forgive those who have wronged me, because if I don't, God will not forgive me (Matt. 6:14–15).

You have healed me and said, "Arise and take up your bed," so that I will know that You have the power to forgive sins on Earth (Matt. 9:6).

Like the servant who owed the king ten thousand talents, I too have been forgiven much. Therefore, I will go and forgive all those who have sinned against me so that I will not be given over to the tormentors (Matt. 18:23–35).

I will forgive any person with whom I have ought, so that when I stand praying, my Father in heaven will forgive me also (Mark 11:25).

If I forgive others, I will be forgiven (Luke 6:37).

Forgive me of my sins because I also have forgiven all those whom I felt were indebted to me. Keep me from temptation, and deliver me from evil (Luke 11:4).

If my brother hurts me, I will tell him that he hurt me. Then if he asks for forgiveness, I will forgive him. If he continues to hurt me and asks for forgiveness each time, I will forgive him every time (Luke 17:3–4).

With Jesus, I pray, "Father, forgive them, for they do not know what they do" (Luke 23:34).

I declare that Satan will not get an advantage over me, because I walk in forgiveness just as Christ did. I am not ignorant of the devil's devices (2 Cor. 2:10–11).

I confess my sins before God, and I know that God is faithful and just to forgive me and to cleanse me from all unrighteousness (1 John 1:9).

I confess my faults to my fellow believers, and we pray for one another so that we will be healed, because the earnest prayer of a righteous person has great power and wonderful results (James 5:16).

I have been sent to the Gentiles to open their eyes, turn them from darkness to light, and deliver them from the power of Satan, so that they may receive forgiveness (Acts 26:18).

Through Christ's blood, I have been redeemed and have received forgiveness for my sins and riches according to His grace (Eph. 1:7).

Father God, you have delivered me from the power of darkness and translated me into the kingdom of Your Son in whom I have been redeemed and forgiven of all my sins (Col. 1:13–14).

HEALING THROUGH OBEDIENCE

I will obey the voice of my Father according to all He has commanded me (Gen. 27:8).

I will arise and obey Your voice and flee from my enemies (Gen. 27:43–44).

I have a special treasure in the Lord because I obey His voice and keep His covenant (Exod. 19:5).

I will obey the voice of the angel of the Lord to keep me in the right way and bring me to a place that God Himself has prepared for me (Exod. 23:20).

I will obey the angel of the Lord, for he will not pardon my sin because the name of the Lord is in him (Exod. 23:21).

As I obey the angel of the Lord and do all that God has spoken through him, my enemies will be God's enemies (Exod. 23:22).

I am blessed because I obey the commandments of the Lord (Deut. 11:27).

I will walk after the Lord my God and fear Him, keep His commandments and obey Him. I will serve Him and cleave to Him (Deut. 13:4).

I will obey the voice of the Lord my God and do all of His commandments and statutes that He has commanded me this day (Deut. 27:10).

I will be left in number if I do not obey the voice of the Lord (Deut. 28:62).

I will return to the Lord my God. I will obey His voice according to all He commands me. With all my heart and soul, from generation to generation, my children and I will obey God. Then the Lord will set us free from any captivity of the enemy, and He will have compassion on us (Deut. 30:2–3).

The Lord my God will put curses on all my enemies because I obey His voice and do all that He has commanded me (Deut. 30:7–8).

The Lord my God will make me plenteous in all the work of my hand, in the fruit of my body, and in the fruit of my land. He will rejoice over me because I obey Him and hearken to His voice (Deut. 30:9–10).

I obey the voice of the Lord, for He is my life, and in Him are the length of days (Deut. 30:20).

I will serve the Lord my God, and His voice I will obey (Josh. 24:24).

I will not refuse to obey the voice of the prophet of God (1 Sam. 8:19).

I will fear the Lord, serve Him, and obey His voice. I will not rebel against the commandments of the Lord. The hand of the Lord is with me (1 Sam. 12:14–15).

My obedience to the voice of the Lord is better than any sacrifice (1 Sam. 15:22).

I will not be like the fathers of Israel. I will be humble and submit to obeying the Lord. I will be mindful of the wonders that God does on my behalf, for He is gracious and merciful, ready to pardon, slow to anger, and of great kindness. He has not forsaken me (Neh. 9:16–17).

I will spend my days in prosperity and my years in pleasures. I will not perish and die without knowledge, because I obey and serve the Lord (Job 36:11–12).

As soon as I heard of the Lord, I submitted myself to Him and obeyed (Ps. 18:44).

The ravens shall not pluck out my eye, neither shall the young eagles eat it. I do not mock my Father, neither do I despise to obey my mother (Prov. 30:17).

I will obey Your voice, and You will be my God. I will walk in all the ways that You have commanded me, and it will be well with me (Jer. 7:23).

I will obey the voice of the Lord, and He will give to me the land that He swore to my fathers—a land flowing with milk and honey (Jer. 11:4–5).

PRAYERS THAT BRING HEALING

You have risen early, O God, and have pleaded with me, "Obey My voice" (Jer. 11:7).

Lord, You have said that if I do not obey You, You will pluck me up and destroy me (Jer. 12:17).

If I do not obey You, You will withdraw the good that You have extended to me (Jer. 18:10).

I will amend my ways and my doings. I will obey the voice of the Lord my God, and the Lord will relinquish the evil that He had pronounced against me (Jer. 26:13).

I will obey the voice of the Lord so that it will be well with me and my soul will live (Jer. 38:20).

Whether I like it or not, I will obey the voice of the Lord my God, that it may be well with me (Jer. 42:6, NLT).

Kingdoms and dominions shall be given to me because I obey and serve the Most High (Dan. 7:27).

I have transgressed the law and departed from God by not obeying His voice. Now a curse has been poured on me and the oath that God made to me (Dan. 9:11).

Those who are far off shall come and build the temple of the Lord, because I diligently obey the voice of the Lord my God (Zech. 6:15).

I declare that as the winds and seas obeyed Jesus, the winds and seas that rise up in my life will obey me (Matt. 8:27).

With authority I will command even the unclean spirits and they will obey me (Mark 1:27).

All those who surround me will fear exceedingly, saying to one another, "What kind of person is this that even the wind and the sea obey him?" (Mark 4:41).

With my mustard seed of faith, I will speak to the mulberry tree and command it to be plucked up by the root and planted in the sea, and it will obey me (Luke 17:6).

I obey God rather than man (Acts 5:29).

God has given me the Holy Spirit because I obey Him (Acts 5:32).

I will not be like the fathers of Israel who would not obey but rejected the man of God and turned their hearts back to Egypt (Acts 7:39).

Let me not be like those who obey unrighteousness, indignation, and wrath, for tribulation and anguish is their portion (Rom. 2:8–9).

Let no sin reign in my body that I should obey its lusts (Rom. 6:12).

Whatever I submit myself to obey, I am slave to it, whether it be sin unto death or God unto righteousness (Rom. 6:16).

I cast off the enemy of my soul, who tries to bewitch me that I should not obey the truth. Before my eyes Jesus Christ has been clearly portrayed before me as crucified (Gal. 3:1).

Let me not run well, then find out at the end that someone or something hindered me from obeying the truth (Gal. 5:7).

My children will obey and honor their father and mother so that it will be well with them and that they may live long on the earth (Eph. 6:1–3).

My children obey me in all things because this is well pleasing to the Lord (Col. 3:20).

I will obey those for whom I work, not with eye service or as a man pleaser, but with sincerity of heart, fearing God (Col. 3:22).

I know God and obey the gospel of the Lord Jesus Christ; therefore, I will not be punished with everlasting destruction and banished from the presence of the Lord and the glory of His power (2 Thess. 1:7–9).

If I do not obey the word of the apostles, I will have no company with the people of God and I will be ashamed (2 Thess. 3:14).

Let me be reminded to be subject to rulers and authorities, to obey, to be ready for every good work, to speak evil of no one, to be peaceable and gentle, showing all humility to all men (Titus 3:1–2).

Let me be a son like Christ, who learned obedience by the things He suffered and was made perfect (Heb. 5:8–9).

I will obey those who have rule over me. I will submit myself to them because they watch out for my soul, as those who must give account (Heb. 13:17).

Like we put bridles in the horse's mouth, let me bridle my whole body that it may obey (James 3:2–3).

Let the wife be subject to her own husband so that even if he is not obedient to the Word, he may be won by the conduct of his wife (1 Pet. 3:1).

For the time has come that judgment must begin at the house of God. And if it first begins with us, what will the end be of those who do not obey the gospel of God (1 Pet. 4:17)?

I have received grace and discipleship from Jesus Christ my Lord so that I can be obedient to the faith among the nations for His name (Rom. 1:3–6).

Jesus, I thank You that by Your obedience many have been made righteous (Rom. 5:19).

My obedience has become known to all, but I still must remain wise in what is right and simple concerning evil (Rom. 16:19).

The mystery of the gospel is now made manifest and made known to all nations for the obedience of faith (Rom. 16:26).

The man of God has greater affection for me because he remembers my obedience (2 Cor. 7:15).

I cast down imaginations and every high thing that exalts itself against the knowledge of God, and I bring into captivity every thought to the obedience of Christ (2 Cor. 10:5).

I punish all disobedience when my obedience is fulfilled (2 Cor. 10:6).

I have been elected according to the foreknowledge of God the Father and sanctified with His Spirit for obedience, and have been sprinkled with the blood of Jesus Christ (1 Pet. 1:2).

HEALING THROUGH WISDOM, KNOWLEDGE, AND UNDERSTANDING

I have been filled with the spirit of wisdom (Exod. 28:3).

I am filled with the Spirit of God, in wisdom, understanding, knowledge, and all manner of workmanship to design artistic works (Exod. 31:3–4).

I have been filled with wisdom of heart to do all manner of work (Exod. 35:35).

I have been brought to the sanctuary of the Lord with other wise-hearted men, for the Lord has put wisdom and understanding to know how to do all manner of work for the service of the sanctuary according to all the Lord has commanded (Exod. 36:1).

I will be careful to observe the statutes of the Lord, for they are my wisdom and understanding in the sight of the nations, who will hear them and say, "Surely you are wise and understanding," for who is the person that God is so near that I may call upon Him for any reason? (Deut. 4:6–7).

Like Joshua the son of Nun, I am full of the spirit of wisdom (Deut. 34:9).

I am wise, according to the wisdom of the angel of the Lord, to know all the things that are in the earth (2 Sam. 14:20).

The wisdom of God is in me to administer justice (1 Kings 3:28).

Like Solomon, God has given me wisdom, exceedingly great understanding, and a heart as large as the sand on the seashore (1 Kings 4:29).

My wisdom excels the wisdom of men (1 Kings 4:30).

Because the wisdom of God is in me, people will come to hear my wisdom, even the kings of the earth (1 Kings 4:34).

The Lord has given me the wisdom He had promised to me, as He did with Solomon (1 Kings 5:12).

Because of the wisdom of God upon my life, people will come

from all around to see the true report of my acts and wisdom and prosperity. People who work with me are happy and will stand before me continually to hear the wisdom of God (1 Kings 10:6–8).

Because of the wisdom of God upon my life, my riches and wisdom will exceed all the kings of the earth. People will seek out my wisdom, which God has put in my heart (1 Kings 10:23–24).

Only the Lord gives me wisdom and understanding that I may keep the law of the Lord my God (1 Chron. 22:12).

Give me now wisdom and knowledge that I may go out before Your people (2 Chron. 1:10).

Because it was in my heart to ask God for wisdom and knowledge that I may serve God's people, and not riches, wealth, honor, the life of my enemies, or long life, wisdom and knowledge have been granted to me (2 Chron. 1:11–12).

After the wisdom of my God that is set in my hand, I will set magistrates and judges for the people of God, so that they may know the laws of God (Ezra 7:25).

May I not die without wisdom (Job 4:21).

May God show me the secrets of wisdom, for they double my prudence (Job 11:6).

Let me be like the aged men, for wisdom, understanding, and strength are with them (Job 12:12–13).

With the Lord are strength and wisdom (Job 12:16).

The price of wisdom is above rubies (Job 28:18).

I fear the Lord, for in that is wisdom, and to depart from evil is understanding (Job 28:28).

Age speaks to me, and the multitude of years teaches me wisdom (Job 32:7).

God, You are mighty in strength and wisdom (Job 36:5).

God, only You can put wisdom in my mind or give understanding to my heart (Job 38:36).

I am made righteous; therefore, my mouth speaks wisdom and my tongue talks of justice (Ps. 37:30).

My mouth will speak of wisdom, and the meditation of my heart will be understanding (Ps. 49:3).

You, O Lord, desire truth in my inward parts, and in the hidden part You will make me know wisdom (Ps. 51:6).

Teach me to number my days so that I may apply my heart to wisdom (Ps. 90:12).

How manifold are Your works, O Lord. In wisdom You have made them all. The earth is full of Your possessions (Ps. 104:24).

I will fear the Lord, for in that is the beginning of wisdom, and all those who do His commandments have good understanding (Ps. 111:10).

I will know wisdom and instruction. I will perceive words of understanding (Prov. 1:2).

I receive the instruction of wisdom, justice, judgment, and equity (Prov. 1:3).

I am wise; therefore, I will hear and increase my learning. I am a person of understanding; therefore, I will attain wise counsel to understand a proverb and its interpretation and the words of the wise and their riddles (Prov. 2:5–6).

I will fear the Lord, for in that is the beginning of knowledge. I will not be a fool who despises wisdom and instruction (Prov. 2:7).

I will turn to the reproof and cries of wisdom. I will not be simpleminded or delight in scorning. I will not be like the fool who hates knowledge, but I will receive wisdom that pours its spirit out upon me. I will receive the words that it has made known to me (Prov. 1:20–23).

I incline my ear to wisdom and apply my heart to understanding (Prov. 2:2).

I cry out for discernment and lift up my voice for understanding. I seek after it as if it were silver or a hidden treasure. Now I know that I will understand the fear of the Lord, and I will find the knowledge of God, because He gives wisdom, knowledge, and understanding out of His mouth (Prov. 2:3–6).

God has stored up wisdom for me, and He shields me because I walk uprightly (Prov. 2:7).

Wisdom has entered my heart, and knowledge is pleasant to my soul. Now discretion preserves me and understanding keeps me, delivering me from the way of evil and from the man who speaks perverse things (Prov. 2:10–12).

I am happy because I have found wisdom and understanding, for it is better than the profits of silver, and its gain than fine gold. Wisdom is more precious than rubies, and nothing I have can be compared to it (Prov. 3:13–15).

Length of days is in the right hand of wisdom, and riches and honor are in the left. The ways of wisdom are pleasant, and all her paths are peace (Prov. 3:16–17).

I lay hold of wisdom, for she is a tree of life to me, and I am happy when I retain her (Prov. 3:18).

By wisdom, the Lord founded the earth, by understanding He established the heavens, and by knowledge the depths are broken up and the clouds drop dew (Prov. 3:19–20).

I will not let sound wisdom or discretion depart from my eyes, for they are life to my soul and grace to my neck. With them,

I walk safely in my way, and my foot does not stumble (Prov. 3:21–23).

I will get wisdom and understanding. I will not forget nor will I turn away from the words of Your mouth. I will not forsake wisdom because she preserves me. I will love her, and she will keep me (Prov. 4:5–6).

Wisdom is the principal thing; therefore, I will get wisdom. And with all my getting, I will get understanding (Prov. 4:7).

I am promoted because I exalt wisdom (Prov. 4:8).

Honor comes to me because I love wisdom (Prov. 4:8).

An ornament of grace and a crown of glory are placed upon my head because I embrace wisdom (Prov. 4:9).

You have taught me in the way of wisdom and have led me in the right paths. When I walk, my steps are not hindered. When I run, I do not stumble (Prov. 4:11–12).

I pay attention to the wisdom of the Lord. I lend my ear to His understanding so that I may preserve discretion and my lips will keep knowledge (Prov. 5:1–2).

I love wisdom like a sister, and insight is a beloved member of my family. They hold me back from immoral behavior and from listening to the flattery of strangers (Prov. 7:4–5, NLT).

Wisdom cries out to me, and understanding lifts up her voice so that I can hear (Prov. 8:1).

I am of a prudent and understanding heart (Prov. 8:5).

I speak of excellent things, and from the opening of my lips are right things. My mouth speaks truth, and wickedness is an abomination to my lips. All the words of my mouth are righteous. There is nothing crooked or perverse in them, because I operate with the spirit of wisdom (Prov. 8:6–8).

The words of wisdom are all plain to me because I have understanding; they are right to me because I have knowledge (Prov. 8:9).

I receive wise instruction and not silver, and knowledge rather than choice gold (Prov. 8:10).

For wisdom is better than rubies, and nothing that I desire can compare to it (Prov. 8:11).

Because I have wisdom I dwell with prudence and find out knowledge and discretion (Prov. 8:12).

Because I have wisdom, counsel and sound wisdom are mine. I am understanding, and I have strength (Prov. 8:14).

I have the beginnings of wisdom because I fear the Lord, and the knowledge of His holiness is understanding (Prov. 9:10).

Wisdom is found in my lips because I have understanding (Prov. 10:13).

I store up knowledge because I am a wise person (Prov. 10:14).

I am not a fool who dies in want of wisdom, but the words from my mouth feed many (Prov. 10:21).

I am person of understanding; therefore, I have wisdom (Prov. 10:23).

My mouth brings forth wisdom (Prov. 10:31).

I am humble, and wisdom is with me (Prov. 11:2).

As a person who has wisdom and understanding, I hold my peace (Prov. 11:12).

Let me be commended according to my wisdom, but I keep my heart from perversion so that I will not be despised (Prov. 12:8).

I till my land and am satisfied with bread. Yet if I follow after frivolity, I will be void of understanding (Prov. 12:11).

Wisdom is with me because I am well advised (Prov. 13:10).

Knowledge and wisdom come easily to me because I have understanding (Prov. 14:6).

I will leave the presence of foolish people when I do not perceive in them the lips of knowledge (Prov. 14:7).

My wisdom is in understanding my way (Prov. 14:8).

Wisdom rests in my heart because I have understanding (Prov. 14:33).

I walk uprightly because I have understanding (Prov. 15:21).

I am instructed of wisdom because I fear the Lord (Prov. 15:33).

It is much better that I have chosen wisdom rather than gold, and understanding rather than silver (Prov. 16:16).

I will not be like the man void of understanding and agree to secure a friend's debt (Prov. 17:18).

I set my sights on wisdom because I have understanding (Prov. 17:24).

I spare my words and have a calm spirit, because I have knowledge and understanding (Prov. 17:27).

I hold my peace and keep my lips shut; even then I appear wise and perceptive (Prov. 17:28).

I will not be like the man who isolates himself and seeks his own desire, raging against wise judgment, for he is a fool who does not delight in understanding but delights in expressing his own heart (Prov. 18:1–2).

The words of my mouth are like life-giving water. In it are

words of true wisdom that are as refreshing as a bubbling brook (Prov. 18:4, NLT).

I am one who gets wisdom because I love my own soul. I will keep understanding so that I will find good (Prov. 19:8).

None of my human wisdom, understanding, or counsel can stand against the Lord (Prov. 21:30).

I will not overwork myself to become rich. I must cease from trying in my own understanding (Prov. 23:4).

I will not speak in the hearing of a fool, because he will despise the wisdom of my words (Prov. 23:9).

I will buy truth, wisdom, instruction, and understanding and will never sell them (Prov. 23:23).

Through wisdom my house is built, and by understanding it is established. By knowledge the rooms will be filled with all precious and pleasant riches (Prov. 24:3–4).

I am strong because I am wise and full of knowledge (Prov. 24:5).

Let me not be like the fool for whom wisdom is too much, but let me be able to speak wisely in the presence of leaders (Prov. 24:7, NLT).

The knowledge of wisdom is my reward, and my expectations for it have been surpassed (Prov. 24:14).

My father rejoices in me because I love wisdom, and I do not keep company with immoral people (Prov. 29:3).

I receive the rod of correction, for it imparts wisdom, but I disgrace my mother if I am left to myself (Prov. 29:15, NIV).

I open my mouth with wisdom, and on my tongue is the law of kindness (Prov. 31:26).

I have given my heart to seek and search out wisdom concerning all things that are done under heaven (Eccles. 1:13).

I see that wisdom excels folly and light excels darkness, for my eyes are in my head but a fool walks around in darkness (Eccles. 2:13–14).

I am good in the sight of the Lord, for He gives me wisdom, knowledge, and joy (Eccles. 2:26).

The wisdom that God gives me is good with an inheritance, and both wisdom and money are a defense, but only wisdom gives me life (Eccles. 7:11–12).

I am stronger than ten mighty men because I have wisdom (Eccles. 7:19).

I am wise and able to analyze and interpret things. Wisdom lights up my face and softens the hardness of my countenance (Eccles. 8:1, NLT).

Day and night I applied my heart to know wisdom and to see the business that is done on the earth. It was then that I beheld all the work of God (Eccles. 8:16–17).

I deliver whole cities with my wisdom, for wisdom is better than strength and weapons of war (Eccles. 9:15–18).

I will not give in to even a little folly else my reputation for wisdom and honor will send forth a foul odor (Eccles. 10:1).

My heart leads me to do right because I am wise (Eccles. 10:2).

Let the wisdom of God bring me success (Eccles. 10:10).

Let me not be like the king of Assyria, thinking that by the strength of my hands I have done it, or by my own wisdom I am prudent (Isa. 10:13). For it is the Lord my God who makes me strong and wise.

The Spirit of the Lord rests upon me, and the spirit of wisdom and understanding, the spirit of counsel and might, the spirit of knowledge, and the fear of the Lord also rest on me because my delight is the fear of the Lord (Isa. 11:2–3).

Wisdom and knowledge are my stability in these times. They are the strength of my salvation, and the fear of the Lord is my treasure (Isa. 33:6).

I will not reject the word of the Lord, for what wisdom is there in that? (Jer. 8:9).

I do not glory in my own wisdom, might, or riches, but I glory in knowing and understanding the Lord. He is the I AM, who exercises loving-kindness, judgment, and righteousness in the earth. In these things I do delight (Jer. 9:23–24).

I thank You, Lord, for You have made the earth by Your power, established the world by Your wisdom, and stretched out the heavens by Your understanding (Jer. 51:15). I know that You will extend Your power, wisdom, and understanding to heal me.

Let it not be to me that I get rich through my own wisdom and understanding. Let my heart not be lifted up because of worldly riches (Ezek. 28:4–5), but let me humbly receive the wisdom and understanding that God gives, so that I will be made whole—body, mind, and spirit.

Let it not be to me that strangers or the most terrible of nations come upon me to draw their swords against the beauty of my wisdom and defile me (Ezek. 28:7), but let me be wrapped in humility and covered by the mighty hand of the only wise God so that all of His promises to heal me will come to pass.

Like Daniel, I am presented before the king as a child with no blemish. I am well favored and gifted in all wisdom, possessing knowledge, and quick to understand (Dan. 1:4).

Like Daniel and his friends, God has given me knowledge and skill in learning and wisdom and understanding in all dreams and visions (Dan. 1:17).

In all matters of wisdom and understanding, I am found ten

times better than all the magicians and astrologers in this realm (Dan. 1:20), for by His might God has empowered me with His Spirit and healed my mind.

Like Daniel, I will answer those who inquire of me with counsel and wisdom (Dan. 2:14).

With Daniel I bless the name of God forever and ever, for wisdom and might are His. He changes the times and seasons; He removes kings and sets them up. He gives wisdom to the wise and knowledge to them who have understanding. He reveals deep and secret things; He knows what is in the darkness, and light dwells with Him (Dan. 2:20–22).

I thank You and praise You, God of my fathers, for You have given me wisdom and might. You have made known to me what I have asked of You (Dan. 2:23).

Secret things have not been revealed to me to show that I am wiser than anyone else, but they have been revealed to benefit the people so that they will understand what is in their own hearts (Dan. 2:30).

Kings and rulers will hear of me and the Spirit of God that dwells in me. They will know that light, understanding, and excellent wisdom are found in me (Dan. 5:14).

I will listen for the voice of the Lord that cries out in my city. I will fear His name because I am wise. I will heed the rod and the One who appointed it (Mic. 6:9, NIV).

Like the queen of the south, I will arise from wherever I am to hear the wisdom of the One greater than Solomon (Matt. 12:42).

Like Jesus, I have been sent out to teach in my own city, and they will ask, "Where did this person get such wisdom and these miraculous powers?" (Matt. 13:54).

Many will wonder where my wisdom and gifts of teaching, healing, and miracles come from (Mark 6:2), and they will know that they come from the Lord God who has healed me.

Like Jesus, I go forth in the spirit and power of Elijah to turn the disobedient to the wisdom of the just (Luke 1:17).

I grow and am strong in spirit, filled with wisdom, and the grace of God is upon me (Luke 2:40).

Like Jesus, I increase in wisdom and stature and in favor with God and man (Luke 2:52).

The fruit of my life shows the wisdom of God that dwells in me (Luke 7:35).

For the Lord will give me a mouth and wisdom, which none of my adversaries will be able to contradict or resist (Luke 21:15).

I am a person of good reputation, full of the Holy Spirit and wisdom (Acts 6:3).

Those who rise up in dispute against me will not be able to resist the wisdom and the Spirit by which I speak (Acts 6:9–10).

Like Joseph, God has delivered me from all my afflictions. He has given me favor and wisdom (Acts 7:10).

Like Moses, I am learned in all wisdom and am mighty in words and deeds (Acts 7:22).

O God, how deep are the riches of Your wisdom and knowledge! Your judgments are unsearchable, and Your ways are past finding out (Rom. 11:33).

I will not be wise according to the flesh, for God has chosen the foolish things of the world to put the wise to shame, the weak things to shame the mighty. No flesh will glory in His presence. I glory in the Lord (1 Cor. 1:26–31).

I do not come with excellent speech or my own wisdom, for I am determined to know nothing else except Jesus Christ and Him crucified (1 Cor. 2:1–2).

My speech and my preaching are not with persuasive words of human wisdom but in demonstration of the Spirit and power, that faith will stand in God and not in the wisdom of men (1 Cor. 2:4–5).

I speak wisdom among those who are mature, but not wisdom of this world or of the princes of this world. I speak the wisdom of God that He ordained before the world for our benefit (1 Cor. 2:6–7).

The things I speak are not in the words of man's wisdom, but those that the Holy Spirit teaches, comparing spiritual things with spiritual (1 Cor. 2:13).

The wisdom I have is not the wisdom of this world, for it is foolishness with God. Therefore, I do not glory in men, because all things are God's (1 Cor. 3:19, 21).

Let it be that I profit from the gifts of the Spirit, for He gives to one the word of wisdom and to another the word of knowledge (1 Cor. 12:8).

I am conducting myself in the world with simplicity and godly sincerity, not with fleshly wisdom but by the grace of God (2 Cor. 1:12).

God has poured out to me all wisdom and prudence, having made known to me the mystery of His will, according to His good pleasure (Eph. 1:8–9).

May God give me the spirit of wisdom and revelation in the knowledge of Him. Let the eyes of my understanding be enlightened so I will know the hope of His calling and the riches of the glory of His inheritance (Eph. 1:17–18).

I preach among the Gentiles the unsearchable riches of Christ with the intention of making known the manifold wisdom of God to the principalities and powers in the heavenly places (Eph. 3:8, 11).

I preach Christ, the hope of all glory, warning every man and teaching them in all wisdom so that they may be presented perfect in Christ Jesus (Col. 1:28).

I will not impose upon myself religious regulations, for in them are the appearance of wisdom, humility, and neglect of the body, but they have no value against the indulgence of the flesh (Col. 2:23).

Let the Word of Christ dwell in me richly in all wisdom, and I will teach and admonish my fellow believers in psalms and hymns and spiritual songs with grace in my heart to the Lord (Col. 3:16).

I will walk in wisdom toward those who are without, redeeming the time (Col. 4:5).

I will ask God for any wisdom that I lack, and He will give it to me liberally (James 1:5).

Let me not be filled with bitter envy and strife in my heart, for this wisdom does not come from above but is earthly, sensual, and demonic (James 3:14–15).

Let me be filled with the wisdom from above, for it is pure, peaceful, gentle, willing to yield, full of mercy and good fruits, and without partiality and hypocrisy (James 3:17).

I say with a loud voice, "Worthy is the Lamb who was slain to receive power, riches, wisdom, strength, honor, glory, and blessing" (Rev. 5:12).

CHAPTER 2

EXERCISING FAITH FOR YOUR HEALING

And He said to her, "Daughter, your faith has made you well. Go in peace, and be healed of your affliction."

—Mark 5:34

FAITH RELEASES THE healing anointing. Unbelief blocks healing. The woman with the issue of blood put a demand on the anointing with her faith. Faith is like a vacuum that draws the anointing. Jesus not only ministered with the anointing, but He also let the people know He was anointed (Luke 4:18). When they heard He was anointed, it was their responsibility to believe and receive. The people of Nazareth did not believe and could not draw from His anointing. (See Mark 6:1–6.) He could do no mighty work in Nazareth because of their unbelief. If they would have believed, they could have drawn from His anointing and been healed.

But the woman with the issue of blood believed. She believed enough to press through the crowds, reach out, and touch the healer Himself. In Luke 8:46, Jesus says, "Somebody touched Me, for I perceived power going out from Me."

Jesus perceived that power ("virtue," KJV) had left Him. The woman drew healing power out of Him with her faith. The word *power* is the Greek word *dunamis*, which means "ability, strength, or might." When you have faith that you will be healed, you draw out the healing power of God. His power is released on your behalf. Thus, the anointing is the power of God.

> When she heard about Jesus, she came behind Him
> in the crowd and touched His garment.
>
> —Mark 5:27

This woman had heard of Jesus. She had heard about the healing anointing that was upon Him. She had heard that a prophet of God was ministering in Israel.

When people hear about the anointing, their faith will increase in this area, and they will then have the knowledge and faith to put a demand on the anointing. We need to know about the apostle's anointing, the prophet's anointing, the evangelist's anointing, the pastor's anointing, and the teacher's anointing. We need to know about the healing anointing and the miracle anointing. We need to know about special anointings given by the Holy Spirit.

Many in this country wonder why miracles occur so much in foreign countries. Many of the ones who attend crusades walk for miles to come to a meeting. Some travel for days. That is putting a demand on the anointing. Healing and miracles happen as a result. In America, many believers will not travel two blocks—and wonder why they don't receive miracles.

> And believers were increasingly added to the Lord, multitudes of both men and women, so that they brought the sick out into the streets and laid them on beds and couches, that at least the shadow of Peter passing by might fall on some of them. Also a multitude gathered from the surrounding cities to Jerusalem, bringing sick people and those who were tormented by unclean spirits, and they were all healed.
>
> —Acts 5:14–16

Here we see people coming "from the surrounding cities to Jerusalem." Where there is a demand, there is a supply. There was enough anointing available to heal *everyone*. These people put a demand on the anointing that flowed from the apostles. When people come to meetings, sometimes from long distances, and put a demand on the gift, they will receive miracles.

> Now it happened on a certain day, as He was teaching, that there were Pharisees and teachers of the law sitting by, who had come out of every town of Galilee, Judea, and Jerusalem. And the power of the Lord was present to heal them.
>
> —Luke 5:17

The word *power* here is *dunamis*, which is the same word translated as *virtue* in Luke 8:46 (KJV). The woman with the issue of blood drew virtue from the body of Jesus with her faith. So we can say that healing virtue was in the house as Jesus taught. When healing virtue (anointing) is present, we can use our faith to put a demand on that anointing. It will then be released for healing.

> Then behold, men brought on a bed a man who was paralyzed, whom they sought to bring in and lay before Him. And when they could not find how they might bring him in, because of the crowd, they went up on the housetop and let him down with his bed through the tiling into the midst before Jesus. When He saw their faith, He said to him, "Man, your sins are forgiven you."
>
> —Luke 5:18–20

Through their faith, they put a demand on the anointing present in that room. As a result, healing virtue was released and the man was healed. There are times when the presence of the Lord is thick like a cloud in a service. When the anointing is present to this degree, all we need to do is use our faith to put a demand upon it. Healing and miracles come as a result of putting a demand on the anointing.

We put a demand on the anointing with our *faith*. The Lord has given us the gift of faith for this purpose. The Lord desires that we use our faith to put a demand (withdrawal) on the gifts of God. Many never use their faith for this purpose.

Congregations that are built up in faith will have a tool they can use to receive from the gifts of God. Faith is a channel through which the anointing flows. Faith is like a light switch that starts the electricity flow. It is like the starter on a car that ignites the power that turns the engine. Faith is the spark that ignites the explosive power of God. It ignites the power gifts of faith, healing, and miracles.

Faith ignites the revelation gifts of word of wisdom, word of knowledge, and discerning of spirits. It ignites the utterance gifts of tongues, interpretation, and prophecy. Faith releases the ministry gifts of apostles, prophets, evangelists, pastors, and teachers.

Faith comes by hearing. The more people hear about the gifts of God, the more faith they will receive to draw from them. I teach on different operations and administrations of the Spirit.

As a pastor, I release people with different anointings and administrations to minister to the people. I teach people concerning these gifts and release them to use their faith to put a demand on these gifts.

It is amazing how profoundly ministers are able to minister in the atmosphere that is created through teaching and releasing. The people use their faith to pull the anointing right out of them, and the flow becomes so great, we have to purposely shut it off until the next service.

DECLARATIONS TO RELEASE FAITH FOR HEALING, PROSPERITY, AND DELIVERANCE

Because of Christ, I am free. Whom the Son sets free is free indeed (John 8:36).

I do not put my trust in man. I do not put my trust in flesh. I put my trust in God (Ps. 56:4).

I live by faith. I walk by faith and not by sight (2 Cor. 5:7).

I am responsible for my decisions and my choices. I make a decision. I choose life. I choose blessings. I choose the Word of God. I choose wisdom.

I thank You, Lord, that I am responsible for making my own way prosperous and having good success.

I have faith to speak to mountains, and they will obey me (Mark 11:23).

My heart will never depart from You. I will always serve God.

Thank You, Lord, for prosperity. I will flourish because I live in the days of the Messiah.

I will have prosperity, and I will have good success because of God's grace in Jesus's name.

INCREASING FAITH FOR YOUR HEALING

I declare that I, like Enoch, have a testimony that I please God through my faith (Heb. 11:5).

Because of my faith, I am pleasing to God, and He will reward me because I seek after Him diligently (Heb. 11:6).

By faith, I will sojourn in the land of promise, as in a strange country, dwelling in tabernacles with Isaac and Jacob, as I am an heir of the same promise (Heb. 11:9).

I will forsake any bondage that seeks to entrap me, looking forward by faith and setting my eyes on Him who is invisible (Heb. 11:27).

I decree and declare that by faith I will walk through my trials on dry ground, and my enemies will be drowned (Heb. 11:29).

I will encircle the immovable walls in my life, and by my faith those walls will fall down (Heb. 11:30).

Like Rahab, I will receive the men of God with peace. I will not perish with those who do not believe (Heb. 11:31).

I will subdue kingdoms, rain down righteousness, obtain promises, and stop the mouths of lions because of my faith (Heb. 11:33).

I declare that I will not only receive a good testimony of faithfulness, but I will also receive all that God has promised (Heb. 11:39–40).

I am established and anointed by God (2 Cor. 1:21).

I activate my mustard seed of faith and say to this mountain of sickness and disease in my life, "Be removed and go to another place." Nothing will be impossible to me (Matt. 17:20).

Because You have anointed me, I have faith and do not doubt that I can speak to any illness, curse it at the root, and cause it to dry up and die, just as You did to the fig tree. I also know that if I tell to this mountain of sickness that is in my way to move and be cast into the sea, it shall be done (Matt. 21:21).

I declare that I have uncommon, great faith in the power of Jesus Christ, faith that cannot be found anywhere else (Matt. 8:10).

Just as Jesus stood in the boat and spoke to the storm, I too can stand in the midst of the storms in my life and rebuke the winds and the waves to command calmness in my life. My faith overrides all my fears (Matt. 8:26).

I will not sink into faithlessness and doubt; I will be upheld by the mighty hand of God (Matt. 14:31).

I pray as Your anointed disciples prayed, "Increase my faith!" (Luke 17:5).

I will not be weak in faith. Like Abraham, I declare that my body is not dead but alive to birth out the gifts and anointing God has set aside for me (Rom. 4:19).

I will not stagger at the promise of God through unbelief, but I will stand strong in the faith, giving glory to God (Rom. 4:20).

My faith increases the more I hear, and hear by the Word of God (Rom. 10:17).

Even though I go through many common trials in this life, God, I declare that You are faithful. You will not allow me to face things beyond what I can stand. You have ordered a way of escape for me, and through Your strength I can bear it (1 Cor. 10:13).

I walk by faith and not by sight (2 Cor. 5:7).

I declare that I feel the substance and see the evidence of the things that I have faith for (Heb. 11:1).

You are Lord of all, and the worlds were framed by Your very words. You spoke into existence unseen things (Heb. 11:3).

I see through the eyes of faith the promise of things afar off. I am persuaded of their reality. I embrace them, knowing that I am a stranger and pilgrim on this earth (Heb. 11:13).

I will stand firm and not waver. I will come boldly before God, asking in faith (James 1:6).

RELEASING LIFE AND WHOLENESS INTO YOUR HEALTH

You have granted me life and favor, and Your care has preserved my spirit (Job 10:12).

My life is brighter than the noonday. Though I was in darkness, I am like the morning (Job 11:17).

My life and breath are in Your hands (Job 12:10).

The Spirit of God has made me, and the Almighty gives me life (Job 33:4).

You keep my life from perishing (Job 33:18).

You will show me the path of life (Ps. 16:11).

You meet me with blessings of goodness. You set a crown of pure gold upon my head. I asked You for my life, and You gave it to me. You gave me length of days forever and ever (Ps. 21:3–4).

Goodness and mercy follow me all the days of my life, and I will dwell in the house of the Lord forever (Ps. 23:6).

The Lord is the strength of my life (Ps. 27:1).

Your favor is for my life (Ps. 30:5).

I desire life and love many days that I may see good. Therefore, I will fear the Lord and keep my tongue from evil and my lips from speaking deceit. I will depart from evil and do good; seek peace and pursue it (Ps. 34:11–14).

Let my enemy, who seeks after my life, be put to shame and brought to dishonor (Ps. 35:4).

Rescue me from destruction and my life from the lions (Ps. 35:17)

You, O Lord, are my fountain of life (Ps. 36:9).

Let the enemy, who seeks to destroy my life, be ashamed and brought to mutual confusion. Let him be driven backward and brought to dishonor (Ps. 40:14).

You will prolong my life and make my years as many generations. I will abide before God forever. Mercy and truth will preserve me (Ps. 61:6–7).

Your loving-kindness is better than life, and my lips will praise You. I will bless You while I live. I will lift up my hands in Your name (Ps. 63:3–4).

My life is preserved from fear of the enemy (Ps. 64:1).

Preserve my life, for I am holy and You are my God. Save me because I trust in You (Ps. 86:2).

I call and You answer me. You are with me in trouble. You will deliver me and honor me. You will satisfy me with long life and show me Your salvation (Ps. 91:15–16).

I will bless the Lord and will not forget His benefits. He has forgiven my sins and healed all my diseases. He has redeemed my life from destruction and crowned me with loving-kindness and tender mercies. God has satisfied me with good things, so that my youth is renewed like the eagle's (Ps. 103:1–5).

I hope in the word You have spoken to me. It is a comfort in my affliction. Your word has given me life (Ps. 119:49–50).

I will not perish in my affliction because I delight in Your law. I will not forget Your precepts, for by them You have given me life (Ps. 119:92–93).

You will restore me and make me live (Isa. 38:16).

You have set before me the way of life and the way of death. I will follow Your way, and I shall live. My life will be my prize (Jer. 21:8–9).

You have given my life to me as a prize in all places, wherever I go (Jer. 45:5).

You have redeemed my life (Lam. 3:58).

You saw me polluted in my own blood and spoke to me and said, "Live!" (Ezek. 16:6).

I will surely live and not die because I walk in the statutes of life without committing iniquity (Ezek. 33:15).

You have brought my life up from the pit (Jon. 2:6).

Your covenant with me is one of life and peace (Mal. 2:5).

I will drink of the water You give me so that I will never thirst again. The water You give me will become in me a fountain of water springing up into everlasting life (John 4:13–14).

I have everlasting life because I have heard Your word and I believe in You. I have passed from death to life (John 5:24).

Jesus, You are the Bread of Life (John 6:48).

I will live forever because I eat of living bread (John 6:51–52).

The Spirit gives me life. His words are spirit and life to me (John 6:63).

Through You, I have life and life more abundantly (John 10:10).

I have eternal life and will not perish. I will not be snatched out of the hand of God (John 10:28–29).

I will live because I believe in Christ Jesus, who is the resurrection and the life (John 11:25–26).

You are the way, the truth, and the life (John 14:6).

I take heart because there will be no loss of life for me (Acts 27:22).

You give life to the dead and call those things that are not as though they are (Rom. 4:17).

Just as Christ was raised from the dead, I walk in the newness of life (Rom. 6:4–5).

The gift of God is eternal life in Christ Jesus my Lord (Rom. 6:23).

I am spiritually minded; therefore I have life and peace (Rom. 8:6).

The Spirit of God, who raised Jesus from the dead, dwells in me. He gives life to my mortal body through His Spirit that dwells in me (Rom. 8:11).

I am the aroma of life leading to life (2 Cor. 2:16).

The Spirit gives me life (2 Cor. 3:6).

The life of Jesus is manifested in my body. Life works in me (2 Cor. 4:10–13).

Christ lives in me. The life I now live I live by faith in the Son of God, who loves me and gave His life for me (Gal. 2:20–21).

I sow to the Spirit, and of the Spirit I reap everlasting life (Gal. 6:8).

My life is hidden with Christ in God (Col. 3:3).

I have a promise of life now and a life that is to come (1 Tim. 4:8).

My Savior, Jesus Christ, has abolished death and brought life and immortality to light through the gospel (2 Tim. 1:10–11).

I have endured temptation; therefore, I am blessed. I am approved and receive a crown of life, which the Lord has promised to those who love Him (James 1:12).

Your divine power has given to me all things that pertain to life and godliness (2 Pet. 1:3).

I have passed from death to life because I love my brothers (1 John 3:14).

I have life because I have the Son (1 John 5:12).

The breath of life from God has entered me (Rev. 11:11)

I freely receive from the fountain of life (Rev. 21:6–7).

I have a right to the tree of life because I do Your commandments (Rev. 22:14).

I take of the water of life freely (Rev. 22:17).

CHAPTER 3

HONORING THOSE WHO COME TO HEAL

> He that receiveth a prophet in the name of a
> prophet shall receive a prophet's reward; and he that
> receiveth a righteous man in the name of a righteous
> man shall receive a righteous man's reward.
> —Matthew 10:41, KJV

HONOR MEANS "VALUE, esteem, precious." To honor a man or woman of God means to value and to esteem them. We must recognize that the anointing is a precious thing. It is priceless. You cannot buy the anointing. It is given by the grace of God. *We must learn to honor ministry gifts*. When you dishonor ministry gifts, you will not be blessed by the anointing that is in them. In other words, if you do not honor the gift of healing, you will not be healed.

> Assuredly, I say to you, no prophet is accepted in
> his own country. But I tell you truly, many widows
> were in Israel in the days of Elijah, when the heaven
> was shut up three years and six months, and there
> was a great famine throughout all the land; but to

> none of them was Elijah sent except to Zarephath, in
> the region of Sidon, to a woman who was a widow.
> And many lepers were in Israel in the time of Elisha
> the prophet, and none of them was cleansed except
> Naaman the Syrian.
>
> —Luke 4:24–27

Elijah and Elisha, two anointed men of God, were in the midst of Israel for years. There were many widows who could have received a miracle through Elijah, but only one did, and she was a Gentile. No other widow put a demand on his anointing. Every leper in Israel could have been healed through Elisha, but no other leper put a demand on his anointing but Naaman. Both Elijah and Elisha had miracle and healing anointings. Those miracles and healings were available to God's people. They were walking reservoirs of the anointing. But no one cast their bucket in to draw from the pool of the anointing. No one used their faith to receive from these men of God except one Gentile woman and Naaman the Syrian.

Jesus said these men were not accepted in their own country. In other words, these men were not *valued* or *esteemed* by Israel. Their ministries were rejected and despised. As a result, many widows perished during the famine, and many lepers died of leprosy. This was not the will of the Lord. It was the will of the Lord for them to receive healing and deliverance.

This kind of rejection was not uncommon to Jesus. As we have mentioned in previous chapters, Jesus was not honored in His own hometown.

Then He went out from there and came to His own country, and His disciples followed Him. And when the Sabbath had come, He began to teach in the synagogue. And many hearing Him were astonished, saying, "Where did this Man get these things? And what wisdom is this which is given to Him, that such mighty works are performed by His hands! Is this not the carpenter, the Son of Mary, and brother of James, Joses, Judas, and Simon? And are not His sisters here with us?" And they were offended at Him. But Jesus said to them, *"A prophet is not without honor except in his own country*, among his own relatives, and in his own house." Now He could do no mighty work there, except that He laid His hands on a few sick people and healed them. And He marveled because of their unbelief.

—Mark 6:1–6, emphasis added

Giving honor to the man of God who is coming to minister is another level of faith in the indwelling power of the Holy Spirit working in us. If you can't show honor, respect, and acceptance to the man of God, you are basically saying, "I don't believe the Holy Spirit is working in you, and I do not receive what you have come to give." You are essentially refusing your healing.

GIVING DOUBLE HONOR

Let the elders that rule well be counted worthy of double honour, especially they who labour in the word and doctrine. For the scripture saith, Thou shalt not muzzle the ox that treadeth out the corn. And, The labourer is worthy of his reward.

—1 Timothy 5:17–18, kjv

Remember, the word *honor* means "value." How much do you value the ministers that God has placed in your midst? Paul is talking here about supporting the ministry. In this case, to *honor* means "to give to and support financially." Congregations who do not bless their ministers financially are dishonoring them. You cannot receive from their anointing if you do not honor them in this way. You will receive more from the anointing, within the men and women of God, if you honor them with your giving.

In Acts 28, the people's giving followed the miraculous healing, but there was unmistakable honor given once they recognized the healing power activated in Paul.

But when Paul had gathered a bundle of sticks and laid them on the fire, a viper came out because of the heat, and fastened on his hand. So when the natives saw the creature hanging from his hand, they said to one another, "No doubt this man is a murderer, whom, though he has escaped the sea, yet justice does not allow to live." But he shook off the creature into the fire and suffered no harm.

—Acts 28:3–5

The men watch Paul for a while longer to see if he would swell up or fall out and die. When neither of these things happened, they were amazed and thought the power he demonstrated was godlike. Not only this, but the leader of this island, Publius, also treated Paul and his companions with great respect and honor. He entertained them and received them courteously for three days. Therefore, there was no hindrance when Publius's father needed to be healed of dysentery. Then the healing just began to trickle down to everyone who was sick on the island.

The giving of honor flowed from the top. The leader of this island knew how to treat guests. He honored them first, and the healings began to flow. But it didn't stop there. The people show additional honor, or double honor, by making sure they lacked nothing for their departure.

> So when this was done, the rest of those on the island who had diseases also came and were healed. They also honored us in many ways; and when we departed, they provided such things as were necessary.
>
> —Acts 28:9–10

It is not hard to see the correlation between giving honor and receiving healing. A gift is given best when it is well received. How much better does a singer or actor perform when their gift is appreciated by the audience? This is why so many Israelites died during the famine. They simply did not appreciate the gifts of Elijah and Elisha.

> And Elisha died, and they buried him. And the bands of the Moabites invaded the land at the coming in of the year. And it came to pass, as they were burying a man, that, behold, they spied a band of men; and they cast the man into the sepulcher of Elisha: and

when the man was let down, and touched the bones
of Elisha, he revived, and stood up on his feet.

—2 Kings 13:20–21, KJV

Elisha had enough anointing in *his bones* to raise a man from
the dead. Imagine the anointing that was available to Israel while
he was alive! Because they did not honor, respect, or receive his
gifts, they did not receive the miracles they needed. Every leper
in Israel needed a miracle. The Lord, in His mercy, saw the need
and provided the man of God with His anointing. It was up to
Israel to put a demand on it. Their needs were not met because
there was no demand. There was no faith. There was no honor.
If they would have honored the prophet of God, they would have
been healed. The anointing was available. It was strong enough.
But there was no demand. As stated earlier, *where there is no
demand, there is no supply.*

RELEASING HONOR TO THE MAN OF GOD

Let my life be precious in the sight of the man of God so that I
will be preserved (2 Kings 1:13–14).

I declare that the man of God in this city is honorable, and all
that he says comes to pass. He will show us the way to go. When
I go to him for direction, I will bless him with valuable gifts
(1 Sam. 9:6–9).

The man of God will pray for me and I will be restored. I will make room in my home for him so that he can be refreshed (1 Kings 13:6–8).

The word of the Lord is in the mouth of the man of God (1 Kings 17:24).

The man of God pursues righteousness, godliness, faith, love, patience, and gentleness. He fights the good fight of faith and lays hold of eternal life (1 Tim. 6:11–13).

The man of God is complete and thoroughly equipped for every good work (2 Tim. 3:17).

I will go everywhere to borrow vessels to accommodate the endless flow of anointing that the man of God has spoken into my household. This anointing will bring prosperity to my children and me (2 Kings 4:1–7).

I will follow the instructions that the man of God gives me, so that my flesh will be restored like that of a little child, and I will be clean (2 Kings 5:14).

The man of God is anointed to minister to the Lord as priest over His people throughout the generations (Exod. 40:15).

The man of God, who is consecrated to minister as priest, will seek God in prayer on my behalf (Lev. 16:32–33).

The Lord will exhalt the horn of His anointed; He will give strength to the man of God (1 Sam. 2:10).

The man of God will be raised up and will do according to what is in the heart and mind of God. God will build him a sure house, and he will walk before God's anointed forever (1 Sam. 2:35).

God forbid that I do anything out of line to the Lord's anointed. I will not stretch my hand out against him, seeing that he is anointed of the Lord (1 Sam. 24:6).

I will not stretch my hand out against the man of God, for he is the Lord's anointed (1 Sam. 24:10–11).

I will not touch the Lord's anointed, and I will do His prophets no harm (1 Chron. 16:22).

Lord God, do not turn away the face of Your anointed; remember the mercies of the man of God (2 Chron. 6:42).

The Lord saves His anointed; He will answer him from His holy heaven with the saving strength of His right hand (Ps. 20:6).

The Lord strengthens the man of God. His is his saving refuge (Ps. 28:8).

God has anointed the man of God with the oil of gladness more than any of his companions (Ps. 45:7).

The Lord has found the man of God. With His holy oil, He has anointed him. With the hand of God, he shall be established. The arm of the Lord will strengthen him. His enemies will not outwit him, neither will the son of wickedness afflict him. The Lord will beat down his foes before his face (Ps. 89:20–23).

The Spirit of the Lord God is upon the man of God, because the Lord has anointed him to preach good tidings to the poor. He has sent him to heal the brokenhearted; to proclaim liberty to the captives and the opening of the prison to those who are bound; to proclaim the acceptable year of the Lord and the day of vengeance of our God; to comfort all who mourn; to console those who mourn in Zion; to give them beauty for ashes, the oil of joy for mourning, and the garment of praise for the spirit of heaviness, that we may be called trees of righteousness, the planting of the Lord, that He may be glorified (Isa. 61:1–3).

God has anointed the man of God with the Holy Spirit and with power. He will go about doing good and healing all who are oppressed by the devil, because God is with him (Acts 10:38–39).

The man of God is established with me in Christ. He has been anointed by God. He is sealed by God and has been given the Holy Spirit in his heart as a guarantee (2 Cor. 1:21–22).

I will rise before the gray headed and honor the presence of an old man (Lev. 19:32).

The man of God honors the Lord; therefore, he will be honored (1 Sam. 2:30).

The man of God will sit in the place of honor among those who are invited (1 Sam. 9:22).

God has crowned the man of God with glory and honor (Ps. 8:5).

The Lord has given the man of God his heart's desire and has not withheld the request of his lips. The Lord has met him with the blessings of goodness and set a crown of pure gold upon his head. He asked God for life, and He gave it to him (Ps. 21:2–4).

The man of God will call upon the Lord, and He will answer him. God will be with him in trouble. He will deliver him and honor him (Ps. 91:15).

Wisdom brings him honor when he embraces her (Prov. 4:8).

The man of God follows righteousness and mercy. He finds life, righteousness, and honor (Prov. 21:21).

The man of God is humble and fears the Lord. He is given riches, honor, and life (Prov. 22:4).

The man of God is humble in spirit; he retains honor (Prov. 29:23).

The man of God will have double honor instead of shame. He will rejoice in his portion instead of being confused. In his land, he will possess double. Everlasting joy will be his (Isa. 61:7).

The man of God honors his Father in heaven. He does not seek his own glory (John 8:49).

Glory, honor, and peace go to the man of God because he works what is good (Rom. 2:10).

Let the elders who rule well be counted worthy of double honor (1 Tim. 5:17).

CHAPTER 4

TOUCHING THE HEM

For she said within herself, If I may but touch his
garment, I shall be whole.

—Matthew 9:21, KJV

THE ROTHERHAM TRANSLATION says, "If only I touch his
mantle." The *mantle* represents the *anointing*. Elisha took
up the mantle that fell from Elijah (2 Kings 2:13). He smote the
waters with Elijah's mantle. When God called Elisha, He used
Elijah to cast His mantle upon him (1 Kings 19:19). This represented the anointing coming upon him to stand in the office of a
prophet. We call this the *prophetic mantle*.

Jesus walked and ministered as a prophet of God. He ministered under a prophetic mantle. This mantle also included
healing and miracles. The woman with the issue of blood pressed
through the crowd to touch His mantle. She was putting a
demand upon His prophetic mantle. As a result, she received a
miracle. There are different mantles given to different people. As
you touch the mantle of a particular office, you will draw virtue
and power from that anointing. I am not referring to touching a
person physically but drawing from them *spiritually*. Faith is the
channel through which you draw. It is the pipeline.

> And when the men of that place had knowledge of
> him, they sent out into all that country round about,
> and brought unto him all that were diseased; and
> besought him that they might only touch the hem
> of his garment: and as many as touched were made
> perfectly whole.
>
> —Matthew 14:35–36, KJV

The Montgomery translation says they "kept begging him." Have you ever had someone continue to beg you? They are demanding something of you. This is how you put a demand on the anointing. To *beseech* means "to beg for urgently or anxiously, to request earnestly, to implore, to make supplication." It means to seek. It is the laying aside of pride. You admit you have a need and beseech someone who has the ability to help you. If you never recognize your need for and utter dependence upon the anointing, you will never put a demand on it.

> And whithersoever he entered, into villages, or cities,
> or country, they laid the sick in the streets, and
> besought him that they might touch if it were but the
> border of his garment: and as many as touched him
> were made whole.
>
> —Mark 6:56, KJV

Everywhere Jesus went people were putting a demand on the anointing. They besought Him to touch His garment. They drew the healing and miracles out of Him. You may say this happened in every city because it was a sovereign move of God. You may think the people had nothing to do with it. But remember, it didn't happen in His hometown of Nazareth. They did not beseech to touch Him in Nazareth. These miracles didn't occur in Nazareth because the people didn't put a demand on the anointing. In other villages and cities, they did, and they were made whole.

If you want to be healed you need to reach out and touch the hem of Jesus's garment. You need to beseech the anointing that He has left on the men and women of God in your life. Pull on their anointings, and demand your healing miracle. Let them pray for you and lay hands on you so that you can be healed.

As I mentioned in the introduction, healing can be transferrable through the anointed cloths or clothes coming from the man or woman of God. The healing anointing is tangible. We used anointed and prayed-over cloths to give to people at my church. We have received many testimonies of healing resulting from this. Paul confirms this phenomenon in Acts 19:11–13. By touching the handkerchiefs and aprons from Paul's body, sick people received miraculous healings. The Bible says that the diseases left these people and demons went out of them. This requires a very high level of faith and an increased demand on the gifts of God's anointed ones. You cannot hesitate to have high expectancy to receive healing by touching a garment. Just like the woman with the issue of blood had, you must *draw* from that touch.

GETTING CLOSE TO THE HEALER THROUGH HIS WORD

And it came to pass, that, as the people pressed upon him to hear the word of God, he stood by the lake of

> Gennesaret…And he entered into one of the ships, which was Simon's, and prayed him that he would thrust out a little from the land. And he sat down, and taught the people out of the ship.
>
> —Luke 5:1, 3, KJV

Faith comes by hearing (Rom. 10:17). That is why we need to *hear* about the healing anointing. We need teaching concerning that anointing. To put a demand on the teaching gift, you must have a desire for knowledge. The New English translation says the people crowded upon Him to listen to the Word of God. These people were putting a demand upon His teaching gift. There was such a demand that He needed to borrow Simon's ship to teach the crowds. How often do people crowd into buildings to hear teaching? Only those who are hungry for the Word will press to hear. Their hunger for the things of God will cause them to put a demand on the gifts of God.

Jesus always responded to people who put a demand on Him through their hunger for the things of God. He never turned them away empty. As I travel, ministering the Word of God, I discern different levels of spiritual hunger in different areas. Some people will press to hear the Word. They will draw the revelation right out of you. You will teach in a higher level of anointing because of the hunger of the people.

I don't want to teach people who are not hungry for the Word. In some places, people will just sit there and look at you. They really don't want anything from God. There is no hunger, no press. If they had to come early to get a seat, you would not see them. The spiritual principle we are sharing in this book is what

I call the *law of supply and demand*. Where there is no demand, there is no supply. Apathetic, passive Christians don't receive much from the gifts of God.

> On the next Sabbath almost the whole city came together to hear the word of God.
>
> —Acts 13:44

Not only can individuals put a demand on the anointing, but entire cities can as well.

This verse excites me because of the possibility of entire cities desiring to hear the Word of God. I believe in these last days the Lord will cause a hunger in cities to hear the Word. When ministry gifts come into the city, people will gather and put a demand on those gifts. This has happened somewhat in the past, but it will happen to an even greater extent in these days, as the Lord pours out His Spirit upon all flesh.

As Paul and Barnabas ministered in Antioch of Pisidia, the Gentiles were the ones who put a demand on their apostolic gifts. The Jews were beginning to harden their hearts. They did not desire to hear the good news of salvation. Paul and Barnabas began to turn to the Gentiles. Ministry gifts will always be wherever the demand is. The Gentiles were the ones who were hungry. The gifts of God were released on their behalf. As a result, they received salvation, healing, and deliverance.

> And the word of the Lord was published throughout all the region.
>
> —Acts 13:49, KJV

As exciting as cities coming together to hear the Word may seem, it is even more exciting for *regions* to be charged by the power of God! Because there was a hunger in the city, and the gifts of God were released as a result, the entire *region* was affected. Mass healings will take place across large geographic areas. I am not satisfied with only my city being taken for God, but I want to affect my region! When there is a hunger for the Word of God in a city, it will affect the entire region, and the anointing for teaching, miracles, and healing can be released. Once a demand is put on the anointing, that anointing will be released on behalf of entire cities and regions.

PRAYERS THAT BRING HEALING BY TOUCH

The Lord will deliver me in six troubles, and in seven, no evil will touch me (Job 5:19).

I am confident deep within myself that if I will but touch the hem of Your garment, I will be made whole (Matt. 9:21).

As the knowledge of who You are spreads, people will send out for the sick and diseased in all the surrounding regions so that they too can touch the hem of Your garment (Matt. 14:35–36).

I press in to touch You, Jesus, and You will heal me of my plague (Mark 3:10).

I will reach for Your clothes and touch them, and I shall be made whole (Mark 5:28).

As Your Spirit goes forth in the villages, cities, and countries, the sick will be laid before You. They will beg to touch even the border of Your garment, and as they touch You, they will be made whole (Mark 6:56).

The blind will come before You, begging to touch You. You will touch them and their sight will be restored. They will see things clearly (Mark 8:22–25).

Multitudes will seek to touch You, and virtue will be transferred out of You, and all of them will be healed (Luke 6:19).

Just like Elisha, even the bones of the man or woman of God You have anointed will be filled with life and healing so much so that, by their touch, the dead will be revived and stand up on their feet (2 Kings 13:21).

Let Your seraphims fly unto me, and touch me with a live coal from Your altar so that all my sin, sickness, and iniquity be taken away (Isa. 6:6–7).

Lord, put forth Your hand to touch me. Put Your life-giving and healing words in my mouth (Jer. 1:9).

You have sent Your angels, and they touched me and strengthened me (Dan. 10:18).

You have put forth Your hand and touched me. I know that I am immediately made clean (Matt. 8:2–3).

The man of God has touched me. My sickness has left me. Now I can arise and minister to those around me (Matt. 8:15).

You touched my eyes, O Lord, and according to my faith, they have been opened (Matt. 9:29–30).

You came and touched me. I will arise and not be afraid. I will lift up my eyes to see no man except Jesus (Matt. 17:7–8).

You had compassion on me and touched my eyes. Immediately I received my sight, and I will follow You (Matt. 20:34).

You took me aside from the multitude and touched my ears and my tongue. And straightway, my ears have been opened and my tongue has been loosed (Mark 7:33–35).

You will come and touch my lifeless body. You have commanded me to arise. Immediately, I will sit up and begin to speak (Luke 7:14–15).

Yes, I have suffered this far, but You will touch my ears and will heal me (Luke 22:51).

Everyone You lay Your hands on is healed (Luke 4:40).

Lay Your hands on the sick and heal them (Mark 6:5).

You lay Your hands on the sick and deformed and immediately they are made straight, and they will glorify God (Luke 13:13).

Like the apostle Paul, may the man of God come and lay hands on me and heal me (Acts 28:8).

PRAYING THE WORD FOR HEALING

The healing of the Lord will spring forth speedily (Isa. 58:8).

I cried out to You, God, and You healed me. You kept me alive (Ps. 30:2–3).

By Your stripes, I am healed (Isa. 53:5).

Speak a word, Lord, and heal me this very hour (Matt. 8:8, 13).

I declare that I am in good health; I am alive (Gen. 43:28).

The fear of the Lord is health to my body and strength to my bones (Prov. 3:7–8).

I will give attention to the words of God. I will incline my ear to His sayings. They will not depart from my eyes. I will keep them in the midst of my heart because they are life to me and health to my body (Prov. 4:20–22).

I will speak with wisdom and promote health (Prov. 12:18).

I will receive and speak only pleasant words. They are like a honeycomb, sweetness to my soul and health to my bones (Prov. 16:24).

I declare that I prosper in all things and am in good health, just as my soul prospers (3 John 2–3).

As heaven and Earth are my witnesses, I choose life so that both my descendants and I will live (Deut. 30:19).

I declare, O Lord, that You are my life and the length of my days. I love You. I choose to obey You. I cling to You (Deut. 30:20).

I declare, O Lord, that You are the restorer of my life and the nourisher of my old age (Ruth 4:15).

You have redeemed my life from all adversity (2 Sam. 4:9–10).

You do not take away life but devise ways so that I will be drawn in close to You (2 Sam. 14:14–15).

I offer sacrifices of sweet savor unto God and pray for my life and the lives of my children (Ezra 6:10).

If it pleases You and as I have found favor in Your sight, let my life be given to me (Esther 7:3).

I gather together with other believers and stand for my life. I destroy, slay, and cause to perish all the powers that would rise up to assault me. I take the spoil of them for prey (Esther 8:11).

CHAPTER 5

DRAWING FROM THE WELL

Jesus therefore, being wearied from His journey, sat thus by the well. It was about the sixth hour. A woman of Samaria came to draw water.

John 4:6–7

THE HEALING ANOINTING that accompanies the ministry gifts is like a well. The Samaritan woman who came to the well that day may not have appeared to have any physical issues, but Jesus knew she needed healing. Her need to draw from the spiritual well that Jesus had within Him was being played out in the natural by her physical need to draw water from Jacob's well.

Jesus was fully operational in the Spirit because the Word of God dwelled in Him—He was the Word (John 1:1–2). Therefore, His level of discernment was able to pierce through the natural and see this woman's spiritual need. (See Hebrews 4:12.) But it didn't stop there. It wasn't just His recognition of her need that got her need met, but it was also about how she began to pull on the well of anointing that Jesus had within Him. She began to inquire, "How is it that You, being a Jew, ask a drink from me, a Samaritan woman?...Sir, You have nothing to draw with, and the well is deep. Where then do You get that living water? Are You greater than our father Jacob, who gave us the well, and drank from it himself, as well as his sons and his livestock?" (John 4:9, 11–12). The more she pressed in and the more she surrendered to the longing for wholeness in her heart, the deeper she dug into the well of the Spirit. At one point she just came right out and demanded, "Sir, give me this water, that I may not thirst, nor come here to draw" (v. 15).

This woman put a demand on the Spirit that will never be refused. The Bible says in Revelation 21:6 that God will freely give the water of the fountain of life to anyone who thirsts. (See also Revelation 22:17.) Are you thirsty for healing? Will you dig deep into the well of the Spirit for your healing?

Just like this woman, you can put a demand upon the healing anointing and draw from it. There is a never-ending supply of the Spirit available to every believer.

> For I know that this shall turn to my salvation through your prayer, and the supply of the Spirit of Jesus Christ.
>
> —Philippians 1:19, KJV

When I look at ministry gifts of the Spirit, I see a *living reservoir*—or *well*. In that well is a supply of the anointing. The Lord has deposited His anointing in individuals for the perfecting of the saints. It is our responsibility to draw from that supply. Just like Jesus at the well, men and women of God have been empowered through the Holy Spirit with miracles, revelation, and deliverance for you in the well. If you put a demand on the anointing in that well, miracles will flow out of them to you.

> And the whole multitude sought to touch him: for there went virtue out of him, and healed them all.
> —Luke 6:19, KJV

These people were putting a demand on the anointing. Virtue came out of Jesus because the people drew from the well of His anointing. They drew it out by seeking to touch Him. You can literally pull the anointing out of ministry gifts by your faith, by fasting and prayer, by worshiping in Spirit and in truth, by walking in obedience to the Word of God, by staying in the presence of God, and by honoring the man or woman of God. If these people would have just sat back and waited for Jesus to put it on them, they probably would not have received anything. Many times believers just sit back and wait for the man or woman of God to do something. He has placed the well in our midst, and we have to draw from it.

SUPPLY AND DEMAND

The Lord spoke to my heart the fact that there is always a supply when there is a demand. The drug problems in our cities would not exist if there were no demand for drugs. Because there is a demand for drugs, there is a supply. It is the same with the anointing. If there is no demand, there will be no supply. Hungry saints who put a demand on ministry gifts will always have a supply of the anointing. I have ministered in churches where there was such a hunger and thirst for the anointing until they literally pulled the power right out of me. I have ministered in other places where there was no demand, and as a result nothing happened. The people just sat back and waited for something to happen, and nothing did. There was no hunger or expectancy for revelation, utterances, or miracles.

As a pastor, I teach the members of our local assembly to draw from the ministry gifts that minister in our services. I tell them to put a demand on the anointing in the apostles, prophets, evangelists, pastors, and teachers. I teach them that these gifts from God have a supply in them, and it is their responsibility to draw from that supply.

Many ministers who have ministered at our local church are shocked by the anointing in which they flow. This happens because I teach the people to pull it out of them. Ministers love to minister in that type of atmosphere. The flow is much easier because the people are pulling *from* you instead of blocking you.

> And behold, two blind men sitting by the road, when they heard that Jesus was passing by, cried out, saying, "Have mercy on us, O Lord, Son of David!" Then the multitude warned them that they should be quiet; but they cried out all the more, saying, "Have mercy on us, O Lord, Son of David!"
>
> —Matthew 20:30–31

These men put a *demand* on Jesus. They cried out even when the multitude was rebuking them, telling them to be silent. They had to press past the opposition of the crowd to receive their miracle. If they had remained silent, they would not have received a miracle. They had to put a demand on the anointing. Jesus was passing by. If they did not put a demand on His anointing, He would have passed *them* by. It is like drawing money from a bank. You must go to the teller with a withdrawal slip and make a demand on the account. That is why they are called demand deposit accounts, or DDAs. If you never make a demand on the account, you will never withdraw anything from the account. A church should never allow a ministry gift to come in their midst and minister without putting a demand on the anointing.

> Then He went out from there and came to His own country, and His disciples followed Him. And when the Sabbath had come, He began to teach in the synagogue. And many hearing Him were astonished, saying, "Where did this Man get these things? And what wisdom is this which is given to Him, that such mighty works are performed by His hands! Is this not the carpenter, the Son of Mary, and brother of James, Joses, Judas, and Simon? And are not His sisters here with us?" And they were offended at Him. But Jesus said to them, "A prophet is not without honor except in his own country, among his own relatives, and in his own house." Now He could do no mighty work there, except that He laid His hands on a few sick people and healed them. And He marveled because of their unbelief. Then He went about the villages in a circuit, teaching.
>
> —Mark 6:1–6

There, right in their midst, was a supply—*a well of the anointing*. In that well was salvation, healing, deliverance, and miracles. Jesus was a walking well of anointing. They had the chance to put a demand on it and draw from it, but they did not because of *unbelief*. They did not see Him as a well of the anointing but as a carpenter, "the Son of Mary, and brother of James, Joses, Judas, and Simon." They looked at Him and judged Him in the natural. However, if they had looked at Him in the spirit, they would have seen Him as a well or a reservoir of the anointing. They would have drawn out of Him miracles and healing *by faith*.

We must begin to view ministry gifts in the spirit. You must see your pastor as a walking well of the anointing. You must put a demand upon the anointing and draw the miracles out of Him. There is nothing wrong with ministers telling people what they are anointed for. If you have a healing anointing, tell the people. Give them a chance to draw from that well of anointing. If you have a prophetic anointing, tell the people. Let them draw the prophetic words out of you. If you have a teaching anointing, tell the people. Let them draw the knowledge, revelation, and healing out of you.

DRAW FROM ANOINTED VESSELS

And there were set there six waterpots of stone, after the manner of the purifying of the Jews, containing two or three firkins apiece. Jesus saith unto them, Fill the waterpots with water. And they filled them up to the brim. And he saith unto them, Draw out now, and

bear unto the governor of the feast. And they bare it.
When the ruler of the feast had tasted the water that
was made wine, and knew not whence it was: (but the
servants which drew the water knew;) the governor of
the feast called the bridegroom, and saith unto him,
Every man at the beginning doth set forth good wine;
and when men have well drunk, then that which is
worse: but thou hast kept the good wine until now.

—John 2:6–10, KJV

The story of the first miracle of Jesus at Cana of Galilee is
prophetic. The six water pots of stone represent the earthen
vessels that the Lord uses (2 Cor. 4:7). Six is the number of man.
Man was created on the sixth day. Jesus commanded the water
pots be filled with water. Water represents the Word (Eph. 5:26).
Servants of God need to be filled with the Word of God. Apostles,
prophets, evangelists, pastors, and teachers are to be filled with
the Word. The Lord will fill you with the Word so that others can
draw from you.

Jesus then told them to draw out of the water pots. As they
drew out, the water was turned into wine. Wine represents the
Holy Spirit. It represents the anointing of God. We are to draw
out of the ministry gifts. *Draw* is the Greek word *antleo*, meaning
to dip water with a bucket or pitcher.

We are to use our buckets and draw out of the earthen vessels
that God has filled with His Word. When I get around anointed
ministry gifts, my bucket is out and I am ready to draw. When
the Lord's vessels come into the local church, we are to draw
from them. We draw because we have needs. We draw because

we need to be healed. The mother of Jesus said to Him, "They have no wine" (John 2:3). There was a need at the marriage feast for wine. When there is a need for the anointing and flow of the Spirit, we must draw out of the earthen vessels the Lord has given us. We must use our faith to draw out the wine when there is a need.

Ministry gifts must spend time filling up on the Word. We must allow the Lord to fill our vessels up with the water of the Word. As we minister, we must allow the saints of God to draw from us. There are so many with needs. They need the wine of the Holy Ghost that will flow from us.

Truly, whether filling up or drawing from the Holy Ghost, we need the power of God flowing in our lives. You are reading this because you have a need. You need the power of God to flow healing into your life. It is my sincere hope and prayer that this revelation will cause you to draw your healing from the Spirit by way of the earthen vessels He has anointed and that you will drink from the water of life God gives so freely so that you can begin to receive in abundance the fullness of God in your life.

DRAWING HEALTH AND LIFE FROM THE WELL OF THE SPIRIT

You have opened my eyes to see the well of the water of Your Spirit. I will fill my cup and drink (Gen. 21:19).

I stand by the well of water from Your Spirit, and what I declare shall come to pass (Gen. 24:43).

I will dig deep into the well of Your Spirit, for you have made room for me and I will be fruitful in the land (Gen. 26:22).

I dig deep in the valley of my circumstances; there I will find a well of springing water (Gen. 26:19).

I will dig and dig until I find the water of Your Spirit (Gen. 26:32).

I am fruitful by the well of Your Spirit. I abide in strength, and the arms of my hands are made strong by the hands of the almighty God (Gen. 49:22–24).

My spirit encamps in Elim by the twelve wells of water and seventy palm trees, for You have healed me and none of the diseases of Egypt will come upon me (Exod. 15:26–27).

With understanding and wisdom, I draw out the counsel that You have placed in the deep well of my heart (Prov. 20:5), and I will find healing.

With joy I draw healing water out of the wells of salvation (Isa. 12:3).

I dug into the well of Your Spirit and drank Your water (Isa. 37:25).

Give me living water, O God, so that I will not thirst anymore or go to earthly wells to draw water (John 4:15).

I drink freely from the water that You have given me. It is a well of water that springs up into everlasting life (John 4:14).

I speak to the well of the Lord deep within me, "Spring up, O well!" I will dig this well according to Your direction (Num. 21:16–18).

Like David, I long to drink of the water of the well of Bethlehem (2 Sam. 23:15).

Let Your rain fall and fill the pools of the well that I have made in my spirit (Ps. 84:6).

My mouth is a well of life (Prov. 10:11). I speak life, health, and prosperity to my mind, body, and spirit.

A fountain of gardens, a well of living waters, and streams from Lebanon dwell within me (Song of Sol. 4:15).

HEALING AND BLESSING FROM THE WATER OF LIFE

I thirst; therefore, I come to You and drink living water (John 7:37).

My belly overflows with rivers of living water because I believe in You (John 7:38).

I come to You with weeping, and You lead me to walk by the rivers of water where I will not stumble (Jer. 31:9).

I am like a tree planted by the rivers of water. I bring forth fruit in my season. My leaves do not wither. Everything I do prospers (Ps. 1:3).

I am like a tree planted by the waters. My roots spread out by the waters. When the heat and drought come, my leaves will stay green and I will not cease to bear fruit (Jer. 17:8).

I have been planted in good soil and by great waters. I am a splendid vine that brings forth branches and bears fruit (Ezek. 17:8).

My mother is like a vine planted by the waters. She is fruitful and full of branches because of the abundant water (Ezek. 19:10).

You have shown me a pure river of water of life, clear as crystal, proceeding out of the throne of God and of the Lamb. In the midst of this river was the tree of life, whose leaves were for the healing of nations—and there shall be no more curse of sickness upon my life (Rev. 22:1–3).

I drink of the water of life freely (Rev. 22:17).

The Alpha and Omega, the beginning and the end, has given to me the fountain of the water of life freely, and I drink (Rev. 21:6).

I serve the Lord my God. He has blessed my bread and my water and has taken away sickness from the midst of me (Exod. 23:25).

Like Moses, I bring my family before the Lord and wash them with the water of the Word (Lev. 8:6).

I will bathe myself in the running water of the Spirit to cleanse myself of any issue—physical, spiritual, and emotional—and I shall be clean (Lev. 15:13).

I will speak to the rock of my salvation, and He shall bring forth His water so that I can drink (Num. 20:8).

I am like groves of palms, like fruitful gardens planted by the riverside, like aloes planted by the Lord, like cedars beside the waters. He will pour out His Spirit over me like gushing buckets of water, and my seed will be supplied with all they need (Num. 24:5–7).

I will be purified with the water of separation (Num. 31:23).

I am like the tree whose roots are spread out by the waters, whose branches are refreshed with the dew. New honors are constantly bestowed on me, and my strength is continually renewed (Job 29:19–20).

God draws the water up into small drops and causes it to rain on me so that I am blessed (Job 36:27–28).

As the deer pants after the water brooks, so my soul pants after You, O God (Ps. 42:1).

My soul thirsts for God, for the living God (Ps. 42:2).

My soul thirsts for God, and my flesh longs after Him in a dry and thirsty land where no water is (Ps. 63:1).

You send Your water that flows out of the abundant river of God. Your water never runs dry, and it brings forth a bountiful harvest (Ps. 65:9–10).

The Spirit of God shall come down upon me like rain upon the mowed grass, like showers that water the earth (Ps. 72:6).

You have turned the desert of my life into pools of water, and the dry ground into water springs. You make me dwell in fertile places. You bless me and multiply my seed greatly (Ps. 107:35–38).

My heart is like the rivers of water in God's hands (Prov. 21:1).

You refresh me like the rivers of water in a dry place. You shelter me like the cool shadow of a great rock (Isa. 32:2).

The dry parched ground in my life will become a pool, and the thirsty land springs of living water (Isa. 35:7).

The Lord will hear me, for I am poor in health and needy and in search of living water. He will not forsake me. He will open rivers in high places and fountains in the midst of valleys. He will make the wilderness a pool of water and the dry land springs of water (Isa. 41:17–18).

You have poured your water upon me because I was thirsty. You flooded my dry ground. You have poured Your Spirit and

Your blessing over my offspring. They will spring up like the grass and like willows by the watercourse (Isa. 44:3–4).

I will not hunger or thirst; neither shall I be overtaken by the heat of the day, because You have mercy on me and will lead me by the springs of water (Isa. 49:10).

The Lord will guide me continually and will satisfy my soul in drought. He will keep me strong and healthy. I will be like a watered garden, like an ever-flowing spring (Isa. 58:11).

You have washed me with water. You have washed off my blood and anointed me with oil (Ezek. 16:9).

You will sprinkle water on me and I will be clean from all my filthiness and idols. You will give me a new heart and spirit (Ezek. 36:25–26).

Let the rivers of Judah flow with waters and a fountain from the house of the Lord so that my valleys can be watered (Joel 3:18).

Let Your angel come and trouble the waters so that I may step in and be made whole of my disease (John 5:4).

I am sanctified and cleansed through the washing of the water by the Word. I have been presented glorious before the Lord, having no spot or wrinkle. I am holy and without blemish (Eph. 5:26–27).

I draw near to the Lord with a true heart full of faith. My heart has been sprinkled clean by the blood of the Lamb and my body washed with pure water (Heb. 10:22).

With You is the fountain of life, and in Your light I see light (Ps. 36:9).

I will heed the advice of the wise, for it is a fountain of life. By obeying, I will avoid the snares of death (Prov. 13:14).

Death will not touch me because I fear the Lord and He is my fountain of life (Prov. 14:27).

CHAPTER 6

ACTIVATING YOUR HEALING GIFT

> Wherefore I put thee in remembrance that thou stir up the gift of God, which is in thee by the putting on of my hands.
>
> —2 Timothy 1:6, KJV

MEN AND WOMEN of God, it is your responsibility to stir up the gift that God has placed in you. You have been touched, healed, and delivered; now it's time for you to give back. Jesus said, "Heal the sick, cleanse the lepers, raise the dead, cast out devils: freely ye have received, freely give" (Matt. 10:8, KJV). Don't hold back from others what you have been given. Stay in the stream of the anointing, and keep your gift stirred up so that someone else can experience a breakthrough in their situation. Don't be passive about your gift. Passivity about the healing anointing can hinder the flow.

Some of the people are too passive, too lazy to stir up the gift. They allow their gift to remain dormant, or they back up when they encounter a little resistance in the spirit. They sit back and wait for the servant of God to do everything. They don't exercise their faith to put a demand on the gift. But you don't have to do that; you can begin to press into the Spirit just as you did for your healing and receive anointing to pass that healing on to someone else. You must resist passivity in order for others to benefit fully from your gift.

Often in ministry, I will *begin* to flow in prophecy, miracles, or healing because I sense a *demand*—and there is a demand for what you have. There is nothing more that people desire and need in the innermost part of their spirits than a touch from God. The more you stay connected to the endless flow of the Spirit, the more miracles will flow out of you. And the people will begin to put a demand on what you have, and you will flow even more. It's that supply and demand cycle all over again. It is like priming the pump. Once the water begins to flow, it comes gushing out. Jesus said that out of our bellies would flow rivers of living water. All we need to do is get the flow started. It will *begin* when there is a *demand*. Once it begins, it will continue to flow until every need is met.

WHAT IS THE ANOINTING?

> But you have an anointing from the Holy One, and you know all things.
>
> —1 John 2:20

> But the anointing which you have received from Him abides in you.
>
> —1 John 2:27

The word *anointing* here is taken from the Greek word *charisma*. It means an unguent or smearing (represented by smearing with oil). It also means an *endowment* of the Holy Spirit. An endowment is a gift of the Holy Spirit. It is the power or ability of God. There are diversities of gifts (endowments or miraculous faculties).

To draw from the anointing is to receive from the gift or ability of God. You can receive healing, deliverance, and miracles in this way. Apostles, prophets, evangelists, pastors, and teachers have an anointing given to them from God. They have endowments or miraculous faculties given to them by grace. These endowments are given for the benefit of the saints.

God will anoint you to have healing virtue in your life, if you ask. The Bible says that we have not because we ask not (James 4:2). When you ask God for this anointing, it will be not only in your hands but also in your clothes. Don't be afraid to go boldly to the throne of grace in your time of need, and you need the anointing of God to be active in your life. You need His anointing so that wherever you encounter sick people and touch them they will get healed. In this kingdom age signs and wonders need to accompany the message of the gospel. Jesus said that whatever works He did, we will do even greater (John 14:12), as we fast and pray that healing virtue will increase in our lives. Jesus had virtue because He spent time fasting and praying. Ask God for an apostolic anointing of healing power, miracles, and virtue to be released in your life. As you go to the hospital, to your home, to your job, believe that the miracles of God will be released through you.

DECLARATIONS TO RELEASE THE GIFT OF HEALING

I pray that God would anoint me to have virtue in my life—not only in my hands but also in my clothes so that wherever I go and encounter sick people, they will be healed when I touch them.

Heavenly Father, I receive an anointing for healing in my hands and in my body. Let virtue be released through me and through my clothing. Let Your power be released through me so that wherever I go people will be healed.

Heavenly Father, as I fast and pray, increase Your healing virtue in my body and in my clothing, that wherever I go and whoever I touch will be healed.

I believe for miracles to flow through my life in Jesus's name.

SUBMITTING YOURSELF TO GOD'S SERVICE

The people are crying for You, Lord. Anoint me like You did Benjamin, and send me to this land as a spiritual captain over Your people, that they might be saved out of the hand of the enemy (1 Sam. 9:16).

You have anointed me and delivered me from the hands of my enemies, just as You did for King David (2 Sam. 12:7).

I will arise and be cleansed, I will be clothed by the Holy Spirit and be anointed as I worship in Your house, and I will eat of the bread of life from the table that You have set before me (2 Sam. 12:20).

Turn Your face toward me, O God, and remember Your mercy toward me as one You have anointed (2 Chron. 6:42).

In Your love for righteousness and hatred of wickedness, You have anointed me with the oil of gladness more than all those around me (Ps. 45:7; Heb. 1:9).

You have anointed me with fresh oil, and now I am strong as a wild ox (Ps. 92:10).

Turn Your face toward me, Your anointed (Ps. 132:10).

My burden shall be taken away from off my shoulder, and the yoke removed from off my neck and destroyed, because of the anointing upon my life (Isa. 10:27).

PRAYERS FOR PERSONAL ANOINTING

Just as the Lord gave a specific anointing to Aaron, so too, by reason of the anointing, I have been given a specific ministry gift to use, which shall be mine—and my children's—by God's ordinance forever (Num. 18:8).

I know that the Lord saves His anointed, and He will hear me when I call and will come to my aid with the saving strength of His right hand (Ps. 20:6).

God has prepared a table before me in the presence of mine enemies: He has anointed my head with oil; my cup runneth over (Ps. 23:5).

The Lord is my strength, and, as His anointed, I will be saved by His strength (Ps. 28:8).

Just like the blind man whom Jesus told to wash in the pool of Siloam, I will demand that God's anointing power will flow through His servants today and touch my eyes, so that I may wash and receive spiritual sight (John 9:11).

I will sing of the mercies of the Lord forever; with my mouth will I make known His faithfulness to all generations, that all will seek after Him for themselves (Ps. 89:1).

I will praise thy wonders, O Lord, and tell of Your faithfulness also in the congregation of the saints (Ps. 89:5).

Lord, keep Your eyes upon Your faithful servants in this land, that we may dwell with You, and help us to walk in a perfect way so that we may serve You and cause many to seek Your anointing also (Ps. 101:6).

Father, make me like Stephen—full of faith and power—that I may do great wonders and miracles among the people (Acts 6:8).

I will stay full of the Holy Ghost and of faith so that many will say, "He was a good man," and because of Your anointing on my life many people will be added unto the Lord (Acts 11:24).

I have been anointed to open their eyes and to turn them from darkness to light, and from the power of Satan unto God, that they may receive forgiveness of sins and inheritance among those who are sanctified by faith that is in me (Acts 26:18).

I thank my God through Jesus Christ for all my anointed leaders, whose faith is spoken of throughout the whole world (Rom. 1:8). May I become like them.

I will allow the power of God's anointing to bring a harvest of the fruit of the Spirit—His love, joy, peace, longsuffering, gentleness, goodness, faith, meekness, and temperance—that draws others to demand His anointing for themselves (Gal. 5:22–23).

I thank Christ Jesus our Lord, who has enabled me, for counting me faithful and putting me into the ministry (1 Tim. 1:12).

I work miracles according to the hearing of faith and not by the works of the law (Gal. 3:5).

God has called me, and He is faithful to do through me that for which I was called (1 Thess. 5:24).

I will receive strength to conceive that seed of the dreams, anointing, and gifts that God has placed in me. I declare in faith that those same dreams, anointing, and gifts will be delivered, because God, who has promised, has declared me faithful (Heb. 11:11).

The anointing of God abides in me and teaches me all things. The anointing reveals the truth to me as I abide in God (1 John 2:27).

I offer excellent sacrifices before You, O God, because You have counted me righteous by my faith. Testify of the gifts You have anointed me with, that even after I am dead my eternal works will speak (Heb. 11:4).

I decree and declare that I will obey God and, by faith, go to where He has called me so I may receive my inheritance (Heb. 11:8).

PRAYERS THAT RELEASE GENERATIONAL ANOINTING

Just as You anointed Aaron and his sons after him, so You have anointed and consecrated my children and me to Your service (Exod. 29:29).

I believe that I have been anointed by God just as He anointed my father, that I may minister unto God in my ministry gifting and that my family may be an everlasting priesthood throughout all our generations (Exod. 40:15).

You have raised me up a faithful priest, and I will do according to what is in Your heart and mind for me to do. You have built a secure house for my family and me, and we will be Your anointed servants forever (1 Sam. 2:35).

You are my tower of salvation, O Lord, and You have shown mercy to me, Your anointed, and to my children for generations to come (2 Sam. 22:51).

Because of Your anointing on my life, You have granted all the future generations of my family and me great deliverance and mercy (Ps. 18:50).

I believe God and take His warnings to heart; therefore, He will shelter my family, and we will all be saved. By faith, we are heirs of His righteousness (Heb. 11:7).

I offer to God my children and declare them His, and in faith I receive the promises of God (Heb. 11:17).

I release blessing upon my children. I have faith in what God is going to do for them in the future (Heb. 11:20).

I will continually speak blessing over my future generations and will worship God, even in my old age (Heb. 11:21).

I cover all of my firstborn—children, dreams, the fruit of my labor—with the blood of Jesus, and the angel of death will not touch them but will pass over (Heb. 11:28).

PRAYERS THAT ACTIVATE YOUR HEALING ANOINTING

I thank You, God, that You have heard my prayers and have released healing to Your people (2 Chron. 30:20).

The Spirit of the Lord God is upon me because the Lord has anointed me to preach good tidings to the poor. He has sent me to heal the brokenhearted; to comfort all who mourn; to give them beauty for ashes, the oil of joy for mourning, and the garment of praise for the spirit of heaviness, that they may be called trees of righteousness, the planting of the Lord, that He may be glorified (Isa. 61:1–3).

O God, You will bring health and healing. You will heal the people and reveal to them the abundance of peace and truth (Jer. 33:6).

I quicken the people of God to fear the Lord, so that the Sun of Righteousness may arise with healing in His wings (Mal. 4:2).

Just like Jesus, I am released to go and preach the gospel of the kingdom and to heal all kinds of sickness and diseases so that the name and fame of Jesus goes throughout the whole world (Matt. 4:23).

Let it be that sick people who are afflicted with various diseases and torments and those who are demon possessed, epileptics, and paralytics come my way that I may heal them in the name of Jesus (Matt. 4:24).

I accept the call: I will go and heal those who need healing (Matt. 8:7).

I am moved with compassion for the sick because they are weary and scattered, like sheep having no shepherd (Matt. 9:36).

I will heal the sick, cleanse the lepers, raise the dead, and cast out demons. As freely as I have received, I will freely give (Matt. 10:8).

I declare that the power of the Lord is present to heal His people (Luke 5:17).

I receive the multitudes. I will speak to them about the kingdom of God and will heal them in the name of Jesus (Luke 9:11).

I will stretch out my hand to heal so that signs and wonders may be done through the name of Jesus (Acts 4:30).

By the word of the Lord, the people are healed (Ps. 107:20).

I will be a faithful ambassador who brings health and healing (Prov. 13:17).

As the sick are laid at my feet, I declare that the healing anointing of Jesus will flow through me, and they will be healed (Matt. 15:30).

I will lay hands on the sick so that they may be healed, and they will live (Mark 5:23).

I rebuke unclean spirits and sickness in children. By the anointing of Jesus Christ, I will heal them and return them to the care of their parents (Luke 9:42).

I may not have silver; I may not have gold, but what I do have is the anointing to heal those who are sick. In the name of Jesus Christ of Nazareth, I speak to those who are ill: "Rise up and walk" (Acts 3:6–7).

I will observe intently and see that those who come have the faith to be healed. I will call them out of their infirmity, saying, "Stand straight on your feet!" And they will leap and walk (Acts 14:9–10).

I will go in to visit the sick and pray with them. I will lay my hands on them and heal them (Acts 28:8).

As the sick are brought before me, I am able, by Your anointing, to heal them because of their faith. I declare to them, "Be of good cheer; your sins have been forgiven" (Matt. 9:2).

I declare that by my great faith, it will be to me as I desire. My children are made whole—body, mind, and spirit—this very hour (Matt. 15:28).

I can see the faith of Your people, God. I speak healing and forgiveness over them (Mark 2:5).

Let it be that those whom I touch will be made well, healed from their infirmity, and set free to live in peace (Mark 5:34).

I walk in the anointing of Jesus Christ, healing people and giving sight to the blind according to their faith in God (Mark 10:52).

I am filled with the Holy Spirit and with power to do good, healing all who are oppressed by the devil, and I know that God is with me just as He was with Jesus (Acts 10:38).

I declare that my faith-filled prayers will deliver the sick and the Lord will raise them up. Their sins will be forgiven (James 5:15).

PRAYERS that ACTIVATE BLESSINGS

BOOK 2

PRAYERS that ACTIVATE BLESSINGS

JOHN ECKHARDT

CHARISMA HOUSE

CONTENTS

INTRODUCTION

A BETTER UNDERSTANDING OF BLESSING AND PROSPERITY

THE SUBJECT OF blessing and prosperity has become very controversial among those in the church. We want to be blessed and live the abundant life Christ died to give us, yet we don't want to approach God as if He is a lottery or a slot machine—if you put in the right amount of prayer, praise, worship, faith, and good works, out comes your blessing. But for some, that is all they see God as, and they get beside themselves when He doesn't come through for them the way they wanted Him to.

Blessing and prosperity are more than money. According to *Strong's Complete Concordance of the Bible*, one Hebrew word for prosperity is *shalom*.

We often associate the word *shalom* with *peace*, but the peace that Christ went to war for on the cross is a complete, whole kind of peace. Also according to Strong's, *shalom* is "completeness, soundness, welfare, and peace." It represents completeness in number and safety and soundness in your physical body. *Shalom* also covers relationships with God and with people.

God's thoughts concerning your peace and prosperity are much higher than you could imagine. It is His desire to bless and prosper you, to give you His grace, favor, and protection. *Favor* means "grace"; "that which affords joy, pleasure, delight, sweetness, charm, loveliness"; and "good will, benefit, bounty, reward." If you look up the Hebrew and Greek definitions of *prosperity*, many of these words carry over into favor as well.

Favor is goodwill. This is God's kindness and benevolence given to those who love Him. Favor will release great blessings, including prosperity, health, opportunity, and advancement. The Bible records numerous examples of God's favor upon His people causing them to experience many breakthroughs. Favor is God's loving-kindness.

Joseph experienced God's favor and went from prison to palace. God will do the same for you. He can change your circumstances in one day no matter where you are in life. This is when the favor of God is on your life.

Job was another man who was blessed and who operated under the full favor and blessing of God. In Job 10:12 he confessed that his life and the favor he had were gifts from God: "Thou hast granted me life and favour, and thy visitation hath preserved my spirit" (KJV). Life and favor are gifts of God. We don't need luck. We need blessing. We need favor. We need the blessing of God. God desires to release new favor on your life. When you have God's favor and blessing, there is nothing in life that can hold you down.

When you begin to walk in the favor and blessing of the Lord, others will recognize it. The favor and blessing of God on your life is one of the most powerful things that can be released to you.

Matthew 6:33 says, "Seek ye first the kingdom of God, and his righteousness; and *all* these things shall be added unto you" (KJV, emphasis added).

Protection was also added to Job. Job 29:17 says, "I brake the jaws of the wicked, and plucked the spoil out of his teeth" (KJV). When the evil plans of the enemy set out to destroy Job, he had weapons to fight back; then he claimed the exponential spoils of the victory.

3

God says, "You don't need money. You need My favor." You need His shalom—the full measure of peace—to operate in your life. This is your gift from Him if you are His child, if you are in covenant with Him. God blesses His people and rescues them. Just as He did with the Israelites, God loved you and chose you in spite of who you are and what you have done. You are elected by God. You were chosen before the foundation of the world. He chose you. It wasn't because of anything you've done. That is His favor!

God talks to the children of Israel in Ezekiel 16:1–14 about how He found them in a rejected state where they had been thrown away and no one wanted them. They were drowning in their own blood. But when God passed by them, He said to them, "LIVE!" Then He blessed them and adorned them with jewels. God is saying this same thing to you. Maybe you were thrown away to die and had no chance at living. Maybe no one wanted you or you were not born with a silver spoon in your mouth. But when God looked upon you, He had mercy on you.

God will not only save you and wash you, but He will also bless you, dress you up, put jewels on you, and beautify you. The grace and favor of God on your life will cause you to go into a place of prosperity. God not only will save you but will also multiply you and bless you.

In this book we are going to talk about how to obtain the covenant blessing of God. We are going to learn confessions and prayers based on God's Word that will activate His shalom over your life. Death and life are in the power of the tongue. We can choose blessing by choosing to live and speak correctly.

God is ready to release new favor, blessing, prosperity, protection, and peace over you. It is His desire to give you good things. Now get ready to receive them.

BLESSING AND FAVOR DECLARATIONS

Lord, You have granted me life and favor.

Lord, I thank You for life and life more abundantly.

I thank You for favor coming upon my life.

I believe that new life and new favor
have been ordained for me.

Today I receive new life and new favor.

I believe favor is a gift of heaven.

I receive the gift of life—the gift of eternal life.

I receive the gift of favor and the gift of grace
upon my life in the name of Jesus.

Thank You, Lord, for new grace and new favor, new prosperity and new blessing coming on my life.

I am the apple of God's eye.

I am one of God's favorites.

God favors me, loves me, and has chosen me from the foundation of the world to receive His grace and favor.

I receive extraordinary favor on my life in the name of Jesus!

PRAYERS FOR THE BLESSING AND FAVOR OF GOD

Let me be well favored (Gen. 39:6).

Lord, show me mercy and give me favor (Gen. 39:21).

Give me favor in the sight of the world (Exod. 12:36).

Let me be satisfied with your favor like Naphtali (Deut. 33:23).

Let me have favor with You, Lord, and with men (1 Sam. 2:26).

Let me have favor with the king (1 Sam. 16:22).

Let me have great favor in the sight of the king (1 Kings 11:19).

Let me find favor like Esther (Esther 2:17).

Thou hast granted me life and favour, and Thy visitation hath preserved my spirit (Job 10:12, KJV).

I pray unto You, Lord, grant me favor (Job 33:26).

Bless me and surround me with
favor like a shield (Ps. 5:12).

In Your favor is life (Ps. 30:5).

Make my mountain stand strong
by Your favor (Ps. 30:7).

Because of Your favor, the enemy will
not triumph over me (Ps. 41:11).

Through Your favor, I am brought
back from captivity (Ps. 85:1).

Let my horn be exalted through Your favor (Ps. 89:17).

My set time of favor has come (Ps. 102:13).

I entreat Your favor with my whole heart (Ps. 119:58).

Let Your favor be as a cloud of the
latter rain (Prov. 16:15).

Let Your favor be upon my life as the
dew upon the grass (Prov. 19:12).

I choose Your loving favor rather than
gold and silver (Prov. 22:1).

Let me be highly favored (Luke 1:28)

Show me Your marvelous loving-kindness (Ps. 17:7).

Remember Your mercy and loving-
kindness in my life (Ps. 25:6).

Your loving-kindness is before my eyes (Ps. 26:3).

I receive Your excellent loving-kindness (Ps. 36:7).

Continue Your loving-kindness in my life (Ps. 36:10).

Let Your loving-kindness and Your truth
continually preserve me (Ps. 40:11).

Command Your loving-kindness
in the daytime (Ps. 42:8).

Your loving-kindness is good: turn unto me according
to the multitude of Your tender mercies (Ps. 69:16).

Quicken me after Thy loving-kindness (Ps. 119:88, KJV).

Hear my voice according to Your
loving-kindness (Ps. 119:149).

You have drawn me with Your loving-
kindness (Jer. 32:18).

CHAPTER 1

BLESSING BY ASKING

ASKING FOR WHAT we need or want from God is a foundational principle of our relationship with Him as king and ruler over all. He has made Himself available to hear our request. Matthew 7:7–11 (KJV) makes that clear:

> Ask, and it shall be given you; seek, and ye shall find; knock, and it shall be opened unto you: for every one that asketh receiveth; and he that seeketh findeth; and to him that knocketh it shall be opened. Or what man is there of you, whom if his son ask bread, will he give him a stone? Or if he ask a fish, will he give him a serpent? If ye then, being evil, know how to give good gifts unto your children, how much more shall your Father

which is in heaven give good things to them
that ask him?

God's covenant leaders understood this aspect
of mankind's relationship to God, and they took
advantage of it when they came into His presence.

JABEZ—OH, THAT THOU
WOULDEST BLESS ME

The story of Jabez is only two verses (1 Chron. 4:9–10),
but it is a powerful reminder of the effectiveness of
fervent prayer. The Bible says that Jabez was an honorable man, more honorable than his brothers. Being
honorable and having a pure heart before God always
play a part in how God answers our prayers. You will
see this theme throughout this book. It's not about
being perfect, but it is about being holy, as we will
uncover later.

The story of Jabez goes on to reveal that he called
on the God of Israel, asking for a blessing, and God
granted him that which he requested. God answered
Jabez. Jabez didn't go into some long exercise of prayer,
reciting the Torah and using big words. He simply
went before God and said, "'Oh, that You would bless
me indeed, and enlarge my territory, that Your hand
would be with me, and that You would keep me from

evil, that I may not cause pain!' So God granted him what he requested" (v. 10). He asked and God gave it to him. Simple.

This teaches us that we can ask God to bless us and that He will grant us what we ask for. Jabez asked for God to bless Him, and He did. God is the source of blessing, and it is the nature of God to be good to His creation. The psalmist says, "The LORD is good, His mercy is everlasting" (Ps. 100:5). A revelation of the goodness of God will cause faith for His blessings.

JACOB—I WILL NOT LET GO
UNLESS YOU BLESS ME

> Then Jacob was left alone; and a Man wrestled with him until the breaking of day. Now when He saw that He did not prevail against him, He touched the socket of his hip; and the socket of Jacob's hip was out of joint as He wrestled with him. And He said, "Let Me go, for the day breaks." But he said, "I will not let You go unless You bless me!"
>
> —Genesis 32:24–26

This event in Jacob's life came after a long battle for the woman of his dreams. He had diligently worked for his wife Rachel for a total of fourteen years. He had hope and expectation behind his efforts. Many of us pray once and immediately get angry with God when He doesn't give us what we prayed for. Not Jacob; he held on to what he knew God had for him at the end of his labor. He had his eyes set on his blessing and wouldn't let go until he had it.

But here we see Jacob once again in the midst of a battle, but this one was not a battle of flesh and blood. He is contending with the supernatural. Jacob had been taught by the fathers of past generations (Abraham and Isaac) about the power and provision of the one true God. He knew that as he came in contact with Him he had an open invitation to request a blessing. And a blessing is what he got.

> So He said to him, "What is your name?" And he said, "Jacob." And He said, "Your name shall no longer be called Jacob, but Israel; for you have struggled with God and with men, and have prevailed." Then Jacob asked, saying, "Tell me Your name, I pray." And He said, "Why is it that you ask about My name?" And He blessed him there. And Jacob called the name of the place Peniel: "For I have seen God face to face, and my life is preserved."
>
> —Genesis 32:27–30

Not only did Jacob come face-to-face with God, but because he asked, he was also blessed with a new name, purpose, future, and destiny. His whole identity was changed. Jacob experienced what is called a bonanza or a "suddenly" of God. He was instantly taken from being second after Esau, having no inheritance of his own, to being blessed spiritually with an eternal birthright full of the riches of the kingdom of God.

That is what God wants to do for you when you come to Him for a blessing. He wants to give you more than what you ask for because He is good and because He knows how to give good gifts to His children. What you ask Him for is only the start of what He wants to do in your life.

MOSES—PLEASE, SHOW ME YOUR GLORY

Moses longed for the glory of the Lord. He longed to dwell in the shadow of the Almighty. He sought hard after God, and God knew him intimately: "...for you have found grace in My sight, and I know you by name" (Exod. 33:17). So when the time came for Moses to make his request to see the glory of God, he didn't have to make a case for how close he and God were. God knew him by name. Does God know you by name?

In Exodus 33:17–23 we witness the exchange between Moses and God. The Lord granted Moses's request because Moses had found favor in His sight, and He caused His goodness to pass before Moses. Goodness is the word *tuwb*, meaning goods, good things, goodness, property, fairness, beauty, joy, and prosperity.

The Lord is abundant in goodness and is anxious to give good gifts to His children. God has laid up His goodness (blessings) for us. If we know Him and He knows us, all we have to do is ask Him for it. His blessings are for His children.

> Oh how great is thy goodness, which thou hast laid up for them that fear thee; which thou hast wrought for them that trust in thee before the sons of men!
>
> —Psalm 31:19, KJV

PRAYERS FOR BLESSING

Lord, You are the source of my blessing.

Lord, I choose blessing by walking in Your covenant.

Lord, command Your blessing upon my life.

Lord, You are the father of lights, and You give good gifts. Release Your gifts into my life (James 1:17).

Lord, I trust in You, and I receive Your blessing.

Lord, I ask and I receive Your blessing.

Lord, I seek and find Your blessing.

Lord, I knock, and the door of blessing is opened to me.

Lord, I ask for blessings in the name of Jesus,
and I believe You give them to me.

Lord, You are a God who blesses and rewards
those who diligently seek after You (Heb. 11).

Lord, You are a fountain of (life) blessing.

Lord, You are a tree of (life) blessing.

Lord, release Your river of blessing into my life.

Lord, rain upon my life, and pour
out Your blessing over me.

Lord, release the blessing of heaven and the
blessing of the deep into my life (Gen. 49:25).

Lord, release the blessing of the breast and
the womb into my life (Gen. 49:25).

Let the blessing of Abraham come
on my life (Gal. 3:13–14).

Let me be blessed with authority (Gen. 49:10).

Let me be a fruitful bough whose branches
run over the wall (Gen. 49:22).

Lord, bless my substance and the work
of my hands (Deut. 33:11).

Lord, bless my land, and let the dew of
heaven be upon me (Deut. 33:13).

Lord, enlarge me like Gad (Deut. 33:20).

Lord, let me be satisfied with favor, and let me be full of Your blessing like Naphtali (Deut. 33:23).

Lord, let me dwell in safety, and cover me like Benjamin (Deut. 33:12).

Let me suck of the abundance of the seas and of treasures hid in the sand, like Zebulun and Issachar (Deut. 33:18–19).

Let me reap a hundredfold like Isaac (Gen. 26:12).

Let me be blessed like Jacob (Gen. 28:1).

Lord, Jabez asked You to bless him, and You did. Bless me like Jabez (1 Chron. 4:10).

Lord, bless me and make me fruitful like Ishmael (Gen. 17:20).

Lord, bless me with a blessing that cannot be reversed (Num. 23:20).

Let my basket and store be blessed (Deut. 28:5).

Lord, bless my beginning and my latter end like Job's (Job 42:12).

Lord, bless me with favor like Esther (Esther 2:17).

Lord, bless me with wisdom like Solomon.

Lord, give me favor like Nehemiah to finish the assignment You have given me (Neh. 2:5).

Lord, bless me to inherit my territory like Caleb and Joshua.

Lord, let me win every battle like David.

PRAYERS FOR THE BLESSING OF GOODNESS

I receive Your blessings of goodness, and You set a crown of pure gold on my head (Ps. 21:3).

I will rejoice because of Your goodness (Exod. 18:9).

Let Your goodness pass before me (Exod. 33:19).

Let Your abundant goodness come into my life (Exod. 34:6).

Let Your promise of goodness be fulfilled in my life (2 Sam. 7:28).

Let me be glad and joyful because of Your goodness (1 Kings 8:66).

I will rejoice in Your goodness (2 Chron. 6:41).

Let me delight myself in Your great goodness (Neh. 9:25).

Let goodness and mercy follow me all the days of my life, for You are my shepherd, and I will not want (Ps. 23).

Remember me for Your goodness' sake (Ps. 25:7).

I will see Your goodness in the land of the living (Ps. 27:13).

Lord, You have laid up Your great goodness for me (Ps. 31:19).

Let Your goodness endure continually in my life (Ps. 52:1).

Crown my year with Your goodness, and drop fatness on my life (Ps. 65:11).

Let me be satisfied with the goodness
of Your house (Ps. 65:4).

I will praise You for Your goodness and Your
wonderful works toward me (Ps. 107:8).

Fill my soul with Your goodness (Ps. 107:9).

I receive your loving-kindness and
great goodness (Isa. 63:7).

Bring me into a plentiful country, and let
me enjoy Your goodness (Jer. 2:7).

Let me enjoy Your goodness, Lord—the
wheat, the wine, and the oil (Jer. 31:12).

Satiate my soul with fatness, and let me be
satisfied with Your goodness (Jer. 31:14).

Let men hear of the goodness and prosperity
You establish in my life (Jer. 33:9).

Let Your goodness be as the morning cloud
and as the early dew (Hosea 6:4).

Make me cheerful with Your goodness (Zech. 9:17).

I have tasted and seen that You are good (Ps. 34:8).

I will not lack any good thing (Ps. 34:10).

Do good in Your good pleasure toward me (Ps. 51:18).

Lord, withhold no good thing from me (Ps. 84:11).

Lord, give me that which is good, and
let me increase (Ps. 85:12).

Show me a token for good (Ps. 86:17).

Satisfy my mouth with good things, and let my youth be restored as the eagle's (Ps. 103:5).

Open Your hand and fill me with good (Ps. 104:28).

Bless me out of Zion, and let me see good (Ps. 128:5).

Let me be satisfied with good by the fruit of my mouth (Prov. 12:14).

PRAYERS FOR BONANZAS AND BREAKTHROUGH

Lord, let my desire come, and let it be a tree of life (Prov. 13:12).

Let understanding be a wellspring of life for me (Prov. 16:22).

Lord, let Your fear give me life (blessing); let me be satisfied, and let me not be visited with evil (Prov. 19:23).

Lord, let humility and Your fear bring riches, life (blessing), and honor (Prov. 22:4).

I will live and not die, and will declare the work of the Lord.

Lord, show me the path of life; in Your presence is fullness of joy; at Your right hand are pleasures forevermore (Ps. 16:11).

Lord, give me life and length of days (Ps. 21:4).

Lord, give me Your favor, for in Your favor is life (Ps. 30:5).

For with You is the fountain of life; in Your light shall we see light (Ps. 36:9).

Let Your wisdom be a tree of life to me (Prov. 3:18).

Let Your words be life to my soul and
grace to my neck (Prov. 3:22).

I will hold fast to instruction because
it is my life (Prov. 4:13).

I have found wisdom, I have found life,
and I obtain Your favor (Prov. 8:35).

Lord, You have redeemed my life from
destruction. You crown me with loving-
kindness and tender mercies (Ps. 103:4).

Let me enjoy the blessing of fruitfulness
and multiplication (Gen. 1:22).

Let Your blessing come upon my family (Gen. 12:3).

I am blessed through Christ, the seed
of Abraham (Gen. 22:18).

Let me be blessed greatly (Gen. 24:35).

Let those connected to me be blessed (Gen. 30:27).

Let me receive blessed advice (1 Sam. 25:33).

I walk not in the counsel of the ungodly, I
stand not in the way of sinners, and I sit not
in the seat of the scornful, but I delight in the
law of the Lord, and I am blessed (Ps. 1).

Bless me, Lord, for I put my trust in You (Ps. 2:12).

Lord, I receive Your blessing for my transgression
is forgiven and my sin is covered (Ps. 32:1).

Lord, bless me; I renounce and turn away from all
guile, and iniquity is not imputed to me (Ps. 32:2).

Lord, bless me; You are my trust. I respect not the
proud nor such as turn aside to lies (Ps. 40:4).

Lord, bless me; I consider the poor. Deliver me
in the time of trouble, preserve me, and keep me
alive. Bless me upon the earth, and deliver me
not unto the will of my enemies (Ps. 41:1–2).

Lord, bless me for You have chosen me and
caused me to approach unto You and dwell
in Your courts, that I might be satisfied with
the goodness of Your house (Ps. 65:4).

Lord, daily load me with benefits (Ps. 68:19).

Lord, bless me as I dwell in Your house
and continue to praise You (Ps. 84:4).

Bless me, Lord; my strength is in You (Ps. 84:5).

Bless me, Lord, and let the light of Your countenance
shine on me; I know the joyful sound (Ps. 89:15).

Let me be blessed by Your correction, and
teach me out of Your Word (Ps. 94:12).

Bless me, Lord, and let me keep Your judgments
and do righteousness at all times (Ps. 106:3).

Bless me, Lord, for I fear You and delight
greatly in Your commandments (Ps. 112:1).

Bless me, Lord; I fear You and walk
in Your ways (Ps. 128:1).

Bless me, Lord; I receive wisdom, watching
daily at wisdom's gates, waiting at the
posts of wisdom's doors (Prov. 8:34).

Lord, I have a bountiful (generous)
eye; bless me (Prov. 22:9).

Bless me, Lord; I wait on You (Isa. 30:18).

I sow beside all waters; bless me, Lord (Isa. 32:20).

Bless me, Lord; I will not labor in vain or
bring forth for trouble (Isa. 65:23).

Bless me, Lord. I trust in You, and
my hope is in You (Jer. 17:7).

Let all nations call me blessed, and let me
be a delightful land (Mal. 3:12).

Anoint me for breakthrough (Isa. 61).

Let me experience breakthroughs
in every area of my life.

Let me break through all limitations and obstacles.

I will expand my tent, lengthen my cords,
and strengthen my stakes, because I will
experience breakthrough (Isa. 54).

The Lord my breaker goes before me (Mic. 2:13).

Let me break through in my finances.

Let me break through in relationships.

Let me break through in my health with healing.

Let me break through in my ministry.

Let me break through in my city.

Let me break through in my emotions.

Let me break through in my praise.

Let me break through in my prayer life.

Let me break through in my worship,

Let me break through in my revelation.

Let me break through in my career.

Let me break through in my giving.

Let me experience bonanzas in my life.

Let me experience Your "suddenlies," Lord.

Do a quick work in my life.

Let me experience great increase
in a short period of time.

I believe in and confess BONANZAS for my life.

Let me find the vein of prosperity
and experience bonanzas.

CHAPTER 2

THE BLESSING OF OBEDIENCE

WE KNOW FROM the story of the Fall in the Garden of Eden that our intimacy with God rests on our obedience to Him. And if we are not close to God through obedience, we are separated from Him through our disobedience and therefore forfeit receiving His blessing.

Adam and Eve were given a simple charge, and that was to stay away from the tree of the knowledge of good and evil. Any other bountiful blessing and experience in the garden was theirs:

> And the LORD God commanded the man, saying, "Of every tree of the garden you may freely eat; but of the tree of the knowledge of

good and evil you shall not eat, for in the day
that you eat of it you shall surely die."

—Genesis 2:16–17

But they did not heed the voice of the Lord and, as
we all know, lost their place of honor, blessing, and
protection from the consequences of sin.

It is even clearer that the blessings of God depend on
our obedience when we go back and review the Book
of Deuteronomy, where God spelled out His covenant
plan to the children of Israel. It almost seems as though
He repeated Himself too much, but we know from the
Old Testament account and our own life experience
that even with His faithfulness in reminding us of
the blessing of obedience, man still goes his own
way and moves himself out of the path of blessing.

In Deuteronomy 11, God laid out His plan for how
His children can receive His blessing. If they were
careful to do all he commanded, His blessings would
flow out to them, the children, their cattle, and their
servants. Everything their hand touched or foot tread
upon would not only be successful—but it also would
be theirs.

Imagine this kind of blessing over your business,
career, or ministry. Imagine this blessing over your
home and finances, your education, and all the things

that concern your family. God desires to release this kind of blessing over you, because it testifies of His goodness among the nations. When God's people prosper, not only do they look good, but God also looks good.

Reading further, you see that the children of Israel would also have the protection of the Lord from all their surrounding enemies (Deut. 11:22–25). He was declaring Himself to be their strong tower. This is what obedience will bring to you as well. Obedience brings protection from death and defeat of all kinds. In Romans 6:23, the Bible says that "the wages of sin is death." So if you obey God, you will be blessed with life. Death is a curse that Jesus died on the cross to release you from. He recaptured the blessing of an abundant life for you. All you have to do is receive His gift and walk in it by being obedient to His Word. The choice is yours.

> See, I am setting before you today a blessing and a curse—the blessing if you obey the commands of the LORD your God that I am giving you today; the curse if you disobey the commands of the LORD your God and turn from the way that I command you today by

following other gods, which you have not known.

—Deuteronomy 11:26–28, NIV

OBEDIENCE AS A SIGN OF TRUE FAITH

We are exercising our confession of faith and commitment of love to God when we choose to obey Him. (See 1 John 5:2–3.) If we only say with our mouth that we believe in God yet do nothing of what He tells us, we are no different from the devils and demons who tremble and believe (James 2:17–19). Active faith is what breeds the perfect environment for the supernatural blessing of God. When you have an active faith, you can receive supernatural healing, deliverance, divine warnings of danger up ahead, provision, and protection.

Your active faith allows you to stay connected to and abiding in the vine. Psalm 91 is a perfect example of one who is walking in the blessing of obedience.

Your obedience to God's direction and instruction for your life says that you trust and believe that He knows what's best for you, that you honor your commitment to follow Him, and that you understand that your perspective on overcoming life's challenges are limited. Anything less than obedience is just lip service.

In order to receive the blessing of God, you must demonstrate that He is Lord of your life. Obedience is the testing ground that proves that. He wants you to be His, and He wants to be yours. He has life for you, but you have to give your broken-down life back to Him and follow His plan for success, prosperity, and peace.

If you are a parent, you may understand it better in these terms: You tell your child to stay close to the front yard. "Stay where I can see you," you say. If your child goes outside of the boundaries you set, how can you protect them if a car comes speeding up the street or a questionable person approaches them with a piece of candy? Obedience is a lifesaver in many cases.

Obedience says, "God, I trust You with my life. Therefore I will love You by keeping Your Word in my heart so that I will not sin against You and risk losing Your favor and blessing, because they are life and breath to me."

> You shall love the Lord your God with all your heart, with all your soul, with all your strength, and with all your mind.
>
> —Luke 10:27

PRAYERS FOR THE BLESSING OF OBEDIENCE

I am willing and obedient. Let me eat
the good of the land (Isa. 1:19).

Like Christ, let me be a son who learns
obedience by the things I suffer (Heb. 5:8).

As an obedient child, I will not conform
myself to the former lusts (1 Pet. 1:14).

May I walk in Your authority so that all
the congregation of the children of God
may be obedient (Num. 27:20).

Let me not be like the nations the Lord
destroyed before me. I will be obedient to the
voice of the Lord my God (Deut. 8:20).

The rebuke of the wise is like an earring of gold and an
ornament of fine gold to my obedient ear (Prov. 25:12).

Through You I have received grace and
apostleship for obedience to the faith among
all nations for His name (Rom. 1:5).

Let me put myself to the test, whether I am
obedient in all things (2 Cor. 2:9).

I know that Your affections are greater for me
as You remember my obedience, how with fear
and trembling I received You (2 Cor. 7:15).

Lord, I pray that You will have confidence
in my obedience, knowing that I will do
even more than You say (Philem. 21).

All that the Lord has said I will do
and be obedient (Exod. 24:7).

Let me not be like those who would not walk in Your ways and weren't obedient to Your law, for like them, I will be plundered and given over to robbers (Isa. 42:24).

I present myself to obey You, Lord; therefore I am a slave of obedience leading to righteousness (Rom. 6:16).

My obedience has become known to all. Let me be wise in what is good and simple concerning evil (Rom. 16:19).

I cast down arguments and every high thing that exalts itself against the knowledge of God, bringing every thought into captivity to the obedience of Christ (2 Cor. 10:5).

Like Christ, let me humble myself and become obedient to the point of death (Phil. 2:8).

Jesus, I thank You that You made me righteous through Your obedience (Rom. 5:19).

Lord, I will obey You so that I may enter into Your rest (Heb. 3:18).

I will not obey unrighteousness. I will obey the truth. Let Your indignation and wrath be far from me (Rom. 2:8).

I will not follow my former rituals, but I will obey the Lord (2 Kings 17:40).

Let me run well, and let no one hinder me from obeying the truth (Gal. 5:7).

Because I obey Your voice, all of my seed will be blessed (Gen. 22:18).

I receive blessing because I obey the commandments of the Lord my God (Deut. 11:27).

Let me not turn my heart back to Egypt,
but let me obey (Acts 7:39).

Because I obey, You are the author of my eternal
salvation. I am perfected in You (Heb. 5:9).

I submit myself as a slave to obey You, Lord,
so that I may be righteous (Rom. 6:16).

I will obey Your voice according to what
You command me (Gen. 27:8).

Thank You, God, that as I obey Your voice,
You will be an enemy to my enemies and an
adversary to my adversaries (Exod. 23:22).

Let me not be the one who does not
obey You and receives seven times more
punishment for his sins (Lev. 26:18).

All the blessings of the Lord come upon me
and overtake me, because I obey the voice
of the Lord my God (Deut. 28:2).

I will spend my days in prosperity and my years in
pleasures, because I obey and serve You (Job 36:11).

I will obey You and incline my ear to You.
I will not be stiff-necked (Jer. 7:26).

I will eat and have enough. I will not
commit harlotry and will increase, because
I seek to obey the Lord (Hosea 4:10).

The Lord will not cast me away, because
I will obey Him (Hosea 9:17).

I will obey Your voice. I will receive correction. I will
trust in the Lord and draw near to my God (Zeph. 3:2).

I will obey God rather than men (Acts 5:29).

The Holy Spirit is given to those who obey Him. I will obey (Acts 5:32).

I will not let sin reign in my mortal body, nor will I obey it in its lusts (Rom. 6:12).

I will be subject to rulers and authorities, to obey them, and will be ready for every good work (Titus 3:1).

To obey is better than sacrifice and to heed than the fat of rams (1 Sam. 15:22).

Whether it is pleasing or displeasing, I will obey the voice of the Lord my God that it may be well with me (Jer. 42:6).

I thank You, Lord, that if I will obey Your voice and keep Your covenant, I will be a special treasure to You (Exod. 19:5).

When I am in distress, I will turn to the Lord my God and obey His voice. He will not forsake me or destroy me, nor will He forget the covenant that He swore to my fathers (Deut. 4:30–31).

I will earnestly obey Your commandments to love the Lord my God and serve You with all my heart and soul (Deut. 11:13).

I will observe and obey all these words You command me, that it may go well with me and my children after me forever (Deut. 12:28).

I will walk after the Lord my God and will fear Him. I will keep His commandments and obey His voice. I will serve Him and hold fast to Him (Deut. 13:4).

Today I proclaim the Lord to be my God; that
I will walk in His ways and keep His statutes,
His commandments, and His judgments; and
that I will obey His voice (Deut. 26:17).

The Lord my God I will serve, and His
voice I will obey (Josh. 24:24).

I will not fear the gods of the Amorites, for You are
the Lord my God in whose land I dwell (Judg. 6:10).

Let me continue to fear, serve, and obey the
Lord, so that the political leaders who rule over
me will also follow God (1 Sam. 12:14).

Let me not be like King Saul, who transgressed against
the commandment of the Lord and feared people more
than God and obeyed their voice (1 Sam. 15:24).

Like Judah, Lord, I pray that You will give me the
singleness of heart to obey the command of my national
rulers, according to Your word (2 Chron. 30:12).

Like Esther, I pray that I will obey the commands of
the spiritual authorities in my life (Esther 2:20).

I return to You, Lord, and I know that You will
not cause Your anger to fall on me, for You are
merciful and will not remain angry forever. I
acknowledge my iniquity and my transgressions.
I have not obeyed You (Jer. 3:12–13).

I will obey Your voice and You will be my God, and
I will walk in all the ways You have commanded
me, that it may be well with me (Jer. 7:23).

I will obey and incline my ear to the Lord
my God. I will not follow the counsels and
dictates of my evil heart (Jer. 7:24).

I will amend my ways and my doings and
obey the voice of the Lord my God; then the
Lord will relent concerning the doom He
has pronounced against me (Jer. 26:13).

Even the wind and sea obey You (Matt. 8:27).

Let no one bewitch me that I should
not obey the truth (Gal. 3:1).

I will obey those by whom I am employed,
not with eyeservice as a man-pleaser, but in
sincerity of heart, fearing God (Col. 3:22).

I will be submissive and obey those who
rule over me, for they watch out for my soul
and must give an account (Heb. 13:17).

I have purified my soul in obeying the
truth through the Spirit in sincere love of
my brothers and sisters (1 Pet. 1:22).

Lord, I pray that my obedience to Your Word
will win my husband for You (1 Pet. 3:1).

Lord, I believe You and will obey You when you say to
go possess the land You have given me (Deut. 9:23).

I will obey the voice of the Lord my God, and none
of those curses will overtake me (Deut. 28:15).

I fear the Lord and obey the voice of His
servant. I walk in light and not darkness. I
trust in and rely on God (Isa. 50:10).

I receive the kingdom and dominion,
because I am a saint of the Most High. I
serve and obey Him (Dan. 7:27).

With authority I will command unclean spirits, and they will obey me (Mark 1:27).

With even my mustard seed faith, a mulberry tree will obey me and be uprooted and planted in the sea (Luke 17:6).

Lord, I will obey You and will proclaim liberty to my brother and my neighbor, because You have proclaimed liberty to me (Jer. 34:17).

PRAYERS FOR A LIFE FLOWING WITH MILK AND HONEY

Bring me into a land flowing with milk and honey (Exod. 3:8).

Let my teeth be white with milk (Gen. 49:12).

Let me enjoy the butter of kine and the milk of sheep (Deut. 32:14, kjv).

Let me enjoy Your blessings like butter and honey (Isa. 7:22).

Let milk flow into my life from the hill of Zion (Joel 3:18).

Bring me into a land filled with wheat, barley, vines, fig trees, and pomegranates; a land of olive oil and honey (Deut. 8:8).

Let me ride on the high places of the earth, eat the increase of the fields, and suck honey out of the rock and oil out of the flinty rock (Deut. 32:13).

Feed me with the finest of the wheat, and satisfy me with honey out of the rock (Ps. 81:16).

Chapter 3

THE BLESSING OF GIVING

THE BIBLE TEACHES a very simple message about being blessed to be a blessing. It is a cyclical law much like sowing and reaping. In Christian circles it has been called the law of the harvest; in the world, karma; and in science, cause and effect: "What goes around comes around." "You get what you pay for." "You get out what you put in." "Whatever you sow, you will reap." Regardless of what man has tried to label it, this law of giving and receiving originated by the hand of God at the foundation of the world. It is not a hypothesis or theory. It is an ingrained law that applies to life on this earth and in heaven regardless of if we are aware of it or not.

What you put out will be given back to you, and even more, you will receive in *proportion* to how you give. If you give (or sow) sparingly, you will receive (or reap) sparingly (2 Cor. 9:6).

If you want to receive the blessing of God, you have to be ready to give. You cannot expect to live a blessed life if all you do is receive, receive, receive. You will end up like the Dead Sea—becoming too salty and too toxic to support any kind of life. A blessed Christian is vibrant, fruitful, and able to give and sustain life. Everything around them is blessed. The spirit of death and staleness does not stay around them very long. Because they are blessed, they give blessing and in turn cause a flow of abundance in the kingdom of God where lack does not exist.

Many churches today say that they have modeled themselves after the New Testament church, but the early church received and responded to the message of giving in a way that many of us today would be reluctant to practice.

In 2 Corinthians 8:14–15, Paul encouraged the Corinthians to continue what they had always done, and that was for those with abundance to give to those who did not have so that no one would go without and that all would be blessed. He called this equality. In Acts 2:44–45 and Acts 4:32–33, it is also called having "all things in common."

There was a living flow of blessings between the members of this church. Those who were blessed gave to those who were in need of a blessing. They did this willingly and cheerfully. (See 2 Corinthians 9:7–15.) In each of these instances you will see that the supernatural grace of God surrounded and blessed the givers and receivers, so that the giving wasn't a burden and the receivers were blessed enough to become givers as well.

THE SEVEN SPIRITUAL PLACES OF ABUNDANCE

In order to receive the blessing of giving, you must first be blessed with abundance. The Old Testament names certain physical places that represented abundance, fertility, fruitfulness, excellence, and beauty. When the people of God dwelled in these places, their lives prospered like never before. They were at peace and protected from their enemies, they had all the food and produce they could eat, their land was well watered, and their cattle were fed. This was true as long as they stayed in this place.

Today, the body of Christ is struggling to understand how to be in a place of blessing and abundance so that they can give the world what it needs as a testimony of God our Father. This lack of revelation concerning His laws and ordinances about giving and receiving is what keeps the church in a position of lack. Many do not feel empowered by God's grace to give cheerfully because they are not dwelling in one of God's spiritual places of abundance.

In the Old Testament God gave made all of His blessings available to His people so that they would be a blessing to the surrounding nations and all who saw how they lived would know there was a true and living God. There were seven places where the abundance of heaven flowed down to the earth. These seven places are still active in the spiritual realm. Your prayers and confessions can begin to release this flow into your life.

Just as the Lord's Prayer says, you are able to release God's will upon the earth as it is in heaven (Luke 11:2). And it is His will to bless and prosper you.

As you learn about these seven places of spiritual abundance, begin to pray that the spirit of abundance that inhabited these places will fall on your life.

1. The plain of Sharon, the fruitfulness of the kingdom

The plain of Sharon was known for its fruitfulness and fertility. In both 1 Chronicles 27:29 and Isaiah

65:10 it was a grazing place, a pastureland for the flocks. It was full and lush, and it seemed to be ever blooming. *Barnes' Notes* on the Bible says that the Hebrew connotation of the word *blossom* in Isaiah 35:2 is that "it shall blossom abundantly... [i.e.,] blossoming it shall blossom." In other words, its fertility, fruitfulness, beauty, and life-giving ability would continue in great measure and without end. When the many-colored flowers are in bloom, it is a scene of rare beauty. What do you need to see blossom abundantly in your life? God wants to bring that beauty into your life.

2. Mount Carmel, the beauty and excellency of the kingdom

Isaiah 35:2 also mentions the excellency of Carmel, meaning that the Lord displayed His glory and splendor in this mountain. The word *Carmel* means "crimson" and also refers often to a "fruitful field." In Isaiah 10:18 and Isaiah 16:10, while the English transliteration is not used, the word *Carmel* is translated directly as a "fruitful field" and a "plentiful field" respectively. It is also referred to as:

- A place of beauty (Song of Sol. 7:5)
- Excellent (Isa. 35:2)

- A plentiful country (Jer. 2:7)
- Carmel by the sea (Jer. 46:18)

Since the *sea* often in Scripture denotes Gentiles, it is interesting to consider the imagery of the strength and beauty of the heights at the edge of the Gentiles as well as the natural imagery.

Song of Solomon 7:5 says, "Thine head upon thee is like Carmel, and the hair of thine head like purple; the king is held in the galleries" (KJV).

In every passage of Scripture that mentions *excellency* or that which is excellent, the word *Carmel* carries with it a connotation of perfection, completion, and fullness.

> But I will bring Israel back to his own pasture and he will graze on Carmel and Bashan; his appetite will be satisfied on the hills of Ephraim and Gilead.
>
> —Jeremiah 50:19, NIV

3. The glory of Lebanon

Fausset's Bible Dictionary describes Lebanon as a fertile valley full of fragrant flowers, aromatic shrubs and vines, cool streams, and a variety of strong and tall trees. It was a place of retreat from the heat of the plains. It was a direct contrast to the vast deserts in the area—an oasis. (See Joshua 11:17; 12:7; Psalm 72:16; 92:12; Song of Solomon 4:8, 11, 15; Isaiah 35:2; 60:13; Jeremiah 18:14.)

4. The valley of Achor

The valley of Achor is the place where the Lord's anger was turned away from Israel after Achan's stoning and they were given a pass to enter the Promised Land (Josh. 7:24–26). In Isaiah 65:10 it was a reward for the people who seek God. According to *Nelson's Illustrated Bible Dictionary*, prophets used it as a symbol of a state of contentment and peace after the coming of the Messiah—a reversal of God's wrath on men for their sins, should they receive His Son and follow His ways. The valley of Achor is like a pass-through between the curse of sin and the blessing of God, between death and life, between the old covenant and the new covenant.

5. Mount Hermon, the blessing of the kingdom, the dew of Hermon

> Come with me from Lebanon, my spouse, with me from Lebanon. Look from the top of Amana, from the top of Shenir and Hermon, from the lions' dens, from the mountains of the leopards.
>
> —Song of Solomon 4:8

The dew of snow-capped, tri-peaked Mount Hermon is compared to unity—reminiscent of the Godhead. When the cool air of the snowy peaks of Mount Hermon meets the warm air of the desert, the clouds dispense a copious dew that is saturating, penetrating, and soaking. Therefore it is no wonder that at the base of Mount Hermon there are luscious gardens, fruitful orchards, and fertile fields. The dew of Hermon penetrates to the roots of trees and plants; it is not just a surface moisture.

6. Zion, the mountain of the Lord

Zion—also known as the city of David, city of peace, and city of God—was a fortress of protection for the Israelites (2 Sam. 5:7). It was the place where King David housed the ark of the covenant. It was a place of holiness, where the presence and goodness of God dwelled.

> Therefore they shall come and sing in the height of Zion, and shall flow together to the goodness of the LORD, for wheat, and for wine, and for oil, and for the young of the flock and of the herd: and their soul shall be as a watered garden; and they shall not sorrow any more at all.
>
> —Jeremiah 31:12, KJV

7. The Garden of Eden

The word *Eden* means "delight." Adam and Eve, the first man and woman, lived in the Garden of Delight. In Genesis 2 and 3 we find that Eden is a place of God's blessing and prosperity. It was plentiful with the original variety, beauty, and fruitfulness of God's creation. Every living thing can trace its beginning in the Garden of Eden. The garden also represents intimacy, a place where man was closest to God. He walked among them in the coolness of the day. There was no dividing wall of sin at the beginning. (See Genesis 3:8.)

ABUNDANCE AND PROSPERITY CONFESSIONS

I will prosper and be in health as my soul prospers.

I will not lack, for You are my shepherd, and I will not want (Ps. 23:1).

Lord, prosper me and let me have abundance.

Lord, You are El Shaddai, the God of more than enough; give me everything I need to fulfill my destiny, and let me have more than I need (Gen. 17).

Lord, You became poor that through Your poverty I might be rich.

Lord, let me not lack any good thing, for I delight myself in You.

Lord, give me the desires of my heart, for I seek You.

Lord, I put first Your kingdom and Your righteousness, and all things are added to me.

Lord, bless my coming in and my going out.

Lord, let me be blessed in the city and blessed in the field.

Lord, let me be blessed to be above and not beneath.

Lord, let me be blessed to be the head and not the tail.

Lord, let me be blessed with dominion and victory over the enemy.

Lord, let every thing my hand touches be blessed.

Lord, let Your blessing overtake my life.

Lord, let Your favor bless my life.

Lord, command Your blessing on my storehouse.

Lord, command Your blessing, even life evermore, on my life.

Lord, let me have plenty of silver.

Lord, multiply Your grace in my life, and let me abound to every good work.

Lord, let me have abundance and not scarceness.

Lord, let there be no holes in my bag.

Let the windows of heaven be opened over my life and pour me out a blessing I don't have room enough to receive. Lord, rebuke the devourer for my sake.

Lord, I seek You; cause me to prosper (2 Chron. 26:5).

Lord, speak over my life and let me prosper.

Lord, send Your angel and prosper my way (Gen. 24:40).

Lord, be with me and let me be a
prosperous person (Gen. 39:2).

Let me have wisdom and prosperity (1 Kings 10:7).

Lord God of heaven, prosper me (Neh. 2:20).

Lord, take pleasure in my prosperity (Ps. 35:27).

Lord, send prosperity to my life (Ps. 118:25).

Let peace and prosperity be within my house (Ps. 122:7).

Let the gifts You have given me
bring prosperity (Prov. 17:8).

Lord, You have called me; make my
way prosperous (Isa. 48:15).

Lord, rule and reign over my life
with prosperity (Jer. 23:5).

Lord, procure Your goodness and
prosperity in my life (Jer. 33:9).

Lord, bless me, and let me not forget
prosperity (Lam. 3:17).

Lord, let me prosper like Abraham (Gen. 24:35).

Lord, bless me and increase me like
Abraham my father (Isa. 51:2).

Lord, let me prosper like Joseph (Gen. 39:2).

Lord, bless me like Asher, and let me
dip my feet in oil (Deut. 33:24).

Lord, bless my house like the house
of Obed-Edom (2 Sam. 6:12).

Lord, bless me and bring me into a
wealthy place (Ps. 66:12).

Lord, give me power to get wealth (Deut. 8:18).

Lord, I am a giver; let wealth and riches
be in my house (Ps. 112:3).

Lord, Your blessing makes rich, and You add no sorrow.

Lord, bless me with enough to eat, with
plenty left (2 Chron. 31:10).

Lord, let me prosper like Daniel (Dan. 6:28).

Let ever journey I take be prosperous (Rom. 1:10).

Let every good seed I plant prosper (Zech. 8:12).

Prayers for the Blessing of Giving

It is more blessed to give than to receive (Acts 20:35).

I give, and it is given to me; pressed down, shaken
together, and running over, men give to me (Luke 6:38).

I sow bountifully, and I reap bountifully (2 Cor. 9:6).

Lord, remember all my offerings (Ps. 20).

I honor You with the firstfruits of my
increase; therefore, let my barns be
filled with plenty (Prov. 3:9–10).

I will not lack; I am a giver.

Let wealth and riches be in my house,
for I am a giver (Ps. 112:3).

I bring the tithe and offerings to the storehouse. Let the
windows of heaven be opened over my life (Mal. 3:10).

I bring the tithe and offering to the storehouse.
Rebuke the devourer for my sake (Mal. 3:11).

I sow into good ground, and I reap an
abundant harvest (Gal. 6:7).

I believe in seedtime and harvest as long
as the earth remains (Gen. 8:22).

I give, so release Your heaps into my life (2 Chron. 31:8).

I have a bountiful eye, and I give; therefore
I receive your blessing (Prov. 22:9).

I give; therefore give me richly all
things to enjoy (1 Tim. 6:17).

I will bring an offering and come
into Your courts (Ps. 96:8).

Let my prayers and giving come up as a
memorial before You (Acts 10:4).

I will support anointed ministers, and my needs are
met according to Your riches in glory (Phil. 4:18–19).

I will minister to You, Lord, with
my substance (Luke 8:2–3).

I am a doer of the Word, and I obey
Your Word by giving (Luke 6:38).

PRAYERS FOR THE BLESSING OF CARMEL AND SHARON

I receive the blessings of Carmel
and Sharon upon my life.

Let the excellency of Carmel be upon my life (Isa. 35:2).

Let my life be a fruitful field like Carmel (Isa. 35:2).

Let the beauty and fruitfulness of Carmel
be upon my life (Isa. 35:2).

Let my life be green and flourishing like
Carmel and Sharon (Isa. 35:2).

"In blossoming it shall blossom," this is Your
promise to me because of Your kingdom.

Let all my desert places bloom and come
alive like Sharon (Isa. 35:2).

Water my life, and let it blossom like Carmel.

Let waters gush forth in every wilderness
area of my life (Isa. 35:6–7).

Let my dry place become a pool (Isa. 35:6–7).

Water will gush forth in the wilderness
and streams in the desert.

The burning sand will become a pool, and the
thirsty ground bubbling springs (Isa. 35:6–7).

Let me feed upon the abundance of Carmel (Jer. 50:19).

Let Your streams flow into my life, and let it
become abundant like Carmel and Sharon.

There are no waste places in my life, but
my life is as abundant as Carmel.

Let joy and rejoicing increase in my life,
the joy of Carmel and Sharon.

Let the majesty and glory of Lebanon be upon my life.

Let all my desert places blossom as the rose (Isa. 35:1).

I receive the abundance and prosperity
of Carmel and Sharon.

Let the winter season come to an end, and let the
flowers appear in my life (Song of Sol. 2:11–13).

Let my life blossom as the fig tree (Song of Sol. 2:11–13).

Let my life be fruitful like the vine (Song of Sol. 2:11–13).

Lord, let Your fragrance manifest in
my life (Song of Sol. 2:11–13).

Let the blessing and prosperity of the myrtle
tree be upon my life (Isa. 55:13).

Let the blessing and fragrance of the
pine be upon my life (Isa. 60:13).

Let me flourish like the palm tree (Ps. 92:12).

Let me grow like the cedar in Lebanon (Ps. 92:12).

Let every area of my life grow like the lily (Hosea 14:5).

I receive the fullness of Carmel, the blessing
and prosperity of the kingdom.

Let fruitfulness increase in every
area of my life like Sharon.

I receive the plenty and abundance of Carmel.

My life is changing and becoming
like Carmel and Sharon.

Let all my fields blossom and be fruitful
like Carmel and Sharon.

Prayers for the Glory of Lebanon

Let the glory of Lebanon come into my life (Isa. 35:2).

Let the excellency of the cedars of Lebanon come into my life (Song of Sol. 5:15).

I receive the majesty of Lebanon because I am in the kingdom.

Let me grow and be strong as the cedars of Lebanon (Ps. 92:12).

Let the beauty of Lebanon be upon my life (Isa. 60:13).

Let me ascend to the heights of Lebanon and live in Your high places (Isa. 2:13).

Let me have the strength of the cedars of Lebanon.

Let the fruitfulness and abundance of Lebanon be upon my life (Ps. 72:16).

Let the glory of Lebanon be released from the building of Your temple, the church.

Lord, You created Lebanon for Your glory, and it is a symbol of the majesty of Your kingdom. Let the reality of Lebanon be released in my life.

Plant me as a tree of Lebanon, and let me grow strong because of Your blessing.

Let all my waste places become like the abundance of Lebanon.

Let the river of God flow from Your holy mountain and water my land, and let it become like Lebanon.

Let the mountain glories of Lebanon come into my life.

Let Your rain fall upon my life, and let
me grow like the trees of Lebanon.

I will clap my hands and praise You, I will
rejoice like the trees of Lebanon.

Let even my clothes be scented like the
cedars of Lebanon (Song of Sol. 4:11).

Let the streams of Lebanon flow into
my life (Song of Sol. 4:15).

PRAYERS FOR THE BLESSING OF ACHOR

Through Christ I am redeemed from the curse,
and my Achor has turned into a blessing.

Let the blessing of Achor be upon my life.

I will lie down and rest in the valley of Achor.

I will live in the valley of blessing and
enjoy the blessings of Achor.

You have brought me to your valley of blessing, and
I will enjoy the peace and prosperity of Achor.

You are my shepherd; I shall not want (Ps. 23:1).

You make me to lie down in green pastures,
and you have restored my soul (Ps. 23:2–3).

I will enjoy the green pastures of Achor.

I will enjoy the abundance and prosperity of Achor.

Achor is my habitation, because I
am a part of Your flock.

Command Your blessings upon me in Achor.

I have left the valley of the shadow of
death, and I have come to Achor.

There is no strife in my valley, but I will
enjoy the blessings of peace in Achor.

Let the beauty of Achor and Sharon be upon my life.

I have come into Your sheepfold; feed
me in Sharon and Achor.

I will be satisfied with Your abundance
in Sharon and Achor.

I have more than enough; I live in the prosperity
and blessing of Sharon and Achor.

PRAYERS FOR THE BLESSING
OF MOUNT HERMON

Let the dew of Hermon descend and
fall upon my life (Ps. 133).

I have come to the top of Amana and Senir; release the
blessing of the mountain upon my life (Song of Sol. 4:8).

PRAYERS FOR THE BLESSING OF ZION

I have come to your holy mountain, let
the blessing of Zion be upon my life.

I have come to Zion, Lord, command Your
blessing, even life forevermore (Ps. 133:3).

Let Your presence be upon my life continually,
and let Your blessing be continual.

I receive the blessing and favor of Zion.

There is no mountain as holy as Zion; I ascend and dwell at Your holy hill.

Zion is Your habitation; I will dwell and live where You are and enjoy Your blessings.

Let everlasting joy be upon my head, for I have come to Zion (Isa. 35:10).

Let gladness and joy overtake my life; let sorrow and sadness flee away (Isa. 35:10).

Let me sing in the height of Zion, and the goodness of the Lord shall flow over me; let my soul be like a watered garden, so that I will sorrow no more (Jer. 31:12).

PRAYERS FOR THE BLESSING OF EDEN

Let all my waste places become like Eden and my desert like the garden of the Lord (Isa. 51:3).

There is no ruin in my life, but I receive and walk in the blessing of Eden.

Let me be like Eden, like a watered garden and like a spring of water, whose waters fail not (Isa. 58:11).

Let the Word sown in my life spring forth, and let me become like Eden (Isa. 61:11).

Lord, I desire that You walk with me in the cool of the day as You did with Adam and Eve in the Garden of Eden (Gen. 3:8).

CHAPTER 4

THE BLESSING OF AUTHORITY FIGURES

You CANNOT HAVE peace and blessing without being under authority. Isaiah 9:7 says, "Of the increase of His government and peace there will be no end." Government means authority.

Israel did not have shalom because they refused to stay in line with God's governing authority and everyone did what was right in his own eyes. But Jesus came to reverse the curse of being out of covenant and to bring peace, blessing, and an abundant life through a new covenant. He brought the authority of the kingdom, full of "righteousness and peace and joy in the Holy Spirit" (Rom. 14:17). In order to receive that, we have to be submitted to Him and to those He puts in authority over us.

When your mind is governed by the Spirit of God, when you think like a saint, when you think good thoughts, and when your mind is not controlled by your flesh and you are submitted to authority, you will receive the blessing of God. The Word of God will help you submit to His authority and not be a carnally minded Christian and expect prosperity and peace.

> For to be carnally minded is death, but to be spiritually minded is life and peace. Because the carnal mind is enmity against God; for it is not subject to the law of God, nor indeed can be.
>
> —Romans 8:6–7

As this Scripture passage says, when you are carnally minded, you are not able to be subject to law and authority. Your mind is ruled by the flesh and determined to go its own way, but at the end of that is destruction (Prov. 16:25). Some people can't prosper because of their minds. They are fleshly. But when you are spiritually minded and have submitted your thoughts to the Lord's authority, you will have life and peace, life and prosperity, life and life more abundantly.

God wants you, as a saint of God, to renew your mind (Rom. 12:1–2). He wants you to be renewed in the spirit of your mind, because "as [a man] thinketh in his heart, so is he" (Prov. 23:7, KJV).

WHO IS YOUR AUTHORITY?

Parents, pastor, professors, local and federal government officials, and boss—whether you like them or not—are whom you are subject to on the earth. You are to pray for them. You are to submit yourself to their instruction and commands as long as they do not stand in direct conflict with God's laws.

Don't think that because you don't like your pastor, boss, governor, or even the president that you don't have to respect their authority. Jesus said to give to Caesar what is Caesar's and to God what is God's. Even when you don't agree with the ruling authority in the natural realm does not mean that God has not sat that person there for a season and a reason. God establishes the authority in the earth and removes it in His time (Dan. 2:21; Prov. 21:2; 1 Chron. 29:11–12).

We may not understand why a person is in a position of authority, but God's ways are higher than ours, so as we are subject to God, we are subject to man. Even Jesus found favor in the eyes of earthly authority (Luke 2:52).

SUBMIT TO AUTHORITY AND BE BLESSED

So often we want to do things our own way. We even attach God's name to it, saying that we are standing up for Him. But God wants us to honor those in authority over us. Daniel is a great example of a righteous man who rose in influence in a heathen nation by being submitted to the rulers of the land yet staying obedient to God. In turn, Daniel had the king's ear for any request. He influenced the laws and codes of the day, and he was protected by angels when his enemies set a trap to take him out.

Daniel asked for special permission to not be defiled by the dietary practices of the heathen nation that held him captive. By *asking* for this, he showed submission to the authority that was over him during that time. But he was also submitted to God by his faith that if he remained obedient to God, he would be blessed in such a way that would bring him favor. And he was right. The Bible says that after Daniel interpreted a dream for King Nebuchadnezzar, the king fell prostrate before Daniel and lavished honor upon him, giving him the highest place in the kingdom (Dan. 2:46–49).

When you submit to authority, you position yourself for the blessing of God. You also are placing yourself under those who have the authority to pronounce blessing over you through prophecy, words of encouragement, promotion, and correction.

SPIRITUAL AUTHORITY CONFESSIONS

I receive the blessing of those in
spiritual authority over my life.

I receive the benedictions (blessings)
of my church leadership.

I receive the blessing of prophecy from those who
minister by the inspiration of the Holy Spirit.

Let my spiritual leaders speak words
of blessing over my life.

I receive the blessing of the Word of God
ministered in my church over my life.

PRAYERS FOR THE BLESSING OF SUBMITTING TO AUTHORITY

Let me not be like the one who mocks his father
and scorns obedience to his mother, for the
ravens of the valley will pick out his eyes and
the young eagles will eat it (Prov. 30:17).

Power and might are in Your hands, Lord. It
is at Your discretion people are made great
and given strength (1 Chron. 29:12).

Lord, You control the course of world events. You
remove kings and set up other kings. You give wisdom
to the wise and knowledge to the scholars (Dan. 2:21).

I will obey and be submissive to those
who rule over me (Heb. 13:17).

I will be subject to the governing authorities,
because they are appointed by God (Rom. 13:1).

I will pray, intercede, and give thanks for all men,
kings, and all who are in authority (1 Tim. 2:1–2).

I will remember to be subject to rulers and authorities,
to obey, to be ready for every good work (Titus 3:1).

I will not be like the dreamers who reject authority
and speak evil of dignitaries (Jude 8).

Let me not speak on my own authority but on the
authority of the Father who dwells in me (John 14:10).

I will not resist authority or the ordinance of God
and bring judgment on myself (Rom. 13:2).

Rulers are not a terror to good works but
to evil. Therefore I will not fear authority,
because I will do what is good (Rom. 13:3).

PRAYERS FOR THE BLESSING OF SUBMITTING TO THE WISDOM OF GOD

Lord, teach me wisdom's ways and lead
me in straight paths (Prov. 4:11).

The Lord's wisdom will save my life (Eccles. 7:12).

I pray for an understanding heart that is
enshrined in wisdom (Prov. 14:33).

I tune my ears to Your wisdom, Lord, and
concentrate on understanding (Prov. 2:2).

I do not put my trust in human wisdom
but in the power of God (1 Cor. 2:5).

In You, O Lord, lie the hidden treasures
of wisdom and knowledge (Col. 2:3).

I listen when those who are older speak, for
wisdom comes with age (Job 32:7).

Lord, Your wisdom is more profitable than silver,
and its wages are better than gold (Prov. 3:14).

Let wisdom multiply my days and add
years to my life (Prov. 9:11).

Let my house be built by wisdom and become
strong through good sense (Prov. 24:3).

I will not be foolish and trust my own insight, but
I will walk in wisdom and be safe (Prov. 28:26).

Let the fruit of my life prove Your
wisdom is right (Luke 7:35).

Let the fear of the Lord teach me wisdom (Prov. 15:33).

I will obey Your commands, so that I
will grow in wisdom (Ps. 111:10).

Fill me with Your Spirit, O God, and give
me great wisdom, ability, and expertise
in all kinds of crafts (Exod. 31:3).

Lord, give me wisdom and knowledge
to lead effectively (2 Chron. 1:10).

Let those who have gone before me teach
me wisdom of old (Job 8:8–10).

True wisdom and power are found
in You, God (Job 12:13).

The price of Your wisdom, O Lord, cannot be
purchased with jewels mounted in fine gold;
its price is far above rubies (Job 28:17–18).

I will keep silent, O God. Teach me wisdom (Job 33:33).

Your wisdom will save me from evil people and
from the immoral woman (Prov. 2:12, 16).

I will embrace Your wisdom, for it is happiness
and a tree of life to me (Prov. 3:18).

I will pay attention to Your wisdom, O Lord. I will
listen carefully to Your wise counsel (Prov. 5:1).

Give me understanding so that Your knowledge
and wisdom will come easily to me (Prov. 14:6).

Grant me wisdom so that I may also have good
judgment, knowledge, and discernment (Prov. 8:12).

Thank You, Lord, that You will certainly give me the
wisdom and knowledge I requested (2 Chron. 1:12).

I will not be impressed with my own wisdom, but I will instead fear the Lord and turn away from evil (Prov. 3:7).

I will not turn my back on Your wisdom, O God, for it will protect and guard me (Prov. 4:6).

Your wisdom is better than strength (Eccles. 9:16).

I thank and praise You, God of my ancestors, for You have given me wisdom and strength (Dan. 2:23).

For You will give me the right words and such wisdom that none of my opponents will be able to reply or refute me (Luke 21:15).

I need wisdom; therefore, I will ask my generous God, and He will give it to me. He will not rebuke me for asking (James 1:5).

I pray that my life pleases You, O God, that You might grant me wisdom, knowledge, and joy (Eccles. 2:26).

CHAPTER 5

THE BLESSING of COVENANT

IN ISAIAH 54 God promised His people a covenant of peace (shalom): "For the mountains shall depart, and the hills be removed; but my kindness shall not depart from thee, neither shall the covenant of my peace be removed, saith the LORD that hath mercy on thee" (Isa. 54:10, KJV). But Israel never walked in that covenant of peace consistently because they continued to violate it. The greatest period of shalom was under King Solomon, whose name actually means peace. He was the most prosperous king of Israel. For a forty-year period Israel lived under that promise of shalom. But then Solomon married other wives and took part in idolatry, and there was a breach or a split from the covenant God had established.

Peace and shalom come from God. Only He can

give it, and He can take it away. We also have the choice to be blessed by walking in covenant with Him or to deactivate the blessings by not walking in covenant with Him.

> I form the light, and create darkness: I make peace, and create evil: I the LORD do all these things.
>
> —Isaiah 45:7, KJV

When you leave God and break His covenant, God will withdraw His shalom and allow disaster. The enemy will come into your land and destroy you. The sword will come in the land and prosperity will be destroyed. We see that this is true based on the Israelites' experiences all through the Book of Judges. But God will send warning and correction. He began to send prophets or "covenant messengers" to a covenant people to warn them of their covenant violation to give them a chance to repent before God's covenant wrath would come upon them. The prophets repeatedly said that there is no peace to the wicked.

If a prophet tells you that you will have a life of peace and you are violating God's Word—His covenant—the prophet is lying, because you will not experience shalom or peace or prosperity if you are not living in covenant with God. When someone is wicked and unrighteous, they are not at peace. Do not be fooled.

ONLY ONE WAY TO TRUE PEACE

God promised Israel that if they would keep His commandments, He would give them that shalom. But they did not listen. However, God had a plan that would not only restore Israel, if they chose, but His plan would also extend to all mankind.

In Jeremiah 31:31–34 God told the people that they would not be able to experience His peace under the old covenant because they continued to break it. He was alluding to the fact that they would only be able to experience God's true peace by way of the Messiah. The Messiah would come to make a new covenant. He came preaching the good news of the kingdom.

The only way you can experience the true shalom of God is through His Son—"the Prince of Peace" (Isa. 9:6). Jesus came preaching the "gospel of peace" (Rom. 10:15; Eph. 6:15)—or the gospel of shalom, the gospel of the kingdom. So we have to repent and receive the gospel of peace.

You are under a new covenant when you have accepted Christ's sacrifice for you and submit your life under His authority. But when you reject Christ and His sacrifice, you reject His new covenant and the very shalom you are looking for—just as the children of Israel rejected Him when He came. In Luke 19:41–42, Jesus cried over Jerusalem because He knew that if they rejected Him, they would not experience shalom but instead experience the sword. He knew that the enemy would build a trench around them and would besiege them on every side, and not one stone would be left upon another. War, famine, poverty, pestilence, and death were coming.

When you reject Jesus, you reject your only hope for peace and prosperity.

GOD ESTABLISHED A COVENANT SO THAT HE COULD BLESS YOU

You must understand how much God wants to bless His people with peace. He is the God of peace. He is Jehovah Shalom. He is the Lord our prosperity. But Israel couldn't see what was right in front of their eyes and missed it. So now this blessing belongs to the new covenant church. We inherit the promise of shalom—prosperity, favor, peace, health, and safety—because we are the ones who through the blood of Jesus enter into a new covenant with God. What Israel could not receive in the natural we receive in the spirit. It now belongs to you!

Covenant means faithfulness. Husband and wife have to be faithful to one another. Divorce comes into the picture because a covenant has been broken. Keep a covenant relationship with God. There is a huge advantage to doing this: blessing comes with covenant. God does not just bless people for any reason. Being in covenant with God is a contract or a promise of His peace, safety, favor, protection, health, and prosperity. And God does not break His promises or go back on His word (Num. 23:19; Isa. 55:11).

Covenant with God is a mutual blessing. God gets a people, and we get God (Lev. 26:12). However, when God doesn't get a people, there is no need for the covenant. We cannot be God's own if we do not walk according to His covenant. He cannot claim us and put His name on us. We can pray for peace all year long, but without Jesus, who is the Prince of Peace, shalom will never come.

> To all who are in Rome, beloved of God, called to be saints: Grace to you and peace [prosperity, shalom] from God our Father and the Lord Jesus Christ.
>
> —Romans 1:7

Notice whom the peace goes to. This peace is not to a physical people but to those "called to be saints." The saints possess the kingdom of God. Are you a saint? This goes beyond being saved. The saints are the holy ones. It doesn't mean that you are perfect or that you don't make mistakes. It means that your lifestyle is holy. You don't *live* a sinful lifestyle. In the New Testament, the saints walked in a level of holiness. They were not liars, drunkards, or whoremongers. They didn't mistreat people. If you are not a saint, you are not saved. The verse says, "Grace [*charis*, favor] and peace to those who are called to be saints." If you are a saint, prosperity belongs to you, not because of anything you did or didn't do, but because of what Jesus did for us all on Calvary. That is the blood covenant.

COVENANT CONFESSIONS

Shalom, prosperity, and peace are
mine through Jesus Christ.

I am a saint of God.

I am a child of God.

I have a covenant with God.

My covenant is a covenant of peace,
prosperity, and blessing.

I walk in covenant all the days of my life.

I enjoy shalom, prosperity, peace, and
safety all the days of my life.

I will walk in covenant.

I will be faithful to the covenant
through the blood of Jesus.

I have a covenant of shalom, peace
and prosperity, in my life.

Prayers for the Blessings of Deuteronomy 28

Lord, You keep covenant and mercy with those who
love You and keep Your commandments (Exod. 20).

Lord, You bless those who obey Your
voice and keep Your covenant.

Lord, I take hold of Your covenant
through Your death and sacrifice.

I choose life (blessing) (Deut. 30:19).

Let Your blessings come upon me
and overtake me (Deut. 28:2).

Let me be blessed in the city and
blessed in the field (Deut. 28:3).

Let the fruit of my body be blessed, and let all
the fruit of my labor be blessed (Deut. 28:4).

Let my basket and store be blessed (Deut. 28:5, kjv).

Let me be blessed coming in and
blessed going out (Deut. 28:6).

Let the enemies of my soul flee before
me seven ways (Deut. 28:7).

Command Your blessing upon my storehouses and
all I set my hand to, and bless my land (Deut. 28:8).

Establish me as a holy person unto
You, Lord (Deut. 28:9).

Let all people see that I am called
by Your name (Deut. 28:10).

Make me plenteous in goods (Deut. 28:11).

Open unto me Your good treasure, and let
heaven's rain fall upon my life and bless
the work of my hand (Deut. 28:12).

Let me lend (give) unto many nations
and not borrow (Deut. 28:12).

Make me the head and not the tail (Deut. 28:13).

Let me be above only and not beneath (Deut. 28:13).

PRAYERS FOR THE BLESSING OF
HEALTH AND HEALING

Lord, bless my bread and water and take
sickness away from my life (Exod. 23:25).

Lord, bless my food and protect me
from illness (Exod. 23:25).

Lord, bless my eyes (vision) and ears (hearing).

Lord, let the body You have created and
given me be blessed, for I am fearfully
and wonderfully made (Ps. 139:14).

Lord, bless my circulatory system, my nervous system, my endocrine system, my muscular system, and my skeletal system.

Lord, let my organs be blessed, and let every part of my body function the way You intended.

Lord, let my heart beat with the rhythm of life.

Lord, You are Jehovah Shalom, my peace, my health, my prosperity (Judg. 6:24).

Lord, you are Jehovah Shammah; let Your presence give me life and health (Ezek. 48:35).

Lord, bless my blood, for the life of the flesh is in the blood.

Lord, bless me with long life and show me Your salvation (Ps. 91:16).

Lord, bless me with strength, and let me not be feeble (Ps. 105:37).

Lord, let my hands and knees be confirmed and strong (Isa. 35:3).

I will love You, O Lord, my strength (Ps. 18:1).

Let Your strength be made perfect in weakness (2 Cor. 12:9).

I will not confess weakness; I am strong (Joel 3:10).

Lord, lift Your countenance (face) upon me (Num. 6:26).

Lord, show me good, and lift the light of Your countenance (face) upon me (Ps. 4:6).

Lord, bless me and make me exceedingly glad with Your presence (Ps. 21:6).

Lord, make me full of joy in Your presence (Acts 2:28).

Lord, let Your glory be upon my
countenance (face) (2 Cor. 3:7).

Lord, in Your countenance (face) is life, and Your
favor is like a cloud of the latter rain (Prov. 16:15).

Lord, hide not Your face from me (Ps. 27:9).

Lord, make Your face to shine upon Me;
I am Your servant (Ps. 31:16).

Lord, I am blessed because my
strength is in You (Ps. 84:5).

Let my flesh be fresher than a child's, and let me
return to the days of my youth (Job 33:25).

Lord, I am blessed with Abraham because
I believe the gospel (Gal. 3:7–9).

Let not my eye become dim or my natural
vigor diminished (Deut. 34:7).

Lord, Your fear (reverence) is health to my flesh
and strength to my bones (Prov. 3:7–8).

Let your fear be health to my nerves
and sinews (Prov. 3:8, AMP).

Lord, I will keep Your word before my eyes,
and in the midst of my heart, let Your words
be health to my flesh (Prov. 4:21–22).

Lord, You are the health of my
countenance (Ps. 43:5, KJV).

Lord, let Your saving health touch my life (Ps. 67:2, KJV).

Lord, let my health spring forth speedily (Isa. 58:8).

Lord, restore health unto me and heal
me of my wounds (Jer. 30:17).

Lord, bring health and a cure to every area of my
life, and give me the abundance of peace (Jer. 33:6).

Lord, let me prosper and be in health,
even as my soul prospers (3 John 2).

Lord, You are the Sun of Righteousness; arise over
my life with healing in Your wings (Mal. 4:2).

Let my soul (mind, will, emotions) be
healed through Your mercy (Ps. 41:4).

Lord, heal every breach in my life (Ps. 60:2).

Lord, I believe all my iniquities are forgiven
and all my sicknesses are healed (Ps. 103:3).

Lord, send Your word to heal me, and deliver
me from all my destructions (Ps. 107:20).

Let my heart be whole, and bind up
all my wounds (Ps. 147:3).

CHAPTER 6

THE BLESSING OF SHALOM

As I mentioned in the introduction, activating the blessings of God has everything to do with dwelling in the peace or shalom of God, which is an all-inclusive word that encompasses prosperity, safety, health, protection, fruitfulness, and abundance. According to the Hebrew definition, we can substitute the word *prosperity* with *shalom* (peace).

Religion has conditioned us to believe that life should be full of trouble and that one day by and by we will go to heaven and then we will have peace. Peace is not only for heaven but also for the here and now on the earth. Your days should not be full of trouble. That doesn't mean trouble will not come, but you can stand up and tell trouble to go. You do not have to live a life of worry and anxiety. Peace is yours.

Prosperity is yours. Even when trouble comes, it will not take away your peace.

The whole world is looking for peace. But there is only one way to peace, and that is through Jesus. He says, "I am the way..." (John 14:6); "I am The-Lord-Is-Peace [Jehovah Shalom]" (Judg. 6:24). Having Jesus in your heart is the way of peace. No Jesus; no peace. That's when prosperity comes; that is when blessing comes. Peace is what you have as a saint of God. You are also a peacemaker, and according to Matthew 5:9, you are blessed. You bring shalom wherever you go because Jesus is inside of you. You can change the whole atmosphere of a room, because the Prince of Peace lives inside of you. This is your covenant.

> How beautiful are the feet of those who preach the gospel of peace, who bring glad tidings of good things!
>
> —Romans 10:15

The gospel is that Jesus Christ came and died so that you could experience the shalom of God. The chastisement—the price—of our peace was upon Him. He was beaten and crucified so we could have peace. All who believe and come under the rule of the Messiah can have peace.

You can have prosperity and live in safety, and all the evil beasts will be driven from your life. You will not be tormented by devils. You will have the blessing of God. It's the guarantee of His covenant of peace. It belongs to the saints of God. So no matter how bad the news gets, don't let the devil take your peace and your shalom away from you.

No matter what goes on, say, "Jehovah Shalom, You are my peace. You are my prosperity. You're the one who gives me shalom. I refuse to be tormented by the devil, to be vexed, harassed, oppressed, poor, or broke. I refuse to not have the peace of God because Jesus was chastised for my peace. I am a saint of God. I am in covenant. I have a right to peace. I can walk in that covenant. A thousand can fall at my side and ten thousand at my right hand, but it will not come nigh me, because I have a covenant of shalom."

Realize that it is not something coming one day. It's here, and it's yours. Jesus is the Prince of Peace. Do you have Jesus on the inside of you? His peace is supernatural. It's already done. All you have to do is walk in faith, and it's yours. This is why Jesus came.

KINGDOM PEACE IN A CHAOTIC WORLD

> For the kingdom of God is not eating and
> drinking, but righteousness and peace and
> joy in the Holy Spirit.
>
> —Romans 14:17

Peace is the kingdom of God. If you're not in the kingdom, you don't have shalom. If you call yourself a child of God, but you keep up a lot of confusion, there's something wrong. A child of God is a peacemaker (Rom. 12:18; Heb. 12:14). Are you a peaceable person? Do you like mess? The church is intended by God to be a model of shalom to the world.

When the world is struggling to find peace, where can they go? Whom can they turn to? Where is the model for peace? Whom can the world look at to see a model for peace? Whom can they look at as a group of people from all different backgrounds—black and white, Jew and Gentile, coming together and living in peace because of the Prince of Peace? There is only one place that this happens—the church, where the wolf lies down with the lamb (Isa. 11:6; Isa. 65:25).

This is a picture that represents the coming of the Prince of Peace into the hearts of people whereby they can love people whom they once hated. You can't be a child of God if you hate people. The church is the one place where we can show the world how to live in peace. That's our calling, and for it we will be blessed. Blessed are the *shalom* makers!

Sometimes we can get so caught up in strife that we begin to think that it's normal to have problems. But it's not. Command good days in your life to be at peace and full of blessing and prosperity. Speak blessing and prosperity over your neighbor, your troubled family member, and your coworkers.

> He who would love life and see good days, let him refrain his tongue from evil, and his lips from speaking deceit. Let him turn away from evil and do good; let him seek peace and pursue it.
>
> —1 Peter 3:10–11

Some don't think they are living unless it's hard. But that is not what Jesus died for you to have. You can have a good life, especially when you "refrain your tongue from evil." Watch your mouth. Don't gossip, argue, fight, or add to confusion. And don't keep company with people who take part in that behavior. Seek peace. Peace is prosperity. You cannot have prosperity if you don't control your tongue. A blessed person is someone who knows how to guard his tongue.

The kingdom of God is a community of peace. Saved people are peaceful people. You can disagree with somebody and still be peaceable. Contention does not belong in the house of God—or in the lives of His people. James 3:17 says, "But the wisdom that is from above is first pure, then peaceable, gentle, willing to yield ["easy to be entreated" (KJV), approachable], full of mercy and good fruits, without partiality and without hypocrisy."

When you're walking in God's wisdom, hearing from heaven and hearing the voice of God…when you're getting your wisdom from above, not earthly or fleshly wisdom…when Christ becomes your wisdom, you will go into prosperity. One of the benefits of wisdom is prosperity. Proverbs 3:16 says that riches and honor are in the hands of the wise. The wise and prosperous are peacemakers.

> Blessed (enjoying enviable happiness, spiritually prosperous—with life-joy and satisfaction in God's favor and salvation, regardless of their outward conditions) are the makers and maintainers of peace, for they shall be called the sons of God!
> —Matthew 5:9, AMP

Prosperous people will walk away from a fight and confusion even if they don't get their point across. They see strife as detrimental to their prosperity. They do not make room for it in their lives. "Follow peace with all men..." (Heb. 12:14, KJV).

Peace is one of the fruit of the Spirit (Gal. 5:22). As a child of God, confusion and strife vex you and don't agree with your spirit. You can't be around that. It is not *normal*. The church is to be God's community of shalom.

> If it is possible, as much as depends on you,
> live peaceably with all men.
>
> —Romans 12:18

Prosperous people are peaceful people. They are blessed. They have more than enough. They love life and see good days. They are citizen of the heavenly kingdom of God because they have been redeemed from the curses of sin and death.

PEACE CONFESSIONS

My life is good and my days are good
because I keep my tongue from evil.

I hate evil, I do good, and I seek after peace.

I commit my life to peace and prosperity.

I will live in peace, I will walk in
peace, and I will seek peace.

Jesus is my peace.

I am a peaceable person.

He is my Jehovah Shalom, my prosperity and my peace.

I will walk in peace all the days of my life.

I will see good, I will love life, and I
will have many good days.

I am blessed and prosperous, because
I am a peaceable person.

KINGDOM BLESSING CONFESSIONS

I am in the kingdom through faith in Christ,
and I receive the blessings of the kingdom.

I receive the inheritance of the kingdom.

I receive the deliverance of the kingdom (Matt. 12:28).

I receive the healing of the kingdom (Matt. 10:1).

I receive and walk in the peace of
the kingdom (Rom. 14:17).

I receive and walk in the joy of the
kingdom (Rom. 14:17).

I receive and walk in the righteousness
of the kingdom (Rom. 14:17).

I receive and walk in the power of
the kingdom (Luke 9:1).

I receive and walk in the authority
of the kingdom (Luke 9:1).

I receive understanding in the mysteries
of the kingdom (Matt. 13).

I seek first the kingdom, and everything
I need is added to me.

I reside and live in a blessed kingdom, and
I receive the blessing of the King.

I receive the favor of the King.

I receive the protection and salvation of the King.

I will serve the King all the days of my life.

I am an ambassador of the King.

I have been translated from darkness into the
kingdom of God's dear Son (Col. 1:13, KJV).

I am in the kingdom of light.

I receive the new wine and milk in
the kingdom (Joel 3:18).

I enter into the rest of the kingdom.

CONFESSIONS FOR THE BLESSINGS OF REDEMPTION

Christ is my redemption (1 Cor. 1:30).

I am the ransomed of the Lord (Isa. 35:10).

I have passed from curse to blessing because
I am ransomed (Isa. 51:10, KJV).

The Lord is my ransom (1 Tim. 2:6).

I am redeemed from the curse, and the blessing
of Abraham is mine (Gal. 3:13–14).

I am redeemed from poverty,
sickness, and spiritual death.

I am redeemed from destruction, and I am crowned
with loving-kindness and tender mercies (Ps. 103:4).

I am redeemed from all curses of the Law.

I am redeemed from the curse of poverty.

I am redeemed from all curses of sickness and disease.

I am redeemed from all curses of insanity and madness.

I am redeemed from all curses of fear and terror.

I am redeemed from all curses of pride and rebellion.

I am redeemed from all curses of
schizophrenia (double-mindedness).

I am redeemed from all curses of rejection and abuse.

I am redeemed from all curses of family destruction.

I am redeemed from all curses of witchcraft and idolatry.

I am redeemed from all curses of failure and frustration.

I am redeemed from cursing, confusion,
and rebuke (Deut. 28:20).

I am redeemed from the pestilence (Deut. 28:21, KJV).

I am redeemed from consumption (Deut. 28:22).

I am redeemed from the fever (Deut. 28:22).

I am redeemed from the inflammation (Deut. 28:22).

I am redeemed from severe burning (Deut. 28:22).

I am redeemed from the sword (Deut. 28:22).

I am redeemed from scorching
and mildew (Deut. 28:22).

I am redeemed from drought (Deut. 28:23–24).

I am redeemed from being smitten
before my enemies (Deut. 28:25).

I am redeemed from vultures and jackals (Deut. 28:26).

I am redeemed from the boils, the
scab, and the itch (Deut. 28:27).

I am redeemed from madness, blindness,
and confusion of heart (Deut. 28:28).

I am redeemed from oppression and
spoiling (Deut. 28:29, KJV).

I am redeemed from having no strength (Deut. 28:32).

I am redeemed from oppression
and crushing (Deut. 28:33).

I am redeemed from being smitten (Deut. 28:35).

I am redeemed from being an astonishment,
a proverb, and a byword (Deut. 28:37).

I am redeemed from planting and
not reaping (Deut. 28:38).

I am redeemed from the worm (Deut. 28:39).

I am redeemed from miscarriage (Deut. 28:4).

I am redeemed from my seed going
into captivity (Deut. 28:41).

I am redeemed from the locust (Deut. 28:42).

I am redeemed from being low (Deut. 28:43).

I am redeemed from borrowing (Deut. 28:44).

I am redeemed from being the tail (Deut. 28:44).

I am redeemed from being pursued and overtaken by curses (Deut. 28:45).

I am redeemed from curses that make me a sign and a wonder (Deut. 28:46).

I am redeemed from hunger, thirst, nakedness, and want (Deut. 28:48).

I am redeemed from the yoke of iron (Deut. 28:48).

I am redeemed from fierce enemies (Deut. 28:49–50).

I am redeemed from the devourer (Deut. 28:51).

I am redeemed from the siege (Deut. 28:52).

I am redeemed from straitness (Deut. 28:53, KJV).

I am redeemed from all plagues (Deut. 28:59).

I am redeemed from all diseases (Deut. 28:60).

I am redeemed from the evil eye (Deut. 28:56, KJV).

I am redeemed from distress (Deut. 28:55).

I am redeemed from serious sicknesses (Deut. 28:59).

I am redeemed from sicknesses that cling (Deut. 28:60).

I am redeemed from sicknesses I have never heard of (Deut. 28:61).

I am redeemed from decrease (Deut. 28:62).

I am redeemed from being scattered (Deut. 28:64).

I am redeemed from serving other gods (Deut. 28:64).

I am redeemed from a trembling heart, failing eyes, and sorrow of mind (Deut. 28:65, KJV).

I am redeemed from fear in the day (Deut. 28:66).

I am redeemed from fear in the night (Deut. 28:66).

I am redeemed from my life hanging in doubt (Deut. 28:66).

I am redeemed from the bondage of Egypt (Deut. 28:68).

My soul is redeemed, and I will not be desolate (Ps. 25:16).

My Redeemer is mighty, and He pleads my cause (Prov. 23:11).

I will not fear because my Redeemer helps me (Isa. 41:14).

My Redeemer teaches me to profit and leads me in the way I should go (Isa. 48:17).

My Redeemer gives me everlasting kindness and mercy (Isa. 54:8).

My Redeemer has turned away my transgressions (Isa. 59:20).

The Lord has redeemed me from my troubles (Ps. 25:22).

I commit my spirit into the hands of my Redeemer (Ps. 31:5).

My Redeemer helps me (Ps. 44:26).

My Redeemer has delivered me from the power of the grave (Ps. 49:15).

I will greatly rejoice and sing, for the Lord has redeemed me (Ps. 71:23).

I am redeemed from deceit and violence (Ps. 72:14, KJV).

My Redeemer remembers me (Ps. 74:2).

I am redeemed from the hand of the enemy
and from them who hate me (Ps. 107:2).

I am redeemed from all my iniquities (Ps. 130:8).

I am converted and redeemed with
righteousness (Isa. 1:27).

No lions or ravenous beasts are in my
path; I am redeemed (Isa. 35:9).

My transgressions have been blotted
out by my Redeemer (Isa. 44:22).

Let the heavens and the earth rejoice and sing,
for I have been redeemed (Isa. 44:23).

I have come to Zion with singing, and everlasting joy
is upon my head, for I am redeemed (Isa. 51:11, KJV).

I have obtained joy and gladness; sorrow and mourning
have left my life, for I am redeemed (Isa. 51:11, KJV).

I have been redeemed without money (Isa. 52:3).

All my waste places will sing, because I
have been redeemed (Isa. 52:9).

I will drink the milk of the nations, for
I have been redeemed (Isa. 60:16).

I am holy, for I have been redeemed (Isa. 62:12).

I have been delivered out of the hand of the wicked
and the terrible, for I am redeemed (Jer. 15:21).

I have been redeemed and ransomed from him
who was stronger than me (Jer. 31:11).

The Lord has redeemed my life (Lam. 3:58).

I will continue to increase, for I
am redeemed (Zech. 10:8).

The Lord has visited and redeemed me (Luke 1:68).

I have been redeemed from iniquity
and purified (Titus 2:14, KJV).

I will sing a new song, for I am redeemed (Rev. 14:3).

I have been redeemed with an
outstretched arm (Exod. 6:6).

I have come to Zion, the holy habitation, for
I have been redeemed (Exod. 15:13).

I have been redeemed by the Lord's great
power and by His strong hand (Neh. 1:10).

I receive abundant redemption (Ps. 130:7).

I am justified freely by His grace and the
redemption that is in Christ Jesus (Rom. 3:24).

Christ Jesus is my redemption (1 Cor. 1:30).

I have redemption through His blood, the forgiveness
of sins, according to the riches of His grace (Eph. 1:7).

PRAYERS FOR THE BLESSING OF SHALOM

Let me know the way of peace (Rom. 3:17).

May the God of peace be with me (Rom. 15:33).

Let mercy, peace, and love be multiplied to me (Jude 2).

Let peace come to me, my household,
and all that I have (1 Sam. 25:6).

PRAYERS TꞭꞧꞦꞧⱵⱵ ⱵⱵ BLESSINGS

O Lord, lift Your countenance upon me
and give me peace (Num. 6:26).

Thank You, Lord, for giving me Your
covenant of peace (Num. 25:12).

I will depart from evil and do good; I will
seek peace and pursue it (Ps. 34:14).

You have redeemed my soul in peace from
the battle that was against me (Ps. 55:18).

Your law gives me great peace, and nothing
causes me to stumble (Ps. 119:165).

Let peace be in my walls and prosperity
within my palaces (Ps. 122:7).

Lord, You make peace in my borders and fill
me with the finest wheat (Ps. 147:14).

I am spiritually minded; therefore life
and peace are mine (Rom. 8:6).

Lord, You are not the author of confusion
but of peace (1 Cor. 14:33).

You, O Lord, are my peace and have
made me one with You (Eph. 2:14).

Let my household be counted worthy, so that
Your peace will come upon it (Matt. 10:13).

The peace You give to me is not what the world gives;
therefore my heart will not be troubled (John 14:27).

I will acquaint myself with You and be at peace,
and good will come to me (Job 22:21).

Thank You, Lord, that You give me
strength and peace (Ps. 29:11).

I pray that I will be meek and delight myself
in the abundance of peace (Ps. 37:11).

Let me be like the one who is blameless and upright,
for the future of that man is peace (Ps. 37:37).

Let my mind be stayed on You, and You will keep me
in perfect peace because I trust in You (Isa. 26:3).

Lord, You establish peace for me (Isa. 26:12).

I will dwell in a peaceful habitation, in secure
dwellings, and in quiet resting places (Isa. 32:18).

My children will be taught by the Lord, and
their peace will be great (Isa. 54:13).

Let Your peace guard my heart and mind (Phil. 4:7).

Speak peace to me, God, and let me
not turn back to folly (Ps. 85:8).

I pray that my ways will be pleasing to You,
Lord, so that You will make even my enemies
to be at peace with me (Prov. 16:7).

Your thoughts toward me are peace (Jer. 29:11).

Bring health and healing to me, O Lord, and reveal
to me the abundance of peace and truth (Jer. 33:6).

I will pursue those things that make
for peace (Rom. 14:19).

The God of peace will crush Satan
under my feet (Rom. 16:20).

You have made a covenant of peace with me, and
it is an everlasting covenant (Ezek. 37:26).

CHAPTER 7

THE BLESSING OF DECLARING "NEVER AGAIN!"

WE HAVE REACHED the final chapter of this book. You should already feel the heavens opening over you. Now, I want you to say with me, "Things will never be the same again in my life, in the name of Jesus!" The confessions that you will recite aloud in this chapter will turn your life around and help put an end to defeat and failure!

Even the Lord said never again.

> I will remember My covenant which is between Me and you and every living creature of all flesh; the waters shall never again become a flood to destroy all flesh.
>
> —Genesis 9:15

The Lord promised Noah that He would "never again" destroy the earth with a flood.

Moses told the people of Israel that they would see Pharaoh no more.

> And Moses said to the people, "Do not be afraid. Stand still, and see the salvation of the LORD, which He will accomplish for you today. For the Egyptians whom you see today, you shall see again no more forever."
>
> —Exodus 14:13

In other words, *never again* would Pharaoh oppress them. This was the word of the Lord first to Moses and then to the people.

I know that whatever God does is final. Nothing can be added to it or taken from it. "The enemy is finished, in endless ruins; the cities you uprooted are now forgotten" (Ps. 9:6, NLT). Cities were destroyed in God's judgment, never to rise again. Kings were removed from thrones, never to sit again.

Jesus told His disciples, "I will give you the keys to the kingdom of heaven, and God in heaven will allow whatever you allow on earth. But he will not allow anything that you don't allow" (Matt. 16:19, CEV; see also Matt. 18:18, CEV).

As a believer you have authority to allow or disallow. Don't allow the enemy to control your life. Take a stand against the wicked one. Use your authority in the name of Jesus. Do it by the power of the Holy Spirit. Don't give place to the devil. Rise up in faith and confess what you believe. Exercise your authority against the powers of darkness, and you will experience the blessings of God. It's time for you to declare, "Never again!"

NEVER AGAIN WILL I ALLOW SATAN TO CONTROL MY LIFE

Never again will Pharaoh (Satan) control me, because I have been delivered from his power.

Never again will I be a slave to Satan; I am now a servant of Christ.

Never again will I allow the devil to do what he desires in my life, but I resist the devil, and he flees from me (James 4:7).

Never again will I listen to or believe the lies of the devil, for he is a liar and the father of lies (John 8:44).

Never again will I listen to the voice of the wicked one.

Never again will I be vexed by unclean spirits (Luke 6:18, KJV).

Never again will I be harassed by the enemy (Matt. 9:36, AMP).

Never again will I be bound, for Christ has made me free. I am free indeed (John 8:36).

Never again will demons operate in and control my life.

Never again will I allow the demons of fear to control my life.

Never again will I allow the demons of pride to puff me up (1 Cor. 4:6).

Never again will I allow the demons of lust to operate in my members.

Never again will I allow the demons of religion to make me act religiously.

Never again will I allow the demons of double-mindedness to confuse me and make me indecisive (James 1:8).

Never again will I allow the demons of rejection to control my life.

Never again will I allow disobedience and rebellion to control my life.

Never again will I allow curses to hinder my life. I break every curse, for I have been redeemed from the curse (Gal. 3:13).

Never again will I open the door for demons to come into my life through unforgiveness (Matt. 18:35).

Never again will I open the door for demons to enter my life through habitual sin.

Never again will I open the door for demons to enter my life through occult involvement.

Never again will I open the door for demons to enter through rebellion and disobedience.

Never again will the demon of mind control affect my thinking, I sever all the tentacles of mind control.

Never again will serpent and scorpion spirits affect my life, for I have power to tread on serpents and scorpions.

Never again will I be tormented by the enemy.

Never again will the enemy be my master; Jesus is my Lord.

Never again will I tolerate the works of the devil in my life, for Jesus came and destroyed the works of the devil (1 John 3:8).

Never again will I allow passivity to keep me inactive.

Never again will I be beneath and not above (Deut. 28:13).

Never again will I be cursed and not walk in blessing, for the blessing of Abraham is mine (Gal. 3:13–14).

Never again will I say yes to the enemy.

Never again will I agree to the lies of the devil.

Never again will I compromise my standards and holiness; the Word of God is my standard, not the standards of the world (2 Cor. 10:2, NIV).

Never again will I act hypocritically (Mark 7:6).

Never again will I condemn the guiltless (Matt. 12:7).

Never again will I give place to the devil (Eph. 4:27).

Never again will I allow the enemy to control my will, but I submit my will to the will of God.

Never again will I allow the enemy to
control my emotions, but I yield my
emotions to the joy and peace of God.

Never again will I allow the enemy to
control my sexual character, but I yield my
body as a living sacrifice (Rom. 12:1).

Never again will I allow the enemy to control my mind,
but I renew my mind with the Word of God (Rom. 12:2).

Never again will I allow the enemy to
control my appetite, but I yield my appetite
to the control of the Holy Spirit.

Never again will I allow the enemy to control my
tongue, but I yield my tongue to the Holy Spirit.

Never again will I allow the enemy to control
any part of my life, but my life is under the
control of the Spirit and Word of God.

Never again will I allow the enemy
to control my destiny, but God is the
revealer and finisher of my destiny.

Never again will I allow the enemy to
abort any plan of God for my life.

Never again will I allow people to draw me away
from the love of God, but I commit myself to
walking in love, for God is love (1 John 4:7–8).

Never again will I shut up my bowels
of compassion (1 John 3:17, kjv).

Never again will I behave unseemly, for love
does not behave unseemly (1 Cor. 13:5, kjv).

Never again will I be easily provoked, for love is not easily provoked (1 Cor. 13:5).

Never again will I seek my own, for love does not seek its own (1 Cor. 13:5).

Never again will I think evil, for love does not think evil (1 Cor. 13:5).

Never again will I lose hope, for love hopes all things (1 Cor. 13:7).

Never again will I give up, for love endures all things (1 Cor. 13:7).

Never again will I act and think like a child (1 Cor. 13:11).

Never again will I be passive with the gifts of the Spirit, but I desire spiritual gifts (1 Cor. 14:1).

Never again will I allow the accuser to accuse me, for I am washed and cleansed by the blood of the Lamb (Rev. 1:5; 7:14).

Never again will I allow sorrow and sadness to control my soul, for the Lord has taken away my sorrow and pain (Isa. 65:19).

Never again will I labor and work in vain (Isa. 65:23).

Never again will the heavens be shut over my life, but the Lord has opened the windows of heaven (Mal. 3:10).

NEVER AGAIN WILL I ALLOW SATAN TO CONTROL MY FINANCES

Never again will I allow poverty and lack to control my life, for my God supplies all my need according to His riches in glory by Christ Jesus (Phil. 4:19).

Never again will I lack, for I have plenty (Gen. 27:28).

Never again will I lack, for I will have plenty of silver (Job 22:25).

Never again will I lack; I will be plenteous in goods (Deut. 28:11).

Never again will I lack, but I will prosper through prophetic ministry (Ezra 6:14).

Never again will I sow and not reap, but I will reap where others have sown (John 4:38).

Never again will I carry a bag full of holes (Hag. 1:6).

Never will I lack glory (*kabowd*), honor, abundance, riches, splendor, glory, dignity, reputation, and reverence (Ps. 84:11).

Never again will I be poor, for the Lord became poor that I through His poverty might be rich (2 Cor. 8:9).

Never again will I live without the desires of my heart, because I will delight myself in the Lord (Ps. 37:4).

Never again will I allow covetousness to control my life, but I am a liberal giver (Prov. 11:25).

Never again will the enemy devour my finances, for the Lord has rebuked the devourer for my sake (Mal. 3:11).

Never again will I hold back from giving, for
I give, and it is given to me, good measure,
pressed down, shaken together, and running
over do men give to me (Luke 6:38).

Never again will I allow fear to stop me from giving.

Never again will I allow debt to control my life, for
I will lend unto many nations and not borrow, for
the borrower is servant to the lender (Prov. 22:7).

Never again will I allow doubt and unbelief to stop me
from believing in the promises of God (Heb. 3:19).

Never again will I think poverty and lack, for as
a man thinks in his heart, so is he (Prov. 23:7).

Never again will my basket and store be empty, for
my basket and store are blessed (Deut. 28:5, KJV).

Never again will I allow slothfulness and
laziness to dominate my life, for slothfulness
casts into a deep sleep (Prov. 19:15, KJV).

Never again will I allow Satan to steal my
finances, but I have abundant life (John 10:10).

Never again will I limit what God can do in
my finances and in my life (Ps. 78:41).

Never again will I tolerate lack, for my God
gives me abundance (Deut. 28:47).

Never again will I have just enough, for El Shaddai
gives me more than enough (Gen. 17:1–2).

Never again will I use my money for
sinful things (Ezek. 16:17).

Never again will the enemy hold back my blessings.

Never again will I doubt God's desire to prosper me, for the Lord takes pleasure in the prosperity of his servant (Ps. 35:27).

Never again will I be the tail and not the head (Deut. 28:13).

Never again will I be a borrower and not a lender (Deut. 28:12).

Never again will I be behind and not in front (Deut. 25:18).

Never again will I believe I don't have power to get wealth, for God gives me power to get wealth to establish His covenant (Deut. 8:18).

Never again will I lack any good thing, because I will seek the Lord (Ps. 34:10).

Never again will I lack prosperity, but whatever I do will prosper, because I delight in the law of the Lord (Ps. 1).

Never again will I lack anointing for my head (Eccles. 9:8).

Never again will I allow the circumstances to steal my joy, for the joy of the Lord is my strength (Neh. 8:10).

Never again will I lack favor for my life, for with favor the Lord will surround me as a shield (Ps. 5:12).

Never again will I walk in the flesh instead of walking in the Spirit (Gal. 5:16).

Never again will I allow my flesh to do what it wants. I am crucified with Christ.

Never again will walk in the works of the flesh, but I will manifest the fruit of the Spirit (Gal. 5:22–23).

Never again will I be weak, for I am strong (Joel 3:10).

Never again will I be oppressed, for I am far from oppression (Isa. 54:14).

Never again will I be depressed.

Never again will I vexed and tormented by demons, for I have been delivered from the power of darkness and translated in the kingdom of God's dear Son (Col. 1:13, KJV).

NEVER AGAIN WILL I ALLOW SIN TO DOMINATE MY LIFE

Never again will I love or enjoy sin.

Never again will I allow sin to reign in my body (Rom. 6:12).

Never again will I depart from holiness (Heb. 12:14).

Never again will I allow lust to dominate me (2 Pet. 1:4).

Never again will I yield my members as members of unrighteousness, but I yield my members as instruments of righteousness (Rom. 6:13).

Never again will I allow lust to war in my members, causing me to war and fight my brothers and sisters (James 4:1).

Never again will I allow fornication, uncleanness,
inordinate affection, evil concupiscence,
and covetousness, which is idolatry, to
operate in my members (Col. 3:5, KJV).

Never again will I sin against my brethren (1 Cor. 8:12).

Never again will I have respect of persons,
which is sin (James 2:9, KJV).

Never again will I develop ungodly soul ties (2 Cor. 6:14).

Never again will I allow sexual sin to reign in my life.

Never again will I allow my eyes to look at
perverse things, but I make a covenant with my
eyes not to behold any wicked thing (Job 31:1).

Never again will I allow perversion and
sexual immorality to control my life;
I flee fornication (1 Cor. 6:18).

Never again will I enjoy that which is
forbidden by the Lord (2 Cor. 6:17).

Never again will I act inappropriately
with the opposite sex.

Never again will I allow worldliness and
carnality to control my life (1 John 2:15).

Never again will I conform to the world (Rom. 12:2).

Never again will I allow anger to control my life, but I
am slow to anger and sin not (Prov. 16:32; James 1:19).

Never again will I let the sun go down
on my wrath (Eph. 4:26).

Never again will I let rage manifest in my life.

Never again will I lose control of my temper,
for he that does not rule his spirit is like a city
broken down without walls (Prov. 25:28).

Never again will I get angry at another person's success,
but I rejoice in the success of others (Rom. 12:10, 15).

Never again will I be possessive or
controlling of another person.

Never again will I allow a person to
dominate and control me.

Never again will I allow selfishness to dominate me.

Never again will I allow disobedience and rebellion
in my life, but I will be willing and obedient
and eat the good of the land (Isa. 1:19).

Never again will I allow addiction to control my
appetite, but I am temperate in all things (1 Cor. 9:25).

Never again will I allow unforgiveness and
bitterness to control my life (Eph. 4:31).

Never again will I allow discouragement and
depression to dominate my life, but I will praise Him
who is the health of my countenance (Ps. 42:5).

Never again will I walk in hate. I am
not a murderer (1 John 3:15).

Never again will I let strife come into
my relationships (Prov. 10:12).

Never again will I let anger rest in my bosom, for
anger rests in the bosom of fools (Eccles. 7:9).

Never again will I be envious, for love
does not envy (1 Cor. 13:4).

Never again will I allow jealousy and
envy to enter my heart, for envy is the
rottenness of the bones (Prov. 14:30).

Never again will I allow malice to operate in my
life, but I walk in sincerity and truth (1 Cor. 5:8).

NEVER AGAIN WILL I ALLOW MY BODY TO BE USED BY THE ENEMY

Never again will I yield my body to fornication.
My body is the temple of the Holy Spirit.

Never again will I yield my body to gluttony and
overeating; I will not come to poverty (Prov. 23:21).

Never again will I allow harmful
substances into my body.

Never again will I yield my body to
slothfulness and laziness, for the lazy man
will be put to forced labor (Prov. 12:24).

Never again will I accept sickness and disease, because
I am healed by the stripes of Jesus (1 Pet. 2:24).

Never again will I join my body to anyone
other than my mate, for I have been saved and
delivered from sexual immorality (1 Cor. 6:16).

Never again will I submit my body to
any ungodly purpose, for my body is the
temple of the Holy Spirit (1 Cor. 3:16).

Never again will I defile my body, which is the temple of God (1 Cor. 3:17).

Never Again Will I Allow Fear to Stop Me

Never again will I be afraid, for the Lord had delivered me from all my fears (Ps. 34:4).

Never again will I be afraid of man, for the Lord is my helper (Heb. 13:6).

Never again will I be tormented by fear (1 John 4:18).

Never again will I be afraid of demons, for I tread on serpents and scorpions and over all the power of the enemy (Luke 10:19).

Never again will I not be afraid of witchcraft (Acts 13:8–11).

Never again will I be afraid to do what God tells me to do.

Never again will I be afraid of the enemy (Ps. 27:2).

Never again will I be afraid to go where the Lord sends me. Here am I; send me (Isa. 6:8).

Never again will I be afraid to prophesy, but I covet to prophesy (1 Cor. 14:39).

Never again will I be afraid to cast out demons (Mark 16:17).

Never again will I be afraid of being rejected, because I am accepted in the Beloved (Eph. 1:6).

Never again will I be afraid to witness
to the lost (Luke 19:10).

Never again will I be afraid of doing what
God tells me to do (Acts 5:29).

Never Again Will I Allow Pride to Control My Life

Never again will I allow pride (Leviathan)
to control my life (Job 41).

Never again will I allow my heart to
become hardened (Job 41:24).

Never again will I allow the Holy Spirit's power
to *not* flow in my life. The scales of Leviathan
have been ripped from my life (Job 41:15).

Never again will I allow stubbornness to control
my life, for stubbornness is as iniquity and idolatry,
and I am not stiff-necked (1 Sam. 15:23).

Never again will I walk in vanity and
vain glory (Gal. 5:26, kjv).

Never again will I walk in selfish ambition (James 3:14).

Never again will I speak in a boastful way (James 4:16).

Never again will I cause another
person to stumble (Mal. 2:8).

Never again will I walk in offense (Ps. 119:165, kjv).

Never again will I give myself to
drunkenness (Eph. 5:18).

NEVER AGAIN WILL I ALLOW FILTHY COMMUNICATION TO COME OUT OF MY MOUTH

Never again will I allow words of doubt and unbelief to come out of my mouth (Mark 11:23).

Never again will I allow cursing and bitterness to come out of my mouth (Rom. 3:14).

Never again will I allow profanity to come out of my mouth (Eph. 4:29).

Never again will I allow lying to come out of my mouth (Eph. 4:25).

Never again will I allow evil words to come out of my mouth (Eph. 4:31).

Never again will I allow a backbiting tongue to be a part of my life (2 Cor. 12:20).

Never again will I murmur and complain (Phil. 2:14).

Never again will I allow my tongue to be out of control, but I will bridle my tongue (James 1:26).

Never again will I allow filthy conversation to come out of my mouth (Col. 3:8).

Never again will I allow critical words to come out of my mouth.

Never again will I allow my tongue to be used for evil (Ps. 34:13).

Never again will I allow gossip in my life (Lev. 19:16).

Never again will I keep silent when I should speak (Eccles. 3:7).

Never again will I speak when I
should be silent (Eccles. 3:7).

Never again will I allow what others say
about me to control my life (Acts 19:9).

Never again will I allow spoken curses to hinder my life,
for the curse causeless shall not come (Prov. 26:2, KJV).

Never again will I be deceived by a
flattering tongue (Prov. 6:24).

Never again will I listen to the words
of the enemy (Ps. 55:3).

Never again will I walk in the counsel
of the ungodly (Ps. 1:1).

Never again will I listen to false teaching and false
doctrine, for the anointing teaches me (1 John 2:27).

Never again will I NOT listen to the
words of the wise (Prov. 22:17).

Never again will I reject correction from
those who love me (Ps. 141:5).

Never again will I listen to people who are in rebellion.

Never again will I make negative confessions, for death
and life are in the power of the tongue (Prov. 18:21).

Never again will I confess sickness and disease, because
Jesus took my sickness and infirmities (Matt. 8:17).

Never again will I confess poverty and lack; I will not
be snared by the words of my mouth (Prov. 6:2).

Never again will I confess defeat; the enemy comes
against me one way but flees seven ways (Deut. 28:25).

Never again will I confess fear, for God has not given me the spirit of fear (2 Tim. 1:7).

Never again will I confess failure, for I will meditate in the Word. I have good success (Josh. 1:8).

Never again will I allow mountains to block me, but I speak to the mountains in faith, and they are removed (Mark 11:23).

Never again will I say, "I can't," because I can do all things through Christ who strengthens me (Phil. 4:13).

Never again will I make excuses for failure (Gen. 3:12).

Never again will I be afraid to say what the Lord is saying, but I will speak what the Lord tells me to speak (Ezek. 2:7).

Never again will I be afraid to preach and walk in the revelation God gives me (1 Cor. 4:1).

Never again will I lose sight of the prophetic words spoken over my life, but I will war according to the prophecies given to me (1 Tim. 1:18).

MORE DYNAMIC TEACHING FROM APOSTLE JOHN ECKHARDT

IF YOU ENJOYED *PRAYERS THAT BRING HEALING AND ACTIVATE BLESSINGS*, YOU WILL LOVE...

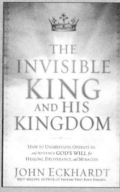

978-1-61638-279-7 / $15.99

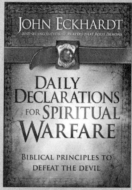

978-1-61638-443-2 / $14.99

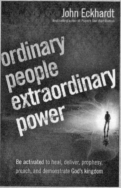

978-1-61638-166-0 / $14.99

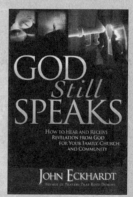

978-1-59979-475-4 / $14.99

The Lost Letter

"The perfect quick read for fans of Regency romances as well as Victorian happily-ever-afters, with shades of Austen and the Brontës that create an entertaining blend of drama and romance."

-RT Book Reviews

"A fast and emotionally satisfying read, with two characters finding the happily-ever-after they had understandably given up on. A promising debut."

-Library Journal

MIMI MATTHEWS

The Matrimonial Advertisement

PARISH ORPHANS *of* DEVON

THE MATRIMONIAL ADVERTISEMENT
A Victorian Romance
Copyright © 2018 by Mimi Matthews

Edited by Deborah Nemeth
Cover design by James T. Egan of Bookfly Design
Interior design by Ampersand Book Interiors

E-Book: 978-0-9990364-4-0
Paperback: 978-0-9990364-5-7

Cover Image: Onésipe Aguado de las Marismas (French, Evry 1830–1893 Paris). Woman from the Back. 1862. Photograph. Salted paper print from glass negative. Gilman Collection, Purchase, Joyce F. Menschel Gift, 2005. Metropolitan Museum of Art.

WWW.PERFECTLYPROPERPRESS.COM

In memory of Orson and Jude

Chapter One

North Devon, England
September, 1859

*H*elena Reynolds crossed the floor of the crowded taproom, her carpetbag clutched in her trembling hands. The King's Arms was only a small coaching inn on the North Devon coast road, but it seemed to her as if every man in Christendom had gathered there to have a pint. She could feel their eyes on her as she navigated carefully through their midst. Some stares were merely curious. Others were openly assessing.

She suppressed a shiver. She was hardly dressed for seduction in her gray striped-silk traveling gown, though she'd certainly made an effort to look presentable. After all, it was not every day that one met one's future husband.

"Can I help you, ma'am?" the innkeeper called to her from behind the crowded bar.

"Yes. If you please, sir." Tightening her hands on her carpetbag, she approached the high counter. A very tall man was leaning against the end of it, nursing his drink. His lean, muscular frame was shrouded in a dark wool greatcoat, his face partially hidden by his upturned collar and a tall beaver hat tipped low over his brow. She squeezed into the empty space beside him, her heavy petticoats and crinoline rustling loudly as they pressed against his leg.

She lowered her voice to address the innkeeper directly. "I'm here to see—"

"Blevins!" a man across the room shouted. "Give us another round!"

Before Helena could object, the innkeeper darted off to oblige his customers. She stared after him in helpless frustration. She'd been expected at one o'clock precisely. And now, after the mix-up at the railway station and the delay with the accommodation coach—she cast an anxious glance at the small watch she wore pinned to the front of her bodice—it was already a quarter past two.

"Sir!" she called to the innkeeper. She stood up on the toes of her half boots, trying to catch his eye. "Sir!"

He did not acknowledge her. He was exchanging words with the coachman at the other end of the counter as he filled five tankards with ale. The two of them were laughing together with the ease of old friends.

Helena gave a soft huff of annoyance. She was accustomed to being ignored, but this was the outside of enough. Her whole life hinged on the next few moments.

She looked around for someone who might assist her. Her eyes fell at once on the gentleman at her side. He didn't appear to be a particularly friendly sort of fellow, but his height was truly commanding and surely he must have a voice to match his size.

"I beg your pardon, sir." She touched him lightly on the arm with one gloved hand. His muscles tensed beneath her fingers. "I'm sorry to disturb you, but would you mind very much to summon—"

He raised his head from drinking and, very slowly, turned to look at her.

The words died on Helena's lips.

He was burned. Badly burned.

"Do you require something of me, ma'am?" he asked in an excruciatingly civil undertone.

She stared up at him, her first impression of his appearance revising itself by the second. The burns, though severe, were limited to the bottom right side of his face, tracing a path from his cheek down to the edge of his collar and beyond it, she was sure. The rest of his face—a stern face with a strongly chiseled jaw and hawklike aquiline nose—was relatively unmarked. Not only unmarked, but with his black hair and smoke-gray eyes, actually quite devastatingly handsome.

"Do you require something of me?" he asked again, more sharply this time.

She blinked. "Yes. Do forgive me. Would you mind very much summoning the innkeeper? I cannot seem to—"

"*Blevins!*" the gentleman bellowed.

The innkeeper broke off his loud conversation and scurried back to their end of the counter. "What's that, guv?"

"The lady wishes to speak with you."

"Thank you, sir," Helena said. But the gentleman had already turned his attention back to his drink, dismissing her without a word.

"Yes, ma'am?" the innkeeper prompted.

Abandoning all thoughts of the handsome—and rather rude—stranger at her side, Helena once again addressed herself to the innkeeper. "I was supposed to meet someone here at one o'clock. A Mr. Boothroyd?" She felt the gentleman next to her stiffen, but she did not regard it. "Is he still here?"

"Another one for Boothroyd, are you?" The innkeeper looked her up and down. "Don't look much like the others."

Helena's face fell. "Oh?" she asked faintly. "Have there been others?"

"Aye. Boothroyd's with the last one now."

"The *last* one?" She couldn't believe it. Mr. Boothroyd had given her the impression that she was the only woman with whom Mr. Thornhill was corresponding. And even if she wasn't, what sort of man interviewed potential wives for his employer in the same manner one might interview applicants for a position as a maidservant or a cook? It struck her as being in extraordinarily bad taste.

Was Mr. Thornhill aware of what his steward was doing?

She pushed the thought to the back of her mind. It was far too late for doubts. "As that may be, sir, I've come a very long way and I'm certain Mr. Boothroyd will wish to see me."

In fact, she was not at all certain. She had only ever met Mr. Finchley, the sympathetic young attorney in London. It was he who had encouraged her to come to Devon. While the sole interaction she'd had with Mr. Boothroyd and Mr. Thornhill thus far were letters—letters which she currently had safely folded within the contents of her carpetbag.

"Reckon he might at that," the innkeeper mused.

"Precisely. Now, if you'll inform Mr. Boothroyd I've arrived, I would be very much obliged to you."

The man beside her finished his ale in one swallow and then slammed the tankard down on the counter. "I'll take her to Boothroyd."

Helena watched, wide-eyed, as he stood to his full, towering height. When he glared down at her, she offered him a tentative smile. "I must thank you again, sir. You've been very kind."

He glowered. "This way." And then, without a backward glance, he strode toward the hall.

Clutching her carpetbag tightly, she trotted after him. Her heart was skittering, her pulse pounding in her ears. She prayed she wouldn't faint before she'd even submitted to her interview.

The gentleman rapped once on the door to the private parlor. It was opened by a little gray-haired man in spectacles. He peered up at the gentleman, frowned, and then, with furrowed brow, looked past him to stare at Helena herself.

"Mr. Boothroyd?" she queried.

"I am Boothroyd," he said. "And you, I presume, are Miss Reynolds?"

"Yes, sir. I know I'm dreadfully late for my appointment…" She saw a woman rising from a chair within the private parlor. A woman who regarded Helena with an upraised chin, her face conveying what words could not. "Oh," Helena whispered. And just like that it seemed the tiny, flickering flame of hope she'd nurtured these last months blinked out. "You've already found someone else."

"As to that, Miss Reynolds—" Mr. Boothroyd broke off with an expression of dismay as the tall gentleman brushed past him to enter the private parlor. He removed his hat and coat and proceeded to take a seat by the raging fire in the hearth.

The woman gaped at him in dismay. "Mr. Boothroyd!" she hissed, hurrying to the older gentleman's side. "I thought this was a *private* parlor."

"So it is, Mrs. Standish." Mr. Boothroyd consulted his pocket watch. "Or was, until half an hour ago. Never mind it. Our interview is finished in any case. Now, if you would be so good as to…"

Helena didn't hear the rest of their conversation. All she could hear was the sound of her own beating heart. She didn't know why she remained. She'd have to board the coach and continue to Cornwall. And then what? Fling herself from the cliffs, she supposed. There was no other way. Oh, what a fool she'd been to think this would work in the first place! If only Jenny had never seen that advertisement in the paper. Then she would have known months ago that there was but one means of escape from this wretched tangle. She would never have had reason to hope!

Her vision clouded with tears. She turned from the private parlor, mumbling an apology to Mr. Boothroyd as she went.

"Miss Reynolds?" Mr. Boothroyd called. "Have you changed your mind?"

She looked back, confused, only to see that the other lady was gone and that Mr. Boothroyd stood alone in the entry-way. From his seat by the fire, the tall gentleman ruffled a newspaper, seeming to be wholly unconcerned with either of them. "No, sir," she said.

"If you will have a seat." He gestured to one of the chairs that surrounded a small supper table. On the table was a stack of papers and various writing implements. She watched him rifle through them as she took a seat. "I trust you had a tolerable journey."

"Yes, thank you."

"You took the train from London?"

"I did, sir, but only as far as Barnstaple. Mr. Finchley arranged for passage on an accommodation coach to bring me the rest of the way here. It's one of the reasons I'm late. There was an overturned curricle in the road. The coachman stopped to assist the driver."

"One of the reasons, you say?"

"Yes, I…I missed the earlier train at the station," she confessed. "I'd been waiting at the wrong platform and…by the time I realized my error, my train had already gone. I was obliged to change my ticket and take the next one."

"Have you no maid with you? No traveling companion?"

"No, sir. I traveled alone." There hadn't been much choice. Jenny had to remain in London, to conceal Helena's absence as long as possible. Helena had considered hiring someone to accompany her, but there'd been no time and precious little money to spare. Besides which, she didn't know who she could trust.

Mr. Boothroyd continued to sift through his papers. Helena wondered if he was even listening to her. "Ah. Here it is," he said at last. "Your initial reply to the advertisement." He withdrew a letter covered in small, even handwriting which she recognized as her own. "As well as a letter from Mr. Finchley in London with whom you met on the fifteenth." He perused a second missive with a frown.

"Is anything the matter?" she asked.

"Indeed. It says here that you are five and twenty." Mr. Boothroyd lowered the letter. "You do not look five and twenty, Miss Reynolds."

"I assure you that I am, sir." She began to work at the ribbons of her gray silk traveling bonnet. After untying the knot with unsteady fingers, she lifted it from her head, twined the ribbons round it, and placed it atop her carpetbag. When she raised her eyes, she found Mr. Boothroyd staring at her. "I always look much younger in a bonnet. But, as you can see now, I'm—"

"Young *and* beautiful," he muttered with disapproval.

She blushed, glancing nervously at the gentleman by the fire. He did not seem to be listening, thank goodness. Even so, she leaned forward in her chair, dropping her voice. "Does Mr. Thornhill not want a pretty wife?"

"This isn't London, Miss Reynolds. Mr. Thornhill's house is isolated. Lonely. He seeks a wife who can bear the solitude. Who can manage his home and see to his comforts. A sturdy, capable sort of woman. Which is precisely why the advertisement specified a preference for a widow or spinster of more mature years."

"Yes, but I—"

"What Mr. Thornhill doesn't want," he continued, "is a starry-eyed girl who dreams of balls and gowns and handsome suitors. A marriage with such a frivolous creature would be a recipe for disaster."

Helena bristled. "That isn't fair, sir."

"Excuse me?"

"I'm no starry-eyed girl. I never was. And with respect, Mr. Boothroyd, you haven't the slightest notion of my dreams. If I wanted balls and gowns or…or frivolous things…I'd never have answered Mr. Thornhill's advertisement."

"What exactly do you seek out of this arrangement, Miss Reynolds?"

She clasped her hands tightly in her lap to stop their trembling. "Security," she answered honestly. "And perhaps…a little kindness."

"You couldn't find a gentleman who met these two requirements in London?"

"I don't wish to be in London. Indeed, I wish to be as far from London as possible."

"You friends and family…?"

"I'm alone in the world, sir."

"I see."

Helena doubted that very much. "Mr. Boothroyd, if you've already decided someone else is better suited—"

"There is no one else, Miss Reynolds. At present, you're the only lady Mr. Finchley has recommended."

"But the woman who was here before—"

"Mrs. Standish?" Mr. Boothroyd removed his spectacles. "She was applying for the position of housekeeper at the Abbey." He rubbed the bridge of his nose. "Regrettably, we have an ongoing issue with retaining adequate staff. It's something you should be aware of if you intend to take up residence."

She exhaled slowly. "A housekeeper. Of course. How silly of me. Mr. Thornhill mentioned the difficulties you were having with servants in one of his letters."

"I'm afraid it's proven quite a challenge." Mr. Boothroyd settled his spectacles back on his nose. "Not only is the house isolated, it has something of a local reputation. Perhaps you've heard…?"

"A little. But Mr. Finchley told me it was nothing more than ignorant superstition."

"Quite so. However, in this part of the world, Miss Reynolds, you'll find ignorance is in ready supply."

Helena was unconcerned. "I should like to see the Abbey for myself."

"Yes, yes. All in good time."

"And I should like to meet Mr. Thornhill."

"Undoubtedly." Mr. Boothroyd shuffled through his papers again. To her surprise, a rising color crept into the elderly man's face. "There are just one or two more points at issue, Miss Reynolds." He cleared his throat. "You're aware, I presume… That is, I do hope Mr. Finchley explained…this marriage is to be a real marriage in every sense of the word."

She looked at him, brows knit in confusion. "What other kind of marriage would it be?"

"And you're agreeable?"

"Of course."

He made no attempt to disguise his skepticism. "There are many ladies who would find such an arrangement singularly lacking in romance."

Helena didn't doubt it. She'd have balked at the prospect herself once. But much had changed in the past year—and in the past months, especially. Any girlish fantasies she'd harbored about true love were dead. In their place was a rather ruthless pragmatism.

"I don't seek romance, Mr. Boothroyd. Only kindness. And Mr. Finchley said that Mr. Thornhill was a kind man."

Mr. Boothroyd appeared to be surprised by this. "Did he indeed," he murmured. "What else did he tell you, pray?"

She hesitated before repeating the words that Mr. Finchley had spoken. Words that had convinced her once and for all to travel to a remote coastal town in Devon, to meet and marry a complete stranger. "He told me that Mr. Thornhill had been a soldier, and that he knew how to keep a woman safe."

Justin Thornhill cast another brooding glance at the pale, dark-haired beauty sitting across from Boothroyd. She was slight but shapely, her modest traveling gown doing nothing to disguise the high curve of her breasts and the narrow lines of her small waist. When first he'd seen her in the taproom, he thought she was a fashionable traveler on her way to Abbot's Holcombe, the resort town farther up the coast. He had no reason to think otherwise. The Miss Reynolds he'd been expecting—the plain, sensible spinster who'd responded to his matrimonial advertisement—had never arrived.

This Miss Reynolds was a different class of woman altogether.

She sat across from Boothroyd, her back ramrod straight, and her elegant, gloved hands folded neatly on her lap in a pretty attitude. She regarded the curmudgeonly steward with wide, doelike hazel eyes and when she spoke, she did so in the smooth, cultured tones of a gentlewoman. No, Justin amended. Not a gentlewoman. A *lady*.

She was nothing like the two sturdy widows Boothroyd had interviewed earlier for the position of housekeeper. Those women had, ironically, been more in line with Justin's original specifications—the specifications he had barked at his aging steward those many months ago when Boothroyd had first broached the idea of his advertising for a wife.

"I have no interest in courtship," he'd said, "nor in weeping young ladies who take to their bed with megrims. What I need is a woman. A woman who is bound by law and duty to see to the running of this godforsaken mausoleum. A woman I can bed on occasion. Damnation, Boothroyd, I didn't survive six years in India so I could live like a bloody monk when I returned home."

THE MATRIMONIAL ADVERTISEMENT

They were words spoken in frustration after the last in a long line of housekeepers had quit without notice. Words that owed a great deal to physical loneliness and far too many glasses of strong spirits.

The literal-minded Boothroyd had taken them as his marching orders.

The next morning, before Justin had even arisen from his alcohol-induced slumber, his ever-efficient steward had arranged for an advertisement to be placed in the London papers. It had been brief and to the point:

> MATRIMONY: *Retired army officer, thirty-two, of moderate means and quiet disposition wishes to marry a spinster or widow of the same age. Suitable lady will be sensible, compassionate, and capable of managing the household of remote country property. Independent fortune unimportant. Letters to be addressed, postpaid, to Mr. T. Finchley, Esq., Fleet Street.*

Justin had initially been angry. He'd even threatened to give Boothroyd the sack. However, within a few days he'd found himself warming to the idea of acquiring a wife by advertisement. It was modern and efficient. As straightforward as any other business transaction. The prospective candidates would simply write to Thomas Finchley, Justin's London attorney, and Finchley would negotiate the rest, just as competently as he'd negotiated the purchase of Greyfriar's Abbey or those shares Justin had recently acquired in the North Devon Railway.

Still, he had no intention of making the process easy. He'd informed both Boothroyd and Finchley that he would not bestir himself on any account. If a prospective bride wanted to meet, she would have to do so at a location within easy driving distance of the Abbey.

He'd thought such a condition would act as a deterrent.

It hadn't occurred to him that women routinely traveled such distances to take up employment. And what was his matrimonial advertisement if not an offer for a position in his household?

In due time, Finchley had managed to find a woman for whom an isolated existence in a remote region of coastal Devon sounded agreeable. Justin had even exchanged a few brief letters with her. Miss Reynolds hadn't written enough for him to form a definite picture of her personality, nor of her beauty—or lack thereof. Nevertheless, he'd come to imagine her as a levelheaded spinster. The sort of spinster who would endure his conjugal attentions with subdued dignity. A spinster who wouldn't burst into tears at the sight of his burns.

The very idea that anything like this lovely young creature would grace his table and his bed was frankly laughable.

Not but that she wasn't determined.

Though that was easily remedied. Folding his paper, Justin rose from his chair. "I'll take it from here, Boothroyd."

Miss Reynold's eyes lifted to his. He could see the exact moment when she realized who he was. To her credit, she didn't cry or faint or spring from her chair and bolt out of the room. She merely looked at him in that same odd way she had in the taproom when first she beheld his burns.

"Miss Reynolds," Mr. Boothroyd said, "may I present Mr. Thornhill?"

She did rise then and offered him her hand. It was small and slim, encased in a fine dark kid glove. "Mr. Thornhill."

"Miss Reynolds." His fingers briefly engulfed hers. "Sit down, if you please." He took Boothroyd's chair, waiting until his loyal retainer had removed himself to the other side of the parlor before fixing his gaze on his prospective bride.

Her face was a flawless, creamy porcelain oval, framed by dark brown hair swept back into an oversized roll at the nape of her neck. Her nose was straight—neither too short, nor too long—and her gently rounded chin was firm to the point of stubbornness. If not for the velvety softness of those doe eyes, she might have appeared prideful or even haughty. And perhaps she was, if her clothing was anything by which to judge.

Granted, he knew nothing of women's fashion—aside from the fact that the hooks, laces, and miles of skirts were dashed inconvenient when one was in an amorous frame of mind. But one didn't have to know the difference between a petticoat and a paletot to recognize that everything Miss Reynolds wore was of the finest quality. Even the tiny buttons on her bodice and the fashionable belt and buckle that encircled her waist appeared to have been crafted by a master.

Next to her, the suit of clothes he'd chosen to wear that morning to meet his intended bride felt rather shabby and third rate. Far worse, he was beginning to feel a little shabby and third rate himself.

"You'll forgive the deception," he said. "As you can see, I'm not the sort of man a woman would wish to find at the other end of a matrimonial advertisement."

"Aren't you?" She tilted her head. The small movement brought her hair in the path of a shaft of sunlight filtering in through the parlor window. It glittered for an instant in her fashionable coiffure, revealing threads of red and gold among the brown. "Why do you say so? Is it because of your burns?"

He was hard-pressed to conceal a flinch. Damn, but she was blunt. He wouldn't have expected such plain speaking from a decorative little female. "You can't claim the sight doesn't offend you. I saw your reaction in the taproom."

Her brows drew together in an elegant line. "I had no reaction, sir."

"No?"

"I was, perhaps, a little surprised. But not because of your burns." Her cheeks flushed a delicate shade of rose. "You are…very tall."

His chest tightened. He was uncertain what to make of her blushes—or of her personal remark. She was such a finely made little creature. He wondered if she thought him too big. Good God, he *was* too big. And too rough, too coarse, and too common and a host of other negative traits, the distastefulness of which he had not fully appreciated until being in her presence.

"You were expecting someone shorter?"

"No, I…I didn't know what to expect. How could I have? You never mentioned anything of that sort in your letters."

Justin recalled the polite and wholly impersonal letters he'd written to her over the past months. He'd described Greyfriar's Abbey, the seasons and the weather and the sound of the waves hitting the rocks beneath the cliffs. He'd mentioned the repairs to the roof, the new outbuildings, and the persistent trouble with keeping servants.

His own appearance hadn't merited a single line.

"Would you still have come, had you known?" he asked.

"About your burns, do you mean?" She didn't hesitate. "Yes, I think so. But there's no way to prove it now, is there? You shall have to take my word for it."

He allowed his gaze to drift over her face, taking in every feature, from the dark mahogany brows winging over her wide-set eyes, to the gentle curve of her cheekbones, and down to the impossibly sensual bow of her upper lip. It was not the face of a woman who had to answer a matrimonial advertisement in order to find a husband.

Take her word for it? "I suppose I must," he said.

"Did it happen while you were in India?"

He nodded once. "During the uprising."

"I didn't like to assume." She paused. "I know something of soldiers from my brother. He often wrote to me about the exploits of his regiment and the hardships of friends who'd been injured in battle. He was a soldier himself, you see."

"Was he, indeed?" Justin regarded her with a thoughtful expression. "I understood that you had no family."

"I don't. Not any longer. My brother was lost last year at the siege of Jhansi." Her bosom rose and fell on an unsteady breath. He noticed for the first time that she was trembling. "Is that where you were hurt, Mr. Thornhill?"

It wasn't a subject he enjoyed discussing, but there was no point in dissembling. She would find out soon enough. "No, at Cawnpore in '57."

Something flickered briefly in the velvet depths of her eyes. Everyone in England knew what had happened in Cawnpore during the uprising, but as the sister of a soldier, she'd have a better understanding than most.

"Were you serving under Major General Sir Hugh Wheeler?" she asked very quietly. "Or did you arrive later, with Brigadier General Neill?"

24

"The former." His mouth curved into a mocking half smile. "You may rest easy, Miss Reynolds. I had no part in the raping and pillaging engaged in by the relieving forces. I was safely tucked away in an enemy prison at the time, being flayed alive by rebel sepoys." She blanched, but he didn't spare her. "The burns and scars you see here are nothing. The ones beneath my clothing are much, much worse, I assure you."

"I am very sorry for it."

"Are you?" He felt an unreasonable surge of anger toward her. "You may not feel quite so much Christian charity toward my scarred body when it's covering you in our marriage bed."

From his place across the room, Boothroyd emitted a strangled groan.

Justin ignored him. His attention was fixed on the scalding blush that swept from the slender column of Miss Reynold's porcelain throat all the way up to her hairline. Doubtless he'd shocked her virginal soul to its very core. He wouldn't have been surprised if she leapt up and slapped his face. He certainly deserved it.

But she did not strike him.

Instead, she met his insolent gaze and held it, unflinching.

"You're purposefully offensive, sir. I believe you're trying to scare me off. I cannot think why."

Because if you don't leave of your own accord, very soon I won't let you leave at all.

And where would he be then?

Stuck at Greyfriar's Abbey, among the crumbling stone and cracked plaster, with a very unhappy lady. A lady reduced to drudgery in a drafty, damp, understaffed ruin. A lady whom he could never hope to satisfy, not if he lived to be one hundred.

"Perhaps," he said finally, "because it seems to me that you have no idea what you're getting yourself into."

"Nonsense. I know exactly what I'll get out of this arrangement. I wouldn't be here otherwise. If you don't wish to marry me, Mr. Thornhill, you need only say so."

"I wonder that you wish to marry me." He folded his arms and leaned back in his chair, surveying the neat little figure hidden beneath her gown. "I hope you're not in trouble, Miss Reynolds."

He heard her catch her breath. The sound was unmistakable.

His heart sank. There was no other way to describe it. The disappointment he felt was that exquisitely painful.

And then, just as swiftly, his temper flared.

"I may be acquiring a wife in a somewhat unconventional way, madam," he informed her in the same frigid accents he'd often employed with disrespectful subordinates in India, "but I have no desire to take on another man's bastard in the bargain."

Her mouth fell open. "*What*?"

"I believe you heard me." He moved to rise.

"You think I'm carrying *a child*?"

Something in her voice stopped him where he stood. He searched her face. "Do you deny it?"

"Yes!" She was blushing furiously now. "The suggestion is patently absurd. As well as being utterly impossible."

Absurd as well as impossible? His conscience twinged. So, she was an innocent after all. Either that or the finest actress he'd ever encountered in his life. "Ah," he said as he resumed his seat. "I see."

She raised a hand to brush a loose strand of hair from her face. She was trembling again.

"What kind of trouble is it, then?" he asked.

"I beg your pardon?"

"Something has plainly driven you to answer my advertisement. If not an unwanted child, then what?"

She dropped her gaze. Her long, thick lashes were black as soot against the creamy curve of her cheek. "You are mistaken, sir."

"And you are trembling, madam."

She immediately clasped her hands in her lap. "I always tremble when I'm nervous. I can't help it."

"Is that all that's wrong, Miss Reynolds? Nerves?"

Her lashes lifted and she met his eyes. "Does it really matter, Mr. Thornhill?"

He considered. "That depends. Have you broken the law?"

"Of course not. I simply wish to be married. It's why I answered your matrimonial advertisement. It's why I've come all this way. If you've decided I don't suit you—"

"You suit me." The words were out before he could call them back.

Try as he might, he could not regret them. It was the truth, by God. She was an uncommonly beautiful woman. He'd been physically attracted to her from the moment she came to stand beside him in the taproom.

On its own that wouldn't have been enough. He was no callow youth to have his head turned by a pretty face. But there was something else about her. Something lost and vulnerable and oddly courageous. It roused more than his ardor. It roused his protective instincts. It made him want to shield her from harm.

Is that why Finchley had sent her to him?

The very idea unsettled Justin deeply. He was no hero. Indeed, his own past conduct fairly disqualified him as a man capable of protecting a woman. Finchley *knew* that.

But if Justin had any lingering doubts about his decision, Miss Reynold's reaction to his pronouncement temporarily banished them from his mind.

Her face suffused with relief. Her soft hazel eyes glistened with what he very much feared were tears of gratitude. "You suit me as well," she said.

"Undoubtedly. Your requirements are not very exacting." He tugged at his collar. It felt damnably tight all of a sudden. "Security and a little kindness, is that right?"

"Yes, sir."

"And that I keep you safe."

"Yes, sir," she said. "That most of all."

Chapter Two

"I can't think what Finchley meant by sending her," Boothroyd said. "If I'd had any inkling, I would've put a stop to it." He gathered up his papers and thrust them back into his leather briefcase, grumbling all the while. "Not at all the thing. A lady like that. A catastrophe in the making. Mark my words."

Justin paced the confines of the private parlor, only half listening to the rantings of his unhappy steward.

Miss Reynolds was gone. Boothroyd had arranged a room for her at the inn. He'd even ordered a meal sent up. She was probably eating it now. Or sleeping. Or perhaps she'd changed her mind? Perhaps she'd already managed to escape back to London or wherever it was she came from?

The possibility sent a bolt of apprehension through him. And it was no mystery why.

He wanted her badly. He wasn't too proud to admit it. He wanted her as his wife. He wanted her in his home and in his bed. He'd been far too long without a woman. And Helena Reynolds, with her doelike eyes and softly curved body, had triggered an overpowering ache inside of him. Good God, he could still smell the faint scent of her perfume lingering in the air. It was delicate, sweet, and disturbingly exotic. Jasmine. It reminded him of balmy nights spent in India.

"I'll contact Finchley and we'll see about the other responses to the advertisement," Boothroyd said. "There were several, if I remember. I shall tell him to forward them all to me. And this time, when you find a suitable female, we'll ask her to send her likeness or—"

"I have no wish to meet any other women," Justin said. "I've already made my decision."

Boothroyd frowned. "If you'll forgive me, sir. Miss Reynolds is not at all the sort of person with whom a man in your position should align himself."

"No?"

"For one thing, she's too young."

"As you keep saying. But a female of five and twenty is hardly a fledgling. Indeed, some might even accuse her of having reached an advanced stage of spinsterhood."

"Yes, but—"

"And her age should be of no surprise to you. She admitted it to Finchley. And to me as well in her first letter. I don't remember your voicing an objection then." Justin stopped pacing and turned to face his steward. His eyes narrowed. "What is it about her that truly troubles you, Boothroyd? That she's a fine lady? That a man like me will be the one to despoil her?"

Boothroyd's spine stiffened. "You do me wrong, sir," he said, very much on his dignity. "It's my job to apprise you of unwise investments and, for a man in your position, marriage to a female of Miss Reynolds's sort would be very unwise indeed. First she'll want a wedding trip. Then a larger staff, new gowns, and a carriage and four. Expenses which you can scarcely afford. And what comes next with a pretty wife? Flirtations? Cuckoldom? Scandal?"

"Good God," Justin muttered.

"If you'll but take the night to think it over, I'm confident that tomorrow, when you consider the matter with your head instead of your—"

"Instead of my what?" Justin prompted, making no effort to hide his irritation. "Not my heart, I gather. We both know I haven't one of those."

Boothroyd's ears turned a dull red. "You appreciate my meaning, sir." He cleared his throat. "Which is to say that this is all perfectly understandable. You're a man in your prime and a man does have his needs, I can attest. But such a bride—though she may temporarily quench a base urge of nature—will make your life a misery. I've seen it time and time again with attractive young wives. While a woman of maturity—a woman who is, perhaps, not quite as handsome—will be content with whatever you have to offer—"

Justin silenced Boothroyd's sputtering with an impatient wave of his hand. The insinuation that he was acting solely out of some primitive need to couple with an attractive woman struck a little too close to home. "I'm in no mood to argue with you. I'm resolved to marry Miss Reynolds and that's an end to it."

"But you know nothing about her, sir!"

"Funny, I seem to recall your telling me that that's what Finchley was for. To investigate the potential candidates and—how did you phrase it?—to weed out the bad apples."

"Yes, but I had not expected—"

"No doubt," Justin said. "We must all adapt, Boothroyd."

Boothroyd's shoulders sagged in apparent defeat.

Justin wasn't fooled for a minute. Boothroyd was adept at getting his own way. It was one of the reasons Justin employed him. "A beautiful wife need not be a liability, you know. Recall how well it served Simon Harding."

Harding had been a partner in one of Justin's earliest, and more successful, business ventures in India. To this day, Justin credited Harding's wife, Rebecca, with the bulk of their good fortune. The daughter of a captain in the Indian army, she'd known everyone worth knowing.

"We wouldn't have had any investors if Mrs. Harding hadn't first made friends of their wives," he said. "And if not for her dinner parties, I would never have met Oliver Smithson, let alone invested my earnings in his cotton mills—the profits of which bought the Abbey, in case you've forgotten."

"Yes, yes, exactly as you say. The right sort of wife is an asset, both in business and in the community. Which is precisely why Finchley and I urged you to marry. And if Miss Reynolds were of the same class as Mrs. Harding, I would have no difficulty—"

"You know nothing about Miss Reynold's class."

"With respect, sir," Boothroyd countered, "neither do you."

Justin shrugged. "I trust Finchley."

"As do I, but—"

"He's assured us both of her character. According to him, she's a respectable gentlewoman with no outstanding debts, nor any problematic entanglements. A gentlewoman who is alone and unable to support herself."

"Her manner and bearing mark her as a lady of some refinement."

Justin raked a hand through his hair. "I can't see that it matters. She has no family, no connections. Regardless of who her people once were, she is now no different from any other impoverished female trying to make her way in the world."

"By marrying a well-to-do gentleman," Boothroyd sniffed.

"Is that what I am now? A well-to-do gentleman?" Justin's mouth twisted into a humorless smile. "You rate me too highly. If Miss Reynolds truly wished to marry well, she could've done far better for herself than an ex-soldier of no birth and little fortune."

"That may be so, sir, but the fact remains that she's chosen you."

"You can credit that miracle to Finchley. He's filled her head with some nonsense about my being a kindly and honorable man." Justin's smile faded. "With any luck we'll be married before she discovers otherwise."

Helena peered out the window as she nibbled on the remainder of one of the cakes that had been sent up with her tea. From her room, she could see down to the inn-yard below. It was relatively empty except for the accommodation coach she'd arrived in and an antiquated carriage to which an ostler was presently hitching a team of four. She watched awhile longer, fully expecting to see a regal red-and-black-lacquered coach pull into the yard.

It did not come.

Which meant absolutely nothing. No one but a fool would drive all the way here when he could take the train instead. But the train to where? To Barnstaple, she supposed, and then the rest of the way by accommodation coach, the same method by which she'd arrived in King's Abbot. She wondered how many days she had. Three, perhaps. Or possibly even four if she was lucky.

With a sigh, she retired from her post at the window and began to undress. She stripped off her traveling dress, stepped out of her petticoats and heavy crinoline, and rolled off each of her stockings. A maidservant had brought up a ewer of water for her to wash with and she didn't know how soon she'd have the opportunity to bathe again.

Clothed only in her chemise, drawers, and corset, she stood in front of the wooden washstand. A small mirror was tacked to the wall above. She looked at herself only briefly as she soaked her sponge. She knew what she would see. A woman who was travel worn, exhausted, and afraid. A woman with bruises circling her throat and her arms.

The worst of them had faded to a yellowish purple. The newer bruises, however, the ones that graced her upper arms and wrists, still bloomed a deep black and blue. They were sensitive to the touch. Even the brush of fabric from the sleeves of her gown was enough to make her wince. And when a woman on the train platform in London had elbowed past her, the pain had been so acute, Helena had nearly fainted.

What was needed was ice and lots of it. Failing that, cool water would have to do.

She wrung out her sponge over her right arm and then her left, repeating the procedure until the cold water began to soothe the deep ache in her limbs. Her eyes fell closed and, for one tired moment, she bowed her head, letting her forehead come to rest lightly against the mirror. She took a long, shuddering breath.

Justin Thornhill was not the man she'd been expecting.

Though what she *had* been expecting, she really couldn't say. She'd hoped he would be kind, of course. And intelligent and honorable and capable of keeping her safe—as Mr. Finchley had promised. But her hopes, such that they were, had never coalesced into the form and figure of a man. She'd never pictured a height, a hair color, or the shape of a chin or a nose. She'd certainly never dared to imagine that her future husband would be handsome.

And Mr. Thornhill *was* handsome.

Though not in the urbane, sophisticated manner of her elder brother and his friends or any of the other gentlemen Helena had met and admired during the course of her five-and-twenty years. Instead, with his rumpled black hair, sun-bronzed skin, and altogether too penetrating gaze, Mr. Thornhill rather resembled a swashbuckling pirate or one of the roguish antiheroes in the penny novels she'd been so fond of reading as a girl.

A woman could easily become infatuated with such a man.

Especially as Mr. Thornhill was not merely handsome. He was tall and powerfully made. Indeed, Helena couldn't remember having ever encountered a gentleman of such majestic proportions. He was all broad shoulders and lean, masculine strength. She felt small and fragile by comparison. If he were to hurt her—to throttle her or shake her violently by the arms—she didn't think she could survive it. He was far too strong. He could snap her neck as easily as breathing.

She swallowed back a rising swell of panic. It wouldn't do to succumb to her fears. Not after having come so far and risked so much.

Yet how could she help but be uneasy after the vulgar things he'd said to her?

She was almost too mortified to recall them. What sort of man spoke of covering a lady in their marriage bed? Not a gentleman, surely. And then to accuse her of being with child! As if she were some sort of deceitful wanton. She whose entire knowledge of the marital act consisted of passages read in medical manuals and a few scraps of overheard masculine conversation.

Righteous indignation rose in her breast. It was a wonderful tonic for the nerves.

Lifting her head from the mirror, she refilled the basin and proceeded to wash her face and body as thoroughly as she could.

Her journey, though not terribly long, had been dusty and dirty. She could still feel the grit in her hair from when the wind had kicked up as she stood on the train platform at Barnstaple. She wished there was time to wash it. Instead, she unpinned it, brushed it out, and twisted it into fresh plaits that she secured at the base of her neck in a large chignon. She was fixing the last hairpin when someone scratched softly at the door.

"Your pardon, ma'am," a maidservant's voice rang out. "The gentleman says to tell you they'll be leaving in half an hour."

Helena's pulse quickened. Mr. Thornhill and Mr. Boothroyd were taking her to see the Abbey. They had even engaged a serving girl to act as her maid during the journey. It was all perfectly proper and aboveboard—facts which did absolutely nothing to calm her quaking heart. "I'll be down directly!"

"Very good, ma'am. Shall I leave your boots at the door?"

"Yes, thank you." At least she'd have clean shoes, Helena thought as she began to dress. Earlier, she'd performed a quick spot clean on her traveling gown, but it still looked as if she'd been wearing it for two days straight. It needed to be properly sponged and pressed. But she couldn't worry about any of that now.

She fastened the final button at the neck of her gown and gave her voluminous skirts one last shake so that they fell gracefully over her crinoline. Her bonnet, gloves, and carpetbag were on the bed. As she moved to retrieve them, her eyes fell on the tea tray. There were three cakes remaining. She swiftly collected them and, after wrapping them in a clean handkerchief, thrust them into her carpetbag with the rest of her worldly belongings.

If things didn't work out with Justin Thornhill, she would need food for the final leg of her journey.

Wherever that journey might take her.

The antiquated coach gave a shuddering jolt as it ascended the cliff road. Bess, the young maidservant in the seat across from Helena, moaned low in her throat. Helena eyed her with concern. The girl's face had gone from stark white to pea green in an astonishingly short span of time. "We're quite safe, Bess," she said again. "Truly."

Her words were instantly contradicted by an ominous rattle. It shook the carriage, causing them both to sway in their seats.

She cast a quick glance out of the window. The carriage wheels were rolling along at the very edge of the cliff road. She could see stones crumbling and falling down to the foaming surf below. Beginning to feel a bit white about the mouth herself, she leaned back in her seat and offered Bess a bracing smile. "If you're afraid, only imagine how poor Mr. Boothroyd feels riding up top with the coachman."

"Lord bless him, miss." Bess pressed a hand to her mouth. Helena couldn't tell if she was stifling a giggle or about to be sick. "If one of the horses loses its footing, he'll be flung off into the sea."

"What a shame that would be," Helena said dryly. A gurgle of laughter escaped from behind Bess's hand.

Mr. Boothroyd had done nothing to endear himself to either of them. From the moment Helena had come down the stairs at the inn, he'd been impatient, irritable, and—when compensating Bess for her time—he'd revealed himself to be surprisingly cheap.

Helena wasn't sure what she'd done to offend him. She knew she wasn't what he'd expected, but she was beginning to think Mr. Boothroyd was somehow opposed to her marrying Mr. Thornhill. Even worse, she suspected that Mr. Thornhill was not entirely agreeable himself.

And yet, despite his vulgar words and his gruff manner, Justin Thornhill had behaved with the utmost propriety since they left the inn. He'd even taken steps to safeguard her reputation during their visit to the Abbey. Not only had he arranged for Bess to accompany her, but neither he nor Mr. Boothroyd had ridden with them inside the carriage.

"Reckon Mr. Thornhill's safer than all of us on that horse of his," Bess said.

"Undoubtedly." Helena looked out the window once more. There was no sign of Mr. Thornhill. He was likely far ahead of them by now, a single horse and rider being much better suited to the treacherous road than a carriage.

Greyfriar's Abbey was a good three miles from the King's Arms and, as Mr. Thornhill had explained when handing her up into the carriage, the cliff road was the only point of access. It ascended along a track just wide enough for a coach and four, curving as it went beneath the branches of trees that seemed to grow at all angles from the cliff face.

It took nearly half an hour to reach even ground. When they did, the horses picked up the pace, the poorly sprung carriage bouncing along behind them. It veered to the left through a sparse woodland and finally slowed to a rattling halt.

Peering out the window, Helena saw that they had come to rest on a small plateau. The sky was thick and gray above, the rocky landscape equally as gray below. In the distance, with only a crumbling stone wall protecting it from the cliffside and the sheer drop down to the open sea, stood Greyfriar's Abbey.

Mr. Thornhill had described it in one of his letters as being a Gothic nightmare of a house and he hadn't exaggerated. It had been built on the remains of a twelfth century monastery, some of which was still standing. There was a tower and a stone stable block which, despite their age, seemed to have needed only minor repairs. The rest of the structure, with its steeply pitched roof and high, pointed arches, appeared to be of a much later date. Helena saw evidence of recent construction, as well as piles of new stone and tools at the ready. She wondered how much of the Abbey's restoration Mr. Thornhill had undertaken himself.

"Have you been here before, Bess?" she asked.

Bess's eyes were very wide. "Oh no, miss," she said in an awed whisper. "No one comes up here."

Before Helena could question Bess further, Mr. Thornhill opened the carriage door. The roar of the sea fairly vibrated in the air around him, and she could hear the mournful cry of seagulls circling above. She lifted her heavy skirts in one hand as he assisted her down the carriage steps. The wind was so strong it nearly swept her off of her feet.

He tightened his grip on her hand to steady her. "Careful."

"Thank you." She stepped to the ground. "I'm all right now."

He nodded and turned to help Bess down.

Helena didn't know many gentlemen who would have troubled themselves with assisting a servant. That Mr. Thornhill did so now struck her as being further evidence of his exemplary character. Mr. Finchley had said he was a good man—a *kind* man. And, despite Mr. Thornhill's gruff exterior, she was beginning to believe it.

She moved back from the carriage, looking all around her. The wind whipped at her bonnet and the skirts of her gown. The cold air stung her face. She was a trifle breathless. Even more so when she felt a large, powerful hand rest briefly on the small of her back. She looked up with a start into Justin Thornhill's smoke-gray eyes.

"You were swaying like a reed in a storm," he said.

"Was I?"

"Take care the wind doesn't carry you away over the cliff."

An icy shiver of fear raced down her spine. The prospect of flinging herself from the cliffs had been at the back of her mind since she boarded the train in London. She didn't know if she would ever have been brave enough—or foolish enough—to do something so rash, but the thought of it had given her comfort in her darkest moments. Now, so close to the jagged cliffs and the raging sea beneath, she couldn't help feeling sick at what she had contemplated.

"Here," Mr. Thornhill said. "Take my arm. I'll not let you fall."

She did as he bade her and, along with Mr. Boothroyd and Bess, they made their way toward the house. As they approached, the front door opened and two enormous black mongrels charged out. The figure of a large man emerged in the arched doorway behind them. He called out, but his words were lost in the wind.

To Helena's horror, the dogs headed straight for them, barking as they ran. They were as large as mastiffs. The kind of dogs that, between them, could easily tear a person to ribbons.

"*Down*," Mr. Thornhill said sharply as one leapt toward her.

Helena pressed her face instinctively into his arm.

"Are you afraid of dogs?" he asked.

Her heart pounded in her throat. Afraid? She was terrified beyond belief. She nevertheless forced herself to turn her head from Mr. Thornhill's sleeve and face the two giant beasts. "I don't know. Should I be?"

"Not of these. Here." He took her gloved hand very gently in his and extended it toward the first dog. The great beast padded forward and tentatively sniffed her fingers. "His name is Paul."

"Paul?" she echoed, still clinging to Mr. Thornhill's arm. "And that one?"

The other dog stood at a distance, watching the two of them. He was growling.

"That's Jonesy," Mr. Thornhill said. "You can make his acquaintance later."

Helena cast a wary glance at the unwelcoming hound as Mr. Thornhill led her up the steps and into the house.

The man who'd let the dogs loose stood in the flagstone entryway, twisting his cap in his hands. He was a strapping fellow of indeterminate years with close-cropped blond hair and a slightly vacant expression in his pale eyes.

"Neville," Mr. Thornhill said. "This is Miss Reynolds. She and her maid will be staying for tea."

Neville bobbed his head at her. "Ma'am."

She inclined her head in return. "I'm pleased to meet you, Neville."

His face reddened. He gave another stilted bow and then, with a wary glance at Mr. Boothroyd, disappeared back into the house without a word. The two dogs loped after him.

"Neville sees to the stables and the livestock," Mr. Boothroyd said as he stripped off his hat and gloves.

"At present, he'll also be seeing to our tea." Mr. Thornhill lifted his own hat from his head and tossed it onto a nearby table. His coat and gloves followed suit.

There was no footman or butler to take their things. She removed her bonnet and gloves and handed them to Mr. Thornhill. "Are Neville and the coachman your only servants?"

"We have a woman who cooks and cleans." He ushered her through the hall. "And we're in hopes of obtaining a new housekeeper within the week, though how long she'll stay is anyone's guess."

The main hall of Greyfriar's Abbey was spacious but spare. Dim light filtered in through the high stone-framed windows to illuminate a console table, a few straight-backed wooden chairs, and a threadbare carpet. The most impressive feature, by far, was a single flight of stairs constructed of what looked to be new oak. It rose to a landing from whence it divided into two separate branches leading to opposite wings of the floors above.

Helena had no idea how large the interior of the Abbey really was, nor how many rooms were currently open and in use. What she did know, even in her limited experience, was

that a house of even half this size could never be run successfully with only a cook, a coachman, and a slow-witted giant
who served as both groom and footman.

"Perhaps Bess might help Neville with our tea?" she sug-
gested.

Mr. Thornhill shook his head. "Your maid stays with you."

He escorted her into a drafty wood-paneled room that bore
some resemblance to a library. Half-filled bookcases lined the
walls and mismatched tables were scattered about with maps
and books lying open on them. A bank of windows draped
with heavy wine-colored curtains looked out toward the sea.

Mr. Thornhill gestured for her to have a seat on one of the
two faded chintz sofas that faced each other in front of a colos-
sal stone fireplace. "Are you cold? Shall I build up the fire?"

"No, thank you. I'm quite comfortable." She sat on the
edge of the sofa cushion, settling her skirts all about her. In
truth, the room was damp and rather chilly, but she didn't
want Mr. Thornhill to think she was difficult to please. Nor
did she wish to give Mr. Boothroyd further cause for disapproval. He'd retreated to a desk in the corner, where he was
presently hunched over a ledger. She had no doubt he was
listening avidly, just as Bess was listening—with a great deal
less subtlety—from her place beside Helena on the sofa.

She and Mr. Thornhill had no real privacy. Was that why
he looked so ill at ease as he took a seat across from her?

"It's all just as you described in your letters," she remarked
for lack of anything better to say.

"Yet still you came."

"Did you think I wouldn't?"

He pointedly did not answer her question, saying instead,
"The Abbey won't be what you're accustomed to."

Helena's eyes fell briefly to her hands, pale and slim, folded one over the other in her lap. What she'd been accustomed to didn't bear thinking of. "Why do you say so?"

Again, he didn't answer her directly. He seemed to be brooding over something, for when she lifted her gaze she found him staring at her with a strangely somber expression.

"There aren't many who can live happily in such a remote place," he said. "The solitude can be…difficult to bear."

She wondered if he was referring to himself. Perhaps *he* found the solitude difficult to bear. Perhaps that was why he'd placed a matrimonial advertisement. "I don't mind it. Indeed, I expect the peace and quiet will suit me very well."

"On occasion, it's more than peace and quiet," he warned. "It's total isolation. There are problems that can arise—" He broke off, raking his fingers through his already disheveled black hair. "I don't want you to think I have misled you."

A troubled frown knit her brow. "Misled me? How?"

"There are risks that come with living in such a place as this. For one thing, it's a treacherous journey from the nearest town. And that's at the best of times. During the winter months, there are days when the road is completely impassable." Mr. Thornhill paused, appearing to weigh his next words with care. "If someone were in urgent need of a doctor, there's every chance they would die before he could be summoned from King's Abbot to attend them."

Helena did not immediately comprehend the significance of what he said. "Has such a thing ever happened before?"

"No. Not that I'm aware. But with a woman such as yourself—"

"I enjoy excellent health," she assured him.

"I'm pleased to hear it. But that's not quite what I meant."

"What *did* you mean?"

"Only that the natural result—" Mr. Thornhill stopped mid-sentence, his attention arrested by Bess. She was tilting forward in her seat, lips half parted, as if he were about to reveal a scandalous secret. His eyes narrowed.

"I understand," Helena said swiftly. "You're concerned I'll injure myself somehow and you won't be able to summon a doctor in time."

He looked more than a little annoyed. "Something like that."

"Is King's Abbot the nearest village?"

"If one travels by land, it is."

Helena went still. "There's a way to get here by water?"

"Anyone willing to brave the currents can sail straight up to the beach from Abbot's Holcombe. If the wind's at your back, the voyage can be made in a fraction of the time it would take a carriage to travel on the cliff road."

"I didn't realize." Her mouth went dry at the implications, her mind already conjuring one thousand and one scenarios—all of them completely unrealistic.

Or so she hoped.

She forced herself to remain calm. "Where is Abbot's Holcombe?"

"Thirteen miles in the opposite direction. It's a resort town. Far more fashionable than King's Abbot."

"They've ever so many shops there, miss," Bess volunteered. "And a dressmaker with all the fashions from Paris."

"If one can afford them," Mr. Boothroyd muttered from his desk.

Helena glanced at the ill-tempered steward. He was still scribbling away in his ledger, seeming to mark his periods and decimal points with extraordinary force.

"I don't expect I'll be too expensive," she said to Mr. Thornhill. "I really require very little."

"And whatever you require, you shall have." Mr. Thornhill's deep voice had an edge to it that was as hard and unyielding as adamantine. Helena suspected his words were intended more for Mr. Boothroyd than for her.

She moistened her lips. "Do you often make the journey to Abbot's Holcombe?"

"Not if I can help it."

"Because of the distance?"

"Because of the people who live there," he said, adding, "I loathe the place."

"Oh?" Helena hesitated. She was a little curious, naturally, but Mr. Thornhill didn't look as if he'd welcome any probing questions. Even if he did, she dared not ask them, lest he be tempted to ask a few of his own. "Then I shall loathe it, too."

The corner of his mouth quirked. "That loyal, are you?"

"Of course," she said. "We are engaged to be married."

Mr. Thornhill regarded her in silence for a moment, an expression in his eyes hard to read. "Would you like to go down to the beach after tea?" he asked abruptly.

She exhaled a breath she hadn't been aware she was holding. "Can we?"

He assured her they could. "There's a footpath along the side of the cliffs. It's steep, but if you think you can manage it we can walk awhile and still have time to get you back to the King's Arms before sunset."

Chapter Three

Justin felt Miss Reynold's hand tighten convulsively on his arm as they descended to the beach. As fetching as she looked in her gray silk gown, the fashion in large, billowing skirts was not at all conducive to navigating a narrow cliff path in a high wind. It was an exercise in self-restraint not to clutch at her every time the stones skittered beneath her boots.

He'd made the mistake once already, much to his regret. The moment his fingers had closed on her upper arm, she'd cried out, pulling away from him so forcefully that she'd slipped and almost fallen.

"I'm sorry!" she'd said when she recovered her footing. "You startled me."

"My fault entirely," he'd muttered in response.

It didn't bode well for their future that she cringed from his touch. He was a physical man and, though he didn't mind playing the gentleman on occasion, when he married—*if* he married—he intended to touch his wife in and out of the bedchamber. He would be damned if he ended up wedded to a fragile porcelain doll who recoiled at the sight of him. Such an arrangement might do for those in the upper classes, but Mr. Bray—the blacksmith to whom he'd been apprenticed as a boy—had been openly affectionate with his wife. Justin had always expected that one day, with his own bride, he would enjoy the same sort of relationship.

Though making any sort of marital example out of the Brays was ludicrous. They'd never treated him particularly well. The long, lonely years of his apprenticeship had been characterized by ragged clothing and a perpetually empty belly. Even so, Mr. and Mrs. Bray had cared for each other, and for their own children, too. As a child himself, Justin had been envious. Had yearned, on occasion, for a gentle word or a consoling touch. But the Brays had had little kindness to spare for the parish orphan in their care.

Had Miss Reynolds's parents been any kinder? Any more affectionate? Justin hadn't the slightest idea. She'd never written a word about her mother and father, or any of her other relations for that matter. He'd not even known she had a brother until she mentioned him during their conversation at the King's Arms. She'd been maddeningly opaque. Though he could hardly blame her. His own letters had been no more forthcoming.

He released her hand so he could jump from the end of the cliff path onto the beach. Miss Reynolds looked down at him from where she stood. The wind had blown some of her hair loose from beneath her bonnet. She brushed it from her face with her fingers.

He stepped toward her with upraised arms. "If you'll allow me."

She nodded her permission and he took hold of her waist, swinging her lightly to the ground. She weighed no more than a feather, the crown of her bonnet scarcely reaching his shoulder, but there was no mistaking her for anything other than what she was—a warm, softly rounded woman.

A woman wearing far too many blasted clothes.

Still, Justin thought, it could be worse. Many women he'd seen of late had skirts that were at least ten feet in circumference. Enormous flounced skirts supported by wire hoops prone to flip upward in a high wind. Miss Reynolds's own skirts were formidable, but he could detect no cagelike contraption beneath them. Indeed, the only bit of armor she seemed to be wearing was in the guise of a tightly cinched whalebone corset, the stiffness of which he could feel beneath his fingers.

"Are you sorry we didn't bring Boothroyd and your maid?" he asked, still holding her.

Her already flushed cheeks turned a deeper shade of rose. "No."

"Nor am I." Justin flexed his fingers on her waist and then reluctantly let her go. He clasped his hands behind his back so he wouldn't be tempted to reach out to her again. "Shall we?"

She nodded and, without another word, they began to walk, side by side, along the dry sand.

They strolled in silence for several minutes. There was nothing but the sound of the seagulls and the tumultuous waves. The wind was high and the sea was rougher than usual. It crashed against the rocks with a resounding roar. More than once, he saw Miss Reynolds stare out at it, a strange expression on her face. "Are you fond of the seaside?" he asked.

"I've never been until now."

He gave her a sharp look. "You've never seen the sea?"

She shook her head. "Not until the accommodation coach crossed a high hill on the way to King's Abbot. I looked out the window and...there it was."

Justin couldn't imagine it. He'd been born on the coast and had spent the better part of his youth clambering along the cliffs and swimming in the open sea. The beach outside of Abbot's Holcombe had been his safe haven; the place he fled to whenever life with the Brays became intolerable. "How does it strike you?" he asked her, genuinely curious.

"Vast," she said. "Limitless. It makes me feel very small."

She resumed looking down the narrow strip of beach as they walked on in silence, staring steadily first up at the cliffs and then down the long, desolate coastline. Justin wondered what it was that captivated her attention to such a degree. There was nothing but stark, isolated rock and empty stretches of sand. He tried to imagine it through her eyes, but it was a fruitless exercise. He was far too cynical and, in the presence of such a fine lady, painfully conscious of his home's many shortcomings.

He'd felt much the same when he'd first seen her inside the Abbey. It was to be her home if they married, possibly for the rest of her life. Yet Queen Victoria herself could not have looked more out of place than Helena Reynolds had, sitting so primly on his shabby library sofa.

"It's not a patch on London, is it?" he asked.

"Isn't it?" She continued to gaze fixedly up at the cliffs.

He thrust his hands into the pockets of his trousers as he lagged a short distance behind her. "There's no comparison. London is vibrant. Full of energy and industry."

"I suppose."

"And then there are the amusements. Shopping on Bond Street. Riding in Hyde Park. Visiting the Zoological Gardens. Whatever one is in the mood for is only a hansom cab's drive away."

"Yes, but—" She glanced back at him. "For those who don't fancy such entertainments, London is rather wasted, don't you think?"

"Are we speaking in hypotheticals?" he asked. "Or are we speaking of you?"

She didn't answer.

He lengthened his stride so he was once again walking at her side. "I refuse to believe there isn't something in London you'll regret having given up. A bookstore, perhaps, or a confectioner's shop where you buy your favorite sweets."

"I don't care for sweets."

"Your favorite books, then. You do like books, I presume." He saw her lip curve upward a fraction. "There are no bookstores in King's Abbot. Nor libraries, either. If one wants to read the newest novels, one must purchase them in Abbot's Holcombe. And since we've both agreed to loathe the place…"

"You have books in your library. I'll simply read those."

"Farming manuals? Architectural journals?"

She cast him a sidelong glance. "Are those really the only kind of books you keep at the Abbey? I was certain I saw a copy of something by Mr. Dickens on your shelf."

He flashed a wolfish grin at her. The brief movement tugged at the burns on the right side of his neck and jaw. It was a sobering reminder that Miss Reynolds would have far more to accustom herself to as his bride than the meager offerings in his library.

"I may have one or two of his novels," he admitted.

"Which one or two?"

"Which are your favorites?"

She folded her hands at her waist, appearing to rest them on the swell of her skirts as she walked. "It's quite hard to choose, really. I did find *Hard Times* to be rather instructive. And I greatly enjoyed reading *The Old Curiosity Shop.*"

Justin raised his brows. "You *enjoyed* the death of Little Nell?"

"No, not her death, but...it's such a moving story." She glanced up at him, her bonnet ribbons blowing in the wind behind her like two silken streamers. "Don't you think so, Mr. Thornhill?"

What he thought was that she looked damnably pretty at the moment. Was it too soon to tell her so? If theirs was a traditional courtship and betrothal, he wouldn't have hesitated. But what were the rules when one became engaged through a matrimonial advertisement? And did those rules even apply anymore? After the crude way in which he'd addressed her at the King's Arms, a soft word or a compliment would likely be as nothing to her. He'd already proven himself to be a vulgar, mannerless brute.

"Justin," he said gruffly.

"I beg your pardon?"

"We're engaged to be married, aren't we? I see no reason why you must continue to call me Mr. Thornhill. My name is Justin. I give you leave to use it."

"Oh." Her voice was faint.

"What about you?" he pressed. "Or am I to address you as Miss Reynolds until we've solemnized our vows?"

"If that's what you'd prefer."

"I wouldn't prefer it. I would dislike it intensely."

She took a quiet breath. "Well, in that case, I suppose you'd better call me Helena."

"Helena," he repeated. He tightened his hands at his back. "We proceed apace."

"Indeed. Everything is moving so quickly."

"Isn't that rather the point?"

She tugged at the fingers of one of her gloves, little agitated movements that expressed her disquiet more eloquently than words ever could. "Yes, but—"

"But?"

"It will take some adjustment, won't it? No matter our intentions." Her eyes found his. "You must be patient with me."

"Of course. Always."

His words seemed to reassure her a little, but Justin would have had to be a fool not to recognize the lingering doubt that shadowed her gaze. She didn't trust him. Not yet. And he couldn't entirely blame her. Thus far, he'd done little to earn her confidence. Quite the opposite. He'd been too sullen. Too volatile. It was all well and good when he was growling orders at Boothroyd, but if he wanted to win the regard of Helena Reynolds, he was going to have to do better.

He made an effort to collect his scattered thoughts. "We were discussing Mr. Dickens."

"So we were."

"*The Old Curiosity Shop*, I believe."

"You were about to tell me you didn't like it."

"I didn't *dis*like it."

"But you didn't find it as moving as I did."

"As to that…" He raised an absent hand to rub the side of his jaw. "It was sentimental, certainly. If one enjoys that sort of thing."

"Which you don't, I take it."

"I dislike suffering for no purpose. Pain and sacrifice should come to something in the end. It should have meaning."

Helena nodded slowly, her expression thoughtful. "Yes, it should. But I'm not convinced it ever does. Not really."

"You take a grim view."

"I can only speak from my experience."

Justin looked down at her, his gaze assessing. It was not in his nature to be sympathetic or consoling, but as he registered the fine lines of tension in Helena's face, he felt the same inexplicable tug of protectiveness that had plagued him earlier at the inn. "You've been reading the wrong novels."

She smiled. "Do you think so?"

"Yes. It won't do, you know. If you're not careful, you'll read yourself straight into a black melancholy."

"Good gracious. I hope you're not one of those gentlemen who believe that a woman must restrict herself to improving books."

"Not in the least."

"What do you recommend, then?" she asked. "Farming manuals? Architectural journals?"

"Either would be better than maudlin tales of innocent creatures dying for no reason, but no. What you need is a steady diet of adventure stories and revenge plots. Suffering always has meaning in those types of books."

"Is that what you read, sir?"

"When time allows. Which is not to say I don't own a Dickens novel or two. I have a copy of *David Copperfield* in my library, and several other of his novels besides. You may read them whenever you wish—and add to the collection, too, as it pleases you."

The glimmer of amusement faded from her eyes. "That's very generous. Thank you."

He acknowledged her thanks with an inclination of his head. She was close enough to him that he could feel the brush of her skirts against the leg of his trousers as they walked, could smell the faint scent of her perfume mingling in the salty sea air.

Was Helena as aware of him as he was of her? Somehow he doubted it. She was looking up at the clifftops again, her thoughts plainly elsewhere.

"Are there no other houses?" she asked after a time.

"Some. Cottages mostly. You won't be able to see them from here. The only building you can see—though not very well— is just there." He pointed to a faint outline in the distance.

She shielded her eyes with her hand. "What is it?"

"The church spire at Abbot's Holcombe."

"But it's so close!" she exclaimed. "I thought you said it was thirteen miles away."

"Only by road. From the clifftops and then by boat, it's no distance at all."

A worried frown worked its way across her brow as her gaze moved along the cliff face and then to the water below. The cliffs at Abbot's Holcombe were some of the most dangerous in the district, only a smattering of rocky outcroppings breaking up what would have otherwise been a sheer, vertical drop into the sea.

"Is there a path down to the beach?" she asked. "Like the one from the Abbey?"

"Nothing so civilized as that. If one wants to reach the beach from the cliffs at Abbot's Holcombe, one must climb down."

"On the rocks? But no one could accomplish such a feat, surely. It's far too steep."

He shrugged one shoulder. "I have done it."

"*You*?" She turned to look at him, her lips half-parted in astonishment.

Had they been conversing on any other subject, Justin might have been amused by her reaction. As it was, he couldn't even muster a smile. "When I was a boy," he said, "no more than nine or ten years of age, my friends and I must have made the climb once a week at least."

"What in heaven's name for?"

Justin looked up at the clifftops, his face a mask of carefully cultivated indifference. In his long quest to purchase the Abbey, he'd never once considered what it would be like to see the cliffs at Abbot's Holcombe every day for the rest of his life. He'd never thought of how it would feel to be reminded. No. He'd been too consumed with thoughts of justice. Too intent on revenge.

He turned back to Helena. "Boys often do foolish things. When have any of them ever needed a reason?"

She shook her head. "I can't believe your parents allowed it."

"We had no parents."

"No parents?" Her brow furrowed. "Do you mean to say that you...that you and your friends—"

"We were parish orphans," Justin said with brutal frankness.

He hadn't meant to tell her. Not yet. But there was no taking it back now. Nor why should he want to? It was who he was. An orphan. A bastard. Had Helena Reynolds been the plain working-class spinster he'd expected, he would have had no qualms about confessing it.

Instead she was a lady. A lovely, impeccably mannered lady. And despite Finchley's assurances that the circumstances of his birth wouldn't matter to her, Justin knew full well that there were not many ladies who would rejoice at the chance to marry a man of dubious parentage. Not unless that man were in possession of a suitably large fortune—which he most assuredly was not.

He watched Helena's face, waiting for the first flicker of revulsion to make its inevitable appearance.

"In Abbott's Holcombe?" she asked.

He nodded, still waiting.

She gave him a long, searching look. "Is that why we loathe the place?"

We.

Justin's chest expanded on an almost painful surge of emotion. He couldn't tell if it was relief or—worse—if it was gratitude. All she'd said was *we*. It was hardly a declaration of undying affection, but to him, in that moment, it was everything. "Yes. That's the reason."

Helena turned her attention back toward the cliff face. "I'm amazed no one was ever hurt."

He followed her gaze, frowning. "Someone was once. Another boy—a childhood friend of mine—slipped on the rocks and fell into the sea. He hit his head on the way down."

"How awful." Her eyes filled with ready sympathy. "Was he injured badly?"

"Yes. Quite badly. He's not been himself since." Justin cleared his throat. "Which is my fault, really. Everyone always said he'd follow me anywhere. And it was I who insisted on making the climb."

"Oh, my dear," she murmured.

His heart gave a desperate, pathetic lurch, believing for a single, fleeting instant that she had addressed *him* as my dear. That her soft, caressing undertone was meant for *him*. But she was merely lamenting the unhappy fate of some unknown boy.

Or perhaps not so unknown.

"Was it Neville?" she asked.

He nodded stiffly.

Helena looked away from him, turning her face back toward the sea. In the distance, white-capped waves rose to crash in the water, leaving nothing but foam to lap up against the sand. It came within an inch of wetting her boots.

Justin reached for her arm to guide her back onto dry ground, but there was no need. She sidestepped the water without his assistance. His hand fell, useless, back to his side.

"How very kind you are," she said.

He started. It was the second time she'd referred to him as kind. "For employing Neville? Hardly. He's not really even a servant. He chooses to work. Insists upon it, in fact."

"He doesn't wish to be idle."

"Neville's stubborn. He always has been. But I won't complain. I'm lucky to have him. Anyone would be. He does the work of five men, all without complaint."

"As I observed." She looked back at him, the lush curve of her mouth hinting at a smile. "Does he often serve tea to your guests?"

Justin grimaced. "No, thank God." Their tea had been the flavorless, watery residue of leaves on their fourth washing. Why Neville hadn't used fresh tea from the canister, he didn't know. He had his suspicions, of course. Suspicions which rested squarely on Boothroyd's shoulders. "Neville prefers being out of doors."

"He did seem rather uncomfortable inside the Abbey. I thought it was because of me."

"He's unaccustomed to seeing women about the place."

"Your cook is a woman."

"Mrs. Whitlock is a sixty-year-old tartar with silver hair and a penchant for cheap gin. Next to you, she may as well be a different species."

"And happy to be so, I have no doubt," Helena said. "There are advantages to being a sixty-year-old woman."

"Are there indeed."

"Of course." She proceeded to enumerate them with the ease of someone who'd given the matter a great deal of thought. "Freedom. Independence. The ability to go where she likes and do what she likes. The ability to be as eccentric as she wishes."

As Justin listened, he couldn't help wondering how highly Helena valued her own independence. *Very* highly, he suspected. She'd mentioned something to that effect in the first letter she'd written him. He could still remember her words, her small even script flowing across the page, so unmistakably feminine:

I never intended to marry, but reversals of fortune have made it impossible for me to remain independent.

Marriage, it seemed, was a last resort for her. And a not entirely agreeable one at that.

"The only type of woman with more independence than an elderly woman," she continued, "is a widow."

"Quite so," he agreed. "Though may I advise—if you are aspiring to widowhood—you consider marrying a man older than two and thirty?"

She gave him a reproving look. "I'm aspiring to nothing of the sort. I'm merely stating a fact. About your cook, I might add."

"Your cook, too, in the very near future."

Her color heightened. "Yes."

They continued to walk side by side at the edge of the water. In a few short minutes, they'd have to return to the house. He'd have to bundle her into the coach with her temporary maid and send her back to the King's Arms. And then…

And then, he'd have to wait.

But for how long? A few days? A few weeks while the banns were called? The prospect was grim, but Helena couldn't very well remain at the Abbey. Not with half the villagers already believing him to be a ruthless, opportunistic monster. Acquiring a wife was supposed to help his reputation, not sink it further into the mire.

"You still haven't answered my question," he said.

Helena glanced back at him, puzzled. "What question?"

"About the things you will miss in London."

"Oh, that." She was quiet for several seconds, seeming to reflect on the matter with uncommon solemnity. "There *was* a place I enjoyed very much once. Though I can hardly pine for it. It isn't even there anymore." She brushed a stray ribbon away from her mouth as she explained, "The summer before my brother first went away with his regiment, he took me to the Crystal Palace."

"The Crystal Palace?" The dazzling structure of cast iron and plate glass had been erected in Hyde Park in 1851 to house the Great Exhibition. It had been a chance for Britain to showcase itself as a leader in industrial technology and design—as well as to display the art and inventions of other nations. "The Great Exhibition was *eight* years ago."

"Yes, I know that, but…it's the only happy memory I have of London."

Justin considered this with a slightly furrowed brow. He couldn't articulate what it was about her statement that unsettled him so. She didn't sound sad or self-pitying, merely matter-of-fact, as if she were commenting on the weather.

"Tell me," he said.

She needed little prompting. "We wandered for hours. First to the Indian Court and then to see the exhibits from Turkey and China. My brother insisted on examining everything. We were like two children. It was all…" She searched for the right words. "Oh, I can't describe it. It was all so marvelous. There was an elephant with grass in his trunk. And an Indian tent filled with rugs of crimson and gold. And then we filed along in a line of a hundred other people to see the largest diamond in the whole world."

"The Koh-i-Noor."

She looked up at him. "Have you seen it, Mr. Thornhill?"

"Justin," he corrected. "And yes. I have. I visited the Crystal Palace that summer as well."

Admission had been only a shilling, which had seemed to him a small price to pay to admire exhibits from all over the world. He remembered having spent a great deal of time in the machinery courts looking at the Harrison Power Loom and the cotton machinery of Hibbert, Platt, and Sons. However, no visit to the Crystal Palace would have been complete without a viewing of its most famous exhibit.

"When I saw it," Helena said, "it was inside a gilded birdcage, illuminated by a ring of little gas jets. People were complaining it didn't sparkle."

"They were doing the same when I saw it." He gave her a wry smile. "Perhaps we were there at the same time?"

She seemed much struck by this idea. "Perhaps we were. Perhaps we were fated to meet again."

"Do you believe in fate?"

"I don't know." Her lashes lowered. "I would like to believe in it."

"It's certainly a more romantic explanation for all of this than your having answered my matrimonial advertisement."

He hadn't said it to embarrass her, but judging by the color that rose in her face, it seemed he'd done so. He cursed himself for an insensitive brute. It was too soon to have mentioned romance in any case. Though why the devil he was mentioning it at all, he hadn't the faintest idea. The whole purpose of a matrimonial advertisement was to meet and marry without the burden of wooing and courtship. That shouldn't change simply because the woman who'd answered his advertisement was sweet and soft and pretty.

"Do you believe romance is necessary in an arrangement such as ours?" she asked.

"Necessary? No. I would say not." He ran his hand along the back of his neck. "Then again, I'm no expert."

Helena bent her head, the brim of her bonnet briefly shielding her face from his view. "What about friendship?"

He thought he detected a note of hopefulness in her voice, but couldn't be certain. "Ah. Friendship, I suspect, is a different matter."

"Then you think it necessary?"

"Not necessary, no, but without some degree of friendship, marriage wouldn't be very comfortable, would it?"

"No, I suppose not," she said. "And yet many gentlemen believe their wives are not their friends, but their inferiors. They treat them as children."

"They want to protect them."

She folded her arms at her waist. "I would that women could protect themselves."

"As do I. But that's not the world we live in." Justin would have said more on the subject, but as they walked closer along the water's edge, his attention was caught by a glint of glass sparkling in the wet sand. He bent to pick it up.

Helena approached, curious. "What is it?"

He gave the glass a quick polish on the sleeve of his frock coat. It shone a gleaming amber. "Sea glass," he said as he stood. "Here. Open you hand." When she obliged him, he placed the glass in the center of her palm. "This looks to be from a broken bottle. Probably French brandy smuggled in during the war with Napoleon."

She traced the rounded edge of the glass with one gloved fingertip. "It's beautiful," she whispered. "Like a jewel."

He dusted the sand from his hands. "Not quite the Koh-i-Noor diamond, I'm afraid."

"No, it isn't," she acknowledged, still staring at the piece of sea glass in her hand. "But it's the loveliest thing anyone—" She broke off with a visible loss of composure.

He took an instinctive step toward her. "Helena," he said, his voice rough with concern.

She raised her eyes to meet his. "How silly I am. I do beg your pardon."

Justin felt a sudden rush of tenderness for her. Had she not already rebuffed him once, he would have been quite tempted to take her in his arms. As it was, he couldn't refrain from reaching out and, very gently, brushing her cheek with his knuckles. He heard her inhale an unsteady breath.

"I'm not a pauper, Helena. I'll be able to give you more than sea glass. But I want you to have no illusions. I'm not a wealthy man. Nor was I raised a gentleman. That I have seen something of the world and know how to go about in society, I owe to Her Majesty's Army not to any accident of birth."

"Why are you telling me this?"

"Because I want you to know what kind of man I am."

"I already know what kind of man you are. Mr. Finchley told me. If I'd had any objections, I would never have written to you."

Justin frowned. In the very near future, he intended to have a few words with Tom Finchley. "He won't have told you everything. He'll have left the worst to me."

He saw the question in her eyes, the unmistakable flash of uncertainty, but she didn't ask him to explain. She didn't ask him anything. Her lack of curiosity puzzled him exceedingly.

"Helena," he said, "you must understand."

"It doesn't matter."

"It *does* matter. The circumstances of my birth—the way in which I purchased the Abbey—even my capture in India. There's been talk, most of it quite unpleasant. Gossips from here to Abbot's Holcombe will be at great pains to apprise you of every sordid detail."

She grew a little paler, but she didn't shy away from him. Nor did she remain silent. Instead, she asked him a question. The same question he'd asked of her earlier at the King's Arms. "Have you broken the law?"

"No." And it was the truth, no matter what the village gossips said about how he'd acquired the Abbey.

Helena visibly swallowed. "And have you… Have you ever hurt a woman?"

His expression hardened at the very suggestion, his reply prompt and fierce. "No," he swore to her. "Upon my honor."

"Then I don't care about the rest." She began to turn away, but he cupped the side of her face with gentle force, compelling her to hold his gaze.

"And what about afterward?" he asked. "A week from now. A month from now. What happens when you realize you hate it here? What happens when you realize you hate *me*? Once we marry, it will be too late for you to change your mind. You will be bound to me for the rest of your life."

"I know that. And I won't change my mind. Only…" She clutched the piece of sea glass against the swell of her bosom. "Please, let us marry quickly."

Justin's heart began to pound with a dizzying strength. "How quickly?"

"As soon as possible," she said. "I don't want to return to London. I want to stay here. At the Abbey. I want us to marry and start our life together."

He regarded her in silence for a moment, his large gloved hand still cradling her cheek with exquisite care. She was trembling beneath his touch, delicate little shivers that he could feel against his palm, that he could hear in her every indrawn breath.

"Please, Justin," she whispered.

He understood then that Boothroyd was right to be concerned for his state of mind—and for the state of his bank account, too—for as he stared down at Helena Reynolds, Justin was struck with a bone-deep determination to move mountains for her. To do anything in the world to make her happy, so long as she would consent to be his and his alone.

"Very well," he said. "If that is what you truly wish, who am I to stand in your way?"

Chapter Four

A quick wedding was not entirely possible, as Justin explained the following morning at the inn. "You'll have to spend another night here, I'm afraid," he said. Helena watched as he divested himself of his hat, gloves, and rain-soaked greatcoat. His hair was wet, an errant black lock falling over his forehead. "The superintendent registrar requires we wait one full day before he'll issue a license."

It wasn't the best of news. She'd already been obliged to stay one night at The King's Arms. One long, awful night spent peering out the window of her room, waiting for someone who didn't come. She'd hardly managed to sleep a wink.

"Though he did agree to marry us tomorrow morning any time before eleven," Justin added. "If that will suit you."

Helena wrapped the heavy folds of her Indian shawl more firmly about her shoulders and began to pace the length of the private parlor. *No*, she wanted to cry. It didn't suit her *at all*. But there was no point in arguing. Justin had already made it quite clear she couldn't stay at the Abbey before they were married. It would harm her reputation, he'd said yesterday. The villagers would *talk*.

"I suppose it must," she said, "since it seems I have little choice in the matter."

"No," Justin acknowledged after a long silence.

She chewed the edge of her lip, lost in thought, as she walked to the end of the room and back again. When she next cast a glance at Justin, she saw he was still standing in front of the cold hearth, observing her agitated pacing with a curiously rapt expression.

He was also clad in riding dress, she realized. A dark coat, drab cloth waistcoat, and light colored breeches clinging to his long, powerful legs. Every garment bore evidence of the inclement weather, from his mud-spattered boots to his damp and slightly wilted cravat.

She felt a flicker of guilt. "Did you ride to Abbot's Holcombe? In this weather?"

He ran a self-conscious hand over his hair. "It wasn't raining when I left."

"And then you rode all the way here?"

"I promised I'd call on you this morning, didn't I?"

Helena wondered if he always kept his promises, no matter how uncomfortable or inconvenient. "You did," she said, moving toward the antiquated bell pull that hung beside the fireplace. She gave it a decisive tug. "And my manners have been appalling."

His brows lifted. "Have they? I hadn't noticed."

"I've left you to stand here shivering while I—" She broke off at the sound of a soft scratch at the door. It heralded the appearance of Bess, who'd grudgingly resumed her duties at the inn earlier that morning after having spent the night on a cot in Helena's room.

"Will you be wanting your tea now, miss?" she asked.

"If you please, Bess. And do send someone in to build up the fire."

"Yes, miss." Bess dropped a curtsy and then withdrew, shutting the door behind her.

Helena turned her attention back to Justin. "Won't you sit down?"

"If you will."

"Of course." She gestured toward two armchairs near the hearth. He nodded and, after she'd seated herself, he did the same. "Oh!" She moved to stand once more. "I should've had Bess take your boots. Shall I summon her back?"

"Don't trouble yourself. I'll only muddy them again on the journey back to the Abbey."

She wanted to tell him it wasn't the mud that concerned her, but the damp. She'd certainly have done so if it had been her brother who'd just tramped in with sodden boots. But Justin Thornhill wasn't her brother. To raise such an indelicate subject as his feet—wet or otherwise—seemed positively indecent.

"I wouldn't like you to catch a chill," she said instead.

A smile tugged briefly at the edge of Justin's mouth. She had a sinking feeling he knew exactly what she'd been thinking. "I'm not so fragile as all that," he said. "If I were, I wouldn't last long here."

"No. I suppose not." She managed a weak smile in return, though smiling was the last thing in the world she felt like doing at the moment.

Tomorrow, if everything went according to plan, this man—this *stranger*—would be her husband. For better or worse, he'd be endowed by law with all of the rights that were a man's privilege over his wife. And he could exercise those rights in any manner he chose. He could beat her if he wished or he could confine her. He could do almost anything short of killing her and no one would say him nay.

This was marriage, as she knew it. And this was what she'd be freely consenting to at the registrar's office in Abbot's Holcombe.

It was impossible to think of it without an accompanying wave of panic.

She swallowed. "I do hope it will have stopped raining by the time you return to the Abbey."

"I expect it will."

Further conversation was interrupted by another scratch at the door. It preceded the entry of a grizzled manservant who informed them he'd come to lay the fire. While he busied himself at the hearth, coaxing a flame from the kindling, Bess arrived with a tea tray.

"Mrs. Blevins says to tell you she made the little cakes fresh this morning," she said, placing the tray on a low table near Helena's chair. "Will you be wanting anything else, miss?"

"No, thank you, Bess. This will do quite nicely. Please convey our appreciation to Mrs. Blevins."

"Yes, miss." Bess offered another stilted curtsy before taking her leave, the manservant not far behind her. The door to the private parlor shut after them with a decisive click.

Helena arranged the teacups and began to pour. As the lone female in a family of men, she'd long been accustomed to presiding over the tea tray. However, in Justin's presence, the familiar ritual felt clumsy and new. She could sense him watching her every movement.

If he noticed her discomfiture, he gave no sign of it. But when she was handing him his teacup, her bare fingers brushed his. He looked at her then and the oddest expression crossed his face.

She stilled in her chair. "What is it?"

"Nothing."

"I've amused you."

"No, you've surprised me." He lowered his teacup to his lap. "Your attentions feel…very wifely."

Her cheeks warmed. "Surely not. I only want you to be comfortable. It's the least I can do after you've ridden out in this weather on my account."

"Not only yours. I'm to be married tomorrow, too, if you'll remember."

"Yes." She prepared her own cup of tea, adding in a liberal amount of sugar. Jenny had always sworn by heavily sugared tea in times of crisis. It was all Helena could remember drinking in the weeks following the news of her brother's disappearance. "But I'm the one who insisted on a hasty wedding. I daresay you would've preferred to wait for the banns to be called."

"Three weeks? You credit me with a great deal of patience."

"Not patience, no, but… Don't you wish to marry in a church?"

He helped himself to a cake from the tray. "Do I strike you as a particularly pious man?"

"One needn't be pious to marry in a church. Merely traditional."

"I'm neither. Which is why a registrar's office will suit me very well."

She took a small sip of her tea. The scalding, sugary liquid burned a path down her throat. It warmed her all over, helping to soothe her frazzled nerves as reliably as it always did. "Even if it's in Abbott's Holcombe?"

"There's not much choice. Not if we want to wed quickly." He looked down into his teacup for a moment, a scowl briefly darkening his brow. "And it's not all bad, really. There's a fine hotel there and several very decent shops. You might want to visit a few of them while we're in town."

"Oh no. That won't be necessary. I meant it yesterday when I said I wouldn't be expensive."

"And I meant it when I said you'd have whatever you require."

She fingered the soft edge of her Indian shawl. It pooled around her in her chair, still half-draped over her arms. "I really don't need anything. I brought enough with me for now. After we're married, I can send for the rest of my things."

"The rest of your things?" Justin looked at her over the edge of his teacup. "How much more is there?"

"A great deal more, stored away in London. It was far too much to bring with me on the train. There was scarcely any room in my carpetbag as it was. And I haven't a maid to sponge and press my dresses. Everything is in a dreadful state." Her words tumbled out in an anxious rush. She couldn't seem to stop them. "I wanted to look my best, but I traveled by myself and I didn't like to draw attention—"

"Helena," he interrupted. "Helena, it's all right."

"I'm babbling, aren't I?" She looked at him, feeling suddenly helpless. "I fear I'm overwhelmed."

"I know. I'll sort it."

"You can't."

He gave her a quick, wry smile. "Try me."

Helena ached to confide in him. To tell him everything. To rest all of her troubles squarely on his broad shoulders. He was willing to bear them, she could tell. He was gruff and forbidding, but he was kind and gentle, too. She saw that now quite clearly. It pricked her conscience that she must deceive him, but she'd fallen victim to seemingly sympathetic gentlemen too many times this past year to trust her instincts now. For all that Justin Thornhill appeared genuinely concerned, she knew in her heart she couldn't fully trust him until they were married.

Which was perfectly fine, she told herself. In less than a day, they'd be man and wife. There would be plenty of time to confide in him then. A lifetime, in fact. Why, she might even grow to like him.

Though whether or not he would like her when this was all over was another question entirely.

She took another sip of her tea. "It isn't any one thing. It's feelings. Nerves."

"All quite natural, I believe."

Her brows lifted. "Are *you* nervous?"

Justin regarded her in silence for a moment. The sensitivity that had shone in his eyes only moments before slowly gave way to something hard and almost predatory. "I'm anxious. I don't think I'll be completely easy until you're mine."

Helena's stomach performed a disconcerting somersault. She took another hasty swallow of her tea, her eyes still locked with his. "Nor I. Until you're mine, that is."

To her astonishment, a dull red flush appeared on Justin's neck, visible just above the line of his cravat. He cleared his throat. "Have I told you— That is, I know I haven't, but

I had meant to—Your gown and your..." He motioned to her shawl. "Is that from India?"

"It is. It was a gift from my brother."

"Yes, well, it looks very pretty," he said. "*You* look very pretty."

She lowered her teacup back to its saucer and returned them both to the tea tray. Her heart was thumping with uncommon force. "Thank you. But you needn't feel compelled to say such things."

"I don't."

"We've already agreed romance isn't necessary in an arrangement such as ours."

"What has romance to do with anything?"

Helena could think of no acceptable answer, so instead addressed herself to the tea tray. She refilled each of their cups and then offered Justin another cake. She chose one for herself, too, and then spent some little time cutting it—quite unnecessarily—into even quarters.

In the back of her mind, Jenny's stern voice admonished her for being so shy and awkward. It wasn't enough just to feed a guest, the voice said. One must engage them in polite conversation as well. Helena knew this. She'd spent years playing hostess, first for her father and then for her brother and uncle. All that was needed was an innocuous remark about the weather. Anything would do at this point.

"I thought it was rather cold last night," she said finally.

Justin's dark brows knit with immediate concern. "You weren't warm enough?"

"Not at first, no. But later Mrs. Blevins brought up an extra blanket for me." She paused to stir more sugar into her tea. "She said that nights at Greyfriar's Abbey will be even colder."

"You won't need extra blankets to keep you warm at the Abbey."

"Oh no," she agreed, remembering Mr. Boothroyd's concern about excess expenses. "Not at all. I'm perfectly capable of making do."

Justin's mouth tilted up in a bemused half smile. She worried he would say something more about economy and was relieved when he turned the subject. "I trust Bess stayed with you last night."

"She did." Helena spread a teaspoonful of Mrs. Blevins's strawberry preserves onto a slice of cake. "Will you engage her as my companion for tonight as well?"

He nodded. "Do you mind it very much?"

"Not particularly," she said, adding, "Bess has been telling me all about the history of the Abbey."

Justin grimaced. "Which version of history would that be? The one with the evil monk? Or the one with the ghost and the buried treasure?"

"The one with the *mad* monk and the papists' gold."

"Good God. Is he mad now?"

"Bess says so."

"And papists too? It grows more gothic by the second."

Helena took a sip of her tea. "Do you know why there's so much local superstition about the Abbey?"

"Not with any certainty. There've been rumors about ghostly monks and buried treasure for as long as I can remember. I believed them myself when I was a boy."

"Is that why you and your friends climbed down the cliffs to sail there every week?"

He crumbled a piece of cake on his plate, seeming to consider his answer. "No. Not entirely. Though Finchley was always hopeful we'd find a hidden cache of gold."

Her eyes widened. "*Mr.* Finchley?"

"Didn't he tell you?"

Helena shook her head. Mr. Finchley had been young and even handsome after a fashion, but his manner, however kind, had been strictly professional. He'd told her nothing about himself, and the information he'd conveyed about Justin had been more in the way of reassurances than confidences.

She recalled how he'd leaned across his desk to hand her his handkerchief, his light blue eyes unerringly sympathetic. "Thornhill will protect you," he'd promised. "Once you're his wife, no one will ever touch you again. That I can guarantee."

"The four of us were in the orphanage together," Justin said. "Me, Neville, Finchley, and another boy, Alex Archer. We were like brothers."

"And you've all remained friends?"

"Not as we once were," he said. "Finchley was articled to a solicitor in London and Neville had his accident. I joined the army and Archer…" His face grew somber. "Archer broke his apprenticeship and disappeared. We none of us know what happened to him. I've long suspected he's dead."

"I'm sorry," she said.

He shrugged. "It's of little matter."

Helena could see that that wasn't entirely true. Justin didn't appear indifferent to the fate of his friend. Quite the opposite. "They were like your family," she said softly.

"We were orphans, Helena. They *were* my family."

"And they accompanied you every week on your sail to the Abbey. But not to look for treasure. Why then?" she wondered aloud.

"We were always sneaking about the Abbey's grounds. Digging holes and crawling in through half-open windows.

I'm rather amazed none of us was ever brought up before the magistrate."

"Was the Abbey empty then?"

It seemed an innocent enough question, but Justin's expression—already so thoughtful and somber—grew shuttered. It was as if he'd firmly closed a door in her face. Not only closed it, but barred it and bolted it, too. When he next spoke, Helena had the distinct impression he wasn't being wholly forthcoming.

"It was owned by a baronet," he said. "Sir Oswald Bannister. He was always well in his cups whenever we came calling."

"But then...how did you come to live at the Abbey? Did you purchase it from him?"

A line of tension tightened Justin's jaw. "In a manner of speaking."

"I'm sorry. It's none of my business."

"You'll hear it eventually from some well-meaning busy-body."

"Perhaps, but—"

Justin cut her off in a hard voice. "Sir Oswald had a propensity for deep play. After he ran through the rest of his assets, he borrowed against the Abbey. I was in India at the time, but when I heard of his predicament..." He gave her a look filled with a bewildering mixture of bitterness, pain, and something very like triumph. "I had Finchley buy up his mortgages and then—when Sir Oswald was at his lowest ebb—I called in all of his debt."

A chill skated down Helena's spine. She leaned back in her chair, unconsciously drawing away from him. "That seems rather heartless."

"It was nothing less than he deserved."

She waited for Justin to explain, but he did not. The silence hung between them, taut and uncomfortable. Helena didn't like it. And she didn't like herself for being so judgmental. She had told him only yesterday that the past didn't matter. He'd tried to confess something about the Abbey then, hadn't he? In her desperation it had all seemed so unimportant. But now…

Now that their wedding was so close and so certain, she felt the familiar fear take hold of her. "There's much we don't know about each other."

Justin was watching her. "Having second thoughts?"

"No," she said. And it was the truth. She hadn't the luxury of second thoughts. "I expect all couples who meet by matrimonial advertisement find themselves in our predicament. They are strangers, after all."

"I'm not concerned." His voice deepened. "You can learn me, if you have a mind to."

Helena's stomach performed another disconcerting gyration. It was butterflies, she realized with some chagrin. A veritable flock of them, each unfurling their wings and taking flight and—

Good heavens.

But she was a woman of five and twenty, not some green girl quivering and fluttering in the presence of a handsome lad.

She lifted her chin. "You will have to learn me as well, sir."

Justin's mouth quirked in that wry, shadow of a smile with which she was fast becoming familiar. "I shall look forward to it, ma'am."

She couldn't tell if he was mocking her. Or flirting with her. Either way, there seemed nothing to say to such a statement. She decided it was safer not to respond at all. She dropped her gaze to the fireplace, attempting to regain some small measure of her lost composure.

The flames crackled ominously in the grate as a log of burned wood snapped in half and fell into the ashes. It was the only sound in the room. Justin appeared to comprehend the significance of this at the same instant she did. He stood abruptly from his chair and walked the short distance to the window. She rose and followed after him.

"It's stopped raining," he said.

She looked out the window at the inn yard. Everything was wet and muddy—including the team of horses an ostler was hitching to a coach—but the rainclouds had drifted past and the sun was shining brightly in the now clear, blue sky. She glanced up at Justin. "Will you have to ride back to the Abbey before the rain starts again?"

"It won't rain again. Not for a while." He tilted his head. "Though judging from the direction of those clouds, it looks like Abbot's Holcombe is in for quite a downpour."

"I hope it won't rain on our wedding day."

"It won't matter if it does. We'll take the carriage." He turned to face her, his eyes lowering briefly to her skirts. "You've dropped your shawl."

She looked down. Her shawl was still threaded through her right arm, but the left end had fallen to the floor in a heap of red and gold cashmere. She moved to retrieve it, but he anticipated her, bending swiftly to sweep the heavy fabric up in his hand

"Here you are," he said as he straightened. "May I?

She nodded and then stood, still as a Grecian statue, while he draped the shawl around her shoulder and back over her left arm. When he finished, she murmured her thanks, but Justin didn't let go of the fabric. He merely stared down at her, holding her questioning gaze for an achingly long moment.

"Helena…"

"Yes?"

"I'd like very much to kiss you," he said. "If I may."

Color crept into her face. He was standing awfully close to her. Just as close as when he'd touched her, so tenderly, yesterday on the beach. Her pulse quickened at the memory. "Very well."

He brought his fingers to the curve of her cheek. She inhaled a shallow breath, holding herself immobile as he traced a path down the edge of her jaw to cup her chin. He tilted her face up. And then he bent his head and brushed his lips very softly and very slowly across her own.

Helena's mouth trembled beneath his, but she did not kiss him back. Nor did she move to touch him in return. She remained still, her eyes closed and her arms at her sides, fingers twisting into the folds of her shawl.

He smelled of the rainstorm. Of horses, leather, and some faint, masculine fragrance that must be his shaving soap. It made her knees tremble and she wondered, absently, how a scent could affect one's knees of all places. But then he kissed her again, warm and firm, and she forgot about her knees. She forgot about everything except the dizzying pressure of his gently insistent mouth.

It lasted only minutes—seconds—and then a horse whinnied shrilly from the inn yard. An ostler shouted: "Catch hold of that bay, Fred! He's a lively one!"

Justin's lips stilled on hers. "The devil," he muttered hoarsely.

She opened her eyes, startled.

He raised his head. His jaw was as hard as granite and she could see a muscle working in his cheek. "I'm sorry, Helena."

"Whatever for?"

"For being so bloody careless." His hand at her waist, he drew her away from the window.

The window.

"Oh no," she said. "Oh, how dreadful."

Who had been out in the yard? She tried desperately to recall. There'd been the ostler, of course. And then there were the grooms and whoever had stopped to changed horses.

What about Mr. and Mrs. Blevins? Had they happened by as well?

"After all I've done to safeguard your reputation," Justin said under his breath.

Helena didn't give a fig for her reputation. Gossip, on the other hand, was an entirely different matter. The last thing she wanted was to make herself memorable here in the village. "Do you suppose anyone saw us?"

Justin glanced back toward the window with a frown. "I don't know."

She folded her arms in front of her to stave off a shiver. The fire had dwindled to a small, struggling flame. She moved to stand in front of it, turning her back to Justin. She could hardly bring herself to look at him. She was growing more embarrassed about their kiss by the minute. Even more so because Justin himself appeared to be relatively unaffected by the intimacy.

"If they did, we've a simple enough explanation." He came to stand behind her. "We're going to be married tomorrow after all."

Helena felt the weight of his hands as he brought them to rest on her upper arms. The jolt of pain was instantaneous. She gasped and pulled away, only to cry out as Justin reached for her again, his fingers clenching around her left arm in a viselike grip.

"Damn it, Helena!" He jerked her clear of the hearth. "Get away from there before you catch your skirts on fire!"

Helena looked up into his furious face, mortified to feel the sting of tears starting in her eyes. He let go of her as soon as she was a safe distance from the fireplace, but the throbbing from her bruises was unceasing. She drew back from him, her hand lifting instinctively to cover her arm. "You mustn't ever grab me like that."

"And you mustn't stand close to an open flame in skirts of this size. One stray ember and you'd have gone up like a torch. Don't you read the papers? Women have burned to death."

"Please don't shout at me."

"I'm not shouting, but—" Justin raked a hand through his hair. "If you don't wish me to touch you—"

"No," she protested.

"If I disgust you or frighten you—"

"No," she said again. "No, Justin." But he wasn't listening to her. He was too angry. No, not angry. He was *hurt*.

"You nearly stepped into the fire rather than let me touch your arm. Your *arm*, Helena. You're an innocent, I have no doubt, but surely you're aware that, as your husband, I'll need to touch more than your arm on occasion. If you're so appalled at the idea, it's better we end this now."

Panic surged in Helena's breast. Everything was beginning to unravel. Months of planning, disintegrating before her eyes.

She didn't know how to make it right. And if he refused to marry her, all would be lost.

She would be lost.

"My arm is bruised," she blurted out.

Justin made a sound like a groan. "Already?"

"No. Not because of you. It was bruised before I came here." She looked at him, silently pleading with him to understand.

And, miraculously, it seemed he did. She saw it in the way his gaze sharpened, fixing on her like a hawk homing in on a field mouse. "How?"

"A silly accident. It's not important."

"Helena—"

"I would have said something on the beach path, but I didn't like to admit how clumsy I am. Always tripping and falling, bruising myself all over. It's not a very becoming trait."

An expression of disquiet darkened his features. "Is that what happened to your arm? You tripped and fell?" He looked skeptical, if not downright disbelieving.

"It was an accident," she said again. "I don't wish to speak of it. And I wouldn't have done so except I can't bear for you to think—"

"That I repulse you? That you can't tolerate my touch?"

She took a steadying breath. When next she spoke, her voice was low and even—and completely sincere. "You don't repulse me."

Justin searched her face. Whatever he found there appeared to satisfy him to some small degree. He still looked troubled, but the hurt and anger were slowly receding. "Don't I? That's something, at least." He ran his hand over the back of his neck. The silence stretched out between them for several uncomfortable seconds. "I beg your pardon for raising my voice," he said at last. "And for my language, as well."

"You've nothing to apologize for."

"I shouted at you like you were a wayward soldier in my regiment." He gave a short, humorless laugh. "I tend to lose my composure when I see a lady walking into an open flame."

Helena's gaze dropped briefly to the burns on the side of his neck and jaw. He'd said he had been flayed alive by rebel sepoys. She wasn't entirely certain what that meant, but if it was half as horrible as it sounded, then it was no wonder he had a healthy respect for the destructive power of fire.

"I'm sorry if I hurt your arm," he said. "I didn't intend—"

"Don't. There's really no need."

"I think there is."

"No," she said. "In fact, I'd as soon we forgot this whole episode. That is…unless you've changed your mind."

"About what?"

"Marrying me."

He huffed. As if the mere idea amused him somehow. "No." And then again, more emphatically, "*No*. But if you're having second thoughts—"

"I'm not," Helena said swiftly. "Truly, I'm not." She forced a tremulous smile, hoping she looked braver than she felt. "Indeed, as far as I'm concerned, tomorrow can't come fast enough."

Chapter Five

By the time Justin arrived back at the Abbey, the rain had started again. The wind was high and the sky was fast becoming gray. His horse, a raw-boned stallion called Hiran, stamped with impatience as he dismounted and led him into the stone stable. It was warm and dry there, the smell of fresh hay permeating the air.

Neville was mucking out one of the loose boxes. He came to the door as Justin entered, a pitchfork clutched in one brawny hand. "Does he want his mash?"

Justin proceeded to remove Hiran's bridle and saddle. "He's earned it."

Neville cast aside his pitchfork and departed for the feed room.

"Where the devil is Danvers?" Justin called after him.

"Sleeping," Neville called back.

Justin scowled. Sleeping off the drink, more like.

Between the coachman and the cook, it was a miracle there was a drop of alcohol left in the place. He had half a mind to give them both the sack. Then again, he was unlikely to find servants willing to replace them. Not in this part of the world, at least. Even worse, if he let the pair of them go, there was every chance they'd end up in the workhouse.

No matter. He preferred looking after Hiran himself. The handsome chestnut had belonged to one of his captors in India. He'd been in the nature of a parting gift. A measure of compensation, dispensed on the day the British recaptured Cawnpore.

It had been nearly one month after the tragic events at Sati Chaura Ghat. When the soldiers raided Nana Sahib's palace, they'd found Justin there, chained to a dungeon wall. He'd been filthy and weak, the burns on his neck and sides festering for lack of care. After freeing him, the soldiers had gone through the palace and grounds, seizing everything of value. They'd taken the horses, camels, and elephants. And, when they were done, they had burned the palace to the ground.

It had been Hiran who'd carried Justin back to the safety of the British camp.

In the days that followed, no one had stepped forward to stake an opposing claim to the stallion. Indeed, no one had stepped forward to say much of anything at all. The camp doctor had treated Justin as best he could in grim silence, dabbing salve onto his burns and dosing him with laudanum. The weight of his judgment had been present in every touch.

Justin had returned to England less than three months later, Hiran in tow.

He was a fine horse with a valiant heart. He was also a constant reminder of what had happened in India. An equine albatross, Finchley had called him.

"You torture yourself more effectively than those sepoys ever could," he often said.

Finchley was an endless fount of wisdom. Full of advice for everyone else, all the while he hid himself away in that office of his, buried in his dusty law books and briefs.

It would serve him right if some well-meaning friend submitted a matrimonial advertisement on *his* behalf.

Justin carried Hiran's bridle and saddle to the tack room and retrieved two stiff brushes. When he returned, he set to work on Hiran's coat, removing the mud and sweat with long, brisk strokes. As he brushed, his thoughts drifted from Finchley's hypothetical matrimonial advertisement to the stark reality of his own impending marriage.

Not that he'd been thinking of much else lately.

He'd tossed and turned all night, knowing that in only a few more days he would have Helena Reynolds in his house and in his bed and wondering why in God's name she'd chosen to marry him of all men.

He still wondered.

He'd thought he would feel easier after seeing her today, but since their encounter at the inn, a whole new set of doubts had begun to prey upon his mind.

She was hiding something. That much had been plain from the moment of their first meeting. What it was, he couldn't tell. But something had compelled her to answer that blasted advertisement. Something—or someone—had frightened her. Had made her desperate enough to marry a stranger. And not just a stranger. A bastard ex-soldier of no birth and moderate fortune. A man with burn scars and a reputation marred by scandal and vicious innuendo.

He wanted to demand she tell him, but who was he to expect Helena to confess all of her dark secrets when he had so many of his own? To do so would be unfair. Hypocritical.

And what did it matter anyway? Theirs was not a love match. And it certainly wasn't a mingling of the souls or any other such drivel. It was a business arrangement. A marriage of convenience. He needed a wife and she needed someone to keep her safe.

But safe from what?

Or from whom?

It had occurred to him as she spouted that nonsense about being clumsy and accident prone that she might already be married. It would certainly explain a great deal. Indeed, the possibility seemed so likely that, for one fleeting moment, the reality of it had squeezed at his heart and his lungs, making it rather difficult to breathe.

And then he'd reminded himself that he trusted Finchley's judgment implicitly. And that Finchley, for all his meddling, would never have sent him a woman who was still bound to her husband—no matter how brutish that husband may be.

No. Helena Reynolds wasn't married. Nor had she ever been. He could tell that much from her kiss. He'd wager his last penny that it had been her first. Her lips had trembled and softened beneath his, her breath uneven and her eyes squeezed shut. She was that inexperienced.

She was also lush and sweet and fairly brimming with untapped passion. He could easily have kept kissing her. And he would have done, too, had he not been recalled to his senses by the activity in the yard. Good God. If they'd been seen…

Well. It was less than ideal, certainly. He had no desire to cause her embarrassment. And he certainly didn't relish the villagers spreading more tales about his being a conscience-less monster. But he couldn't regret kissing her. It was the finest thing he'd experienced in a very long while. Finer still because there was the promise of more to come.

Tomorrow, Helena would be his wife. And no matter her secrets, he wouldn't be sorry she was the one who'd answered his advertisement.

Neville returned a moment later with a bucket of warm bran mash. The water sloshed over the rim as he placed it in Hiran's loose box. "Justin?"

"Yes?"

"Are you going to marry that lady?"

Justin shot his old friend a distracted glance. He'd long since ceased to be surprised at Neville's ability to discern the substance of his thoughts. "I am. Tomorrow morning."

"At the church?"

"At the registrar's office in Abbot's Holcombe. You're welcome to come if you like."

Neville vehemently shook his head.

His refusal wasn't a surprise. He hated coach journeys. And he hadn't set foot in Abbot's Holcombe in years. "Suit yourself," Justin said.

Neville retrieved his pitchfork and resumed turning over the straw. "Where will she live?"

"Here at the Abbey." Justin ran a brush over Hiran's flank.

The sound of the rain, falling hard and fast on the roof tiles, nearly drowned out Neville's quiet reply. "Where will *I* live?"

A needle of guilt pricked at Justin's conscience. When it came to Neville, it was a feeling that was as familiar as breathing. "Here at the Abbey," he repeated. "Nothing's going to change."

"But Miss Reynolds—"

"You have a home with me for as long as you want one. It makes no difference if I marry." He paused, adding, "Or who I marry."

Neville leaned his pitchfork against the side of the loose box and let himself out into the aisle. "Do you like her?"

Justin was taken off guard by the question.

Like her? He was attracted to her, certainly. He felt protective of her as well. Any halfway decent gentleman would. But *like* her?

He thought of their conversation on the beach. Their discussion of Charles Dickens and the Great Exhibition. He remembered the way she'd smiled at him in commiseration over the watery tea Neville had served. And the way she'd responded to the revelation that he'd been a parish orphan in Abbot's Holcombe.

"Is that why we loathe the place?" she'd asked.

His chest infused with warmth at the memory. It was equal parts unnerving and...quite wonderful.

"Yes," he said. "I do like her. Very much." He cast aside his brushes and went to untie Hiran's halter. "What about you, Neville?" he asked as he led him to his loose box. "What do you think of Miss Reynolds?"

Neville followed after him. "She's prettier than Miss Bray."

Justin frowned. "Miss Bray?" That was a name he hadn't heard in a long while. He released Hiran and withdrew from the box, shutting the door behind him. Hiran immediately thrust his nose into his bucket of mash. "What makes you think of her?"

Neville shrugged.

"You admired her once, I believe."

Neville dropped his gaze and shrugged again.

"It was a lifetime ago," Justin said. They had been orphan boys. Shabby and ignorant. He supposed all of them had fancied Cecilia Bray at one time or another. She was of an age with them and had been reckoned a burgeoning beauty in those days. She'd also been thoroughly unpleasant, never missing a chance to tell them how common they were and how it was no wonder their parents had abandoned them.

Justin had had to bear the brunt of it. When he'd been apprenticed to her father, she'd taken great pleasure in subjecting him to her acid tongue. By the time he left to join the army, he'd long forgotten what it was about her he'd ever imagined to be pleasing.

Mr. Bray had died ten years ago. Justin heard about it in a letter from Finchley. As for Cecilia, Justin supposed she was still living somewhere in Abbot's Holcombe, along with her mother and younger sisters. No doubt she was married by now with half a dozen children. He neither knew nor cared. He wished he could say the same for Neville.

Helena drew her knees up to her chest and wrapped her cashmere shawl tighter around her shoulders. Her flannel nightgown was long-sleeved and covered her from her chin to her toes, but it did absolutely nothing to keep her warm. The King's Arms was no modern London hotel. Her room was damp and drafty, with a fire that produced more smoke than heat.

She glanced over at Bess. The young maidservant was huddled on her cot by the door, looking frozen through and utterly miserable.

"I wish you'd come up and share the bed," Helena said. "You'll catch your death on the floor."

"Oh no, miss. Mrs. Blevins says I'm to stay right here."

"Surely the inn can't be that unsafe."

"Indeed, miss. A gentleman in his cups had a mind to try the doors once. He scared an old lady something fierce."

"Hmm." Helena was skeptical. If a wandering drunkard decided to force his way into her bedchamber, she didn't see how Bess's presence in front of the door would prevent him. The young maidservant couldn't weigh much more than seven stone. "At least let us build up the fire, then. There's no reason you must freeze to death in service to my safety."

She turned up the oil lamp at her bedside, illuminating the room in a soft yellow glow. When Bess made no move to get up, Helena did so herself. The wooden slats of the floor were ice cold beneath her bare feet. They creaked in protest as she padded across the room to the fireplace. She picked up a poker and jabbed at the struggling flames in the grate.

"Aren't you afraid, miss?"

"Of what?"

"Going to live at the Abbey. What with all them monks and things."

Helena was tempted to smile. She had many things to fear, but spectral monks were not among them, thank goodness. There was enough to trouble her in this world without contemplating the vagaries of the spirit realm. "I don't believe in ghosts."

"Why not?"

"I simply don't." She bent to put another log on the fire. "They're not real. You can't see them or touch them."

Bess turned over in her cot to watch as the flames sprung to life. "I've never seen one," she said. "But my friend Martha…"

Helena rose and returned to her bed. She climbed in, settling herself beneath the blankets. "What about your friend?"

"Martha walks out with Bill, the fishmonger's son. And he told her—" Bess broke off. "But Mrs. Blevins says I'm not to gossip."

Helena reached to turn down the lamp. "That's a shame. How else am I to learn about the village?"

"Do you truly want to know, miss?"

"Of course."

Her words were all the permission Bess needed to disregard Mrs. Blevins's warning. "Well, miss." She continued her tale in a hushed voice. "Bill was down in the cove off the beach at Abbot's Holcombe and—what do you think happened? He looks up and sees the ghost of Sir Oswald himself walking the Abbey cliffs!"

"Oh? I wasn't aware Sir Oswald had died."

"Years and years ago," Bess said. "When Mr. Thornhill returned from India, like."

A frisson of uneasiness tickled at Helena's spine. She knew Justin had taken the Abbey from Sir Oswald in a somewhat unscrupulous manner, but he hadn't mentioned anything about the man's death. "I see." She was silent for a long moment. "How did he die?"

"He fell off the cliff, miss. The very ones where Bill seen his ghost. Everyone says as how…" Bess trailed off. "But Mr. Hargreaves says it was an accident. And he knew Sir Oswald and all."

Helena licked lips that were suddenly dry. She was almost afraid to ask. "Who is Mr. Hargreaves?"

"The magistrate, miss. From the inquest."

The inquest? Helena couldn't credit it. If there had been such a scandal, surely she'd have heard about it before now. If not from Justin himself, then at least from Mr. Finchley.

Her stomach, already in knots at the thought of her impending nuptials, proceeded to knot itself even tighter.

Could it be she'd simply traded one untenable situation— one violent and dangerous man—for another? Was life with Justin Thornhill going to be no safer than the life she was leaving behind?

She refused to believe it.

Since her arrival in Devon, Justin had shown himself to be a gentleman in dozens of ways. And not only where she was concerned. He was kind to his servants and his dogs. He took care of Neville. And though he had, admittedly, been vulgar at their first meeting, no man of a crass and violent disposition could ever have touched her face with so much tenderness as he had on the beach yesterday. Or kissed her so softly, so gently, as he had earlier today in the private parlor.

But how could a woman ever know for certain? It was impossible. At some point, she must simply put her faith and her trust in a man. The prospect frightened Helena more than any ghost ever could.

"Will you go back?" Bess asked.

"What?"

"To London, miss. If you do, I can come with you. You'll need a maid on the journey. And I've always wanted to see London and to work in a grand house."

"How do you know I have a grand house?"

"Just by looking at you." Bess flopped onto her back. "Your gowns. I never seen such fine fabric. And your hands. So white and soft. My aunt Agnes trained for a lady's maid in Bath. She taught me how to lift an oil stain out of silk. If you take me with you to London, I can look after your clothes. I'm a fast learner, miss."

Helena buried her face in the scratchy fabric of her pillow. Tears had sprung to her eyes several times during her flight from Grosvenor Square to Devon, but tonight, for the first time, she truly felt like weeping. "Thank you, Bess," she said. "But I'm not going back to London. Not ever."

Chapter Six

They were married the following morning at the district registrar's office in Abbot's Holcombe. Helena wore a plain gray silk day dress with a dark cloth paletot trimmed in braid. It was a long way from the white ruffled wedding gowns she'd often admired in the pages of the *Englishwomen's Domestic Magazine*, but it was not wholly unhandsome. Or so Bess had said when first she beheld her descending the stairs at the King's Arms earlier that morning.

"You look like a queen, miss," she'd declared.

Helena didn't see how she could. She'd hardly managed to sleep a wink the previous night. She was exhausted and emotional and scared out of her wits. She very much feared something would happen at the last moment to prevent her marriage to Justin. Indeed, she *expected* it.

As she stood beside him at the registrar's office, she couldn't seem to stop trembling. Justin himself was outwardly calm, even if he did seem unnaturally still and grave. He'd dressed for the occasion in a somber black suit. The burns on his neck were hidden by the high collar of his white linen shirt and a severe black cravat. She could see the glimmer of a pocket watch chain at the front of his waistcoat.

She listened to his deep voice as he disavowed any impediment to their marriage. At the registrar's prompting, she did the same. And then Justin was taking her left hand in his. She looked up at him with a start as he slid a plain gold band onto her finger. She was so dreadfully nervous she didn't realize the registrar had pronounced them man and wife until Justin raised her hand to his lips and pressed a kiss to her wedding band.

Helena felt the same mortifying rush of emotion she'd felt when he'd given her the piece of broken sea glass two days before. There was no reason for him to kiss her hand in such a gallant manner. Theirs was not a romantic union. Yet, he held her knuckles against his lips for a long moment, his eyes fixed steadily on hers.

Suddenly, she wanted nothing more than to tell him how tired she was and how much she'd been afraid. He was her husband now. Mr. Finchley had said he would protect her. That nothing would ever harm her if Justin Thornhill gave her his name.

But it wasn't the time. Not here. And certainly not in front of Bess and Mr. Boothroyd.

She swallowed back her feelings of relief and, as Justin lowered her hand, she managed a weak smile. "Well," she said.

His mouth hitched in a fleeting half smile of his own. "That's done, then."

"Officially."

He squeezed her hand. "There's no turning back now, Mrs. Thornhill."

Mrs. Thornhill.

Helena's stomach clenched. This was never what she'd wanted. Like every other young woman of her acquaintance, she'd dreamed of meeting a handsome gentleman who would assiduously court her and win her affections. She'd believed she would marry for love or not at all.

Mr. Boothroyd cleared his throat. "It's not quite official, sir." He cast a pointed look at the large leather-bound book lying open on the high counter. "You've yet to sign the register."

Her smile faded. She wished Mr. Boothroyd hadn't been necessary as a witness. His dour presence had only served to worsen her anxiety during the brief ceremony. Even now, as they moved to the register, she could feel him behind her, judging her every step.

The superintendent registrar handed her a quill pen. He was a white-haired gentleman with a truly impressive set of side-whiskers. "Mind you write your married name now," he said. "There's many a female who forgets."

"I won't forget." She dipped the pen into the inkwell and signed her new name for the first time with an unsteady hand.

Helena Elaine Thornhill.

"Though it still doesn't feel quite real," she murmured as she passed the quill to Justin.

He signed his own name in the register with far more decisiveness. "You'll soon grow accustomed to it."

"You'll have forty or more years to do so," the superintendent registrar said. "God willing."

Forty or more years? Helena glanced at Justin, expecting to find some expression of apprehension on his face. But Justin didn't seem at all alarmed at the prospect of spending such a length of time with her.

He exchanged a few words with the superintendent registrar while Mr. Boothroyd and Bess stepped forward to sign their names in the register, attesting to their role as witnesses.

And then they all waited—some with more impatience than others—as a clerk painstakingly copied out their marriage lines onto a sheet of paper.

When he'd finished, the superintendent registrar directed them each to affix their signatures and then, with an air of solemnity, he presented the paper to Helena.

"Your proof of marriage, madam. Keep it safe."

Helena took the certificate, awash with a profound sense of reverence—and relief. It seemed such an unexceptional document. And yet its existence could mean the difference between respectability and ruination.

Or, in her case, life and death.

She folded it carefully into her reticule. "I shall."

Justin touched her lightly on the small of the back. "Will you give me a moment to speak with Boothroyd?"

"Of course." She waited near the counter, watching as he crossed the room to address his steward. He said something to Mr. Boothroyd. Something which made the older man purse his lips in irritation. Moments later, Mr. Boothroyd departed the registrar's office with Bess in tow.

"Where are they going?" she asked when Justin returned to her.

"To the livery stable. To hire a carriage to take them back to King's Abbot."

Her pulse skipped. The idea of being left alone with Justin without a chaperone was too new. It felt illicit. Dangerous. "Aren't we…?"

"We're going to dine at the Stanhope Hotel. It's only a short walk. And you'll find the food far superior to anything

Mrs. Blevins has been serving at the King's Arms." He took her hand in his and tucked it through his arm. "I trust you're hungry."

"I am," she admitted. "I didn't eat a single bite this morning."

"Nor did I." He gave her another brief smile. "Wedding day nerves, I believe."

The street outside the registrar's office was all but empty save for a lone gentleman driving a smart-looking gig in the opposite direction. The rain had stopped, but the sky was gray, dark clouds heavy with the promise of another deluge.

"It's never been as popular as Torquay," Justin said. "But in the summer, these streets are teeming."

Helena could well believe it. What she'd seen of Abbot's Holcombe thus far had put her in mind of fashionable resort towns like Bournemouth, Brighton, and Margate. She'd never visited such places herself, but they were often depicted in lady's magazines. During the past months, she'd read a great deal about seaside fashions, the use of bathing machines, and the relative propriety of sea bathing at a public beach. She'd thought to prepare herself for her new life along the coast.

"Is it always so empty during the colder weather?" she asked.

"There are those who remain for their health. But they're invalids, generally, and don't venture outside when the temperature drops." He guided her around an uneven piece of pavement. "The private hotels hereabouts do a steady business catering to the wealthy and idle who fancy themselves ill."

"And this is where you grew up? Where you spent your childhood?"

He flashed her a wary look. "Not in this part of town, no. The orphanage is closer to the church. Or, rather, it was. It's not there anymore."

"Did it close down?"

"Something like that," he said vaguely.

They walked along for some little time, down one street and then crossing over to another, before reaching the Stanhope Hotel. It was a handsome structure of pristine white stone with an entrance faced in carved Corinthian marble. As they approached the doors, a footman trotted forward to welcome them, ushering them into the warmth of the hotel's luxurious, wood-paneled foyer.

The clerk at the front desk greeted them with upraised brows. "How may I assist you, sir?"

"I have a reservation," Justin said. "For Thornhill."

The clerk consulted a large book on the counter. "Ah yes. A room with a view."

Helena's eyes flew to Justin's face. *A room?* But they were merely dining together, weren't they? Simply sharing a meal to celebrate their wedding day. Unless…

Unless her new husband meant for them to share a bed.

The possibility sent a jolt of apprehension through her.

She watched as the clerk gave Justin the key to their room and wished them a pleasant stay. Her mouth opened in protest only to shut again almost at once. She wouldn't make a spectacle of herself by questioning her new husband in front of an audience. Better to wait until they were alone.

"The dining room is filled with local tabbies and London gossips," Justin explained. "Even at this time of year." He led her across the marble-tiled lobby floor toward the main staircase, a grand affair lined with artwork and potted palms. "We'll have more privacy if we dine in one of the rooms. We'll be more comfortable there as well." He paused. "Unless you object?"

Helena gathered her skirts in her hand as they climbed the carpeted steps. Husband or no, she didn't think she was ready to be alone with Justin in a hotel room, but if the alternative was exposing herself to gossip that might find its way back to London…

"I don't object," she said.

A footman directed them to their room on the third floor. It had an elegantly appointed sitting room with a rich Oriental rug and furnishings of heavy mahogany. Pale green draperies framed a window that looked out toward the sea. Helena moved to stand in front of it, uncertain of what to say or do in such a situation.

She heard Justin thank the footman for his assistance. And then he shut and bolted the door.

"Our meal will be sent up in a quarter of an hour," he said. "I took the liberty of ordering it yesterday when I made the reservation. Soup, roast chicken, and I don't know what else. If you'd prefer some other dish—"

"No." She turned to face him. He had removed his hat. His hair was rumpled and, for a fraction of a second, it seemed to her that he looked remarkably unsure of himself. "I'm not particular about food."

"No favorites, then?"

Helena untied her bonnet strings from beneath her chin and lifted her bonnet from her head. She placed it on an overstuffed chair near the window. "I like freshly baked bread. But I expect it has more to do with the smell than the taste."

"Ah." He appeared as much at a loss as she was herself.

She tugged off her right glove and then her left. It caught briefly on the ridge of her wedding band—a sharp reminder of her new status. As if she needed a reminder! Good heavens.

She was alone in a hotel room with a gentleman she'd only just met two days before.

"Is there somewhere I can wash my hands?" she asked.

"Through the bedroom," Justin said.

Helena retreated into the adjoining room, averting her eyes from the mahogany four-poster bed as she made her way to the adjacent bath. She was pleased to find that it was plumbed for water. There was a claw-footed tub and a marble basin with brass taps for hot and cold. Beside the basin was a stack of fluffy white towels, several cakes of scented soap, and a small selection of glass vials containing perfumed oil for one's bathwater.

It was the work of a moment to wash her face and hands and to repair her hair, but she took her time about it. When she finally emerged from the bedroom, her paletot draped over her arm, their meal had arrived. It was arranged in covered silver serving dishes on a cloth-draped table at the center of the room. Justin was standing nearby, his hands clasped behind his back.

He gave her a look of inquiry. "Shall we eat?"

She dropped her paletot on the chair alongside her bonnet and gloves and joined him at the table. He pulled out a chair for her before taking a seat himself.

"There's champagne," he said. "Or lemonade, if you prefer."

"Champagne, if you please."

Justin filled her glass and then his own. She thought for a moment that he might propose a toast to their marriage. It seemed the traditional thing to do.

He didn't propose a toast.

Helena supposed this sort of marriage was not the kind to inspire one. The thought depressed her a little. She raised her glass to her lips and took a drink, watching as Justin did the same.

She'd never had champagne before. The bubbles tickled her nose. For an instant, she feared she might sneeze. But then she took another swallow and the sensation subsided.

Justin began to remove the covers from the serving dishes. The smell of roast chicken and potatoes wafted into the air, making her mouth water. And, "Ah look," he said. "Fresh bread."

Helena leaned forward in anticipation as he filled her plate.

And then, for the next two hours, they ate and drank and talked, discussing everything and nothing.

Helena hadn't realized how hungry she was. Nor how deeply she yearned for conversation. And Justin Thornhill, for all his gruffness, seemed in a particular mood to oblige her. He filled her glass when it was empty and encouraged her to take second helpings of food. And he talked to her—about the weather, the history of King's Abbot, and the tumbledown state of Greyfriar's Abbey.

"It must have needed a fair amount of work," she said. They'd finished their meal and were halfway through a strawberry tart. She felt as if her corset was going to burst.

"A vast understatement," he said.

She set her fork down beside her plate, giving Justin her full attention. "Why did you want it, then? You weren't still looking for the treasure, were you?"

"God no. I doubt there was ever any treasure to begin with." He looked down into his glass, frowning. "I suppose, you might say I bought Greyfriar's Abbey for sentiment. I spent most of my young life thinking it was the grandest house in England."

"It *is* very grand."

"Once, perhaps. Now it's merely expensive."

"Did you never consider buying a property that was in better condition?"

"No." He lifted his gaze to hers. "I was foolishly single-minded in my pursuit of the Abbey. Once I learned there was a way to make it mine, I didn't stop to consider the village superstitions or the fact it had fallen into such disrepair." He paused. "Nor did I consider how it would suit a wife."

Helena leaned back in her chair. She was feeling thoroughly sated. Gorged, in fact. And, for the first time in months, in perfect harmony with the world about her. "I cannot speak for other wives," she said, "but I like it very well."

"You shall like it a great deal better in a moment. We've managed to hire a housekeeper. A woman named Mrs. Standish. You may recall her from that first afternoon when she came to meet with Boothroyd at the King's Arms."

Helena remembered her well enough. She was the sour woman of middle years who'd glared at her with so much scorn.

"I thought you were going to marry her," she said.

Justin was surprised into a hoarse crack of laughter. "*What?*"

"When I came to the private parlor at the King's Arms, she was inside with Mr. Boothroyd. She gave me such a look."

He ran a hand over his face. "Good God."

"I was so disappointed."

"No doubt."

"Truly. I almost left. And I would have done if Mr. Boothroyd hadn't called me back."

"Ah." The humor in his voice faded. "I wondered what that was about."

"You were watching me?"

"Naturally."

"I thought you were reading your newspaper." She gave him a speaking glance. "You might have introduced yourself."

"Didn't I?"

"And earlier, at the counter. I suppose you knew I was there in answer to your advertisement from the moment I entered the taproom."

Justin drained his glass in one swallow. "Actually, I didn't. Not until you asked to see Boothroyd."

Helena remembered the way he'd glowered down at her before grudgingly showing her to the private parlor. She reached for her glass, raising it to her lips and taking a measured sip of champagne. "Were you disappointed?"

The words were no sooner out of her mouth than she wished she could call them back again. It was a stupid, girlish question. And a pointless one, too. Justin was a gentleman. He was her husband now as well. There was only one way he could answer her.

He looked into her eyes. "Deeply disappointed," he said with unexpected gravity. "You see, I was expecting a slightly younger version of Mrs. Standish."

Helena nearly choked on her champagne.

Justin grinned at her. "It serves you right for asking."

She set down her glass and reached for her napkin. "You're a perfect beast to tease me about it," she said as she dabbed her mouth. "Any lady in my situation would wonder. Especially when the man she's come to marry makes such an effort to frighten her off."

"I was trying to be noble."

"You were trying to send me running back to London."

"More fool I."

Heat suffused her face at the memory of his coarse words. She lowered her napkin. "What on earth possessed you to say what you did to me?"

Justin looked mildly abashed. "I didn't plan to outrage your sensibilities."

"Then why?"

"I was out of my depth. I knew at once that you were too good for me. To own the truth, I *was* expecting a younger version of Mrs. Standish."

That made her laugh again. But Justin wasn't smiling anymore. She could no longer tell if he was teasing or serious. "Poor Mrs. Standish," she said. "We really shouldn't make sport of her. Especially if she's to be our housekeeper."

"A commendable philosophy. You may feel less charitable in the days to come."

"When does she start work?"

"She was at the Abbey when I left this morning."

"Already?"

"Boothroyd was lecturing her on her duties, the first of which, you'll be pleased to know, is a thorough cleaning of our bedroom."

She stared at him. "*Our* bedroom?"

He set aside his glass. "I've shocked you. Forgive me. Is it too indelicate a subject?"

"No, no. It's not that…" Her head was spinning. It occurred to her that she might have had too much to drink. "I beg your pardon, but are you saying that you and I…that we're to share a single bedchamber between us?"

Understanding registered on Justin's face. It was followed closely by another emotion which flickered for an instant and then disappeared. Helena thought it might have been disappointment. "Ah. I see." He fell silent for what seemed an eternity. "Do you object to our sharing a bedroom?" he asked finally.

She looked down at her hands, now folded tightly in her lap. The long pagoda sleeves of her silk gown concealed the bruises on her arms and her cuffed muslin undersleeves covered the marks on her wrists, but they did nothing to mask the deep ache she felt from having endured so much rough handling. It was a painful reminder of the circumstances that had brought her to North Devon.

"No," she said. "I don't object."

"But you would prefer a room of your own."

Would she? She'd had a room of her own her entire life. It's what she'd expected to have at the Abbey. A room she could go to when she wished to be alone. A door she could lock if she was feeling afraid.

After all, even a wife was afforded her privacy. A husband might visit her at night, but he didn't impose his presence on her any longer than was necessary. It was how respectable married couples conducted themselves. Or so she'd always understood.

"I don't know what I'd prefer," she said. "I've never shared a room with anyone before."

"Mr. and Mrs. Bray—the couple I was apprenticed to as a boy—shared a room for the whole of their married lives. I'd assumed…" Justin rubbed the side of his jaw with his hand. "But that was wrong of me, wasn't it? I shouldn't have assumed. I should have consulted you." His frown deepened. "I take it your parents kept separate rooms?"

The unknowing question gripped at Helena's heart like a vise. Her mother had died when she was just a girl, but she could well remember the small icy room, stripped of everything save an iron bedstead. It was an image that had populated many a childhood nightmare.

She moistened her lips. "They lived apart, yes. But you and I... We needn't..."

"It will be however you wish," he said. "I'll not make unreasonable demands on you. You'll not find me a brute."

"I know that. You've been very kind to me. I'm more grateful than I can say."

"Grateful," he repeated.

"Yes. And so very much obliged to you."

"I see."

Helena sensed she'd said something wrong, but she hadn't the least idea what. She wished she had someone to advise her. A sensible female to tell her what to say and what to do.

She needed Jenny.

Then again, Jenny was only two years older than she was and, for all her strident proclamations, knew as little about men and marriage as Helena did herself.

"Justin, I..." She struggled to formulate the words. "I don't want to disappoint you."

His expression softened. "You haven't. You won't." He stretched his arm across the table, his palm up in invitation.

His hand was large, his fingers long and almost elegant. It was the sort of hand that could wield a sword or a pistol as easily as it could write a letter or caress a lady's cheek. Helena's pulse fluttered as she reached out to take it.

Justin's fingers closed protectively around hers. His clasp was reassuringly warm, his skin tanned from the outdoors and calloused from hard work. Her own hand looked small and pale in comparison.

"There's no manual for marriage by advertisement," he said. "We shall have to feel our way along." His thumb moved slowly over the curve of her knuckles. "But if we're honest with each other, we stand far less risk of being unhappy."

She swallowed. He wanted honesty. Of course he did. And she was going to tell him everything. She'd planned to do it tonight, when they were back at the Abbey. When she was safe in his home and there was no chance he could send her away. But now…

She bit her lip. "There's so much I haven't told you."

"I know. I've been somewhat less than forthcoming myself."

"Yes, but at least you *tried* to tell me about your past. I've made no effort at all to tell you about mine." She searched his face. "Doesn't that worry you?"

"Probably not as much as it should."

"Why ever not?"

He shrugged. "Your dark secrets can be no worse than my own. Besides which, I trust Finchley with my life. He'd never have sent you to me if you were a murderer or a lunatic escaped from Bedlam."

She jerked her hand from his and, abruptly, rose from her chair. For a moment she feared she would be sick. She clutched her hand to her mouth and turned away from him.

Justin was at her side in an instant. "What is it? What's wrong?"

She shook her head.

He rested his hand at the small of her back, guiding her to an overstuffed sofa near the fireplace.

Outside, the skies darkened and thunder rent the air. It was followed by the sound of driving rain. It fell hard and fast against the windows of their room.

Helena hardly noticed the worsening weather. She sank down on the damask-covered sofa. "I fear I've drunk too much champagne."

More lies. It wasn't strong drink that made her stomach roil and caused perspiration to spring to her brow.

"I'm not used to it," she said. "I never even drink wine, except at Christmas."

Justin sat down beside her. "I wish you'd told me. I would have stopped filling your glass."

"I wasn't thinking."

He touched her cheek with the back of his hand. His gray eyes were dark with concern. "You've gone white as a ghost."

She ducked her head away from him. "Have I?"

"Shall I summon a doctor?"

The suggestion sent a jolt of alarm through her. "No. Absolutely not." The last thing in the world she wanted was to be examined by a doctor. She hated the breed and trusted them even less.

"He might be able to prescribe something for it."

Of course he would prescribe something. A bleeding, no doubt. In her bitter experience, medical men never passed on an opportunity to apply leeches or open a lady's veins. "No," she said again. "Truly, Justin. I don't need anything. I'm only a little lightheaded."

"Then just sit here a moment." His hand moved gently on her back. "It'll pass. It always does."

Helena tried to focus on his words. To quell the rising panic in her breast. All would be well. When they returned to the Abbey, she would explain everything. He wasn't an unreasonable man. Surely he would understand.

"You sound as though you were speaking from experience," she said.

"Naturally. When I first arrived in India, I often drank too much." A wry smile edged Justin's mouth. "I was a British soldier in a devilish hot climate. It was practically obligatory."

She looked up at him. "Were you terribly homesick?"

"There was nothing to be homesick for."

"Not even for England?" she asked. "Not even for the sea?"

He seemed to consider. "I confess I did miss the sea. I daresay I should have joined Her Majesty's Navy. But to a boy who'd spent the whole of his life staring out at the water, sailing away on a ship didn't seem like much of an adventure. I didn't want weevily biscuits and watch and watch about. I wanted the desert. The sound of foreign tongues and the taste of food rich with spices."

"And drink," she said.

"And drink," he concurred. "Champagne is nothing compared to bhang and brandy. The few occasions I was foolish enough to indulge, my batman was obliged to make me a special physic. A noxious substance. A highly effective one, too. I'd attempt to replicate it, but I'd probably end up poisoning you."

She huffed with unwilling amusement. "I shouldn't like that."

"Nor would I." He drew his knuckles along the edge of her jaw. "I've only just acquired you. I'm not quite ready to let you go."

A queer sort of ache settled in Helena's heart. "I'm not going anywhere."

He scanned her face, a hint of a smile still playing on his lips. "You're getting your color back, at least."

She was blushing. And he knew it, the rogue. She wasn't accustomed to sitting so close to a man. Nor was she used to being touched with so much tenderness. The kiss they'd shared at the inn yesterday had been the most intimate experience of her whole life. "I'm feeling a little better."

"Just a little?"

"A great deal better."

He tipped up her chin with his fingers. He was no longer smiling. He looked deadly serious. Rather determined, in fact. "Are you sure you're quite recovered?"

"Yes," she whispered.

"Good." Justin bent his head and captured her mouth in a slow, and devastatingly thorough, kiss.

Helena's eyes fell closed and her body tilted against his. He was a big man, tall, lean, and broad of shoulder, but though she was so much smaller, there was no awkwardness between them. They fit together perfectly. She wouldn't have thought it possible.

Indeed, she could scarcely think at all.

His lips were warm and firm on hers. It made her heartbeat quicken and skip. She forgot about what it was that had upset her. Justin's touch seemed to have that effect on her. Merely being close to him, feeling the heat from his body and inhaling the scent of his shaving soap, reassured her somehow. Made her feel safe and protected and…

Beloved.

No, not beloved. He didn't love her. How could he? But the way he touched her, the way he leaned over her, enveloping her in his strength. It was something very like love. Or, at least, the way she imagined love might be.

"Justin…"

He drew back to look at her. His eyes were heavy-lidded, his chest rising and falling on a harsh breath. "Too much?"

"No. Not that."

"Too fast?" he asked. "Have I overwhelmed you?"

Helena nodded. She felt suddenly foolish, and far younger than her five-and-twenty years. "I-I don't know what to do."

His gray gaze softened to a caress. He brought both hands to cradle her face. "Slower then," he murmured. "More gently."

Her lashes fluttered as he brushed kisses over her jaw, her cheek, and her temple. They were whisper-soft kisses. Courting kisses. But there was an underlying desperation to them, most evident when he took her mouth once more.

Helena made a soft sound low in her throat. Yesterday she'd received his kiss with passivity. She'd been constrained by her sense of propriety—inhibited by her lack of experience. But today, the rules that had governed her youth no longer applied. She was a grown woman. And she was married. Whatever the future held, Justin Thornhill was her husband.

This time, when his lips found hers, she put her arms around his neck and she kissed him back.

*C*hapter *S*even

*A*ny doubts Justin had about whether or not Helena could stand his touch promptly went up in flames. Her hands curved insistently on his neck, tugging him down to her uplifted face and returning his kisses with an innocent ardor that made his blood surge in his veins.

She wanted him.

It shouldn't matter, but it did. She was his wife. The first person on earth to ever truly belong to him.

He set his arm about her waist and drew her closer, crushing her heavy skirts against his legs in a waterfall of silk and horsehair crinoline. She was pillow soft and pliant, tasting of champagne and smelling of Indian jasmine, starched petticoats, and warm, willing woman. It was the most enticing blend of fragrances he'd ever encountered. It made her seem some exotic combination of respectable British lady and mysterious, Far Eastern siren.

He slid his hand behind her neck as his mouth moved on hers, gentling her and coaxing her, until her lips half parted beneath his. He might have made a sound at that. A murmur of approval, perhaps, or—heaven help him—a growl of pleasure. It was wholly inappropriate and far too much too soon, but—good Lord!—she was so soft and so sweet.

And she was his.

All his.

He raised his head. "Would you like to spend the night here?"

Helena's arms were still around him. Deliciously so. He could feel her fingers threaded in his hair. "At the hotel?"

"I've reserved the room."

She pulled back, her hands sliding from his neck to rest on the front of his waistcoat. He saw her throat spasm in a visible swallow. "I thought we were going home."

"To the Abbey?" Justin glanced toward the window. "If the rain continues, there's every chance the road will be impassible by nightfall."

"Does that mean we're stuck here?" She didn't look pleased by the idea.

"No. But it means we'll need to leave fairly soon if we're to make it back safely." He hated to ask. "Do you want to go?"

"I had rather hoped we might." Her hands fell to her lap. "I haven't been sleeping very well since I left London."

Justin felt a flicker of disappointment. He wanted to point out that there was a perfectly serviceable bed in their hotel room, but he knew very well that that wasn't the crux of her objection. She simply didn't wish to share a bed with him. Not yet, at any rate.

He was going to have to woo her.

A damnable prospect.

What did he know of wooing? His romantic past—what there was of it—consisted of brief interludes with willing widows or impersonal tumbles with tarts. He'd never properly wooed anyone. He'd never even kept a mistress. It had seemed far too much trouble. Especially when his heart had never been engaged. And after Cawnpore…

He hadn't felt himself worthy of kindness or gentleness. And he'd been even less inclined to offer it. Not to a willing widow or a tart. And certainly not to a wife.

Good God, but a matrimonial advertisement was supposed to alleviate the need for any of this emotional claptrap. If he'd wanted to embark on a courtship, he'd have found a woman at a village assembly somewhere. A plain, no-nonsense sort of female. The daughter of a tradesman or the widow of a soldier. He'd never have chosen a lady of such beauty and refinement. He knew what he was. And what he deserved.

But as Helena gazed up at him, her lips rosy from his kisses and her eyes soft as velvet, he realized that whether he deserved her or not, she was his. And he'd be damned if he made her unhappy.

He took hold of her hands. They were pale and slender in his. "We won't have much privacy at the Abbey. Boothroyd will likely importune me as soon as we return. He has no sense of timing. Nor does Neville, come to that."

"Life at the Abbey sounds very…informal."

The corner of his mouth lifted. "That's one way of putting it." His thumbs slid over the silken skin on the backs of her hands. "It won't be what you're used to."

"You've said that before. I hope you're not still trying to warn me off."

"Would it work this time?"

"We are married, sir. I am your wife."

"Ah," he said. "I thought I recognized you."

A smile glimmered in her eyes. She tugged at his hands until he obediently bent his head. And then she kissed him, her lips clinging to his, warm and sweet.

His heart thundered in his chest. "Take care," he said huskily. "Much more of this and I'll begin to think you're growing fond of me."

Her hands moved in his, returning the clasp of his fingers. "Would that be so bad?"

"Who can say? It's uncharted territory. No woman has yet developed a tendre for me."

"I don't believe that."

"Of course you don't. You find me irresistible."

A blush rose in her face. "I find you infuriating. Especially when you tease me."

He nuzzled her cheek. "And I find you beautiful beyond words."

It was quite the most revolting thing he'd ever said to a woman. The sort of treacle an ardent swain would spout to his sweetheart.

It was also the absolute truth.

"How did such a lovely creature ever come to answer my advertisement?" he asked, rubbing his cheek against hers.

Her breath was a delicate whisper against his ear. "It was fate."

"Mmm. I remember. Something to do with our having both gone to see the Koh-i-Noor in the summer of '51, wasn't it?"

"Don't laugh."

"I'm not laughing." And he wasn't. His heart was too full, the moment too perfect.

Their fingers intertwined and he leaned forward to brush his lips over her brow.

He didn't believe in fate. He didn't trust it. The universe had never dropped good fortune into his lap. The only luck he'd ever had was what he'd made for himself. Even then, success had often left him hollow.

If she wanted to believe they'd been fated to meet, he wouldn't argue. But he had no illusions. He recognized their union for exactly what it was. It wasn't fate or destiny or providence. It was blind chance. As fleeting and ephemeral as a vapor of ether.

He intended to savor every precious second of it.

"I'm a cad," he said several kisses later. They were both breathing heavily. "I'll keep you here until the weather makes it impossible to return."

"You wouldn't."

He kissed her once more. "I can be quite ruthless when it comes to getting what I want. Make no mistake."

"And what you want is to remain here at the hotel."

"And you want to return to the Abbey."

"I do," she said. "I know it's silly, but I feel safe there. I can't explain it."

Justin didn't require an explanation. He already knew how much she valued her safety. It was why she'd married him. Not because she cared for him, nor even because she found him particularly attractive. It was because she needed a man to protect her. And Finchley, for whatever reason, had promised her that Justin was that man.

"*He told me that Mr. Thornhill had been a soldier,*" he'd heard her say to Boothroyd. "*And that he knew how to keep a woman safe.*"

Bitterness swirled like acid in his stomach. He felt all at once the full weight of his responsibility for her—and the full extent of his own unworthiness. If she trusted him at all, it was only because she didn't know him. He'd kept the worst of himself locked away. His past couldn't bear close scrutiny. And if ever he shared it with her...

Well. It certainly wouldn't inspire the sort of tender embraces they were enjoying now.

"Are you certain you're up to the journey?" he asked. "It's thirteen miles of poor road."

"I can manage."

"Then I'd best send for the coach before the weather worsens." He moved to release her, but she squeezed his hands, her expression uncertain.

"You really don't mind, Justin?"

He minded like the very devil. He only hoped he didn't show it. "No, I don't mind." He raised one of her hands to his lips, adding, "At the moment, I have the rather imbecilic idea that I'd do anything in the world to make you happy."

And so he would.

Three quarters of an hour later saw them bundled in the coach and on the road back to King's Abbot. The rain was unrelenting, making the drive along the cliff's edge a far more delicate business that it was in less treacherous weather. The coachman held the horses back to a walk on the turnings and, by the time they arrived at the Abbey, the sun was sinking.

They were greeted in the entry hall by Mr. Boothroyd and Neville, along with the elderly cook, Mrs. Whitlock, and the new housekeeper, Mrs. Standish. Mrs. Standish looked at Helena down the length of her nose. She was retiring for the night, or so she informed her, and didn't wish to be disturbed.

"I've been given the evening off," she said, "to allow me time to settle into my quarters."

Mrs. Whitlock was somewhat more welcoming. She was also slightly inebriated, the faint scent of cooking sherry lingering about her wiry person. She promised them stew for their supper and fresh bread and butter before teetering back to the kitchen below.

Helena watched the two women leave with a sense of chagrin. She'd expected that one of them would show her to her room. And she'd cherished some small hope of ordering a bath.

If she hadn't been feeling so dreadfully vulnerable at the hotel, she might have taken advantage of their excellent plumbing and had a bath there. As it was, she'd been unable to stop thinking about who might be staying in the other rooms. Countless strangers, any one of whom might recognize her.

But that wasn't going to happen now. She was safe at the Abbey. The rain made her safer still. With any luck, the cliff road would be impassible by the time she retired. And then tonight, for the first time in a long while, she would be able to fall asleep without fear.

"We weren't expecting you back this evening, sir," Mr. Boothroyd said.

Justin stripped off his gloves. "A minor change of plans."

Mr. Boothroyd pursed his lips. He looked her way, disapproval etched into his face. "Mrs. Thornhill. You'll be wanting to freshen up, I suppose. Neville? Show your mistress to her—"

"I'll see to my wife." Justin offered her his arm. "If you'll allow me?"

She tucked her hand in the crook of his elbow. He said not a word as he escorted her up the staircase to the second floor. He'd been equally quiet in the coach. At the hotel he said he'd do anything to make her happy, but it hadn't been long into their journey before he'd fallen into what could only be described as a sullen silence. She was certain he was displeased with her.

Lord knew he had ample cause.

Between her reaction to the prospect of their sharing a bedchamber and her unwillingness to remain at the hotel for the night, she no doubt appeared to be every bit as spoiled and flighty as the frivolous creature Mr. Boothroyd had accused her of being at their first meeting.

"This way." Justin turned left at the top of the stairs, leading her down a wide hall papered in patterned-yellow silk. Their path was lit by evenly spaced wall sconces flickering with gaslight.

"I had no notion the Abbey was fitted for gas," she said.

"Only in the corridors and the drawing room."

She shot him an inquiring look. "Is that dictated by design?"

"It's dictated by the limitations of my pocketbook," he said grimly. "To bring a house of this antiquity up to snuff takes an inordinate amount of time and money. The modernizations have had to be gradual. I'm afraid they don't extend throughout the house just yet." He stopped in front of a wood-paneled door and opened it. "Your room, ma'am."

Helena entered ahead of him into a spacious bedchamber. It smelled of lemon polish, starched linens, and washing soda. At its heart was a magnificent carved Elizabethan bed with a half tester of red damask. She glanced back at Justin.

He cleared his throat. "From the sixteenth century. But the carpets are new. As are the wall hangings. And just in here"—he led her through another open door—"is the bath."

Given the Abbey's age, she'd expected nothing better in terms of plumbing than a water closet and a tin tub. But what lay before her was a thoroughly modern room, with black-and-white tiled marble flooring and mahogany paneling stretching halfway up the walls. There was a tall cabinet, a washbasin and beveled mirror, and an enameled tub with a rolled rim that looked large enough to accommodate a person twice her size.

Justin stepped forward and twisted a brass spigot. Water gushed out into the tub.

"Running water," Helena said softly. "Oh, how marvelous."

He turned off the tap. "You can have a bath if you like."

"I would like that. Above all things." She wandered back into the bedchamber. Justin followed. A queer sort of electricity seemed to pulse between them. She moistened her lips. "Was this to be our room?"

"It *is* our room. I'll simply be sleeping elsewhere for the time being."

"Where?"

"In the adjoining chamber."

Her conscience twinged. "It should be me who sleeps elsewhere. Not you."

"I think not."

"It would only be fair."

"For me to force my new wife to sleep in the second best bedroom?" His brows lifted. "What sort of man do you think me?"

"One who is very much put upon."

"Helena, I was a soldier. Shall I tell you some of the places I've slept during the course of my career? A slightly shabby bedroom is a paradise, I assure you."

"Yes, but this room has clearly been refurbished. You've taken a lot of trouble—"

He caught her hand in his as she walked past him. "Do you like it?"

She stopped and turned to face him. It was there again. That faint hint of almost boyish uncertainty lurking behind his eyes. It moved her deeply. "It's more than I ever dared hope for."

Justin held her gaze for several seconds. "I'm glad it pleases you." His voice was deeper than usual, if that was possible. For a moment, it looked as if he wanted to say something more. She waited, but in the next instant he released her hand. "We dine at seven. Shall I come and fetch you?"

"Do, please. I'll never find my way to the dining room otherwise."

Justin inclined his head to her and left the room. The door clicked shut behind him.

Helena exhaled heavily. She looked around the bedchamber again, trying hard not to compare it to her luxurious room in Grosvenor Square. Was Jenny still there? Was she, even now, sitting in front of the marble fireplace and knitting a pair of mittens for one of her charity cases? She'd promised she would remain. That she would wait to hear from Helena.

"*Once you're married, you send a note to Mr. Finchley. He's an enterprising sort of fellow. He'll see I get it. And then, my love, if you need me, I'll be on the next train to Devon.*"

But what if Jenny had already gone? What if—after Helena's disappearance—they'd cast her off into the street?

Or worse.

Much subdued by her thoughts, Helena returned to the bathroom.

A half hour later, she emerged from the tub in a much more positive frame of mind. Tonight, after dinner, she would tell Justin everything. She wouldn't let another day pass without him knowing the truth. And if he was angry or disappointed...

Well, then, she would just have to bear it, wouldn't she?

She unpinned her hair, giving it a half-hearted brushing as she made her way back into the bedroom. The rain sounded far lighter than the deluge that had marked their drive from Abbot's Holcombe. She drew back one side of the heavy damask curtains and peered out the window. Raindrops streaked down the glass in haphazard squiggles. Through their watery blur, she could see out over the drive and down to the stable beyond.

It was still muddy, gray, and miserable, but the rain *had* lessened, even if only by a small amount.

Perhaps the road to the Abbey wouldn't be impassible after all?

She propped her hip on the window embrasure and, through sheer force of habit, stared out at the view a little longer. It was stupid to continue keeping such a vigil. No one would dare come here in pursuit of her. Even if they knew where she was, they wouldn't brave the roads. Not in this beastly weather.

Besides, she was a married woman now. The only man who had any legal rights over her was Justin Thornhill. No other man could compel her to do anything. They simply hadn't the power. Not to hurt her—to confine her or to lay hands on her. And certainly not to force her to return to London.

She moved to rise.

And then she saw it. Lights blinking unsteadily at the bend of the cliff road.

She squinted, trying to make them out. It wasn't necessary. They grew brighter before her eyes, coming closer and closer still. They were advancing toward the Abbey at an unrelenting pace.

An icy cold trickle of fear skated down her spine.

They were carriage lamps And they were attached to a coach that was, even now, turning into the drive.

She watched, frozen where she stood, as it came to a halt in front of the entrance to the Abbey. A footman leapt down from the box and opened the door to the coach. He lowered the steps and then stood back as a man in a heavy black coat descended. Another man followed close behind. A hulking and all-too-familiar figure. He lifted his head to scan the face of the Abbey and—

Oh, God!

Helena backed away from the window, her heart in her throat.

And she didn't think. She couldn't. All rational thought seemed to have fled in the face of so much terror. Nothing was left but instinct.

So, she did what she had always done.

She ran.

Chapter Eight

Justin leaned against the fireplace mantel, arms folded across his chest. Things would have been so much easier if Helena had consented to remain at the hotel. He'd had it all so carefully arranged. The comfortable room. The champagne. The complete absence of interruption. Now, instead of enjoying privacy with his new wife, he was standing in a slightly damp library, contemplating two equally damp men.

One of whom was the local magistrate.

"Captain Thornhill," he said.

"Hargreaves," Justin said in reply.

George Hargreaves had been the magistrate since Justin was a boy. There was no love lost between the two of them. Indeed, upon entering the library, the man hadn't even offered to shake Justin's hand.

Not that Justin had been any more welcoming. He hadn't asked either man to sit down. And he certainly had no intention of offering them something warm to drink.

"Bloody awful weather," Hargreaves said.

"Not the best time to be paying a call," Justin pointed out.

"Couldn't be helped." Hargreaves removed his hat. He was ruddy-faced and fleshy, with a balding pate and white side-whiskers curving down to a double chin. "A bad business, this."

The fair-haired man who stood beside Hargreaves said not a word. He was a brawny brute of a fellow, the seams of his overcoat straining across the broad expanse of his back and shoulders. He was not as tall as Justin. Nowhere near it. But his neck was thick as a tree trunk and his gloved hands appeared to be the approximate size of dinner plates.

He was looking about the library, perusing the contents of the room with all the subtlety of a bailiff.

"The matter is straightforward enough," Hargreaves continued. "If you would—"

"Where is Lady Helena?" the brutish gentleman asked.

Justin turned his gaze on the man, even as his heart slammed against his ribcage. *Lady Helena?* It was only through sheer force of will that he was able to keep his countenance. "And you are?"

"This is Mr. Horace Glyde," Hargreaves said. "He represents the Earl of Castleton. His lordship is looking for his missing niece."

"The Earl of Castleton!" Boothroyd exclaimed from his place in front of the closed library doors. "Do you mean to say that Miss Reynolds—"

"*Lady* Helena is his lordship's niece," Mr. Glyde said. "And I'm empowered by law to retrieve her. Even if I have to tear this place apart."

Justin stood to his full height. Anger was rising steadily within him, coiling in his muscles and imparting a dangerous edge to his voice. "Are you indeed. And tell me, Hargreaves, since when does British law allow a stranger to come into a man's home and threaten to lay hands on his wife?"

"She's here, I knew it." Mr. Glyde's lifted his face to the ceiling, as if he could see straight through it to the floors above. "Do your duty, Hargreaves. Or I shall go up and fetch her myself?"

"I wouldn't advise it," Justin said.

Mr. Glyde's eyes glittered. "Oh you wouldn't, would you?"

Hargreaves stepped between them. "Now, now, gentlemen. Let's handle ourselves like civilized human beings. I've no doubt that once Thornhill understands the ruse that's been perpetrated, he'll willingly cooperate."

"Ruse? What ruse?" Boothroyd had been hanging back, listening, but at the mention of some deception lost no time in entering the fray. He crossed the floor to join Justin near the fireplace.

"Lady Helena disappeared from her uncle's house in London three days ago," Hargreaves explained. "Mr. Glyde traced her as far as King's Abbot. It was there he learned of your impending marriage, Thornhill."

"And I went straight to the magistrate," Mr. Glyde said. "You'll find that the law is on his lordship's side in this matter."

Hargreaves sighed. "I'll say this, sir. We've traveled a mite too much for my taste today, with it raining as if the world's about to end. First to Abbot's Holcombe and then back here. That cliff road's a menace, Thornhill."

"It is," Justin agreed. "Yet still you came."

"Couldn't be helped. After visiting the registrar's office and learning of your marriage—"

"Such that it is," Mr. Glyde interjected.

"What's this?" Boothroyd jerked his head to the magistrate. "Is the marriage not valid, sir? And why not, pray? Is the lady not of age?"

"Lady Helena is of age," Hargreaves said. "But Mr. Glyde possesses documents which appear to show that her ladyship hasn't the capacity to consent to marriage."

"Lord Castleton was in the process of having her committed to a private asylum," Mr. Glyde said. "She'd be incarcerated there now, had she not fled in the night like the veriest criminal."

Justin's blood ran cold. "I don't believe it."

Hargreaves turned to Mr. Glyde. "Show him the documents, sir," he said with some impatience.

Mr. Glyde reached into the interior of his overcoat and withdrew a packet of papers. He thrust it at Justin. "There's your proof."

Justin took the packet without a word. The topmost paper within was thin and yellowed with age. When he unfolded it, he saw what appeared to be a woman's death certificate, the names and dates written in a spidery script.

"Honoria Reynolds, the late Countess of Castleton." Mr. Glyde came close enough to jab his thick finger at the faded name on the death certificate. "Died in an asylum in 1844."

Justin raised his gaze to Mr. Glyde's face, looking first at him and then at Hargreaves. "What the devil does this prove?"

Mr. Glyde snorted. "It's her mother, isn't it? Madness is in the blood. His lordship's doctors will attest. Here, you see. A report written by Dr. Philemon Collins, the earl's personal physician. And another by Sir Luther Fortescue, from St. Andrews University."

Justin skimmed the doctors' reports. They'd both been written in the past year. And they were both oddly alike, using eerily similar turns of phrase to describe Helena's condition. Words like *hysteria* and *melancholia* leapt out from the pages. One notation mentioned *prolonged delusion*. Another made reference to *hydrotherapy* and *electrotherapy*.

"*First treatment a success*," Dr. Collins had written. "*Patient greatly subdued.*"

Justin's jaw clenched as shock swiftly gave way to rage.

"A bad business, as I said." Hargreaves struck a conciliatory note. "But we need take no more of your time with it, Thornhill. Simply fetch Lady Helena and we'll be on our way."

Boothroyd opened his mouth to speak, but Justin shot him a quelling glance. He could deal with this himself. And he would deal with it, for at last he understood the precise reason Helena had married him. "She is my wife," he said.

Mr. Glyde snatched back his papers and returned them to the pocket inside his coat. "Lord Castleton will naturally have the marriage annulled. He's even arranged a modest compensation for you. For your troubles, as it were."

"Compensation," Justin repeated. The word stuck in his throat.

"Small, but generous," Mr. Glyde said. "You won't find his lordship tightfisted. In exchange for your silence and cooperation, he's prepared to advance you a sum of five hundred pounds, another five hundred to be paid upon the dissolution of the marriage."

"Generous indeed," Hargreaves remarked. "One thousand pounds would go a long way toward renovating the Abbey, aye, Thornhill?"

Mr. Glyde gave Justin a complacent smile. "His lordship has as much interest in keeping this scandal quiet as you do, sir. He has no wish to see his family name splashed across the broadsheets."

"Is an annulment possible?" Boothroyd asked.

"I don't see why not," Hargreaves said. "We've managed to intervene before the wedding night. And with the marriage left unconsummated—"

Justin cleared his throat. "As to that…"

Three sets of eyes flashed to his, staring at him with varying degrees of alarm.

"There will be no annulment," he said.

Hargreaves gaped. "Do you mean to say…?"

"Quite," Justin replied.

"It's a lie!" Mr. Glyde burst out. "You've had no opportunity—"

"I'll not discuss my marriage with either of you," Justin said. "Except to say that, if you doubt its validity, you may inquire at the registrar's office in Abbot's Holcombe." He paused for effect. "If that isn't sufficient, I direct you to The Stanhope Hotel, where my wife and I had the pleasure of sharing a room together after our wedding ceremony."

"A hotel room?" Mr. Glyde was aghast. "In broad daylight?"

Hargreaves motioned for him to be silent. "See here, Thornhill. This changes the complexion of things. If the marriage has already been consummated, extricating you from this predicament won't be as—"

"I have no wish to be extricated." Justin glanced at Mr. Glyde. "You may tell the Earl of Castleton that Lady Helena is mine now. And I keep what's mine."

Mr. Glyde reddened with outrage. "Who the bloody hell do you think you are, sir?"

"A bastard," Justin said quietly. "In every sense of the word. If you require further clarification, no doubt Hargreaves can provide it during your journey back to King's Abbot."

Slow-dawning comprehension registered in Hargreaves's eyes. "By God, Thornhill, does your ambition know no bounds? First you drive a good man to his death in order to acquire this house. And now you wed a feeble-minded lady in order to…what? Worm your way into the aristocracy?" He shook his head in disgust. "Have you no shame, sir?"

"None whatsoever," Justin said. "Will that be all, gentlemen?"

Mr. Glyde was beginning to look apoplectic. He took a menacing step toward him, fists clenched at his sides.

Justin didn't budge an inch. He had no wish for the proceedings to devolve into violence, but if it was a fight Mr. Glyde wanted, he was more than happy to oblige him. In truth, he rather felt like putting his fist through something. And, at the moment, Mr. Glyde's sneering face seemed a particularly desirable target.

"Ahem." Boothroyd edged in front of Justin. "If I may interject, sirs. You will observe that the thunder we've been hearing is now accompanied by lightning. If the rain doesn't relent, the cliff road will soon wash out."

Hargreaves cocked his head toward the windows, listening to the heavy rain beating relentlessly against the glass. He heaved another sigh.

Sensing his capitulation, Mr. Glyde puffed up even further. "I won't leave without seeing Lady Helena. His lordship commands—"

"Enough, Mr. Glyde," Hargreaves said. "I've no wish to be stuck in this godforsaken abbey for the next four days." He looked at Justin. "Lord Castleton is a powerful man, Thornhill. If his niece lacked the capacity to consent, no judge in England will consider this marriage valid."

"The courts will void it," Mr. Glyde said. "It won't matter if it's been consummated."

"Some legal remedy will be found," Hargreaves concurred. "You may depend upon it."

"The cliff road, Mr. Hargreaves," Boothroyd murmured. "Conditions are worsening by the second."

Hargreaves settled his hat back on his head. "As you say, Mr. Boothroyd." He touched the arm of his still fuming companion. "Come, Mr. Glyde. Nothing can be done tonight. We will return after you've received further instruction from his lordship. And when this foul weather has abated."

"Tell Lady Helena I'll be back for her," Mr. Glyde said over his shoulder. There was unconcealed menace in his words. "She may depend upon it."

"Yes, yes," Hargreaves muttered. "We must away, Mr. Glyde."

Boothroyd ushered the two men out of the library and into the hall, where Neville was waiting to show them out. A resounding crash of thunder only served to hasten their departure.

Justin watched them go, the reality of the situation sinking into the very marrow of his bones. He felt oddly numb. As if the entire encounter had happened to another a person.

When Boothroyd returned, he appeared to be equally affected. His face was a studied blank. He shut the library doors behind him and, after a long moment of silence, repaired to a nearby table which held a decanter of sherry and two glasses. He poured himself a generous measure and drank it in one swallow. "The Earl of Castleton. It beggars to belief."

"Do you know the man?" Justin asked.

"I know the title. One of the oldest and most distinguished. One of the wealthiest as well." Boothroyd poured himself another drink. "What do you propose to do, sir?"

Justin knew what he had to do. He had to talk to Helena. He had to demand answers. But beyond that…

"What do you advise?" he asked.

Boothroyd pursed his lips. "I've had my doubts about her suitability. I've made no secret of that. Nevertheless…I don't believe she's mad."

"Nor do I," Justin said.

"But she lied to you, sir."

"She never lied to me."

"Withholding the truth is tantamount to dishonesty."

"She *never* lied to me," Justin said again. "No more than I lied when I refrained from telling her about Sir Oswald or about what happened at Sati Chaura Ghat."

Boothroyd bent his head over his glass. "Ah. So, you haven't told her."

Justin huffed. "Did you think I'd be proclaiming it from the rooftops?"

"Beg pardon, sir, but what *I* thought is that marriage would make your life easier. I didn't anticipate"—he made a vague gesture—"all of this."

"Things have never been easy, Boothroyd."

"No, but…"

"We've managed before."

"Yes, we've managed, but…honestly, sir. Her uncle is the Earl of Castleton. He's no Oswald Bannister."

Justin's lips twisted in a brief parody of a smile. "Lucky him."

Boothroyd opened his mouth to respond. Before he could do so, the library doors opened in a clatter and Neville entered the room. He was in his shirtsleeves, his blond hair wet from the rain and his trousers streaked with mud. He met Justin's eyes from across the room.

"Justin?"

"What is it now?"

Neville's face crumpled in distress. "Paul and Jonesy have run off."

"In this weather?" Boothroyd gave a disapproving cluck. "Damn fool dogs."

"They chased a rabbit," Neville said thickly. "Paul ran over the cliff."

Bloody blasted hell. As if he didn't have enough to deal with. Justin strode forward to place a hand on his friend's shoulder. "There are no rabbits at the cliff's edge, Neville. If the dogs ran out—"

"They ran to the cliffs and Paul leapt over the side. Jonesy's there, but he won't come back."

Justin cast Boothroyd a frustrated glance. "I have to speak with Helena. Can you…?"

"Those dogs don't obey me," Boothroyd said. "Where's Danvers, Neville? Can't he assist you?"

Neville ignored Boothroyd. Or perhaps he simply didn't hear him. He was becoming increasingly distressed. "It's Paul, Justin. You have to come."

Justin hesitated for a moment. And then, with a sigh of resignation, he squeezed Neville's shoulder. "Yes. Of course, I'll come. Let me fetch a lantern."

The sun set early this time of year. It wasn't much past five and already dark. Even with their lanterns held aloft, Justin could scarcely see anything through the driving rain. It didn't help that both dogs were black as pitch.

"Paul!" Neville shouted. He waved his lantern in front of him as he walked. "Paul!"

Justin had insisted Neville put on his hat, coat, and gloves. Not that his own were doing him much good. What use was a hat when the rain was falling sideways? He raised his lantern higher. "Jonesy!" he called. "Here, Jonesy!"

The wind whistled over the cliffs. They were closer to the edge now. "Have a care, Neville," Justin said.

"He was here, Justin." Neville trotted ahead, heedless of the danger. "Down here."

With a muttered curse, Justin charged after him, half-slipping in the mud. Damnation, but he couldn't see a blasted thing! Confound those dogs. For all he knew they were already back at the Abbey, curled up in front of a fire.

"Paul!" Neville cried. "Paul!" He stepped forward blindly.

Justin reached out in the nick of time, seizing him by the back of his coat and hauling him backward, away from the cliff's edge. Neville's feet slid out from under him. He fell with an undignified splat onto his rear end.

"He was there, Justin! That's where I saw him!"

Justin peered into the darkness. In the halo of light cast from their lamps, he could see the jagged edge of the cliffs. It was a particularly dangerous spot. A person who wasn't paying attention could easily lose their footing. He wouldn't have thought a dog would be in danger. Then again, Paul was still young and over-exuberant. For all Justin knew, he might have chased a shadow down over the side.

"Stay here, Neville," he commanded.

Neville nodded his assent. "I won't move."

Justin ventured forward, choosing his path with care. And then he heard it. A high-pitched sound. It was not quite a bark. It was more of a whine. A plaintive, distinctly canine whine.

"Jonesy?" Justin shouted as he approached the cliff's edge. "Paul? Where the devil are you?" He extended the lantern over the side and peered down. "What in blazes…"

The dogs were there. Both of them, perched on a narrow outcropping. He could see their dark silhouettes in the rain—Jonesy sitting and Paul lying down, his muzzle resting on his paws. They didn't acknowledge him. Their attention was fully occupied on the small white figure at the other side of the ledge.

Justin's heart leapt into his throat. Good God, it was Helena.

She was huddled against the wall of the cliff with her knees drawn to her chest and her arms wrapped tight around herself. Her forehead was pressed to her knees, her unbound hair a wet, tangled mass all around her. She was wearing what looked to be nothing more substantial than a dressing gown. She was soaked to the skin. He could see the shivers coursing over the delicate curve of her back and shoulders.

He uttered a blistering oath. She must have fallen. There was no other explanation. He sank to his knees on the wet grass, dropping his lantern down beside him. "Helena? My God, Helena. Are you hurt?"

She didn't respond.

"Helena? Can you hear me?"

She gave no sign that she could.

A sickening feeling of foreboding settled over him. He thought of Neville, falling from the cliff face and striking his head. The scene had replayed in his mind thousands of times over the years. Is that what had happened here? Had Helena slipped over the side and struck her head on the rocks?

He tossed aside his hat and stripped off his coat and gloves. "I'm going to climb down to you. Stay exactly where you are."

"Don't."

Justin froze. "What?"

Her words were faint and slightly muffled. "Don't come any closer."

"I have to. If you're injured, it's the only way to get you off of the ledge." Justin moved to swing a leg over the side. He heard her mutter something. He couldn't quite make it out. "You needn't worry about me," he assured her. "I've been climbing these cliffs since I was a lad."

She lifted her head then and looked up at him. Her beautiful face, usually so composed, so regal, was white and frightened in the light of the lamp. "If you come any closer, I'll throw myself over the side."

The fine hairs rose on the back of Justin's neck. He stared down at her, fully registering the extent of her terror for the first time. He'd thought her fear had to do with her position on the ledge. He'd thought she was hurt or afraid of falling or—

"I mean it," she said. "I won't go with you. I'd rather die here."

He swallowed hard. "Yes, I can see that."

She pressed her forehead back against her knees, her arms drawn even tighter around them. He could hear her teeth chattering.

"What do you propose I do with you, then?" He was amazed at the steadiness of his voice. "Leave you here to freeze to death?"

"I don't care. I won't let them take me back to London."

Them.

Justin cursed himself for an idiot. She wasn't running from *him.* And she wasn't threatening suicide if he touched her. She was afraid of *them.* Of her uncle and the brutish man he'd sent to retrieve her.

"My dear girl, do you think I'd let anyone lay so much as a finger on you?"

She looked at him again. The desolation in her expression tore at his heart. He knew then, with a painful certainty, that she didn't believe he could protect her. That she'd thought he would hand her over to that man without so much as a by your leave.

"You're my wife, Helena," he said gruffly. "You married me to keep you safe and that's precisely what I intend to do."

"Mr. Glyde...I saw him..."

"He's gone. I sent him away."

Her breath shuddered out of her. "He'll come back."

"Not tonight he won't. And not tomorrow. The road will be impassable."

"He'll come back," she said again.

"He'll have to get through me first." Justin swung his other leg over the edge of the cliff. "I'm going to climb down now."

Helena made no reply.

Justin kept one eye on her as he proceeded to feel his way along the rocky outcroppings of the cliff face. He hadn't climbed in ages. And he wasn't certain he'd ever done it in the rain. It wasn't much of a distance, but it was slippery as all hell.

"Justin?" Neville's voice boomed out from somewhere above.

Justin started and nearly lost his balance. He swore violently. "Blast it, Neville! Didn't I tell you to stay put?"

"Did you find Paul?"

"Yes." Justin lowered his booted foot to the ledge. "He and Jonesy are here." Both dogs looked up at him, their tails thumping in greeting. Justin touched Paul's head with a reassuring hand before edging carefully toward Helena.

Her face was pressed to her knees again. She wasn't moving.

"You're not going to make this easy for me, are you?" Justin crouched beside her. Wet hair was covering her like a shroud. He lifted a hand to brush it from her face. Her skin was cold as ice. "That's all right," he said under his breath. "I can manage. If you'll allow me…" He slid one arm around her waist and the other under her knees, gathering her to his chest. Her body was stiff and unyielding, but she made no move to struggle. Heaven help him if she had. The ledge was not big enough. There was every chance they'd both plummet straight over the side.

"I'm going to hand you up to Neville," he said. "Neville? Lean down here, would you?"

Neville's face appeared over the side of the cliff. "Is that Miss Reynolds?"

"She's Mrs. Thornhill now," Justin said as Neville reached out his arms. "Be careful with her."

Chapter Nine

For the longest while, Helena wasn't aware of anything save the sound of her own teeth chattering. Her hair and clothes were wet and she was shaking all over. She didn't know how she'd managed to end up on the ledge. She'd been running away. The grass and mud had been slippery under her feet. She'd tried to keep her bearings. But it was growing dark so quickly. The rain was hitting her face. She couldn't see properly. And she was too terrified to stop.

The cliff's edge had rushed up in front of her. It seemed to come out of nowhere. She'd gasped and—

Fallen.

The next thing she knew, the dogs were there. Paul and Jonesy. Enormous black figures across from her on the ledge. She could smell their wet fur, could hear them whining at her.

The wind was cold on her face, the cliff face hard against her back. She thought she must have scraped or twisted her leg. There was a stinging sensation and what felt like a trickle of blood.

Time passed. A profound sense of futility weighed down on her, crushing her hopes beneath it like a heavy, suffocating blanket.

There was no escape. There never had been. It was always going to come to this. Whether she'd stayed in London or whether she'd run to Cornwall, or Paris, or Timbuktu.

She clutched her knees tight to her chest. She had no mettle, that was the problem. She was weak and useless and utterly lacking in courage. It was no wonder she was in this predicament. When it came to the point, she hadn't even enough strength of will to throw herself over the side.

Not but what she didn't threaten to do just that.

But then Justin was there, his deep voice sounding from somewhere above the ledge. "My dear girl, do you think I'd let anyone lay so much as a finger on you?"

She nearly wept then. Not because she was safe, but because he meant it. He truly meant it. He believed he could prevent them from hurting her.

His head bent low over hers as he carried her through the rain, walking in long ground covering strides.

He bounded up a short flight of steps. A door creaked open. "Great heavens!" Mr. Boothroyd exclaimed. "What's happened?"

"An accident."

"I'll fetch Mrs. Standish."

"No," Justin said. "No. I don't want anyone to see her like this."

Helena hadn't thought she was capable of being hurt any more. Not today, at least. But his words managed to find that one small, soft part of her still nurturing a miniscule shred of hope and skewer it with ruthless precision.

I don't want anyone to see her like this.

It was the last thing she remembered before darkness engulfed her.

When she regained her senses, she was tucked under an eiderdown blanket in the great Elizabethan bed, her head propped up on a pile of pillows. Her hair was still wet, but no longer dripping. Her dressing gown and shift were gone. Someone had removed them. She was now wearing some sort of odd-fitting linen nightdress.

She touched the curved neckline of the garment. It had a short row of buttons. It also had sloping shoulders and what felt like gussets under the arms.

Good gracious.

It was a gentleman's shirt.

She raised her head in alarm. The oil lamps had been lit and a fire was blazing in the hearth. In the flickering glow, she saw Justin. He was seated in a winged-back chair beside the bed, watching her.

Their eyes met and held.

A rush of color flooded her face. Oh, but she was beyond embarrassment. "Did you…?"

"It couldn't be helped." There was no warmth in his voice.

"I see." She lay back against her pillows. Her cheeks burned and her stomach quivered with butterflies run amok. But she resolved to be mature and reasonable about the business. So he'd seen her without her clothing. It was not the end of the world. He was her husband. There was no reason to be missish.

She'd been wet through, she supposed. And, since she couldn't remember much of anything, she assumed she'd either fainted or been in some manner of shock. Someone would have had to get her out of her sodden things. If Justin wished to keep her dreadful state hidden from the servants, he would have had no choice but to do it himself.

Though he didn't look best pleased with the experience. Quite the opposite. He looked…angry.

He stood and moved to a marble-topped table near the bed. She heard the clink of crystal, followed by a splash of liquid. "Here." He extended a glass to her. "Drink this."

She took it from his hand. Their fingers brushed. It was the barest touch, but more than sufficient to set the butterflies soaring once more. "What is it?"

"Brandy," he said. "Excellent for shock."

She tilted the glass to her lips and took an obedient swallow. It burned like fire all the way down her throat. She stifled a cough.

"All of it," Justin prompted.

She didn't argue. She lifted the glass to her lips once more. As she downed the remainder of the rich golden liquid, an equally golden warmth slowly suffused her stomach, chest, and limbs.

He gave her an appraising look. "Better?"

"I-I think so."

He nodded once and resumed his seat. He was still angry. It was evident in the set of his shoulders and the rigidness of his jaw.

Tears pricked at the back of her eyes. She was the one who'd brought him to this pass. She'd lied to him. Tricked him into marriage. And now that he knew, it was plain that he hated the very sight of her. "Justin, I'm so—"

"Where did all of the bruises come from?" he asked.

Her unfinished apology disintegrated on her lips.

Her heart gave a painful contraction.

So that's what he'd seen. Not her body. Not whether her unclothed form was pleasing. Just her bruises. Just the damage that had been done to her. She shouldn't be surprised. Nor even disappointed. It was what defined her now. She only wished she didn't feel so much shame.

"They're everywhere. Around your arms. Around your neck." Justin's deep voice was taut with control. As if he were holding onto his temper by nothing more substantial than a half-frayed thread. "Who put his hands around your neck, Helena? Was it Mr. Glyde?"

"No." She returned her empty brandy glass to the bedside table. "He wouldn't. Not there."

"But elsewhere?"

She saw no reason to deny it. She had the sense that they'd reached the end of the road, the two of them. The moment of reckoning. "Yes. On my arms and wrists."

"And your neck?"

Her fingers fluttered to her throat. She had a visceral memory of how she'd felt when it happened. Despite all the indignities she'd suffered thus far, all the threats and abuse and betrayals, that act had terrified her as nothing else had before. "That was my Uncle Edward."

"The Earl of Castleton."

He knew who her uncle was then. Of course he did. It would have been one of the first things Mr. Glyde would have told him. "Since last September, yes. That's when he inherited the title." She paused, her heart thudding heavily. "What else did he tell you?"

Justin shook his head. "I want to hear it from you."

He was regarding her with unwavering intensity. Helena had been on the receiving end of just such a look from the doctors her uncle had hired. It made her want to scream in frustration. It made her want to shout that *she was not mad*.

But it never worked to simply blurt it out. She must speak to him calmly. She must explain the circumstances without emotion.

She returned his gaze with what she hoped was equal solemnity. As she did so, some small part of her brain registered the absence of his coat and cravat. He was clad only in his shirtsleeves and a pair of black trousers. It was outrageously intimate.

"Until two years ago, my father was the Earl of Castleton," she said. "When he died, my brother Giles ascended to the title."

"The brother who perished at the siege of Jhansi."

"Yes," she said. And then, "No."

Justin's brows lifted slightly, but he said not a word.

She wasn't helping her cause, she knew it. And her appearance couldn't be helping much either. Her wet hair was matted and wild all about her. She must look like a veritable madwoman, even if she didn't sound like one.

"The British army believes him dead. Another officer gave an eyewitness account. It was evidence enough for my uncle to succeed to the title. But the army never found Giles' body. Without it—without some physical proof—I couldn't accept that my brother had died. And that…" She took a breath to steady her voice. "That's when this whole nightmare began."

Helena attempted to explain it to Justin as clearly and succinctly as she could. It was an impossible feat. She couldn't speak of such things in a dispassionate manner. Not about the loss of her brother. And certainly not about what came after.

"I took the news of Giles's death very hard," she said. "For weeks, I kept to my room. I wept unceasingly. When the solicitor came to Grosvenor Square with my brother's will, I could scarcely bring myself to attend the reading. My uncle was there. He didn't take any notice of me. Not at first. But when the terms of Giles's will were revealed, he reacted...rather badly."

She closed her eyes for a moment, the events of that day materializing as clear as crystal in her mind. The blinds had been half-drawn in her brother's study. The footmen had arranged chairs in front of what had once been his desk. She'd been seated in one of them, a veiled mourning bonnet on her head and a black lace handkerchief clutched in her hand.

"The property belonging to the earldom is entailed," she said. "The family seat in Hampshire, the hunting lodge in Wiltshire, and the townhouse in London all went to my uncle, along with a dozen other properties. But the money—the bulk of it, anyway—was my brother's to do with as he liked."

Comprehension flared in Justin's gray eyes. "He left it to you."

"All of it. Free from any encumbrance. I didn't pay attention to the legal whys and wherefores. I was too distressed. It was then my uncle turned to me. He saw I was weeping behind my mourning veil. Weeping more than the occasion deserved, or so he said."

"You were close to your brother."

"He was my best friend. I loved him dearly. Perhaps I did grieve overmuch. In other circumstances it wouldn't have mattered. But my mother behaved in just such a fashion after

Giles was born. The excessive weeping and low spirits. It only worsened after I arrived. She fell into a melancholy from which she never recovered. My father... He had her put away."

"Into an asylum," Justin said bluntly.

"Yes. A private asylum in Highgate." She lowered her gaze to her hands. "It was an awful place. They confined her to a room with nothing but an iron bedstead. She was subjected to treatments. I don't know the extent of it. I was just a child. But my father made us visit her. And every time I saw her, she was worse. *They* made her worse. And I couldn't—" Her voice broke.

Justin leaned toward the bed. "You don't have to say any more."

"I must. Else you won't understand why—"

"I do understand."

"Not everything."

His expression was grim. "I expect I can guess the rest."

She lifted her gaze back to his. "You believe I inherited my mother's melancholia." There was a note of accusation in her voice. "It's what he'll have told you."

"He did say that," Justin acknowledged.

"It's not true. I have a sadness in me, but I'm not melancholic. I'm not suffering from hysteria. I merely feel things deeply. I feel them here." She pressed a hand to her breast. "And when I love someone—and when they're taken away from me—I can't just forget them as though they'd never been."

"Helena..."

"So I grieved for my brother. But when they couldn't find his body, I began to doubt. And then I began to hope. And when my uncle demanded I sign my inheritance over to him, I refused to do it. No amount of threats or violence could persuade me. It's Giles's money, don't you see? If there's even a small chance he's still alive…that he might come back one day…"

She couldn't go on. If she did, she feared she might start sobbing. And that would only make her look more unbalanced than she already did.

"How does Mr. Glyde fit into all of this?" Justin asked.

She folded her arms around herself to stave off a shiver. "He works for my uncle. He was sent to find me on the first occasion I ran away."

Justin stared at her. He said nothing for a long moment. "The first occasion," he repeated at length. "Exactly how many occasions were there?"

"Several. I lost count."

"They weren't all related to matrimonial advertisements, I trust."

Helena couldn't tell if his question was in earnest. His deep voice had no inflection at all. "No. Your advertisement was the first I answered. Jenny found it in the *Times*."

His gaze sharpened. "Jenny?"

"My companion. She came to live with us shortly before my father died. She's a distant relation. A second cousin four or five times removed. I've known her most of my life."

Companion was an inadequate word to describe Jenny. She'd been a friend. A confidante. The only person to help her when events with her uncle had taken such a dark and frightening turn.

"It was Jenny who posted the letters I wrote to you. She made the travel arrangements with Mr. Finchley. If not for her, I would never have managed to get out of London."

"And the other times you ran away?" he asked.

Helena inwardly winced. He made her sound like some variety of desperate criminal. A lunatic bent on escape. Well. And perhaps she was.

"In the beginning, I wasn't running. If I left the house at all it was to pay calls on gentlemen who had been friends of my father. I needed an advocate. I was sure someone would help me. But my uncle is the earl now. No one wished to go against him. Not on my behalf, anyway. My mother's illness looms rather large."

"Your uncle appears to have exploited that fact."

"He has. Quite ruthlessly. And when no gentleman of my acquaintance was willing to come to my aid, he felt quite at liberty to begin soliciting treatment for me. Some of the treatments were administered at a private asylum called Lowbridge House. The doctors, they—" She inhaled a tremulous breath. "Well. It makes no difference what they did, except that, after they'd done it, I hadn't very many plans left. I simply ran."

"Where did you run to?" Justin asked. "Where exactly were you going?"

"Away," she said. "Just…away."

He frowned, seeming to contemplate some facet of the matter with greater than usual attention.

Helena sank farther back into the pillows. The full effect of the day's events was catching up with her. Her limbs were heavy and her eyes threatened to drift shut at any moment.

Was it really only this morning that she and Justin had been married? That he'd kissed her so passionately in their room at the Stanhope Hotel? And now, here she was telling him about her mother and her uncle and Mr. Glyde. All after having fallen over the edge of a cliff and—quite possibly—fainted from the shock of it.

"So," Justin said at last. "Marrying me was a last resort."

She turned her head to look at him. "It was my very last hope, yes."

"And when you arrived at the King's Arms—when you saw me—it didn't matter that I was burned. Or that I was a bastard. You needed a husband to give you the protection of his name. Any man would have done."

He was leaning forward in his chair, his elbows resting on his knees. His hair was disheveled and his jaw shadowed with evening stubble. Helena had never seen him looking so somber. So vulnerable.

"But it wasn't just any man at the King's Arms," she said softly. "It was you, Justin. It was you."

Chapter Ten

Justin bowed his head, his throat contracting on a convulsive swallow. Helena's words were as tender as a caress. For a brief moment, they managed to calm the rage that had boiled in his veins since he first beheld the bruises that covered her bare neck and arms.

Many of those black-and-blue marks had been in the shape of a man's fingers.

It had been all Justin could do to keep from going after Mr. Glyde. From pulling the man from his carriage and beating him to a bloody pulp.

"Have you ever hurt a woman?" she'd asked him on the beach.

It had been little more than three days ago. He'd suspected then that someone had treated her harshly, but he could never have imagined the extent of it.

No wonder she'd been desperate. A lady of her quality would have had to be to consent to marry a man like him.

"I'm so very sorry, Justin," she said. "I know I should have told you."

He could only nod. His mouth had gone dry and there was a lump in his throat the approximate size of a boulder. He was feeling—

Bloody hell.

He was *feeling*. He didn't know what. Anger, hurt, and the bitter ache of longing were all inextricably knotted in his chest. He couldn't tell where one ended and the other began. Then again, he was not a man accustomed to examining his emotions.

And he had no wish to start doing so now.

He rose from his chair. "You should sleep. We can continue this discussion tomorrow."

Helena's eyes flickered with something like alarm. "Where are you going?"

"I'm leaving you to rest."

She moved to sit up against the pillows. "Justin—"

His stopped where he stood. "What is it?"

"Please don't go. Don't leave me here by myself."

He scanned her face in the lamplight. Her brow was drawn, her cheeks pale as alabaster. She was afraid. No, he realized. Not afraid. Hell and damnation. She was *terrified*. "Helena," he said. "He's not coming back."

"You don't know that."

"I do, actually. The cliff road is washed out. And even if he somehow managed to get through, Paul and Jonesy would tear him apart before he ever reached the entrance to the Abbey."

She was silent a moment. And then, "You said the dogs were gentle."

"Ah. So I did." He cleared his throat. "And they can be. Er…when the occasion calls for it."

"Hmm." She did not sound entirely convinced.

Justin speared his fingers through his hair. It was already standing half on end. He'd had no chance to bathe after carrying Helena into the house. His every attention had been on her. Only when she was warm, dry, and safely tucked up in bed had he taken time to change out of his own wet clothes.

"The point is," he continued, "the dogs are more than capable of—"

"The dogs aren't you."

Not the most flattering compliment a lady ever gave to a man, but at this moment—and with this particular lady—it might as well have been a sonnet.

His mouth hitched briefly. "I smell enough like one. After rescuing you from the cliffs, I was obliged to haul up both Paul and Jonesy."

"I don't mind it."

"Don't you?" His smile faded faster than it had appeared.

He knew what he was going to do only a fraction of a second before he did it.

"Move over," he said.

"*What?*" Helena touched a hand to the collar of her makeshift nightdress. It was a modest gesture, rendered somewhat comical by the fact that she was already wearing his shirt.

"Helena, today I traveled to and from Abbot's Holcombe in a thunderstorm. I was married. I was visited by the magistrate. I rescued two dogs and one new wife from over the side of a cliff. If you wish me to remain, you're going to have to move over."

She looked at him for several seconds.

Several seconds during which his heart teetered on the brink of an abyss.

"Very well," she said at last. She edged over slightly on the mattress. "Though I don't see why it's necessary for me to move. There's plenty of room for you already."

Justin's heart resumed beating in a rather erratic fashion. More erratic still as he watched her pull back the blanket for him. "Yes, well…it was the abbot's bed."

"Was it? I didn't realize Elizabethan abbots were quite so large."

"This one was. Either that or very grand."

He took a moment to turn down the oil lamps. A fire was still crackling in the hearth. It provided plenty of light for him to see his way back to the bed. He'd already removed his boots when he changed his clothes. There was nothing to do now but climb in beside her.

The mattress dipped beneath his weight as he lay down. They were so close that he could feel the warmth emanating from her body.

Devil take it. She was wearing absolutely nothing under that linen shirt of his.

He'd been concerned about her health when he'd removed her wet clothing. And then he'd been focused on the bruises, seething with anger at whoever had hurt her. But he wasn't blind, for God's sake. And though he lived in an abbey, he sure as hell wasn't a monk.

She shifted onto her side to face him. The faint fragrance of jasmine tickled his nose.

"Better?" His voice had deepened to a husky undertone. He hardly recognized the sound of it.

"Yes," she whispered back. Her long lashes were already fluttering closed. "I have so much more to tell you, Justin."

"I know."

"So much more to explain."

"Rest now," he said. "It will keep until tomorrow."

It had been a harrowing day. She was exhausted and, very probably, still in shock. He'd seen the symptoms before. Frankly, he was amazed she'd managed to stay awake and coherent for as long as she had. He would lie beside her for a short while and then—

"Will you stay with me?" she asked.

His chest tightened. It was a bad idea. Things were far from settled between them. Besides, he hadn't shared a bed with another person since his days in the orphanage. Not to sleep, at any rate. It would do nothing but confuse the issue and—

"I think I can bear it," he said.

She murmured something then as she drifted off. It sounded vaguely like another apology. Or possibly a few words of thanks. He didn't know which was worse. He didn't want her guilt and he had no use for her gratitude. What he wanted…what he needed…was something else altogether.

Justin woke well before sunrise. The fire had gone out in the hearth and the room was cold. Helena had huddled against him for warmth. Her cheek was on his chest, her arm draped over his midsection. His own arm had somehow managed to insinuate itself around her. His hand was resting, rather possessively, on the swell of her hip.

It should have felt presumptuous. She was a lady. The niece of an earl. The daughter of an earl and the sister of an earl, as well. When he'd cleaned the scrape on her knee last night, he was frankly amazed the blood he'd swabbed away hadn't been blue.

As a boy, the closest thing to a title he'd ever encountered had been in the person of Sir Oswald. A mere baronet. The first time he'd seen him riding through the gates of the orphanage on a magnificent black hunter, Justin had been in awe. It was an emotion that hadn't lasted long.

"Out of the way you motherless beggars!" Sir Oswald had bellowed.

Justin had been standing in the drive with Finchley, Archer, and Neville. Sir Oswald had swung his crop to disperse them. The leather tassel had cracked against Archer's cheek. Justin had had to grab his friend by the arm and haul him out of the path of the horse.

Finchley, meanwhile, hadn't moved an inch. He'd been the smallest and thinnest of them, but was then, as now, possessed of an unnatural steadiness of the nerves. He'd squinted at Sir Oswald's retreating figure through the second-hand spectacles he wore perched on his nose. "Who's that?"

"The king," Neville had said.

"It's not the king," Archer had retorted. "The king is an old man."

Justin had watched the tall, impeccably clad gentleman dismount at the entrance to the three-story stone building where the orphans of Abbot's Holcombe were housed. "Maybe it's someone's father," he'd said. "Come to fetch him home."

It felt like a lifetime ago. That brief morning encounter that had set the events of the next two decades in motion. All because they'd been fascinated by the appearance of a fine gentleman. Because they'd been dazzled by wealth and rank.

But if Justin was dazzled by Helena, it had nothing to do with her wealth and aristocratic lineage. How could it? He hadn't known about either of them until the appearance of Hargreaves and Glyde. Up until then he'd known only that she was a lady. A woman of quality.

She was too good for him by any measure. Anyone could see it. But touching her didn't feel presumptuous. It felt natural and right. As if she'd been specially fashioned to lie in his arms.

He bent his head to her hair and inhaled deeply.

She didn't stir. Not even when he released her and slowly extricated himself from the bed. She'd said she hadn't slept well since she left London. And, considering what she'd been through, he didn't doubt it. After yesterday's events, he was feeling a little tired himself.

But there wasn't time to linger.

He kindled a fire for her in the hearth and then, after collecting a few articles of clothing from the dressing room, withdrew to the bath. Within fifteen minutes, he was washed, shaved and dressed. He tossed a change of clothes into an old leather portmanteau and headed downstairs.

Boothroyd was in the kitchen, just as he always was at this time of morning. He sat at the wooden table, his napkin tucked into his shirt as he spread jam on a piece of toast. Neville was seated across from him, finishing off a plate of eggs and bacon. Paul and Jonesy milled at his booted feet.

At the sight of Justin, Boothroyd stilled. His eyes fell to the portmanteau. "You're going, then."

"I think I must," Justin said.

Boothroyd returned his toast to his plate. He tugged the napkin from his collar and tossed it onto the table. "For how long?"

"It shouldn't take above two days."

Neville looked up from his breakfast. "It's still raining, Justin."

"So, it is." Justin strode across the flagstone floor to join them at the table. He poured himself a cup of tea and drank it standing. "Not to worry. I won't melt."

"Do you think it wise to leave, sir?" Boothroyd asked.

"Wiser to do it now than when the road dries out." Justin said. "I'll hire a carriage to take me to Barnstaple. I can catch a fast train from there to London."

"And how do you propose to get down to King's Abbot?"

Justin shrugged. "The same way I always do when the cliff road washes out."

Boothroyd pursed his lips. "Forgive me for saying so, sir, but one of these days you're going to break your neck."

"Justin won't fall," Neville said. His brow creased. "Will you, Justin?"

"Indeed I will not." Justin shot a warning glance at Boothroyd. There was no reason to alarm Neville. The truth was, though the cliff road was impassible by horse or carriage, someone who knew the terrain—someone who was both fit and exceedingly careful—could navigate his way down on foot. It was a touch risky. But it was less than three miles. And it wasn't as if he'd be scaling down the cliff face.

"You'll be all over mud by the time you arrive in King's Abbot," Boothroyd said.

Justin's finished his tea. "Very likely." He turned to Neville, placing a hand on his shoulder. "I have a special task for you, Neville."

Neville sat up taller in his chair. "What is it?"

"While I'm gone, you're to look after Mrs. Thornhill."

Boothroyd lifted his brows.

Justin ignored him. "I want you to watch over her. You, Paul, and Jonesy." He held Neville's gaze. "Do you understand?"

Neville gave a solemn nod. "Yes, Justin."

"Good man." He looked at Boothroyd. "No one will come. There's no one in King's Abbot who would dare risk the cliff road. Nevertheless…be vigilant."

"As always, sir." Boothroyd stood. When Justin left the kitchen, he followed after him. "What shall I tell Mrs. Thornhill?"

Justin frowned. It occurred to him that he should have left a note for her. An oversight on his part, but one that was easily remedied.

He headed upstairs to the library, taking the steps two at a time. There was money in Boothroyd's desk that he would need for his journey. There was pen and paper as well. As Boothroyd counted out coins, Justin dipped a sharpened quill into the inkwell and scratched out a short message to Helena.

> Gone to see Finchley. Will return in two days.
> Yr. obedient, etc.,
> Thornhill

He paused, quill poised in his hand. After a moment's reflection, he added a postscript.

> P.S. — Trust me.

Chapter Eleven

London, England
September, 1859

Finchley shared his premises in Fleet Street with another solicitor, a gentleman by the name of Mr. Keane. Upon arriving, Justin was shepherded into Keane's office by his clerk, a harried fellow with uneven side-whiskers, who was juggling a stack of law books.

"Shall I bring in tea and biscuits, sir?" the clerk asked.

Mr. Keane rose from behind a heavily cluttered barrister's desk, causing several pieces of paper to spill over from their respective piles and waft down to the floor. After casting a questioning look at Justin, he waved the clerk out. "Mr. Thornhill, I apologize for the disarray. We've been at sixes and sevens this week." He motioned to a chair. "Won't you sit?"

Justin remained standing. His clothes were stained from travel. He'd come directly from the station. "Where's Finchley?"

"Ah." Mr. Keane's face fell. He sank back into his chair. "Most distressing, sir. And very unlike him. I've been obliged to —" He stopped. "But I won't complain. There's been many an occasion when he's taken it upon himself to manage my cases when I've been called away. Only last Christmas, when my mother was ill—"

"Called away?" Justin interrupted. "To where?"

"It's his sister, I believe. Some difficulty at home. He was needed quite urgently."

Justin's eyes narrowed. Finchley didn't have a sister. He didn't have any family at all. None of them did.

"She arrived here Tuesday morning in a terrible state," Keane continued. "He took her away at once. And then— quite extraordinarily—a message arrived, informing me that he wouldn't be returning until matters at home were resolved. Naturally, I expected him back directly. He's never absented himself for longer than the space of an afternoon. I can only guess that the crisis is of a grave and serious nature. An illness or, possibly, a death."

Justin listened to Keane rattle on, a sense of amazement rendering him temporarily mute. Good God, was it possible his work-obsessed friend had at last taken a mistress?

"Did he say where he was going?" he asked.

"Home, I expect. To be with his family." Keane opened a drawer of his desk and shuffled through the contents. "He gave me his sister's direction. Said it was confidential. That I wasn't to share it with anyone. Excepting you of course. Or Mr. Boothroyd, if he should… Ah. Here it is."

He withdrew a folded piece of notepaper from the drawer and extended it to Justin. An address was scrawled on it in black ink.

Justin departed Fleet Street moments later in a hansom bound for what turned out to be a small but quite elegant house in Half Moon Street. When he arrived, he vaulted up the steps and applied the knocker with no little force. Long seconds passed before the door was cracked open, not by a servant, but by Finchley himself.

"Thornhill!" His eyes flashed with relief behind his silver-framed spectacles. "I knew you'd come."

He was clad in a frock coat and matching trousers, his cravat neatly tied and his usually wild dark brown hair forced into compliance by a liberal dose of Macassar oil. He looked clean and pressed—and quite unlike himself.

"What the devil's going on?" Justin asked.

Finchley waited for him to enter and then shut and bolted the door behind him. "Come through to the sitting room. We can discuss things there."

Justin dropped his portmanteau in the hall and followed Finchley upstairs. There was a cozy parlor there, furnished with a plump chintz sofa and chairs, a tufted ottoman with tassel-trim, and an array of heavy wooden tables on which various collections of dried flowers and stuffed birds were displayed under glass domes.

A fire of hot coals glowed cheerfully in the grate. On a carved mantelshelf above it, a gilt-trimmed clock softly chimed the hour.

Justin's gaze roamed over the room. "Very homey," he said dryly.

"I thought so." Finchley sank into a chair. "I've just signed a three-month lease."

Justin sat down across from him. "For your sister, I presume."

A dull flush tinted Finchley's neck. He cleared his throat. "There's time enough to explain that. But first, tell me…did you marry her?"

"Miss Reynolds? Otherwise known as *Lady* Helena?" Justin rubbed the side of his face. "Bloody hell, Tom. What in blazes were you thinking to perpetrate such a scheme?"

"It wasn't a scheme. It was a mission of mercy."

"At my expense."

"I don't see how you can view it in those terms. Lady Helena is extraordinarily beautiful. Her disposition is pleasing and her intelligence appears to be well above average. Add to that her wealth and breeding and you have what amounts to an ideal candidate for a wife. Any man would think himself lucky to have her."

A sudden flare of irritation turned Justin's voice cold. "With so many superior qualities, I'm amazed you didn't marry her yourself."

Finchley briefly removed his spectacles to massage the bridge of his nose. There was a slight bump in the ridge, evidence of an old break he'd suffered during their time in the orphanage. "Yes, well, given the circumstances, I'm not altogether sure I'd have suited the lady."

"Because she's reckoned to be mad."

"No." Finchley settled his spectacles back on his face. "Because Lady Helena didn't require a solicitor. What she needed was a hero."

Justin drew back with a flinch. "Ballocks. I'm the farthest thing there is from a hero and well you know it."

"So you claim. But in times of trouble, when have you ever been anything less than heroic? And don't dare say India. You're forever raking yourself over the coals for what happened in Cawnpore. It's become a little self-indulgent, to be honest."

Justin stiffened. "Is that so?"

"Yes, it is. But I don't care about that right now. All I care about—all I really want to know—is whether or not you married her."

"Of course I did."

Finchley exhaled. "Thank heaven. Where was it done, and how?"

"Yesterday morning, at the registrar's office in Abbot's Holcombe. We returned to the Abbey in the early evening. Hargreaves arrived an hour later."

"Alone?"

"No. He had a large man with him who threatened to tear apart my home and forcibly remove my new bride."

"That would be Mr. Glyde." Finchley frowned. "I assume you didn't allow him to take her."

Justin gave his friend a speaking glance.

Finchley's lips quirked. "Quite. As a matter of curiosity, how did you manage to put him off?"

"It was in the midst of a thunderstorm. The cliff road was on the verge of washing out. In addition…" Justin tugged at his cravat. "I may have intimated that we'd already consummated the marriage."

Finchley lifted his brows. "Have you?"

"It's what I'll swear to."

"The answer is no, then."

"Does it make any difference? Glyde and Hargreaves mentioned something about Helena lacking the ability to consent." Justin paused. "My God, Tom." He ran a hand through his hair in a burst of frustration. "Is this marriage even legal?"

Finchley's face grew serious. "It is, even without consummation. But there's nothing to prevent them from arguing that it's not. And winning that argument too."

"She's frightened to death."

"And well she should be. That uncle of hers… He won't scruple to have her put away."

"All because of the money her brother left her."

"That's the crux of the matter," Finchley said. "It's no small sum, Justin."

"Why the hell does he need it? Didn't he inherit all of the property? Helena mentioned estates and hunting lodges and the like."

"The income from the estate isn't enough. Not for a man like Castleton. He has debts, apparently. He might manage well enough if he retired to the country, but he's a man who likes to cut a figure in town. Lavish balls, fine bloodstock, a yacht on the Thames. His lifestyle is luxurious by any measure. And the expenses…well. Suffice to say that the earl has every reason to want his niece—and her money—back in his clutches. And given his status in society, there's little anyone can do to stop him."

Justin stared into the fireplace for a long moment. He was close enough to feel some of the warmth from the burning coals. But he didn't feel it. The prospect of losing Helena left him cold to the heart. "It's a mystery to me why you ever involved yourself in this affair."

"I wouldn't say I involved myself. I never sought Lady Helena out. She simply answered your advertisement." Finchley hesitated. "Or, rather, her companion answered it."

"But you met her, didn't you? You must have done. She speaks highly enough of you."

"Naturally I met her. You don't think I'd send a lady all the way down to Devon to marry you sight unseen?"

Justin was silent.

"Well, I wouldn't," Finchley said. "Lady Helena came to my office some days later. She wasn't exactly what you had in mind in terms of a wife, but she was exceptionally fine. And an earl's daughter, too. You can't do much better than that. Except for a duke's daughter, or the daughter of a marquess, I suppose. But there's not many of them who'd consent to marry a man like you, I'm afraid."

"Helena was desperate."

"True. She's also kind and intelligent and—"

"Yes, yes, I've heard your recitations," Justin said with a scowl.

"My point is, you would never have been content with an average woman. Some part of you has always believed you were entitled to something more. It's what's driven you for the whole of our lives." He paused for a long moment. "Besides, I think it would do you enormous good to successfully rescue a female from harm."

Justin glared at him. He didn't know whether to be outraged or amused. "If rehabilitating my self-image was your goal, you might have chosen a female I'm actually capable of saving."

Finchley shrugged. "There's some minor difficulty, certainly, but nothing that can't be resolved if we employ a little ingenuity."

"Some minor difficulty? Is that what you call it?"

"Yes, well…" A fleeting expression of embarrassment passed over Finchley's face. "The fact is…I didn't fully comprehend the extent of the business until after Lady Helena had already departed for Devon."

"*What?*"

"I was working on a case. Quite fascinating, really. A dispute over a right of way which turned on a novel theory of law.

When Lady Helena arrived to meet with me, I was in the process of finishing my brief. I may have been a bit…distracted."

"Too distracted to ask why an earl's daughter was answering a matrimonial advertisement?"

"Give me some credit," Finchley said. "I did ask. And Lady Helena's answers—and those of her companion—seemed more than sufficient."

"What did they tell you?"

"That Lady Helena's uncle was a brute. That he'd been rough with her. Trying to force her to sign some document. I understood there to be a substantial sum of money involved."

Justin's jaw tightened. "Her uncle and that attack dog of his have been more than rough with her, Tom. They've terrorized her."

"Yes. I know that now." Finchley sounded suddenly tired. "But, unfortunately, those particular details weren't made clear to me until…er…two days ago."

Justin looked at his friend, but it was Helena that occupied his thoughts. His mind was flooded with images of her bruised arms and throat. Of her face, white with fear, as she gazed up at him from the cliff's ledge during the storm.

I'd rather die here, she'd said.

A lead weight settled in the pit of his stomach. He knew what it was to be afraid. When he'd been hung up in Nana Sahib's dungeon. When he'd been burned with a glowing hot poker across his bare chest, neck, and jaw. He'd been afraid then. He'd felt powerless. Toward the end, he'd even prayed for death. But he was a man. And—self-indulgence be damned—he'd *deserved* it. While Helena…

She didn't deserve this. She hadn't harmed anyone. She hadn't committed any crime.

"Is there any chance her brother is alive?" he asked.

"You'd know better than me," Finchley said. "How chaotic was it during the rebellion? Could a man who was still alive be reported dead?"

"Probably, but it's less likely to have happened with an officer. Even less so for one sporting a title. Whoever reported her brother's death would have had to recognize him."

"And his body?"

Justin shook his head. He truly didn't know. At that time, in that place, anything was possible. "It might have been burned on a pyre with the other dead. It might have been dismembered or left out in the sun to rot. Chances are there wasn't enough left of him to send home to England."

"Then we must proceed on the assumption that Giles Reynolds, 6th Earl of Castleton is not coming back to save the day. Which means—"

"Which means," Justin said grimly, "I must prepare to fight an unwinnable legal battle with a member of the peerage."

"Not necessarily." Finchley looked thoughtful. "There's a chance—a very small chance—this battle won't have to be fought in the courts."

Justin met Finchley's eyes. A weighted look passed between them. An unspoken acknowledgement of all the untenable situations in their past that had been resolved through Finchley's intellect and Justin's daring. "What do you advise?" he asked.

They spent the next thirty minutes talking. Or, rather, Finchley did the talking. Explaining the legal whys and wherefores, as Helena would have called them. He was so focused on the intricacies of his plan he didn't notice the passing of the time until the little clock on the mantle delicately chimed the hour. At the sound of it, he looked up with a start.

"Damnation, is that the time?"

"Do you have somewhere else to be?"

"No, but I was supposed to send for her shortly after you arrived." Finchley grimaced. "It's been a full hour. She'll be thinking I've forgotten. Or worse, that I've decided to exclude her."

"Who the devil are you talking about?"

"Miss Holloway. Haven't I mentioned her?" Finchley moved to rise. "Blast it. You know how forgetful I am once I start discussing the law."

At that very instant, the parlor door opened. A woman stepped through. She was tall and slim, clad in a prim black day dress with a lace collar. Her thick hair was twisted into intricate plaits at the back of her head.

Her thick *auburn* hair.

Justin shot Finchley a sharp glance as the two of them stood. His friend had long had a weakness for auburn-haired females. Up until now, he'd never indulged it. As far as Justin knew, the only mistress Finchley had ever had was his work.

"I beg your pardon," she said to Finchley. "But I've been waiting for some time."

Justin regarded the woman with mild annoyance. He had urgent matters to discuss with Finchley and had no intention of discussing those matters in company. Least of all in the presence of the man's mistress.

But this woman didn't sound like anyone's mistress. Quite the opposite. Her words were brisk and businesslike, her voice as crisp as a fresh apple.

Finchley crossed the room to meet her. "My apologies, ma'am. The hour got away from me." He ushered her into the parlor. "Allow me to introduce my friend, Mr. Justin Thornhill."

The woman fixed Justin with an appraising stare. She appeared to take in his face, his frame, and his burns in one comprehensive, and rather cool, glance.

Realization dawned slowly in Justin's brain. "Ah," he said. "You must be Jenny."

Chapter Twelve

North Devon, England
September, 1859

Helena spent the next two days inside the Abbey with Mr. Boothroyd, Neville, and the housekeeper and cook. She had little to occupy herself with.

Each morning, Mrs. Standish brought breakfast to her room on a tray. She built up the fire and drew the curtains.

"This is a maidservant's job," she grumbled.

Midmornings were spent pacing the house. Walking from stone-framed window to stone-framed window and gazing out across the drive, the stables, and the sea. She spent so much time walking the upper floors she felt as if she'd been transformed into one of the Abbey's ghosts. A colorless wraith, silently roaming the halls.

She wasn't alone in her wanderings. Indeed, since Justin's departure, she'd scarcely been alone for five minutes outside of her bedroom. Neville and the dogs followed after her wherever she went.

On the second day, her impatience with the situation finally got the better of her. She stopped in the long gallery and turned to face Neville. "You needn't stay with me," she said. "I'm more than content to be on my own."

Neville reddened with embarrassment. "I have to. I promised Justin."

"That you would watch me?"

He nodded. "Me, Paul, and Jonesy."

Helena cast a dubious glance at the two giant black dogs. They strolled along lazily in Neville's wake, their tongues lolling out of their mouths. She wasn't deceived by their languor. She'd seen them explode with energy on her first visit to the Abbey. And she knew firsthand how fearless they could be. The younger one—Paul—hadn't hesitated to leap after her when she'd tumbled over the side of the cliff. The elder dog had followed, the two of them guarding her as intently as a marrowbone.

"If that's the case," she said, "you'd better walk alongside me."

Neville looked vaguely startled by the suggestion. "Ma'am?"

"There's no need for you and the dogs to trail behind me like a royal retinue. I'd rather see you and talk to you. Come. Tell me about the animals at the Abbey."

"The dogs?"

"And the horses. You tend to them, don't you?"

As a question designed to loosen Neville's tongue, it succeeded admirably. He gradually began to relax his guard and, with occasional prompting, told her about Jonesy's appearance at the Abbey as a starving stray and about Paul's arrival a year later, an exuberant puppy Justin had found wandering the back alleys of King's Abbot.

He told her about Justin's horse, Hiran. About Mr. Boothroyd, Mrs. Whitlock, and—rather reluctantly—about himself and how he'd come to live at the Abbey when Justin acquired it nearly three year before.

Their conversation was slow and halting. Necessarily so. Whatever damage Neville had incurred during his childhood fall from the cliffs at Abbot's Holcombe had made formulating complex sentences an ordeal. It was as if his words were submerged in a deep London fog. He visibly struggled to find each one and draw it out. It was a painstaking process that seemed to both embarrass and frustrate him.

But Helena never doubted his intelligence. Indeed, the more they talked, the more she came to regret her first impression of him. He was slow, and perhaps a bit childlike in some respects, but he was no halfwit. He comprehended everything she said.

He also took Justin's directive to watch over her very much to heart.

Though why Justin had given such an order, she didn't know. Was he worried she would escape again? Fling herself from the cliffs or otherwise disappear without a trace? Or was he afraid someone would come for her?

But how could they? He'd said when the cliff road washed out there was no way a carriage or a horse and rider could get through. And yet…

And yet, Justin had managed to find his way through without difficulty.

Then again, comparing the abilities of other men to those of Justin Thornhill seemed unfair at best. All she had to do was recollect how he'd rescued her—and the dogs—from the ledge of the cliff during the thunderstorm. After that, a walk from the Abbey to the village was surely child's play.

"Will he be back today, do you think?" she asked.

But Neville didn't know anything more than she did. He only reiterated that Justin had gone to see Mr. Finchley and would return in two days.

That afternoon, she sat at the window in the library, her cashmere shawl wrapped tight around her shoulders. Raindrops slid down the glass, one after the other in quick succession. The sight only served to further depress her spirits. Along with the gray skies, the cold, and the damp, it made her feel isolated and alone. It should have made her happy. The poor weather guaranteed that the cliff road wouldn't be drying out any time soon. Which meant that no one would come to the Abbey.

It also meant no one could leave.

She was in two minds about that fact. Part of her wanted to run. To take the next coach departing from King's Abbot and flee to Cornwall, Taunton, or Exeter. Anywhere, really, as long as the town was large enough for her to disappear in.

The other part of her desperately wanted to wait for Justin. *Trust me*, he'd said in his hastily scrawled note.

There was no reason she should. After learning the truth about her, he'd left. Gone to see Mr. Finchley in London. Did he wish to annul their marriage? Or was he seeking legal counsel on the matter of her sanity?

Hadn't he seen, just from talking to her, that she was perfectly sane? She might have been wet and numb with shock, but she thought she'd explained things to him in a calm and reasonable manner. Perhaps he simply didn't believe her.

The prospect did nothing to improve her mood.

She hated feeling helpless. In the past she'd combatted the sensation by coming up with a plan. To be sure, toward the end, she and Jenny had made endless plans. None had ever come to fruition of course. None but the last—and, considering Justin's absence, even that was debatable. But still, such plans had always given Helena hope.

She didn't have a plan now. She was completely at sea. There was nothing to do but wait.

Perhaps that waiting would have been easier if she could be left alone with her worries. However, even when Neville was obliged to tend to his duties outside of the house, she was not permitted to be on her own. Instead, she was relegated to Mr. Boothroyd's care. He was in the library with her now, albeit an entire room away. His gray head was bent over his desk. She could hear the scratch of his quill as he made notations in his ledger.

She turned from the window with a sigh. "Shall I order tea?"

"What's that, my lady?" Mr. Boothroyd asked.

Her conscience flickered. And so did her temper. He'd been addressing her as *my lady* at every opportunity. As if she needed to be reminded of her dishonesty. "I asked if you would care for some refreshment."

Mr. Boothroyd looked up, his pen poised in his hand. "Is it midday already?" He glanced at the clock. "Yes, yes, a spot of tea would not be amiss."

Helena rang the bell for Mrs. Standish. The housekeeper might not like serving breakfast trays and tea trays, but there was no one else to do the job at present.

She arrived a short time later, a dirty apron over her dress and a cobweb-strewn cap on her head. She'd been cleaning out a study down the hall—a room that appeared to have been sealed off since the dawn of time. "You'll be wanting your tea, I expect," she said crossly.

"Yes, thank you Mrs. Standish."

Mrs. Standish departed the library as quickly as she'd come into it.

Helena sat down on one of the sofas near the fireplace. "Won't you join me?" she asked Mr. Boothroyd.

He looked at the blaze in the hearth for a moment. And then he rose from his desk and moved to take a seat on the faded sofa across from her.

"It can't be comfortable to sit at that desk day and night," she said.

"I'm accustomed to it."

"When Mrs. Standish has properly cleaned the study, perhaps you might use it for your work? It's smaller than the library and has a fireplace of its own. I daresay you'd be warmer there."

Mr. Boothroyd smoothed a hand over the front of his rumpled waistcoat. "Possibly."

He was no more effusive when their tea arrived.

Helena poured out a cup for him. "Mr. Boothroyd," she said, making yet another attempt at civil conversation. "I understand you've worked for Mr. Thornhill since he purchased the Abbey."

"That's correct." Mr. Boothroyd took a sip of his tea. "It's going on three years now."

She poured a cup for herself, adding in a liberal dose of sugar. "And before that?"

"Before Mr. Thornhill bought Greyfriar's Abbey?" Mr. Boothroyd's brow furrowed. "Why, I was here, my lady."

"Here?" Helena looked up at him, confused.

Mr. Boothroyd lowered his teacup back to its saucer with an audible clink. "I was employed by the Abbey's previous owner."

She stared at him, stunned. "Do you mean to say you worked for Sir Oswald Bannister?"

"I was his private secretary." Mr. Boothroyd's face betrayed a flicker of distaste. "In which capacity I resided here at the Abbey for nearly a decade. The study, as you call it, has the dubious distinction of having once been my office."

She waited for him to say more, but he didn't appear inclined to elaborate. "Really, Mr. Boothroyd," she said in exasperation. "Must I pry the details out of you?"

"The story is not mine to tell, ma'am. If Mr. Thornhill wishes to relate it to you at some point in the future, I daresay he will. Until then, I must respect his wishes."

"He's asked you not tell me?"

Mr. Boothroyd shifted in his seat. "Not in so many words. But Mr. Thornhill is a private man. I've already exposed him enough by placing that unfortunate matrimonial advertisement. I'll not compound my sin by spreading gossip about him."

Helena was sure she hadn't heard him correctly. "Forgive me. Are you saying it was *you* who placed the advertisement?"

"It was, my lady." He raised his cup to his lips, taking a casual sip of his tea. "Mr. Thornhill was not at all pleased."

Her eyes met his. He looked steadily back at her. They were no longer simply having tea, she realized. They were two adversaries, engaged in a polite battle of wills.

"Didn't he wish to marry?" she asked.

"No, indeed. However, he soon came to agree that there were benefits to having a wife. The right lady would make his life easier, both at the Abbey and within the community. She would help to relieve the weight of his burdens."

She returned her teacup and saucer to the tea tray. "If I remain here at the Abbey—"

"*If* you remain?"

"—I shall, of course, address myself to alleviating some of those burdens."

"You are one of them, my lady," Mr. Boothroyd said.

Helena stilled, her breath stopping in her chest. So, it was not to be mere innuendo, then. He wished to confront the situation head-on.

An hour ago, she might have welcomed a little plain speaking. Now, however, she found she didn't have the stomach for it.

"Yes. Yes, I know." She tightened her fingers in the soft cashmere folds of her shawl. "I never meant—"

To lie? To scheme? To take advantage of Justin's kindness?

No, she hadn't *meant* anything. She'd thought only of herself. Of escaping from her uncle. Of finding a decent, honest gentleman who'd give her the protection of his name.

In doing so, she'd been worse than selfish. She'd been cruel. If she had any doubt of that, all she need do is recall the look on Justin's face as he sat at her bedside, his elbows resting on his knees and his head bent under the weight of her betrayal.

But she wouldn't make excuses. Not to Justin's steward of all people. She had some pride left, after all.

"My lady?"

She rose from her seat on the sofa. Mr. Boothroyd swiftly stood as well. "I'm going for a walk outside."

His brows shot up. "In this weather?"

"It's only a drizzle."

"You would do better to remain in the house."

"Undoubtedly." She smoothed the skirts of her gray silk gown and wrapped her shawl more firmly about her shoulders. "I shall walk to the stables to see Neville. Surely that's within the bounds of my confinement."

Mr. Boothroyd's lips pressed together in a line. "I don't think it wise of you to caper about out of doors. If you were to have another fall…"

It would solve a great many problems. Possibly even her own. But she wouldn't say such things to Mr. Boothroyd. What would be the point? He'd resolved to think ill of her. She certainly didn't blame him.

"You may come if you like," she said.

She didn't wait to see if he followed her.

Helena strode down the drive, her boots crunching on the wet gravel and her skirts whipping violently about her in the wind. The rain had relented, she was thankful to see. Especially as she was wearing neither bonnet nor gloves. She'd left the Abbey in a rush, too distressed by her conversation with Mr. Boothroyd to stop and find her cloak and other outdoor accessories.

She would find a way out of this. There had to be a way.

Though she couldn't for the life of her think what that way might be.

She and Jenny had racked their brains for months. Only when Jenny had found Justin's advertisement had there seemed to be a light at the end of the tunnel.

"See here?" Jenny had said, pointing at the newspaper. "He's a soldier, like your brother. And quiet too, with a remote property in the country. Better still, Helena, look at this. He's not concerned with a woman's fortune. And he doesn't say anything at all about her looks. Rather promising, don't you think?"

Helena had been lying listless on her bed after a visit from Dr. Collins, curled on her side, staring at the silk-papered wall of her bedroom.

"Won't you look at it?" Jenny had asked. "We've always said your uncle could do nothing if you were married. A stranger isn't ideal, I know. But we're running out of time. And Fleet Street isn't so far. I can pop round to the office of this Mr. T. Finchley Esquire and find out all the particulars. It may all be a hum, but surely it's worth investigating."

Helena had made no response. She'd felt so defeated. She'd scarcely had the will to move.

Jenny had sat beside her on the bed, smoothing her hair from her forehead. "Don't give up," she'd said softly. "Please don't give up."

Helena hadn't given up. Hope had flickered in her breast at the thought of her escape, a small, struggling flame fed by her own meeting with Mr. Finchley and then, later, by Justin's letters.

Dear Miss Reynolds, he had begun each one. Except for the last letter. The one confirming her journey to Devon to meet him. That had been addressed to *My Dear Miss Reynolds*.

My Dear.

An extraordinary intimacy from her future husband.

Or so it had seemed at the time.

Would that she had known then how handsome Justin would be. How tall and powerful and charismatic. Would that she had known how passionately he would kiss her at the Stanhope Hotel, his large hands cradling her face with a gentleness that made her heart ache to recall it.

I could fall in love with him.

The realization settled in her chest, warm and bright. It was not as alarming as she would have imagined it would be. Quite the opposite. For Justin Thornhill wasn't only a handsome man capable of bestowing kisses that made her melt into a mass of treacle. He was a *good* man. Unutterably kind and steadfast, and fiercely protective of everyone in his care.

She'd learned that about him during their time apart. It had been an unspoken thread in every conversation she'd had with Neville, Mr. Boothroyd, and Mrs. Whitlock. Justin took care of people. He protected them.

Despite his growls and grumbles and his often-grim countenance, despite the ignominy of his birth, Justin Thornhill was as true a gentleman as any she'd ever met. Too good for her by half.

Fall in love with him? She could think of nothing more ill advised. Not when she'd lied to him in such stupendous fashion. Not when she'd tricked him into a marriage he didn't want.

No. It was far better to steel herself against him. That way, when he rejected her—when he sent her away—her heart wouldn't shatter into smithereens.

She continued toward the stables, her head bent against the rising wind. The drive curved in a gradually winding slope, leading down past the cliffs. The cold air nipped at her face as she traversed its edge. She inhaled a bracing lungful, breathing in the wild, salty smell of the sea. It was only a few more steps to the stable. It would be warmer there and—

"What the devil are you doing out here?"

She looked up with a start.

Justin was standing several yards off, clad in a mud-spattered greatcoat, a portmanteau slung over one shoulder. His black hair was wet, his hat held carelessly in one gloved hand.

Any thought of hardening her heart vanished into the ether.

"*Justin.*" She ran to meet him in a flurry of silken skirts, reaching him in only a few hasty strides and flinging her arms around his neck. It was not an easy feat. He was so much taller than she was. He must have leaned down to her or bent his head. She was too overcome to know which. "You came back."

"Of course I did." His voice was gruff. He brought one arm around her waist to steady her. "Helena, I'm all over mud."

"I don't care."

He held her for a long moment. She felt the rain splashing down on her back and shoulders and soaking into the rolled and braided coils of her hair. Her wide pagoda sleeves slid toward her elbows, the light muslin of her undersleeves growing damp on the collar of his coat. The front of her bodice was dampening as well.

She drew back from him at last, lowering from her tiptoes and releasing the death grip she had on his neck. She wiped the raindrops from her cheeks with her hands. She prayed he didn't think she was weeping.

"What are you doing outside?" he asked again. "Where's Neville?"

"In the stable. I'm going—I was going—to sit with him while he works."

Justin gazed down at her, his expression hard to read. "And your hat and gloves?"

"At the Abbey."

He dropped his portmanteau from his shoulder and removed his greatcoat. She held herself immobile as he draped it over her shoulders. It was lined with wool, still warm from his body heat, and so large it fairly swallowed her whole.

"Draw it up over your head," he said. "Come. I've been dreaming of a warm fire and a cup of tea for the last two and a half miles."

They returned to the Abbey, walking side by side up the drive. With each step, Helena felt a little more ridiculous about the exuberant greeting she'd given him. For all she knew, he'd already decided to annul their marriage.

Either that or have her committed.

The prospect sent a chill down her spine. She cast a sidelong glance at Justin's face. He looked thoughtful. Grave. Like a man with a great deal on his mind.

She reminded herself of the words he'd uttered when he rescued her from the cliff's ledge.

"You married me to keep you safe and that's precisely what I intend to do."

That night he'd meant it.

Did he still mean it?

He'd told her to trust him. And, except for leaving her without a word, she had no real reason not to. Not unless she counted the sins of other men against him. But that wouldn't be fair, would it? Justin was not her uncle or Mr. Glyde or any one of the half dozen gentlemen in London who'd refused to help her. It would be unjust to tar him with the same brush.

They climbed the front steps of the Abbey in silence. He opened the door, allowing her to precede him into the hall. She removed his greatcoat from her shoulders and handed it back to him. "You'll want to wash and change. I'll have a tea tray brought to the library in half an hour. Unless you'd like more time?"

"I daresay we'll need it." His gaze dropped to the front of her gown. "I'm not the only one who must wash and change."

She looked down at her bodice. "Oh dear." It was worse than damp. It was streaked with mud all across the collar and bosom. She gave him a rueful grimace. "It serves me right for embracing you." She attempted to inject humor into words, but her voice only succeeded in sounding hollow. "I don't know what I was thinking."

"Helena—"

"Mr. Thornhill?" Mr. Boothroyd emerged from the library. "I wasn't aware you'd returned. And I see you've found her ladyship. Splendid." He came across the hall to speak with Justin, full of questions about his visit to Mr. Finchley.

Helena stood listening for a moment, but she felt excluded. As if her very presence was superfluous to the conversation. She excused herself to go upstairs and change. Neither man made any objection. She wondered if they even noticed when she quietly slipped away.

Once in her bedroom, she stripped off her wet under-sleeves and bodice and stepped out of her muddied skirts. She deposited the whole in the bathroom and, after washing up and repairing her hair, returned to her bedroom and quickly donned a clean dress. It was the last of the three she'd brought with her from London and the only one that wasn't gray.

"Ashes of roses," the modiste had called the dusky shade of pink.

It was silk like the others, with long, loose sleeves that fastened tight at the wrists and a plain bodice, confined at the waist by a ribbon belt of dark plum velvet. The same dark velvet edged the single deep flounce at the bottom of her skirts. It was a beautiful dress. The cut set off her figure and the color made her hair shine and her skin look rich as cream. But that wasn't why she'd brought it. The simple fact was, it was one of the only gowns she owned that she could get into and out of without the assistance of a lady's maid.

If she remained, perhaps she could offer the position of lady's maid to Bess. Hadn't the young maidservant said she knew something about removing stains from silk? It was a skill that would be particularly useful now, given the current state of Helena's gowns.

But she didn't know if she'd remain.

In order to find out, she'd have to go downstairs and confront the situation. Part of her—a rather large part, admittedly—would have preferred to crawl under a blanket and hide. The news from town could not be good.

I don't want to know.

A stupid, childish thought. She was becoming a coward. It simply wouldn't do. She straightened her spine and crossed to the door. She was halfway there when someone knocked. The sound echoed through the room, strong and firm.

Not a servant, then.

She shouldn't be surprised. Unlike her, Justin was no coward. If there was bad news to be relayed, he would not scruple to do it himself.

"Come in," she called out.

Justin entered. She watched, heart thumping, as he slowly closed the door behind him. "You left rather quickly," he said. "I trust there wasn't anything—"

And then he stopped and looked at her. Simply looked at her. The sort of scorching look that took in every detail of her appearance, from the top of her head to the hem of her flounced skirts.

Her pulse beat heavy at her throat.

"You've changed your dress," he said.

A vague sense of self-consciousness assailed her. Did he think she was trying to entice him? To use her feminine wiles to influence his decision about their marriage?

"I hadn't much choice." She smoothed both hands over her skirts. "I hope I haven't kept you waiting."

He dropped a brief glance at the muddied legs of his trousers. "Hardly. I haven't yet had a chance to change myself. I've been talking to Boothroyd."

"Have you?"

He gave her another long, measuring look. "I'd like to talk to you as well."

"By all means."

"Why don't you order tea while I wash up? We can have it here. In our room."

Our room.

She swallowed. "Very well."

Her eyes followed him as he walked to his dressing room. Most of his clothes were there. She'd examined them in his absence. Frock coats, waistcoats, trousers, riding breeches, and a collection of pristine white shirts. It was all impeccably organized. Especially considering he didn't keep a valet.

"What about Mr. Boothroyd?" she asked.

"What about him?"

"Will he be joining us?"

Justin stopped at the door to the dressing room. His brow furrowed. "No. Why should he?"

"I assumed…" Her voice trailed away. He was coming back to her, crossing the room in a few long strides. He reached inside of his coat.

"I have something for you," he said. "I'd almost forgotten." He withdrew a small envelope, stamped with a red wax seal. "You can read it while I change for tea."

She took it from his hand. "What is it?"

"You'll see," he said. "And Helena?"

"Yes?"

His lip quirked. "Don't assume."

She flushed. But he didn't linger to see it. He was gone through the dressing room door in a trice, leaving her alone with the mysterious letter.

She took it to the window. A shaft of sunlight filtered in through the glass. Still standing, she broke the seal, spread the paper open in her hands, and began to read.

> *My dearest Helena,*
>
> *This evening I met your Mr. Thornhill. We didn't get on at all. Nevertheless, he's promised I shall see you again when the rains cease. Do the rains ever cease in Devon? Perhaps it's all a ploy to silence my unruly tongue. No matter. Mr. Finchley says that if Thornhill should prove disagreeable, he will bring me to you himself.*
>
> *I've so much to tell you and no time in which to write it all down. Your new husband won't wait on a longer letter. He's impatient to see you again. Does this mean what I think it means? If so, you'll forgive me for gloating. Didn't I tell you it would all come right?*
>
> *With boundless affection,*
> *Jenny*

Chapter Thirteen

After washing and changing into a clean suit of clothes, Justin returned to Helena's bedroom. *Their* bedroom. She was seated on the settee near the fireplace, her skirts settled all about her like a dusky pink cloud. She was still looking at Miss Holloway's letter. He stood a moment in the door of the dressing room and watched her.

He didn't know what Miss Holloway had written. He hoped it was something that would lift Helena's spirits. When he'd seen her walking down the cliff road, her face had been pale, her eyes despairing. And when she'd thrown her arms around him in greeting, he'd felt a small portion of what she must have been feeling in his absence. She'd been alone. Afraid. Uncertain of him.

Justin's fist clenched reflexively at his side. He'd handled things badly. And, quite probably, hurt her in the process. "I should have woke you before I left."

Helena looked up, startled. "I beg your pardon?"

He crossed the room to join her on the settee. The tea tray was sitting on a low table near the fire. A swirling vapor of steam floated up from the spout of the teapot. "A note was inadequate," he said. "I can see that now."

Helena refolded Miss Holloway's letter and set it aside. Her eyes found his. "Why didn't you say something?"

He sank down beside her, half crushing her voluminous skirts against his leg. It was no use dissembling. "Because I knew if I woke you—if I saw how frightened you were—I wouldn't be able to leave you."

"Oh," she said softly.

"Leaving you here was the safest thing to do. With the rainstorm and the road… It was the only way I could see Finchley."

"And Jenny?"

"She happened to be there as well."

"With Mr. Finchley?"

"Yes. Er…it's rather a long story."

Helena poured him a cup of tea. When she handed it to him, their fingers brushed. "I'm listening."

He waited to speak until she'd poured a cup out for herself. "When your uncle discovered your absence, he confronted Miss Holloway. When she wouldn't divulge your whereabouts, he fell into a rage, ransacking her rooms for some sign of where you'd gone."

Helena's face drained of color. "Did he hurt her?"

"No. But when he found the evidence he was looking for—"

"What evidence? There wasn't any, I'm sure of it. We were exceedingly careful."

"There was a letter," Justin said. "Miss Holloway kept it in a locked drawer of her dressing table."

Helena shook her head, unwilling to believe it. "There must be some mistake. I brought all of your letters with me."

"Did you?" He filed that bit of information away to examine later. "But this wasn't a letter I wrote to you. This was the letter Finchley wrote in reply to Miss Holloway's initial inquiry about the advertisement. It mentions me by name. It also mentions North Devon and the King's Arms."

"Why in heaven would Jenny have kept *that*?"

"I didn't ask," Justin said.

Not that he didn't have his suspicions.

"So," Helena said, stirring a generous helping of sugar into her tea, "after reading that letter, my uncle would have all but had your direction."

"That's the size of it."

"He would have sent Mr. Glyde after me straightaway." Her expression was meditative. "And what about Jenny? You say he didn't hurt her—"

"He didn't. Not physically. He turned her off without a reference. He gave her half an hour to collect her things and then had a footman escort her from the premises. She had no money and no one with whom she could take shelter."

"Which is why she went to see Mr. Finchley," Helena concluded.

Justin's lips tilted in a wry smile. "You know her well."

She shrugged. "It's what I would have done."

A sharp twinge of emotion caught him unaware. He recognized it at once for what it was. He'd experienced the exact same sensation when Finchley had prattled on about Helena's beauty.

Jealousy.

It was damned disconcerting. He had no earthly reason to be jealous of Finchley, nor of any man. Nevertheless...

"You think a great deal of him," he said.

"Of Mr. Finchley? Yes, I suppose I do."

"Why? You scarcely know him."

"No, but he was kind to me when I needed it most. I shan't ever forget it."

Justin's fingers tightened reflexively on the handle of his teacup. He forced them to loosen, imposing relaxation on himself as he raised the dainty porcelain cup to his lips and took a deep drink. The brew was strong—unlike the tea they'd shared on her first visit to the Abbey. "Ah yes, kindness." He returned his cup and saucer to the tea tray. "One of your primary requirements in a husband, as I recall."

A dull flush rose in Helena's cheeks. "Where is Jenny now? What has Mr. Finchley done with her?"

"He's procured a little house for her near Piccadilly."

Helena's mouth fell open. "He's done *what?*"

"It's all perfectly respectable," Justin assured her.

Or so he'd been led to believe.

Then again, Finchley *had* been in residence when Justin had come calling in Half Moon Street. And he *had* admitted to spending time alone with Miss Holloway without benefit of a chaperone.

"She needed somewhere safe to stay," he explained, as much for his own peace of mind as for Helena's. "A place where your uncle and his hired villains wouldn't think to look for her. And Finchley could hardly offer her board and lodging with him, could he?"

Helena was suitably appalled. "I should hope not!"

"He's been careful not to compromise her."

"I'm certain he has, but…" She pressed her fingertips to her forehead, as if to stave off an impending headache. "Oh, but this is all my fault. If not for me, Jenny would never have been put in such a predicament."

"It's not as bad as it seems."

"Isn't it?"

"No," he said. "Not by half."

She raised her eyes to his, a glimmer of hope shining in their hazel depths.

His pulse kicked up a notch, his blood responding to the warmth in her gaze with an equal warmth of its own. He cleared his throat. "For one thing, I've taken over the lease from Finchley. And before you object, I would remind you that Miss Holloway is, in some degree, your cousin, which makes her my relation by marriage. It's perfectly appropriate for a gentleman to look after an indigent relation, is it not?"

"Yes, but—"

"I've also left her money for a railway ticket. If worse comes to worst, she can always take the train to Devon."

The tension in Helena's face softened. She dropped her hand back to her lap. "Oh, Justin."

"I hoped that would ease your mind."

"It does. So much. But it's all been achieved at such great inconvenience to you. How can I ever—"

"You needn't."

"But after everything I've—"

"What's done is done." He strove for a bracing tone. He didn't think he could bear it if she offered to repay him. And he sure as hell didn't want to hear her express her gratitude. "We can only go forward."

She held his gaze. "Can we?"

"We can try," he said gruffly. "Which is precisely why I went to see Finchley. We can't just drift along without a plan. Not when it comes to matters of law."

"Is it a matter of law?" she asked. "Even though we're married?"

"It may be. It depends..." He ran a hand over his hair. It was still damp from the rain. "There's an issue of consent."

She blanched.

"You understand the concept, I trust."

"Yes, I do. It's only..." She returned her teacup to the tea tray. Her hands were trembling. "The night they came, I heard Mr. Glyde as I was passing through the hall. He said I was unable to consent to marriage." Her voice grew thin. "Which means you and I are not married at all."

Justin took her by the hand. "Listen to me. I'm going to explain everything that Finchley and I discussed and everything we propose to do. But first I want you to hear me. To really listen."

She nodded.

He threaded his fingers through hers. His words were fierce and low. "No one is ever going to take you away. Do you understand me? Not your uncle or Mr. Glyde. Not the courts. There's always a way, Helena. And there's nothing I wouldn't risk—nothing I wouldn't dare—for the people I care about."

Helena's fingers flexed in his. "How can you care for me?"

"You're my wife. How can I not?"

"I'm only your wife because I played you false. Because I took advantage of your kindness and generosity."

He snorted. "Good God, Helena. Do you think me as innocent as a babe? I knew you were hiding something the day I met you. Have you forgotten how I spoke to you at the

King's Arms? If I were squeamish about marrying a woman with secrets, I'd have turned tail and run."

"I can't understand why you didn't."

Justin didn't wonder. He scarcely understood himself.

All he knew was that he'd always had a weakness for fine things. An incessant yearning for something more. Something better.

It had never led to anything but misery. He'd had ample proof of that over the years. Everything he'd acquired—all the way down to Greyfriar's Abbey itself—had ended as no better than a millstone round his neck.

Which was precisely why Boothroyd had warned him against marrying her. He knew Justin's weakness. Had always known it.

And this time it was worse. His desire to possess the refined, beautiful creature who had answered his advertisement was all mixed up with his instinct to protect her, to keep her safe.

Hadn't Finchley said it would do him good to successfully rescue a female from harm?

Curse the man and his opinions.

After what had happened in Cawnpore, Justin doubted he had the capacity to keep anyone safe, least of all a vulnerable woman.

But he was sure as hell going to try.

"Perhaps it was because I wanted to help you. Either that or because I fancied you like mad." His mouth hitched. "Probably a little of both, if I'm honest."

Her blush deepened, turning her cheeks a brilliant shade of rose. "The news from London must be very bleak indeed."

"Whatever gives you that idea?"

"Common sense. You're clearly trying to soften an impending blow. I wish you'd just tell me, Justin. It's worse not knowing."

His smile faded. He'd meant what he'd said. Every blasted word. But…

"You're right. We must speak plainly, you and I. From now on, if this is to work, there are to be no more secrets between us."

Her expression turned wary. "If what is to work?"

"This plan of Finchley's. He believes there's a way to rout your uncle without resorting to a protracted lawsuit. It won't be comfortable. Not for either of us. It requires exposure. Drives in the park, nights at the theater, and even a ball or two, if we garner the requisite invitations. And that's not all, I'm afraid."

Helena was looking at him as if he'd just spoken to her in ancient Greek. "Balls and the theatre," she repeated faintly. "In Abbot's Holcombe, do you mean?"

"Not Abbot's Holcombe," he said. "When the weather clears, you and I are going to London."

Helena drew back from him in white-faced shock. "We are not."

"Helena—"

"No." Her voice was sharp and brittle to her ears.

She rose from the sofa and walked away from him. She didn't know where she was going. All she knew was that she needed to put distance between them. The mere mention of London was enough to make her want to run. She didn't care where.

"Helena, wait." Justin stood to follow her. "Let me explain."

She stopped in front of the bedroom window. The heavy curtains were drawn back to reveal the rain-streaked glass. She stared unseeing out over the drive. "I can't go back there. I won't."

Justin came to stand at her side. He was just outside of her line of vision. She could feel him there, big and warm and masculine.

"What are you afraid of?" he asked.

She folded her arms at her waist. "You wouldn't understand."

"Try me."

She shook her head, refusing to explain. But there was no keeping the words to herself. They tumbled out in spite of her resolve. "Everything bad that's ever happened to me has happened in London. My mother…and Giles…and my uncle and Mr. Glyde…" She cast an anguished glance at Justin over her shoulder. He was standing there, grave and still. "Don't you see? I've never been more alone in my life than when I was in that wretched city. And if I go back now…I know my uncle will take me. I'll be no better than an animal walking straight into a trap. They'll lock me away in Lowbridge House and this time there'll be no escape. Nothing I can do to save myself."

Justin moved in front of her, filling her vision. His large frame blocked out the light as he leaned back, half sitting on the window embrasure. "You're not alone anymore."

Helena's throat tightened with emotion. She bit her lip. She wasn't going to cry. She hadn't shed a tear since those weeks after Giles's death. And she certainly wouldn't do so now.

Justin reached out to her. "Come here."

She took his hand, allowing him to draw her into an embrace. Her skirts pressed against his trousers, the deeply flounced hemline pooling over the toes of his polished leather boots. She rested her cheek on the soft woolen fabric of his waistcoat, feeling his arms close around her, holding her safe against the broad expanse of his chest.

He said nothing for a long while. He merely held her, one large hand moving idly over her back until she began to relax against him, her breath coming slow and even.

"There's a gentleman in London by the name of Charles Pelham," he said at length. His voice was a deep rumble. She could hear it as well as feel it, emanating from his chest as he held her close. "He's a passing acquaintance of Finchley's."

A fine hum of tension coursed through her body. "Is he a doctor?"

"God no." He bent his head down to hers. His cheek brushed over her hair. "He's a newspaperman. An editor at the *London Courant*, and a well-respected one, at that. For the past year, he's been investigating abuses in the management of private asylums."

She stiffened.

"Easy," he murmured. His hand moved up the curve of her back. "Just listen to me."

He was gentling her into submission, like a high-strung horse being readied for the bridle. She wasn't entirely sure she liked it.

"Pelham has been documenting cases of wrongful confinement. Cases where family members have paid to have a relation put away in order to gain control of their money or property. Finchley believes that, when Pelham's editorial is published, there will be mass outrage. He expects it to instigate some sort of reform."

She had a sinking feeling in her stomach. "What does any of this have to do with me?"

THE MATRIMONIAL ADVERTISEMENT

"If you would talk to Pelham—if you would agree to an interview—he would feature your story along with the others. Once the details of what your uncle has done are made public—"

This time she did draw back, but only far enough to look in Justin's eyes. "You can't possibly think that would work!"

"I think it might."

"My uncle would never permit such a story to be published. He'd bring suit against the paper or shut down the printers—or worse. You don't know what he's capable of."

"What I know," Justin said, "is that your uncle has shown a marked interest in concealing his crimes. He wants to keep what he's done to you his own filthy secret, even to the extent of offering me a bribe to remain quiet about our marriage."

"*What?*"

"The point is, he doesn't wish to have his name dragged through the mud. He doesn't want to take a chance that the tide of public opinion will turn against him. Which is precisely why you need to tell your story to the press. When coupled with all the rest of the cases Pelham has dredged up, people will have to believe it. And when they do—when your uncle is exposed—he won't dare attempt to meddle with you or your money again."

She huffed. "You make it sound so simple."

"It won't be. You'll have to share some of the more unpleasant details of your ordeal with Pelham. He'll want to know everything about you."

"So he can publish it, for all of London to see?"

"That's the idea."

Her stomach clenched at the thought of it. She envisioned her former acquaintances reading the sordid tale at the breakfast table or in the smoke-filled lounges of their clubs. She imagined groups of fashionably clad ladies tittering about it over tea and biscuits. Pitying her. Laughing at her.

Her mouth went dry. "Must we go there? Couldn't Mr. Pelham come here?"

"Regrettably, no. People will need to witness you out and about. That's where the balls and the theatre come in. It will give them a chance to see that there's nothing irregular about your behavior. Then, when the editorial is published, they'll be more inclined to believe you."

She took a deep breath. It did absolutely nothing to quell her rising sense of panic. "I can't do it, Justin."

"Why not?"

"For a lady to expose herself in such a way…to make a spectacle of herself for the public's amusement…" Everything within her recoiled at the thought. "It isn't decent."

He looked at her in disbelief. "You're worried about your reputation?"

"Yes," she said. And then, "No." She focused on the topmost button of his waistcoat, watching it blur before her eyes as unshed tears clouded her vision. "It's all just so shameful. I can't bear for anyone else to know."

His hand tightened at the curve of her waist. She could feel the weight and warmth of it through the layers of silk and corsetry, settling like a brand against her skin. "It's not meant to shame you, Helena. It's meant to set you free."

"By robbing me of what's left of my dignity."

He was silent for several seconds. "I'll be with you," he said at last. "If that's any consolation."

She lifted her eyes back to his. "You can't want to go to London. Not for this."

"Not particularly, no. But it's not forever. A few weeks inconvenience, merely. It will be over before you know it."

"A few weeks? Is that all?" Even a day was too much. Even an hour. "And what's to prevent my uncle from—"

"I'll be with you," Justin said again. His gaze bore into hers. "Every moment."

Helena didn't know why she continued to resist him. He seemed to have a creditable plan. And who was she to naysay when her own plan had failed so miserably? "It wasn't supposed to be like this," she blurted out.

"No? What did you expect to happen?"

"I expected to marry you. To have a life here. Safe. Far away from London. I hoped I would never see my uncle—or Mr. Glyde—ever again."

For the briefest instant, Justin's face betrayed a flicker of surprise. "You truly intended to stay here with me as my wife?"

"Of course. Did you think it all a trick? That after we wed I'd disappear?" She was sorely tempted to laugh. "I have nowhere to go, Justin. No one willing to render me protection. I *needed* a husband. It was the only way to keep my fortune and my name."

"Ah yes. Your fortune."

"My *brother's* fortune."

"And how do you know I won't squander it now I've gained control?"

"You won't," she said. "You couldn't."

"Finchley's assurances again, I take it."

"Was he wrong?"

"No," Justin admitted. "He wasn't wrong. Still…it was a hell of a risk tying yourself to a stranger."

"What else was I to do? The only other choice was to flee with nothing. At least, by marrying you, there was a chance it would all come right. And now…"

The prospect of a trip to London loomed large in her mind. It sucked all the light from within her, leaving behind nothing but cold and darkness and roiling fear.

She shivered in Justin's arms. "Must I go back there? Is there no other way?"

He didn't answer immediately. He appeared to consider the matter, to truly examine the alternatives. "There are other ways. But in this case, they aren't likely to lead to success."

"This plan may not succeed either."

"No. There are no guarantees, but I agree with Finchley. We have better odds of defeating your uncle in the court of public opinion than besting him in a court of law. All that's required is a little courage."

"Pity I haven't any left."

Justin bent his head, his voice a husky murmur against her ear. "Take mine."

She closed her eyes. She wanted to say yes. To tell him that she'd go with him to London. That she'd bare her soul to whichever newspaperman he wished. She owed him that much. She owed him her very life.

But it wasn't easy.

Justin seemed to understand. His hand slid from her waist to her back, a heavy, comforting weight. "Think on it. There are a few more days of rain yet."

"Only a few?"

"It will give us time to talk."

Talk? She didn't know why the prospect should affect the rhythm of her heart, but it did. Most decidedly so. She moistened her lips. "To speak plainly, isn't that what you said?"

"Precisely."

"With no more secrets between us."

Justin looked down at her, his gray eyes solemn as the grave. "No more secrets."

Chapter Fourteen

The rain stopped sometime during the night. By morning, the dark clouds had drifted away and the sun was shining in a clear blue sky. Helena woke early, alone in the great Elizabethan bed. She was cold and hungry—and quite unwilling to wait on the grudging service of Mrs. Standish.

After washing and dressing, she made her way down to the kitchens to see about something to eat. Mrs. Whitlock was there, fluttering about the stove in a grease-stained apron. Mrs. Standish stood near the sink, filling a teakettle with water from the tap. The smell of frying bacon wafted through the room.

"My lady!" Mrs. Standish swiftly disposed of the teakettle. "What are you doing in here? And at this hour?"

Mrs. Whitlock wiped her hands on her apron. "She'll be wantin' her breakfast."

"And I'll be bringing her a tray at nine of the clock, won't I?" Mrs. Standish retorted. "Though it's a maidservant's job, if I do say so."

"Are you hungry, ma'am?" Mrs. Whitlock asked. "Shall I fix ye a plate of eggs and bacon?"

"Her ladyship prefers porridge," Mrs. Standish said.

Mrs. Whitlock turned back to the stove. "We've that too, and plenty of it." She stirred the contents of a steaming pot with a wooden spoon. "Won't be a minute, my lady."

Helena seated herself at the long wooden table. "Have the gentlemen already eaten?"

"Not as yet, ma'am," Mrs. Whitlock said. "Mr. Boothroyd and Neville should be down any moment."

"And Mr. Thornhill?"

"Up at dawn, he was, and dressed to go riding."

Mrs. Standish removed the tea canister from the cupboard. "Meanwhile, that wretched Mr. Danvers is still abed and still the worse for drink. He'll never improve, lest he eats something. And so I told him, the vile creature."

"He needs a wife to look after him," Mrs. Whitlock said.

"A wife?" Mrs. Standish scoffed. "Who would have him?"

Mrs. Whitlock looked over her shoulder at Helena. "He were a good man once, was Bill Danvers. Drove the mail coach, he did. No man could handle a team of horses so well." She scooped a ladleful of porridge into a bowl and handed it to Mrs. Standish. "He lost his wife and two little sons to fever in '55. Lost his job soon after. Hasn't been the same since."

Mrs. Standish set the bowl of porridge down in front of Helena along with a folded napkin, a spoon, and fresh butter and sugar. A pot of hot tea followed, accompanied by a chipped porcelain teacup and saucer. "We've all suffered hardship. It's no excuse to fall into vice."

Helena listened to the two women bickering as she ate her porridge and drank her tea. The servants at Greyfriar's Abbey were so unlike the servants at her uncle's townhouse in Grosvenor Square as to be almost a different species. They talked, argued, and gossiped with impunity, and seemed to have no fear of being turned off without a reference. It was little wonder the house was in such a state.

In other circumstances, a new wife would set about restoring some semblance of order. Helena was certainly up to the task. She'd had the charge of her father's household from the age of fifteen and, when Giles had ascended to the title, he'd happily let her continue in the role. If Giles were still alive, she'd likely be in Grosvenor Square now, conducting weekly meetings with the housekeeper and cook and toiling over the household accounts.

If Giles were still alive.

The hand holding her spoon froze midway to her mouth.

Good gracious, had she truly thought such a thing? Of course Giles was alive!

She slowly lowered her spoon and rose from the table, leaving her porridge half-finished.

"No appetite, my lady?" Mrs. Whitlock asked.

"Not as much as I thought I had," Helena said. Indeed, a leaden weight seemed to have settled in the pit of her stomach. She felt vaguely ill.

"Up too early, that's the trouble," Mrs. Standish grumbled. "Ladies aren't meant to rise before ten."

"And how many ladies have you waited on?" Mrs. Whitlock replied tartly. "Not many, I'll wager."

Helena retreated from the kitchen to the sound of their continued arguing.

She fetched her bonnet, shawl, and gloves from her room and made her way back downstairs. The entry hall was empty, the sun shining in through the stone-framed windows, casting dust motes in dancing beams of light.

If Justin was dressed for riding, he must have gone to the stable. With any luck he'd be there still.

With that in mind, she headed out the door and down the front steps, tying on her bonnet as she went. The air was crisp and cool on her face. There was no hint of moisture in it. Perhaps the rain had truly stopped?

An anxious tremor went through her. She envisioned Mr. Glyde waiting for the moment he could swoop in and take her. He'd bring the magistrate with him again, and this time there would be no thwarting him.

Justin had told her that, after visiting the Abbey that fateful, stormy evening, Mr. Glyde had returned to London on a night train. He'd probably gone straight to see her uncle. To make his report. She supposed he could have come back. Perhaps he was even now lingering about the village? Drinking at the King's Arms. Biding his time until the roads dried out.

Or perhaps he was still in London, anticipating her return?

There were countless places for him to hide in the city. If she went back, she'd have to remain forever on her guard. At the slightest sign of weakness or inattention, Mr. Glyde would seize her and take her to Lowbridge House. She'd be locked away with no hope of regaining her freedom.

But she couldn't think about that now. For one thing, she hadn't even agreed to Justin's scheme. There might yet be another way.

She tightened her shawl around her shoulders as she marched down the drive. There was activity at the stable. She could see the dogs lying in the stable yard, watching Mr. Danvers polish the carriage. Contrary to the disparaging report rendered by Mrs. Standish, he appeared very much awake and not at all the worse for drink.

He tipped his cap to her as she entered the stable.

Justin's horse, Hiran, was tied in the aisle, his chestnut coat gleaming like a freshly minted penny. Justin was at his side, swinging a saddle onto his back. He was clad in Bedford cord breeches and black top boots, his white linen shirt worn open at the collar to reveal a shadowed glimpse of the burns on his neck.

He caught Helena's gaze over the top of Hiran's withers.

"Good morning," she said brightly.

"You're up early."

"Not very."

"No?" He settled the saddle in place and reached under Hiran's belly to catch the girth. "Do all fine ladies rise at half seven?"

"This one does." She walked to the other side of the aisle, watching as Justin tightened the girth. "Sometimes even earlier."

"Shocking."

She shrugged one shoulder. "I've never enjoyed lolling about in bed in the morning. There's too much to be done."

"I'd have thought that was what servants were for."

"Servants can't do their work without direction."

Justin scratched Hiran on the shoulder, his expression thoughtful.

"Where do you ride?" she asked. "When you exercise him, I mean."

"It depends. Usually I take him into King's Abbot."

"And today?"

"Today I thought I'd ride on the beach." He moved to a nearby hook to retrieve Hiran's bridle. "Do you ride?"

"Not since…" She faltered. "Not in a long while."

"But you do know how?"

"Of course. I used to ride with Giles before he left for India. We'd go out in the early morning for a canter in Hyde Park. After he left, I sometimes rode there with a groom."

Justin bridled Hiran. He had an expert hand, cradling the big horse's face as he eased the bit into his mouth and slipped the bridle over his ears.

"Would you like to ride with me?" he asked.

"Now?"

"Why not?"

"I've nothing to wear," she said. "I didn't pack my riding habit."

Justin gave her a cursory glance. "What's wrong with what you're wearing?"

"This?" She pressed her hands to her voluminous skirts. The gray silk dress she'd donned this morning was service-able enough for a walk, but it would never do for riding. "I'm knee deep in petticoats and crinoline."

"I know. It's very becoming."

Her cheeks warmed at the compliment. "Yes, it's very pretty. And wholly impractical, too. I'd never be able to sit a sidesaddle in these skirts."

Justin untied Hiran and turned him around in the aisle. The giant horse swished his tail with impatience. "A sidesad-dle. I hadn't thought of that."

"You don't have one?"

"We don't. There hasn't been a lady in residence at Grey-friar's Abbey in three decades or more."

She followed Justin as he led Hiran out of the stable and into the yard. Danvers was gone, but the coach was still there, the dogs resting languidly beneath it. "Was Sir Oswald not married?"

Justin stopped. He looked out toward the cliffs for a moment, his eyes squinting against the sun. "No, he wasn't married." He paused. "He was rather a famous bachelor around these parts."

"Oh." She didn't know what else to say. "May I watch you exercise Hiran?"

"If you like. It's nothing very exciting. You'd do better to go back to the house where it's warm."

"I'd rather stay with you." An embarrassing admission, but an honest one. Ensconced in the Abbey, she felt safe. In Justin's presence, she felt doubly so. He was her husband. Her protector. Now he'd returned from London, she was loath to let him out of her sight. "If you don't mind," she added.

"Why should I mind?"

Helena could think of several reasons. After their discussion yesterday, she'd rarely been out of his company. She'd even sat in the library, curled up in the window embrasure with a book, while he'd discussed business matters with Mr. Boothroyd. He might simply want his privacy. A few minutes alone, free from her and all of the problems she'd brought into his life.

"Here," he said. "I'll walk down with you."

"You needn't."

He gave her an amused look. "After nearly a week of rain?" He offered her his hand.

She took it gratefully.

The path to the beach was muddier than it had been on the day of her arrival in Devon. She might have slipped and fallen had she not availed herself of Justin's arm. Hiran had better luck. He picked his way along the path with surefooted ease. When they reached the end, he jumped from the edge down to the beach. Justin followed.

She waited for him to assist her down as he had the last time. Instead, much to her dismay, he caught Hiran by the bridle and vaulted into the saddle. He spun the horse around to face her.

"If you can manage to shed a petticoat or two, I'll take you up with me," he said.

She blinked. "What?"

"I daresay you'd enjoy it more than sitting on the sidelines watching me ride."

"I daresay you're right. But I'm not certain…"

"Are you frightened?" Justin asked. Hiran pranced beneath him, mouthing at the bit. "You shouldn't be. He's perfectly safe."

Helena wasn't so sure about that. Hiran was a giant brute of a horse, not at all suitable for a lady of her dimensions. "It wouldn't be entirely proper. Me riding pillion in a day dress."

"You won't be riding pillion. I intend to put you up in front of me."

She gave a short laugh. "Oh, well, I suppose that makes a difference."

He flashed a grin. "As for your dress…"

Her stomach fluttered. Was she really going to do this? And why not?

"May I have a moment of privacy?" she asked.

Justin readily obliged, turning his horse—and himself—away from her.

She lifted her skirts and swiftly unfastened the tapes of one of her petticoats. It slid down over her hips, falling to her booted feet. She unfastened a second petticoat as well. And then, just to be safe, she removed her crinoline.

MIMI MATTHEWS

Without the layers of support, her silk skirts fell in unstructured folds down to drag on the ground. She gathered them up out of the way as she stepped out of her petticoats and crinoline. She shook the sand out of each of them before folding them carefully into a little pile.

"You may turn back around now," she said as she dropped her bonnet atop the stack of discarded undergarments.

Justin walked Hiran in a half circle, riding up to the edge of the path. His gaze roved over her with approval. "There's much less of you, my lady."

"I should think so. I've just removed half of my underpinnings." She willed herself not to blush. "My skirts are going to tangle up awfully."

"I'll see they don't." He reached down to her, his large black-gloved hand outstretched. He was all seriousness now. "Take hold of my hand. And place your foot on my boot."

She clasped his hand, feeling it close strongly around hers. She was still on the path and of a height to reach his boot without too much trouble. No sooner had she set her foot atop his than he lifted her up in front of him with an effortless grace, seating her sideways in front of his saddle.

One of his arms curved around her midsection, holding her in an iron grip. His other hand grasped the reins with the casual skill of a career British cavalryman.

Helena's heart beat with a mixture of fear and excitement. "Have you done this before?"

"Not with a lady."

She gasped as Hiran surged forward.

Justin held her fast against the hard wall of his chest. "You're safe."

"I know I am." Which did nothing to prevent her fingers from tightening on his arm.

He guided Hiran along the water's edge. "I've had to take up injured soldiers on occasion. Though they weren't usually seated. Most were unconscious from their wounds. The poor lads had to be draped over the front of the saddle like sacks of grain."

"How dreadful." She turned her head to look up at Justin's face. He met her eyes briefly. "Was it during the uprising?"

"It was." He resumed looking straight ahead. "Would you like to canter?"

She gripped his arm tighter. "You won't let me fall?"

"Never."

"Then yes," she said.

Justin gave no discernible cue to Hiran. He was too accomplished a rider. A subtle shift in the saddle, a faint pressure of the legs, and Hiran sprang from a walk into a long, ground-covering canter.

Helena's pulse leapt. She clung to Justin's arm, but true to his word, he didn't let her fall. Indeed, she scarcely budged from her perch in front of his saddle.

Hiran's stride was smooth as glass, a rarity in a horse so big. The soft sand churned under his hooves as he ran, the sea roiling and crashing alongside them. The wind whipped at Helena's skirts and through her tightly plaited hair. She didn't know when she began to smile, nor when she started to laugh. By the time Justin brought Hiran back down to a walk, she was doing both.

"I feel quite giddy," she said, catching her breath.

Justin's smile was broad—and a little smug. "You enjoyed that."

"I did, rather."

"I knew you would."

"You knew better than I." She loosened her grip on his arm. "Forgive me for clutching at you. I can't seem to help myself."

"It's what I'm here for."

She laughed. "You may feel differently tomorrow when you see the bruises left by my fingers."

He looked down at her, his gray eyes suddenly solemn. "And how are your bruises? Better, I hope."

Her smile dimmed. She was painfully reminded of the night he'd rescued her from the cliff's ledge. It was a shameful memory and one she wished they could both forget. "They're fading." She kept her voice light. "Every day they ache a little less."

"I'm glad. I don't want you to be in pain."

"Nor I you." She let her gaze drift to the open collar of his shirt. The burns on the column of his neck were the same sort as on his jaw. They were puckered and red, disposed in thick, slashing lines, one over the other. "Do they hurt?"

"Rarely."

"How…?"

"A hot poker," he said brusquely. "They held it in the fire and then they held it against me."

She bowed her head. "Oh, Justin." She wanted to weep for him. "How on earth could you bear it?"

"I had little choice in the matter, my dear."

"I know that, but—"

He squeezed her waist. "It's over now. Part of the past. I don't refine on it too much. You shouldn't either."

Hiran chomped at his bit and tossed his head.

"He thinks we're dawdling," Justin said.

Helena swallowed back her emotions. If Justin didn't wish to dwell on his time in India, she had no business forcing him to do so. She reached down to give Hiran a scratch on the neck. "He likes to run, does he?"

"He enjoys nothing better."

"Are all his gaits as smooth as his canter?"

"His gallop isn't bad."

Her heart pounded. "Can we…?"

But she didn't have to ask. Justin was already urging Hiran forward, first into a canter and then into a gallop.

The pace fairly stole her breath away. She'd never gone so fast on a horse. It was like flying. As if his hooves never even touched the ground. The sand and the sea slipped by them in a blur of color. She wondered if this was how jockeys felt when they raced at Newmarket and Epsom.

After a time, Justin drew Hiran back to a canter. They had galloped the length of the beach. The treacherous cliffs of Abbot's Holcombe loomed ahead, the surf frothing violently beneath them amidst a jagged array of stone.

As Hiran slowed to a walk, Helena gazed up at the cliffs. She could sense Justin looking up at them as well.

"How far up was Neville when he fell?" she asked.

"He was nearly at the bottom. The rock crumbled beneath him. His head struck one of the stones and then he plunged straight down into the sea. It was the space of an instant. One moment he was there and the next—gone beneath the waves."

"Was it you who went in after him?"

Justin nodded stiffly. "I thought I could pull him to shore, but the sea was too rough. I couldn't find him in the water. It was Archer who finally rescued him. He saved his life."

Helena's heart ached for Neville. For all of them. "You're not responsible for what happened. You know that, don't you?"

"You think not?"

"None of you were responsible. You were only little boys. You should never have been allowed to climb on the cliffs. Any fool could see how dangerous it was. An adult should have stopped you. Someone at the orphanage. Neville's accident is on their head, not yours."

"No one could have stopped us. Not even if they'd tried. We were that determined."

"But why?" she asked. "I still don't understand."

"We wanted to get to the Abbey. It was the fastest way."

She turned her head and looked into his eyes. "Was it something to do with Sir Oswald? He seems to be tied up with everything somehow."

"He owned the Abbey. Didn't I tell you?"

"It's more than that. Mr. Boothroyd said he'd been Sir Oswald's secretary. He wouldn't explain how he came to work for you. He said it wasn't his story to tell. As if it's all some sort of secret."

Justin fell silent.

"We promised each other there would be no more secrets," she reminded him.

His muscles tensed. Hiran reacted by sidestepping into a prancing trot. Justin absently brought him back to a walk. "What would you like to know?"

"Any number of things," she said. "To start with, why were you and your friends so driven to visit the Abbey? You've said it had nothing to do with the tales of buried treasure. I think it must have something to do with Sir Oswald. I know you disliked the man."

"You think I didn't like him?" Justin gave an incredulous laugh. "Helena, I didn't dislike Oswald Bannister. I *hated* him. We all did. Finchley, Neville, Archer, and I. We hated him so much that we drove him to his death."

Justin was glad he couldn't see Helena's face. It was bad enough to sense the shock coursing through her body. He didn't need to see it registering in her eyes.

He guided Hiran down the beach at an easy walk. Helena was half-turned in front of him, as if she were truly riding sidesaddle. Her back fit snugly against his chest, her plaited hair a silken torment beneath his chin. All he need do was tip his head and he could nuzzle the soft curve of her cheek. He could capture her mouth with his.

God knew he wanted to. Memories of the kisses they'd shared at the Stanhope Hotel had intruded on his thoughts far too often of late. The feel of her in his arms. The taste of her on his lips. The way she'd looked at him as her fingers twined in his.

If he could recreate those moments…rekindle the tenderness between them…perhaps she would forget about his past. She would cease her questions about Oswald Bannister and they could truly contemplate some sort of a future together.

And perhaps Hiran might sprout wings and fly.

"What do you mean, drove him to his death?" she asked. "You didn't—"

"No. We didn't kill him. Though you must know there are those who think we did. Or, more precisely, that *I* did."

"Bess told me he fell from the cliffs. She said there was an inquest."

"Did she?" Justin wasn't entirely surprised. There weren't many in the village who would pass up the chance to apprise his future wife of his dastardly reputation. "Sir Oswald was ever disobliging. Not long after I returned from India, he drank himself into a stupor and staggered over the cliffs outside of the Abbey. People still enjoy speculating about it."

Helena turned her head. Her hazel eyes were soft with concern. "Why did you hate him, Justin? Did he hurt you somehow?"

A bitter laugh bubbled in Justin's chest. Hurt him? Good God.

He reined Hiran to a halt by the water. He lifted Helena down to the ground and dismounted. She waited, her drooping skirts draped over one arm, while he caught Hiran's reins.

"Oswald Bannister was a brute and a bully," he said. "He hadn't a single shred of honor."

"Many gentlemen don't. I know that well enough. One can't hate them all."

"Yes, well…it's rather different when the gentleman in question is one's father."

Helena's brows shot up. "Sir Oswald Bannister was your *father*?"

"I believe so, yes." Justin ran a hand over the back of his neck. "Mine and, possibly, Alex Archer's. Probably both. I don't know."

She drew away from him. "Who was your mother? Was she…" Her voice sank to a scandalized whisper. "Was she his mistress?"

"Nothing so refined as that." Justin couldn't keep the bite of anger out of his words. The last thing on earth he wanted to do was confess his disreputable origins to the daughter of an earl. Not when that lady was his wife. Not when he was coming to care for her so very, very much.

He knew she would never look at him the same way again.

"My mother was his fifteen-year-old scullery maid," he said. "Sir Oswald regularly debauched his female servants. So much so that the orphanage in Abbot's Holcombe was under his patronage. It made a convenient place to dispose of his bastards."

Helena's countenance went pale as parchment. No doubt it was the most vile, despicable thing she'd heard in her whole life.

"Forgive me," he said gruffly. "This isn't the sort of thing one speaks of in front of a lady, is it? Yet another failing you may mark down to my lack of breeding."

She didn't appear to register his apology. "What of your mother?"

He shrugged. "A child herself and happy to be rid of an unpleasant burden. She likely went on to find employment somewhere more respectable. Either that or was sent to the workhouse. I never discovered what became of her. I couldn't even manage to find out her full name. The orphanage didn't keep very good records, you see. The proprietor was one of Sir Oswald's cronies. He counted us little better than vermin."

Helena said nothing. She merely looked at him, her mahogany brows knit in an elegant line. He hadn't the slightest idea what she was thinking or feeling.

He stroked Hiran's neck. Every instinct told him to cease talking. To keep the rest of the sordid history to himself. No good could come from sharing it. But something deep within him urged him to continue. He wanted her—needed her—to know him for who he really was.

"The first time we encountered Sir Oswald, he was riding through the gates of the orphanage, mounted atop the finest piece of horseflesh we'd ever seen. His clothes were equally fine. I can still recall the gloss on his boots. A blacking made with champagne, we surmised. Something mixed up special by his valet." Justin managed a wry smile. "He rode past us like he was royalty. You can imagine the effect such a dashing figure would have on the imaginations of four young boys. Neville thought he was the king. But I—pathetic fool that I was—hoped he might be my father."

"Because you resembled him?"

"I did, in a general way. He had black hair and blue-gray eyes. And he was tall—though I suppose every man seems tall to a lad. But I'd be lying if I said that was the reason. The truth is, I'd always dreamed I was destined for better things. A lost heir or some such nonsense. I could never accept my circumstances. It had to be a mistake, I reasoned. A mix-up by a local midwife or some cruel revenge plot which resulted in my being stolen from my well-to-do parents and hidden in an orphanage." He gave a humorless chuckle. "I read a great many penny dreadfuls as a boy."

Helena didn't seem to find this fact amusing. "How did you discover who he was?"

"We followed him. We eavesdropped on his conversation with Mr. Cheevers, the fellow who ran the orphanage. Later, Finchley went through the files in the orphanage office. There wasn't much to be found there, but there was enough to confirm our suspicions. The following week, we climbed down the cliffs at Abbot's Holcombe. A fisherman kept an old boat tied in a cove nearby. We used it to row to the Abbey."

Hiran chose that moment to nudge him in the shoulder with his muzzle.

"He's growing impatient for his oats," Justin said. "We'd better start back."

He offered her his arm and she took it. Hiran walked along beside them on a loose rein.

"Why did you go to the Abbey?" Helena asked. "Was it because you wished to see him?"

"I wanted to meet him. To explain to him who I was. I thought, if he properly met me, if he could see how intelligent I was, how capable, he'd realize I didn't belong in the orphanage."

Her hand tightened on his arm. "What happened?"

"Suffice to say, it wasn't the homecoming I'd envisioned. Sir Oswald was in the garden, tending his rosebushes. He wouldn't admit to having sired me, or any of us. He wouldn't even allow us into the house. When we pressed him on the subject of our mothers, he became vulgar and abusive. He ended by cursing the lot of us and chasing us off the property."

Sir Oswald's scathing response to the mere suggestion that Justin, or any of the orphans, might come and stay at the Abbey echoed in Justin's mind.

"*Are you mad? Do you think I'd let the bastard brat of some slut of a scullery maid live in this house? You aren't fit for my stables, lad.*"

"But you kept going back," Helena said.

"So we did."

"To what purpose?"

"In the beginning? We thought we could bring him round to us. It didn't quite work out that way."

Justin refrained from sharing the precise details. There was little point in telling Helena how Sir Oswald had thrashed Archer on their next visit. Or how, on their third, he'd leveled a pistol at Justin in a drunken rage.

"After that, we began to go there purely out of spite. The very sight of us riled Sir Oswald like nothing else. We'd play on his beach and muck about in his outbuildings. We'd dig holes in his gardens, or sneak in through a half-open window and replace his liquor with seawater. Stupid childish pranks." Justin looked up at Greyfriar's Abbey looming in the distance. "It escalated from there."

"My goodness," Helena said. "He could have had you arrested. Or worse. I can't imagine why he didn't."

"Boothroyd talked him out of it."

She frowned. "I hadn't realized Mr. Boothroyd's tenure as Sir Oswald's secretary was of such long duration."

"He'd come to work at Greyfriar's Abbey a year or two earlier."

"And now he works for you," she said. "I find that very strange."

Justin could see how it might seem so. To anyone who knew the substance of Boothroyd's character, however, it made perfect sense. "He corresponded with Finchley and me over the years. He advised us on investments and the like. Boothroyd had a conscience, you see. He was a decent man—a loyal servant looking for a worthy master. It hadn't taken him long to realize what sort of man Sir Oswald was."

"Yet he remained in his employ."

"A fact he regrets to this day. You might say that working for me is his penance. God knows it's a thankless enough job."

"He *is* faithful to you," Helena conceded. "But that hardly excuses his having stood by and done nothing when you were a child."

"Don't judge him too harshly. After Neville's accident, it was Boothroyd who arranged apprenticeships for Finchley, Archer, and me. He knew it was the only way to be rid of us." Justin paused, adding, "Solving problems is Boothroyd's particular skill."

"He seems to have failed in this case. You're here now, aren't you? You own the Abbey."

"True, but it kept us out of trouble for a time. With Finchley gone to London and Neville hurt, it was just Archer and me. And then, one day, Archer was gone. He broke his apprenticeship. Disappeared without so much as a word. I could find no trace of him anywhere."

"Is that when you joined the army?" Helena asked.

He nodded.

"You must have done very well there."

"Well enough." He'd always been willing to put himself in danger. To take extraordinary risks. Some had called him heroic. The truth was, in the beginning, he simply hadn't cared whether he lived or died. As a result, he'd earned the respect of his superiors—and risen swiftly through the ranks of enlisted men.

"How did you gain your captaincy?"

"A field promotion during the early days of the rebellion."

"And Sir Oswald?"

Justin hesitated. It wasn't a pleasant story. "I went to see him one last time before I left for India. It was the only occasion I ever confronted him alone. We stood, facing each other at the top of the drive. He'd been drinking."

"How well you remember."

"I could hardly forget. It was the day he admitted that I was his son. He said some foul things about my mother, and then he laughed. He told me that no one wanted me. That I was nothing, not to him or anyone. That I never would be. That's when I promised him—" Justin broke off.

The memory left a taste in his mouth as bitter as poison. Never before, not even in his darkest days in the orphanage, could he recall having felt so alone. So unwanted. So *angry*.

"What did you promise?" Helena asked softly.

Justin looked down at her. "That I would come back to Devon one day. And that, when I did, I wouldn't just take Greyfriar's Abbey from him. I would take everything."

Chapter Fifteen

Helena's mind was in turmoil. She spent the rest of the morning on her own. She required time to think. To make sense of everything. She needed to make a decision about her future.

Such serious thinking was no small matter. She was restless with it. Unable to be still. She went to her room and sorted out her clothes. Her underthings would have to be laundered. As for her gowns...

She held up her other gray silk dress to the light, examining the wrinkles in the fabric and the stains on the bodice and skirts. Dirt, merely. A remnant of her tramp out in the rain yesterday and her ill-advised encounter with Justin's muddy clothes.

"Gin," Mrs. Standish said when she arrived to take away the laundry. "If there's any left after Mrs. Whitlock's had her tipple."

Helena shot the housekeeper a questioning glance. "Gin?"

Mrs. Standish draped Helena's soiled petticoats over her arm. "A boiled mixture of gin, soft soap, and honey. I'll brush it over the stains. After it's soaked awhile, I'll give the silk a good sponging." She narrowed her eyes at the gray silk dress Helena was currently wearing. "Those stains will be more difficult."

Helena looked down at her skirts. Among the wrinkles and horsehair, she saw what looked to be oil stains. "Can you get them out?"

"They'll need pipe clay, my lady. Or French chalk." Mrs. Standish waited for Helena to strip out of her bodice and skirts. "I'm not a lady's maid, ma'am."

"No, indeed." Helena handed the housekeeper her dress. "Thank you, Mrs. Standish."

There was little point in explaining why she presently had no lady's maid of her own, and really no need to do so. Mrs. Standish was the sort of servant who'd think less of her for making excuses. She'd only softened toward Helena when she'd heard Boothroyd referring to her as "my lady." She expected a certain amount of aristocratic disdain.

It was not Helena's way. She'd never been particularly top lofty with servants. They mayn't have been her friends or her family, but in the absence of her mother, the staff at the family seat in Hampshire had looked after her. The cook had spoiled her with chocolate and biscuits in the kitchens. And the housekeeper had fussed over her like an old mother hen.

She would never look down on Justin because of his parentage. The fact that his mother had been a scullery maid in Sir Oswald's household troubled her, it was true, but not because she was concerned with matters of wealth, rank, and breeding. It troubled her because it troubled Justin. The circumstances of his birth were clearly a source of pain to him.

It had seemed inadvisable to offer him words of comfort. Justin wasn't the sort of gentleman who would appreciate a lady's pity. But as he'd told her about his mother, and about his childhood hopes and dreams, she'd ached with sympathy for him.

Their upbringings couldn't have been more different. She hadn't been an orphan, and she certainly hadn't been poor, but she could understand loneliness. She'd felt enough of it in her life. And after Giles had left for India…

She'd spent far too much time being listless and brooding. It was no wonder people had been so willing to believe she'd inherited her mother's melancholy.

Would they be equally as willing to believe she was well? If they saw her in London, attending the theatre or dancing at a ball, would it be enough to convince them?

Her mind conjured an image of waltzing with Justin in a gaslit ballroom. She in a sleeveless, low-necked dress trimmed in Honiton lace and he in an elegant black evening suit, whirling about the floor to the swelling sounds of a twenty-piece orchestra.

A romantic daydream, nothing more. But it caught at her heart.

She'd always been somewhat reserved with people. It wasn't in her nature to giggle and flirt. Nevertheless, she'd once taken great pleasure in the entertainments of the season. She'd attended the theatre, played the pianoforte at recitals, and danced in crowded ballrooms. It had been expected of her. And she'd never minded it. She'd always been sure of herself and of her place in the world.

If only she could return to London with Justin and be as she once was. Confident and carefree. There were so many things she'd like to show him. So much she longed to experience with him at her side.

Why must it be a daydream? Why couldn't such pleasures be real?

All it wanted was a little courage, Justin had said. Courage enough for her to face her uncle and Mr. Glyde. Courage enough to speak to the man at the newspaper. To risk her reputation.

Was a chance at happiness—at freedom—worth such an outrageous gamble?

She slipped on her one remaining dress and, after arranging her skirts over her crinoline and adjusting the plum velvet ribbon at her waist, she made her way downstairs. She found Justin in the library with Mr. Boothroyd, dictating a letter.

He'd changed from his riding clothes into black woolen trousers, a clean white linen shirt, and a black waistcoat. His frock coat was disposed over the back of a nearby chair. As if he'd removed it while working.

He didn't hear her enter, but as she crossed the floor to the window, he turned his head and looked at her.

"Please don't mind me." She retrieved the copy of *David Copperfield* she'd been reading the previous day and settled herself in the window embrasure, her legs drawn up under her skirts.

After a long moment, Justin resumed dictating his letter. His voice was a deep, rich baritone. The lines of her book blurred in front of her as she listened. The substance of his words was unimportant. Something about a board of directors and a percentage of railway shares. But it didn't matter what he said or to whom he was saying it. It was his tone which soothed her. The same tone in which he'd recited his marriage vows to her.

"Mr. Fothergill will require a duplicate of that," he said to Mr. Boothroyd. "And see that Mr. St. John's solicitor gets a copy."

She gazed out the window. The rain had stopped for good, or so it seemed. How many days would it take for the cliff road to be passable?

And how many days before Mr. Glyde would once again make an appearance?

The familiar fear settled over her. She tried to suppress it. To drive it back with cold rationality. She was married now. Justin would never let anyone take her. He'd promised her that.

Even so, she couldn't help but worry.

There was no guarantee that Mr. Finchley's scheme would work. In the end, the cost to her reputation—and to her peace of mind—might all be for nothing. She could be ostracized. Or worse. Her uncle could seize control of her again and have her locked away somewhere.

But what was the alternative? A lifetime of living in fear of her uncle and Mr. Glyde? Of peering out of windows? Never knowing from one day to the next whether or not she was safe.

Was such a life even worth living?

She resumed reading her book. Her nerves were all a-jangle, but she was determined to forget her problems, even if only for a while.

Several absorbing chapters later, she heard the library doors close behind Mr. Boothroyd. She marked her place in her book and set it aside as Justin came to stand in front of her.

His expression was guarded. "Are you enjoying your novel?"

"Very much," she said. "I confess, I've read it before."

"Of course you have." He leaned his shoulder against the window frame. "You seem very comfortable here."

"I hope I'm not disrupting your work."

"Not at all. Though I do think it must be boring for you. Trapped here in this house, with nothing to do but read books you've already read."

"I'm not bored."

"Not even after listening to me drone on about the North Devon Railway?"

She smiled. "I like hearing your voice."

At her admission, a faint flush of color appeared at Justin's neck. She could see it, gradually creeping above the line of his turned-down shirt collar and sensibly tied black cravat.

He cleared his throat. "I hadn't realized it was so affecting."

His embarrassment only served to feed her own. She felt her cheeks warming. "You'll tease me mercilessly now, won't you?"

"I shall be sorely tempted." He sat down next to her. The hem of her skirts brushed his thigh. He gave the rose-colored fabric a soft tug with his fingers. "This dress again."

"It's the only one that's clean. Mrs. Standish is washing the two others I brought with me. She's going to treat the ordinary stains with gin."

"Have we any?"

"She isn't certain. She says Mrs. Whitlock may have drunk it all."

"True enough." His eyes found hers. There was no humor in them. "Helena...About those things I told you on the beach..."

"Yes?"

"I beg your pardon for speaking so candidly. It was badly done of me."

"Don't be silly. I asked you about your past. I want to know. Naturally, I didn't mind your telling me."

"You disappeared afterward."

"Because I needed time to think," she said. "Which I have done."

"And?"

"It wasn't easy for you to share all of that with me, was it? The truth about Sir Oswald and your mother and your friends from the orphanage."

"There are certainly more pleasant topics."

She uncurled her legs from beneath her and shook out her skirts. "Yes, well…it's made me think about our situation. About *my* situation. Which is selfish, really. Except that our lives are now so inextricably tied together." She took a breath. "What I'm trying to say is I've decided that, yes, I will go to London with you. I'll speak to the gentleman at the paper."

Justin fell silent for a moment. His expression was solemn, his gray gaze holding hers with greater than usual intensity. "What changed your mind?"

"When I hear how thoroughly you've persevered, how brave you've been, it makes me feel brave, too. I'm not brave, though, am I? I'm scared to death of going back. But I'll do it. Only…I'll probably cling on your arm even worse than I did when we were riding on Hiran."

He took her hand in his, engulfing it in the strong clasp of his fingers. Butterflies fluttered in her stomach as he raised it to his lips and pressed a kiss to her knuckles.

"What was that for?" she asked.

"For trusting me. In spite of it all."

She pressed his hand. "I do trust you, Justin. With all my heart."

Over the next two days, as the roads dried out, preparations for their journey to London began in earnest. Financial arrangements were made, clothes were laundered and packed, and Boothroyd and Neville were both given instructions on managing things in Justin's absence.

The morning of their departure, Danvers brought the carriage round to the front of the Abbey. "We'll drive to the railway station in Abbot's Holcombe," Justin explained as he handed Helena up into the cab. He climbed in after her, settling in the opposite seat. "It's a shorter distance than driving all the way to Barnstaple."

Helena looked out the window. She didn't appear to be fully attending what he was saying. Her face was pale, her gloved hands twisted together in her lap.

Danvers gave the horses the office to start. The antiquated carriage rolled forward with a shudder.

"We can wire Finchley to let him know we're on our way," Justin went on. "No doubt he's already found us a house to let for the duration of our stay."

"Was he that certain I would agree to come?"

"Finchley always plans for every eventuality. He's much like Boothroyd in that respect."

Helena fell quiet for a moment. Her expression was shadowed. "A house in a fashionable street will be expensive. And we don't yet know if the bank will release any of my funds."

"Let me worry about expenses."

She gave him a pained glance. "There will be so many of them."

Justin well knew it. Boothroyd had been subtly reminding him of that fact for the past several days. "It doesn't signify. Finchley and I have everything well in hand."

Or so Justin hoped.

He knew precious little about fashionable society. He knew even less about the law. In truth, he half expected a dozen of the earl's solicitors to greet them on their arrival in London and produce legal documents that not only dissolved his marriage to Helena, but gave them the authority to take her away. He could too easily imagine what it would feel like to stand there watching, powerless to help her.

He'd been in that position before.

But this wasn't Cawnpore. It was England. And Finchley *did* know the law. He was confident in the plan he'd proposed. Boothroyd had given the plan his vote of approval as well. All Justin had to do was execute it. What could possibly go wrong?

Everything, he thought grimly.

But it wouldn't do to dwell on worst-case scenarios. Not when Helena's nerves were already taut as a bowstring.

He made an effort to turn the conversation to more trivial topics, keeping up a constant—and quite uncharacteristic—patter until they arrived at the station in Abbot's Holcombe.

After disembarking from the carriage, they stopped at the booking office to purchase two first-class tickets. True to her word, Helena clung fast to his arm. She was frightened and trying hard not to show it.

"We've a half hour until the train arrives," Justin said. "Would you like to stop at the bookstall? They have penny novels. You could get one for the journey."

She shook her head. "I couldn't read a word. I'm far too nervous."

He covered her gloved hand with his, giving it a reassuring squeeze.

The train arrived at ten past eleven in a cacophony of screeching metal, smoke, and steam. A crowd of passengers disembarked, ladies and gentleman of every description rushing this way and that. It was nowhere near as crowded as King's Cross or Waterloo Station in London, but it was far busier than Justin had anticipated. For once, he was grateful for his imposing height. He easily caught the attention of one of the porters and summoned him to load their luggage onto the train.

"That's our carriage, just there," he murmured to Helena. "We can board in a moment. You'll feel more at ease when we've taken our seats."

They walked down the platform toward the first-class railway carriage. A group of ladies was huddled together nearby, talking loudly amongst themselves. As Justin and Helena passed, he saw one of them detach herself from the group.

"Can it be?" she exclaimed. "What a mercy. Look, Mama. It's Thornhill. And that must be his new bride!"

For an instant, time stood still. Justin might have been an orphan boy, newly apprenticed, hearing the shrill voices of Mrs. Bray and her daughter as they heaped abuse on him.

But the two ladies who approached looked nothing like the ones in his memory.

Mrs. Bray's hair had turned gray and her sturdy figure had gone to fat. She was clad in unrelieved black, a jet brooch pinned at her jiggling throat. Cecilia Bray was likewise garbed in black, her taffeta skirts stretched over an enormous wire crinoline. She was still possessed of the golden curls and pouting lips that had marked her as a village beauty in her youth; however, next to Helena, such paltry charms appeared decidedly second-rate.

There was no way to avoid introductions.

"Helena," he said. "May I present Mrs. Bray and her daughter? I was apprenticed to Mrs. Bray's husband for a time when I was a boy. Madam? Allow me to introduce—"

"Your wife," Mrs. Bray interrupted. "We know all about your marriage, sir." Her gimlet eyes fixed on Helena, examining her with undisguised curiosity. "You're an earl's daughter, are you? Don't know how you ever met Thornhill."

Miss Bray tittered. "Oh, Mama. Where are your manners?" She turned to Helena and, to Justin's astonishment, dropped a deep curtsy. "I'm honored, your ladyship."

Helena responded to the ludicrous gesture with a subtle inclination of her head. "Miss Bray."

"Oh, no." She tittered again. "I haven't been Miss Bray in donkey's years. I'm Mrs. Pettypiece now. My husband owns the draper's shop in Abercrombie Street." She slanted a cool glance at Justin, adding, "He's ever so rich."

Justin didn't know any draper by the name of Pettypiece. He nevertheless felt a flash of pity for the man.

"If you haven't yet been to the shops here in Abbot's Holcombe, Cecilia will gladly accompany you," Mrs. Bray said. "You'll be lamenting the lack of society, living at the Abbey.

You *are* living at the Abbey, aren't you? A cold, dank place, far past its days of glory. Not a proper residence for a lady, as my daughter can tell you."

Mrs. Pettypiece nodded vigorously. "The best people hereabouts live in Abbot's Holcombe," she informed Helena. "You may take my word for it. I was once friendly with a viscount's daughter. Miss Elizabeth Parker. Do you know her, my lady? She moved in the very best circles."

"I've not had the pleasure," Helena said.

"Hmm." Mrs. Pettypiece touched a finger to her chin. "Let me see… Who else am I acquainted with in the peerage?"

Justin's eyes narrowed. Good God. Had the Bray women always been such toadeaters? "If you'll forgive us, madam. We have a train to catch."

"Are you traveling first class?" Mrs. Pettypiece inquired of Helena. "That *is* the first-class carriage, isn't it?"

"First class." Mrs. Bray clucked her tongue. "Thornhill always did put on airs. When I saw the announcement of his marriage—"

Justin's attention snapped to Mrs. Bray. "What announcement?"

"It's in this morning's paper." Mrs. Pettypiece gave a little laugh, her eyes averted from his face. "Didn't you know?"

Justin exchanged a glance with Helena. "Finchley," he said under his breath.

Helena nodded. "Perhaps we should procure a newspaper?"

She didn't need to ask twice. After bidding a curt adieu to Mrs. Bray and her daughter, he and Helena walked back to the bookstand. He purchased a copy of the *North Devon Post*.

Helena leaned over his arm as he rifled through the pages. The announcements of births, marriages, and deaths were located at the back.

"Here it is." He straightened the page, holding it up so they could both read it at the same time.

On the 27th September at the District Registrar's Office in Abbot's Holcombe, Burlington-street, Captain Justin Thornhill, of King's Abbot, to Lady Helena Elaine Reynolds, daughter of the late Earl of Castleton, Hampshire.

Helena drew back with a short, anxious laugh. "You were right. Mr. Finchley *is* thorough."

"He's making sure everything appears aboveboard." Justin's brow furrowed as he read the marriage announcement over again. "See here? This is a reprint. The original announcement appeared in the *Times* three days ago."

Helena's hand tightened on his forearm. "My uncle takes the *Times*."

"It won't have been news to him. He'd have already heard of our marriage from Mr. Glyde."

Helena looked troubled, but there was no time to discuss the matter. The stationmaster was already calling out the first warning for the London train. At the sound of his shout, they began making their way toward the first-class railway carriage.

Mrs. Bray and her daughter were still standing on the platform. Justin tipped his hat to them as they passed.

He'd always imagined that if he encountered them again, he'd feel the same storm of emotion he'd felt as a child. The same sense of helpless rage at the injustice of his situation. Now, in their presence, he was obliged to acknowledge a hard truth.

The old hurt at how they'd treated him was gone. Even the longing he'd had as a boy, the deep desire to be included in their family, had faded away to nothing. They were just two silly females. Strangers, really. And yet…

The anger still remained.

He was reluctant to let it go. He'd nursed old grievances for far too long. They'd been his guiding light since his childhood. His impetus for bettering himself, for accumulating his modest fortune. Without them, he had a sense that he'd become unmoored. Lost in a great pit of nothingness.

"What a peculiar pair of women," Helena said once they'd settled across from each other on the train.

Their compartment was paneled in rich, dark wood. The floor was carpeted and there were parcel racks installed above the upholstered seats. It was a level of luxury reserved for first-class carriages, and only then for those on newer trains.

"By peculiar, I assume you mean odious," he said.

"I'd certainly never say *that*." A suppressed laugh vibrated in her voice. The sound of it made Justin smile.

He liked to think he could make her laugh. He didn't much care how he accomplished it. "You don't have to. I'll say it."

Helena untied her bonnetstrings. "Have they always been so unpleasant?"

"I confess, they seemed more so in my youth." Justin dropped his tall beaver hat on the seat cushion beside him. "They never looked at me, did you notice? Not if they could help it."

"They seemed rather fascinated with my honorific."

"They were. But it wasn't only that." Justin ran a hand over his rumpled hair. At his right side, elegant fabric shades with tassel pulls were drawn up to reveal newly washed windows. He could see his reflection within the glass. The sight of it made him grimace. "It's the burn scars."

"Nonsense," Helena said. "One hardly notices them."

She removed her bonnet. Her hair was parted in the center, the bulk of it drawn back into an oversized roll at her nape. A few curling strands had worked loose at her temples and cheek. She smoothed them back into her coiffure with an expert hand.

His own hand clenched at his side. She was achingly lovely; imbuing even the most commonplace tasks with an elegance and femininity that made his heart beat faster.

"You noticed them," he said. "The day we met in King's Abbot."

She made a dismissive sound. "For precisely five seconds. Such things fade away when you get to know a person."

"Do they?"

"In my experience." She straightened her skirts. "Do the scars bother you so much?"

"Sometimes, when they pull or ache. But the appearance of them…no. I never much cared how they looked until the day you arrived."

Her brows lifted. "What on earth have I to do with it?"

"I feared they would put you off."

She gave him a look of gentle reproof. "You were afraid you repulsed me. That's what you said at the inn."

Good God, had he? "It feels like a lifetime ago."

She rested her hands in her lap. She was still wearing her gloves. They were made of fine kidskin, secured at her wrists with delicate, pearl-sized buttons. "I nearly told you the truth that day, did you know that? About my uncle and Mr. Glyde."

"I wish you would have."

"And if I had…would you still have married me?"

Justin stilled. Her question hung in the air between them for several uncomfortable seconds. He couldn't bring himself to lie to her. "I don't know," he admitted.

Helena turned her head to gaze out the window. He could no longer see her eyes. He couldn't tell if his words had hurt her. "When all of this is over," she said, "I'll consent to an annulment, if that's what you wish."

His heart stopped. *What in blazes?* He sat up straighter in his seat, his body tensing, as if anticipating a blow. "Is that what *you* wish?"

"I haven't thought that far ahead. I can't. Not with all that's looming in front of me. I'm already overwhelmed." Her throat contracted in a visible swallow. "But you needn't worry I'll hold you to your vows. Not when they were given under false pretenses. If you want to dissolve our marriage, I'll agree to it without any fuss. I owe you that much."

His jaw hardened. Bloody hell. Is that what she believed? That she was in debt to him somehow? Was that the reason for her kindness? For her kisses? "You don't owe me anything."

"Don't I? You've saved my life on more than one occasion. First by marrying me and then by rescuing me from the cliffs." She looked at him briefly. "I owe you everything, Justin."

He frowned. "No," he said, shaking his head. "No. That isn't how any of this works. It isn't a tabulation of debts and repayments. I advertised for a wife and you answered. It doesn't signify what drove you to it. That ceased to matter the moment we exchanged vows in Abbot's Holcombe. We're married now, in law if not in deed. I'd walk through fire for you, and you wouldn't owe me a thing."

She finally turned from the window. "Because I'm your wife."

"Yes. And because you're you. A lady who makes me smile. Who's kind and thoughtful and loyal as all hell. A lady whose hand fits perfectly in mine. And who returns my kisses so very sweetly. For all of those reasons, yes. I'd go to the ends of the earth for you, Helena. You must know that."

A flush of color worked its way from her throat all the way to the roots of her hair. She bent her head. "I-I didn't know."

Justin tugged at the knot of his cravat, brutally suppressing a swell of embarrassment. He wasn't accustomed to making pretty speeches. "Well, you do now," he said gruffly. "No more secrets, remember?"

"I remember." She worried the finger of one of her gloves. "And I like you very much, too, Justin. For those exact same reasons. I hope we might be friends."

"We *are* friends."

Her blush deepened. "Then I hope we might be more."

Their eyes met and Justin felt his heart lurch back to life. It pounded swiftly. Painfully. "We are," he said again.

The train chose that moment to grind into motion. A shrill whistle pierced the air and the conductor shouted, his words unintelligible over the roar of the engine. Their railway carriage rattled as the train began moving slowly on the track.

Helena's fingers tightened together in her lap.

There was no turning back now. Their journey to London had officially begun.

Justin rose and moved to take the empty seat beside her. "You seem very far away all of a sudden. Here. Take my hand."

She flicked an anxious glance out the window as she slipped her hand into his. The train was picking up speed, rapidly leaving the station behind. "I feel like Daniel must have felt, walking into the lion's den."

"You're a little scared, that's all."

"I'm petrified."

"But you're not alone. Far from it. You have Finchley on your side. And Miss Holloway."

"And you." She pressed his hand.

"And me." He returned the firm clasp of her fingers. "For as long as you require, in whatever manner you require."

Chapter Sixteen

London, England
October, 1859

"There's been a slight change of plans in regard to your lodgings," Mr. Finchley said as they stood outside of Waterloo Station. The cabstand was nearby, but he didn't hail a hansom. The three of them would never have fit inside one. Instead, he raised his hand to a coachman who was sitting on the perch of a four-wheeler parked across the way.

The coachman brought the carriage round and waited as they all bundled in. There was wet straw on the floor of the cab and the interior smelled heavily of cheap perfume. Helena was tempted to press her handkerchief to her nose.

"What do you mean?" Justin asked. He was seated beside her on the forward-facing seat.

Mr. Finchley sat across from them. He was wearing a handsome wool overcoat and carrying a silver-topped walking stick.

He looked a great deal more fashionable than when Helena had seen him last. "There was some difficulty in finding a house to let," he said. "But it's nothing to concern yourselves with. Not when there's a perfectly suitable residence available in Half Moon Street."

"With Jenny?" Helena's mood brightened a little.

"If that's acceptable to all parties." Mr. Finchley exchanged a glance with Justin. "It's a genteel enough address for our purposes, and there's plenty of room. I've hired a skeleton staff. People I know and trust."

Mr. Finchley's idea of a skeleton staff was a stern-faced married couple of middle years who looked like they'd seen a fair bit of hardship. The husband was to act as both butler and footman, and the wife was to perform the duties of a cook-housekeeper.

Helena hardly noticed them. When they arrived at the little house in Half Moon Street, she went straight to Jenny, enfolding her friend in a fierce embrace.

Jenny hugged her tightly. "You reek of cheap scent," she said with a laugh. "But how well you look."

Helena took a step back to examine her friend. Jenny was wearing a sensible, unflounced poplin skirt and a black velvet caraco. The loose, thigh-length jacket nipped in at her waist and flared down over her hips. She didn't look any the worse for her altercation with Uncle Edward, but Helena knew that looks could be deceiving. "Are *you* well?"

Jenny smiled. "He didn't touch me. I promise."

Helena saw nothing about which to smile. "It's quite enough that he shouted at you and turned you out."

"I'll admit, it wasn't pleasant. But I'm not made of spun sugar. You know that. Besides, I was far more worried about you." Jenny held out her hand. "Come upstairs with me. I have something to show you."

Helena looked back at Justin. He and Mr. Finchley were talking quietly with each other, their faces serious. He caught her gaze and smiled slightly.

"Go ahead," he said.

"Must you ask his permission?" Jenny inquired in a low voice as they climbed up the stairs to the third floor.

"No. Of course not. But I've been clinging to him awfully since we left Devon. I'm amazed he has any circulation left in his arm."

"You do like him then?"

"I do," Helena said. "Rather too much."

"There's no such thing as too much, is there? Unless he doesn't like you back. In which case, you must at least try to appear indifferent." Jenny drew Helena into one of the bed-rooms. "Look."

It was a large room with an equally large curtained bed. On the opposite wall, a tall pier-glass mirror was mounted between two windows draped in chintz. On the left an oil lamp with a cut-glass shade reposed on a marble-topped walnut chiffonier. On the right was a dressing table and an oversized burled walnut wardrobe. The doors of the wardrobe were open, revealing a profusion of muslin, fine woolens, and silk.

Helena's jaw dropped in amazement. "My clothes!"

"They were delivered yesterday," Jenny said. "Everything but your jewels. Lord Castleton has taken to keeping those in his safe."

"But how...?" Helena went to the wardrobe, her gaze skimming over the familiar petticoats, bodices, and skirts. Some articles of clothing hung on pegs installed at the back of the wardrobe, others were folded on the wardrobe shelves, each item carefully separated by tissue paper. "Uncle Edward can't have allowed it."

"Heavens, no. It was Mrs. Butterfield who arranged it. She had Martha and Maisy pack everything in trunks while your uncle was at his club. Two of the footmen carried the trunks down and put them in a hired carriage."

Mrs. Butterfield had been the housekeeper at the Earl of Castleton's residence in Grosvenor Square for many long years. She'd served Helena's father and then her brother and had seemed happy to continue in service to Helena's uncle when he ascended to the title. She'd never once indicated, neither by word nor deed, that she disapproved of Uncle Edward's cruelties.

"I wouldn't have thought Mrs. Butterfield would take such a risk," Helena said. "She's never been anything but loyal to my uncle."

"Mrs. Butterfield is loyal to all the Earls of Castleton. That doesn't mean she's without a conscience."

Helena refrained from commenting. Her final months living in her uncle's house had been a living nightmare. She couldn't recall any of the staff being remotely sympathetic. Indeed, most of them—including Mrs. Butterfield—had been unable to look her in the eye.

"I've put most of your things away," Jenny said. "I'll finish unpacking for you this afternoon. I intend to play lady's maid, you know."

"Don't be silly."

"I'm in dead earnest. Do you think Mrs. Jarrow has the first inkling of how to arrange a lady's hair? She can cook, though, I'll give her that. And she's a dab hand at the mending." Jenny straightened one of the little glass cosmetic pots on the dressing table. "Mrs. Jarrow and her husband would do anything for Mr. Finchley. He saved their son from going to prison."

"Did he?" Helena glanced at Jenny. "How?"

"By writing a legal paper. A brief or some kind of argument. I don't understand it. Neither do Mr. and Mrs. Jarrow, frankly. Most of what Mr. Finchley does seems a mystery."

Helena wandered around the room, taking in the heavy furnishings, thick carpet, and patterned wallpaper.

Jenny trailed after her, still talking. "Take this house, for example. Mr. Finchley insisted on having it. I told him I'd be quite happy with a room in a boarding house somewhere, but he wouldn't be dissuaded."

"He thought you'd be safer here."

"Even so…" Jenny sat down on the edge of the bed. "I shouldn't have permitted him to spend a single penny on my behalf. It's utterly scandalous to be in debt to a single gentleman. If word got out, I would be ruined."

"You're not in debt to Mr. Finchley." Helena sank down beside Jenny. The counterpane rumpled beneath their combined weight. "Justin has taken over the lease. Didn't he tell you?"

"It doesn't change the fact that I've been living here for the past week. *And* I've been permitting Mr. Finchley to visit. Everyone on the street will have seen him entering the house. They'll think I'm his fancy woman."

"Foolish people. He might be your brother."

A rare blush tinted Jenny's cheeks. "It doesn't feel as if he's my brother."

Helena lifted her brows. "He hasn't made any overtures, has he?"

"Not a single one," Jenny said with a grimace. She waved her hand in a dismissive gesture. "But let's not talk about him. I want to hear about you. Tell me everything about Greyfriar's Abbey. And about Mr. Thornhill, too."

Helena spent the next half hour describing life at the Abbey. She talked about the cliffs and the sea and appalling weather. She talked about Mr. Boothroyd, Neville, the servants, and the dogs. She even talked about the night Mr. Glyde had arrived with the magistrate.

But despite Jenny's request, she shared little about Justin. Her conversations with him were too private. Too precious. And she certainly wasn't going to discuss his kisses. Not even with a bosom friend.

"You sound as if you're happy there," Jenny said when she'd finished.

Helena smoothed a wrinkle in the counterpane, her thoughts drifting back to the grim reality of her situation. "I think I could be. If only—"

"If only you were free of your uncle and Mr. Glyde." Jenny paused. "I saw him yesterday."

Helena's gaze snapped to hers. "My uncle?"

"No. Mr. Glyde. He was walking in Piccadilly, as bold as you please. The great brute. I had half a mind to shove him in front of an omnibus."

"He didn't see you, did he?"

Jenny shook her head. "I was very careful."

Helena rose from the edge of the mattress. She began to pace the room. "You can't underestimate him, Jenny. I know he looks like a stupid lummox, but he's dangerous. Not to mention, he has a grip like an iron vise. Only recall how he used to grab my arms and haul me about. I still have the bruises."

"At least he never throttled you. Not like your uncle did that day."

"Uncle Edward was out of temper. He'd been drinking and he'd just lost a fortune in play. He was desperate for me to sign those papers."

Jenny's eyes kindled. "Don't you dare make excuses for him! He might have killed you. I thought he had for a moment."

Helena didn't like to think of it. Her uncle had grasped her throat and shaken her like a terrier might shake a rat. She'd been paralyzed with terror. Unable to scream. Unable to breathe.

"I'm not making excuses. I'm simply stating a fact. My uncle may be devious and even violent on occasion, but Mr. Glyde is ruthless. He came all the way to the Abbey in the middle of a storm, Jenny. He's determined to drag me back to Uncle Edward so he can lock me away somewhere and throw away the key."

"He won't succeed." Justin's deep voice sounded from the door.

Helena turned abruptly, her pulse leaping at the sight of him.

He didn't enter the bedroom. Merely stood there, his shoulder propped lazily against the doorframe. "Come downstairs to the parlor," he said. "Finchley would like to speak with you."

"That's your plan?" Helena stared at Mr. Finchley, incredulous. "To keep my uncle tied up with legal documents until the newspaper article goes to print?"

She was seated next to Jenny on an overstuffed chintz sofa in the parlor. Mr. Finchley was in a chair across from them, the pomade in his dark brown hair gleaming in the light of the gas lamps. Only Justin remained standing. He leaned against the carved mantelshelf, idly turning a little lacquered box in his hand. Helena had no doubt but that he was listening to the proceedings with rapt attention.

"It's not foolproof," Mr. Finchley said. "Indeed, it's rather flimsy on its face. Nothing has yet been submitted to the courts. At this stage it's little more than a furious exchange of letters between Castleton's attorneys and myself. The point is, they understand there's a strong legal basis for our claim."

Helena was at a loss. "What claim? I thought we weren't going to engage my uncle in the courts."

"We aren't. But his attorneys don't know that. As far as they're concerned, the battle has been engaged."

She gave him a bewildered look.

Mr. Finchley leaned forward in his chair. "Think of it like this. You are, essentially, a piece of property, the ownership of which is in dispute."

A spark of indignation stiffened her spine. "I don't care to think of myself as a piece of property, sir."

"It's not a personal aspersion, my lady. It's a legal reality. In the eyes of courts, you're the property of your husband. Your uncle's only hope of gaining control of you—and thereby your fortune—is to first prove that your marriage to Thornhill is invalid. His attorneys strike me as competent fellows. They'll have advised him to steer clear of you until the courts have had their say in the matter."

"In other words," Justin said, "your uncle shouldn't be coming to our door with the magistrate anytime soon."

"Or so we hope." Mr. Finchley briefly removed his spectacles. "Unfortunately, it won't stop him from sending one of his henchmen to abduct you and spirit you away to a private asylum somewhere."

Justin returned the lacquered box to the mantelshelf. "Which is why you're not, on any account, to leave this house unaccompanied."

Helena compressed her lips. His property, indeed. But she wouldn't dispute the sense of his edict. "You needn't worry about that. I have no desire to go anywhere without you."

Mr. Finchley's legal stratagem didn't make her feel very much safer. She still spent the evening pacing and peering out the window of her bedroom. Only by repeatedly reminding herself of Justin's presence in the adjoining room and of Jenny's presence down the hall could she finally get to sleep.

The next morning, Mr. Finchley returned to the house in Half Moon Street. He wasn't alone. With him was a handsome dark-haired gentleman possessed of the bluest eyes Helena had ever seen.

"Lady Helena," Mr. Finchley said. "May I present Mr. Charles Pelham?"

Helena shook Mr. Pelham's hand. He was of a height with Justin, with a serious face and a gaze so penetrating it felt as if he were attempting to plumb the depths of her soul.

And perhaps he was.

"Shall we all repair to the parlor?" Jenny asked. "Unless you'd prefer to speak to Mr. Pelham alone."

The notion of sharing the details of her ordeal in front of a room full of people made Helena slightly nauseated. But these weren't strangers. They were her friends. People who cared for her.

"That won't be necessary," she said.

Justin's hand found the small of her back as they all made their way upstairs. She hadn't had a moment alone with him since they disembarked from the train. She missed him. Which was stupid, really. He hadn't gone anywhere. At any given moment, he was no more than a room away. And yet…

Somehow, in a very short span of time, his presence had become essential to her happiness. To her sense of safety and well-being. She needed to be with him. To hear his voice and feel the touch of his hand holding hers.

Would he think less of her when he learned the full extent of the indignities to which she'd been subjected? Would he feel that it tainted her, somehow?

It was how she felt herself. As if she'd been stained with a foul substance that couldn't be washed away.

Justin's hand fell from her back when they entered the parlor. He stood nearby as she situated herself on the sofa, but he didn't sit beside her. He would have had to displace Jenny. Instead, he strolled to the coal fireplace at the opposite side of the room and leaned against the carved mantelshelf as he had the previous evening.

Mrs. Jarrow brought them tea and Jenny poured. Helena's hands were trembling too badly to hold the teapot.

Mr. Pelham took no more than a sip before he returned his teacup to the tray and withdrew a small notebook and pencil from an inner pocket of his coat. He looked at her steadily. "I can ask you questions, if you prefer, but it might be easier for you if you simply started your tale at the beginning."

Helena moistened her lips. "Very well."

The gilt-trimmed clock on the mantelshelf chimed eleven o'clock.

When it chimed twelve, she was still talking.

Mr. Pelham occasionally asked a question or requested clarification, but the majority of the time he merely listened—all the while jotting notes in his little book.

"You describe the first treatment at Lowbridge House as a cold water treatment," he said at one point. "Can you explain what that entailed?"

Helena nodded. "If you like." She folded her hands in her lap. They were shaking quite out of control. "The matrons at Lowbridge would put me into a tub filled with ice cold water. There was a…a sort of lid. It had a hole in one end for a person's head. It allowed them to keep a patient in the cold water for as long as they pleased. Mr. Glyde said—"

Mr. Pelham raised his head from his notebook. "Mr. Glyde was present during this treatment?"

"Yes. It's part of the reason my uncle employs him. Whenever I resisted one of the treatments, he would take me by the arms and shake me into compliance. Then, when I was quite subdued, he would drag me wherever it was I'd been ordered to go. At Lowbridge, when I wouldn't…when I wouldn't undress and get into the tub, the matrons called him. He—" She broke off, briefly losing her composure.

Jenny took her hand and squeezed it. "It's not decent. You shouldn't have to repeat it."

"It's your choice, my lady," Mr. Pelham said quietly. "But know this: you are not alone. I've spoken to countless others, both men and women, who have been subjected to equally appalling treatments at private asylums just like Lowbridge House."

Helena gave him an almost imperceptible nod. "It's all right, Jenny. I need to finish." She gently extricated her hand and folded it back in her lap.

She wanted to do this on her own, without clinging to Jenny or Justin. It seemed somehow important that she maintain a sense of independence—of control—in the telling of her story, however illusory that control might be.

"Mr. Glyde was outside with the carriage," she continued. "The matrons summoned him and, with his help, they… they stripped me down to my shift and…forced me into the tub. They put the lid over me, trapping me inside." Her voice trembled, but she kept on. "There was n-no way to get out. I was frozen. Numb. I b-begged them to let me go, but it only strengthened their resolve to keep me in the water. Mr. Glyde said he knew of a lunatic who'd once been kept in the cold baths for three days straight."

Mr. Pelham looked up at her, his expression grave. "How long were you kept in the bath?"

"Two hours, that first time."

"And subsequent cold water baths?"

Helena shot a brief glance at Justin. He was still standing by the mantelshelf. His arms were crossed, his jaw hardened. Even from a distance, she could see the rhythmic spasm of a muscle working in his cheek. "Three, maybe four hours," she said. "One loses count."

"Were these cold baths always administered at the asylum?" Mr. Pelham asked.

"Yes. It was only the bleeding and the electrotherapy that were done at Grosvenor Square."

"By Dr. Collins, Lord Castleton's private physician?"

"That's correct."

Mr. Pelham's pencil flew across the pages of his notebook. She wondered if he was writing in shorthand. "I'll need you to describe those treatments as well," he said. "I understand it's difficult."

Mr. Finchley withdrew his pocket watch and looked at the time before dropping it back into the pocket of his waistcoat without a word. He'd remained silent throughout the interview, sitting nearby with a notebook of his own in which he occasionally jotted something down.

"Are you able to go on?" Mr. Pelham asked her.

Helena assured him that she was. She spent the next hour telling him everything about the other treatments to which she'd been subjected. The leeches and lancets which had bled her until she was faint and listless. The purgatives which had left her sick and weak. And the electric shocks which had terrified her almost as much as the ice baths at Lowbridge House.

"Dr. Collins had an electrotherapy machine," she said. "A portable device in a wooden box. I don't know quite how to describe it. It operated by magnet, I think. He would turn a little crank on the side of the box and it would produce a jolt of electricity. He applied it with a pair of brass handles placed over a wet piece of sponge."

"Where on your body did he apply it?" Mr. Pelham asked.

"My arms or my…my legs. The shock wasn't severe, but if he turned the crank very fast, he could make it stronger."

Justin made a low sound of displeasure from his place by the mantel. "It sounds more like torture than medicine. All of it does."

"It's quackery," Mr. Finchley told him. "Plain and simple."

"Finchley's right," Mr. Pelham said. "Unfortunately, anyone with enough coin can purchase an electrotherapy machine. They're advertised as being capable of curing every ill, from cancer to toothache."

Jenny's lips thinned with anger. "It looked like something out of the Spanish Inquisition. An infernal contraption, operated by a doddering old fool. And after every treatment, Lord Castleton would appear in the room with that dratted paper."

Helena well remembered. "He promised that everything would stop if only I'd sign it. He so desperately wanted that money."

"Did your courage never fail you?" Mr. Pelham asked.

She gave him a puzzled frown. "You think it was courage that kept me from signing? I assure you it wasn't. I was never more frightened in my life than in the months after my brother disappeared. By the end, I would have signed anything my uncle put before me, and gladly. But I knew it wouldn't make a difference. He'd already gone too far, you see."

Mr. Pelham's face was inscrutable. "You believe he would have put you away regardless."

"Yes," she said. "I know he would have."

"Do you think she's all right?" Finchley asked.

Justin crossed the parlor and sat down. Helena had retired to her room to rest. Pelham's interview had exhausted her. She'd been left pale and drained, still trembling long after he'd gone. "No. I don't."

"Perhaps you should go to her."

"Miss Holloway is with her," Justin said. "Her presence has made mine rather superfluous." He was unable to keep the twinge of aggravation out of his voice. Since their arrival at the house in Half Moon Street, Miss Holloway had supplanted him as Helena's advocate and protector. She seemed to feel it was her right to always be at Helena's side.

"Ah. Well, I suppose it's for the best. Given what's transpired, Lady Helena will appreciate the support of another female." Finchley slipped his notebook and pencil back into the interior of his coat. "We've asked the unthinkable of her, you know. Most ladies can't speak about their bodies—or anyone else's—without falling into a faint. Even Keane's wife, as sensible a female as you'll ever meet, refers to chicken breast as chicken bosom. It's ridiculous, but there it is."

Justin was unable to be philosophical about the matter. His blood was still boiling at the thought of anyone putting their hands on Helena. At her description of how Glyde had forced her out of her clothing and into the cold bath, he'd been hard pressed not to charge out into the street, find the blackguard, and tear him to pieces. It had taken every ounce of his self-control to keep his countenance.

"Ladies are delicate, by nature," Finchley went on. "I suppose that's what I admire about Miss Holloway. She's a strong, efficient female, with no nonsense about her."

"She's a managing female."

Finchley set his spectacles more firmly onto his nose. "Not every fellow wants to go about rescuing damsels in distress. We can't all be heroes. Some of us aspire to nothing more than a congenial companion with whom to share the yoke of life."

"How appealing you make it sound. Share the yoke of life, indeed. As if you were two oxen." Justin leaned back in his chair, stretching his legs out before him. "Good God, Tom, you need to get out more."

"This from the fellow who was obliged to find love through a matrimonial advertisement."

A heavy silence fell over the room.

Finchley's brow furrowed. "You do love her, don't you?"

Justin sighed. The last thing he wanted to do was to discuss his feelings for Helena with Tom Finchley. The man was his best friend. Practically a brother. But the bonds of friendship only stretched so far. "I care for her. Very much."

"But you don't love her."

Justin rubbed his forehead. "I don't know," he admitted after a long moment. "I often wonder if I'm even capable of the emotion."

Finchley's face set into a meditative frown. It was the exact expression he wore when puzzling over a particularly thorny legal issue. "Perhaps you merely don't recognize it. Neither of us has had much experience with loving anyone or being loved in return. I know I haven't."

"Nor I," Justin said. "What a depressing pair we are."

"I don't know," Finchley mused. "We seem to have done all right between us. And who's to say? Love might well do more harm to our lives than good. It's the cause of endless strife. I can tell you that much from my experiences in the law. Violence, murder, mayhem. All committed in the name of love."

"I'd as soon have loyalty," Justin said. "It seems a far more valuable quality."

"Loyalty is essential, yes. And friendship wouldn't be amiss. It's steadier. Less volatile than love."

"Precisely."

"Are you and Lady Helena friends?"

"We are. Quite good friends, or so I have reason to hope."

"Huh." Finchley considered this. "Since you've said that, I'll admit that, in addition to friendship, I wouldn't disdain a small degree of tenderness from a woman. A soft word or look."

"Or touch."

"That, too." An ironic smile flickered in Finchley's eyes. "No doubt I should follow your example and find a proper wife."

Justin regarded his friend with reluctant amusement. "And if you did…would Miss Holloway be a candidate for the position?"

"*What?*" Finchley's ears reddened. "No." He shook his head. "No. She's far beyond my reach."

"She's a lady's companion."

"Who happens to be a distant cousin of the Earl of Castleton."

"I beg your pardon," Justin said. "My hearing must be defective. For a moment, it sounded as if you said you couldn't court a woman because she's distantly related to a member of the peerage. You. The man who facilitated my marriage to an actual earl's daughter."

"It's not the same."

"The hell it isn't."

"Your father was a baronet," Finchley retorted in irritation. "Mine may well have been the village drunk. Or worse."

Justin was ready with a sharp reply, but he had no opportunity to utter it. The door to the parlor pushed open before he could speak and Helena stepped in. She'd changed into a fashionable black silk walking dress trimmed in embossed velvet. A plumed velvet bonnet was clutched in her gloved hand.

Both he and Finchley immediately rose to their feet.

"Forgive the interruption," she said.

Justin's gaze swept over her. She was still pale, but she was no longer trembling. Indeed, she looked rather determined. "You're not interrupting anything."

"Were you unable to rest?" Finchley asked.

"I've had enough of rest." Helena lifted her chin a fraction. "I would like to go for a walk."

Justin went to her, his voice low. "Now?"

"If you please."

He gave her a long, assessing look. "Very well. I'll fetch my hat."

Chapter Seventeen

Helena took Justin's arm as they exited the house and proceeded to walk along Half Moon Street in the direction of Green Park. They kept a sedate, comfortable pace, as if they often strolled along together in the heart of fashionable London.

"I've resolved not to cling to you anymore," she said.

He glanced down at her. "Any particular reason?"

"Aside from sparing your poor arm?" She stared straight ahead. "I'm sick to death of being such a frightened, poor-spirited creature."

"There is nothing poor-spirited about being afraid. You've had ample cause."

"Perhaps. But such fears have touched every aspect of my life. I've been so frightened, and so angry about the injustice of it all. It's changed me. I scarcely know who I am anymore."

Justin made no reply. His eyes had grown distant, as if he were contemplating some troublesome dilemma of his own.

She walked at his side in silence, her silk and velvet skirts swaying gently with every step. Half Moon Street was a small and rather quiet street, lined with narrow, elegant houses. Two young gentlemen in plaid trousers were walking together toward Piccadilly and a severe-looking nurse was pushing a perambulator toward Curzon Street. Other than that, the street was deserted.

At least, it appeared to be so.

If there were suspicious characters lurking about, she certainly didn't see them. Not that Mr. Glyde was likely to be hiding behind a lamppost in the broad light of day.

"Do you truly believe such feelings can change a person?" Justin asked abruptly.

Helena took her time responding. She had a sense that his question had more to do with his own demons than with hers. "Yes, I do. Fear and anger shouldn't be the guiding principles of one's life."

"What's the alternative? To forgive and forget?"

"Ideally."

His gaze rested on her face. "Can you forgive your uncle for what he's done to you? Can you forgive Mr. Glyde?"

"Mr. Glyde? Definitely not. But my relationship with my uncle is rather more complicated. He wasn't always the man he is today."

"No?" Justin sounded skeptical.

"Indeed. When I was a girl, I thought him a jolly fellow. Whenever he came to visit, he'd hide treats in his pockets for me to find. He was always bringing me little presents. A paper fan or a miniature horse carved out of ebony. Once, when I was very small, he even brought me a spaniel puppy." Helena smiled slightly to recall it. "My father objected, of course. He didn't want anyone to spoil me. But Uncle Edward insisted I be allowed to keep her."

"You have fond memories of the man."

"Despite everything, yes. I do."

"But you can't forgive him."

"No," she said. "Not yet. Possibly not ever. But I must find a way to get past it and go on living. I can't allow the pain they've inflicted to pull me down into the mire."

"It won't. You're too strong for that."

"I'm not strong, Justin. I'd already half given up by the time I met you. The night of the storm, when you found me on the cliff's ledge, I was quite prepared to die."

"You were terrified. And understandably so."

"Yes," she acknowledged quietly. "But I can't continue being terrified. Even if there's cause. I have to find a way back to the person I was before this nightmare began. If I don't, my uncle and Mr. Glyde will have won."

That night, they visited the Haymarket Theatre. The only production Mr. Finchley had been able to procure tickets to on such short notice was a new play entitled *The Lamented Friend*. It was billed as a *comedietta*, but there were not many scenes which inspired humor. The storyline featured an unhappy widow who, though lately married to a marquis, did nothing but lament the loss of her dear departed first husband. The audience hissed their displeasure far more than they laughed or applauded.

With Jenny's help, Helena had dressed carefully in an evening gown of blue *glacé* silk with deep triple flounces and short laced-trimmed sleeves. The heart-shaped neckline was fashionably low, revealing a greater expanse of her bosom than she'd ever displayed in Justin's presence—unless one counted the night he'd stripped her out of her wet clothes.

It was nothing more or less daring than what she'd worn on previous visits to the theatre, but it nevertheless made her feel vaguely self-conscious.

"I'd be more comfortable with a bertha," she'd told Jenny. A lace bertha collar was wide and round, attaching at the throat and covering the neck and shoulders. Many ladies paired them with their dresses.

"Why? Your bruises have faded well enough. The ones that haven't are well-hidden by your gloves and your sleeves."

"It's not the bruises that concern me. It's my modesty. I'd prefer to cover up."

"And have everyone remark on it?" Jenny had shaken her head. "No. It's bad enough you have no jewelry. I'll not have people say you've become a dowd."

Seated in the second tier private box that Mr. Finchley had managed to obtain for them, Helena didn't feel very dowdy. Even so, she had no doubt that people were talking about her. In the light of the gas lamps and the glittering pendant chandelier, she'd seen many a pair of opera glasses trained on her—and on Justin, too.

"They'll drop in at the interval," she said. "They'll want to meet you."

Justin appeared unperturbed by this information. In his black evening coat and trousers, a cream silk cravat knotted at his neck, he looked perfectly at home among the throng of well-dressed gentlemen and fashionably clad ladies. He also looked remarkably handsome. "It's what we're here for."

She looked at him a moment longer, a queer ache of longing twisting in her chest. When he turned and caught her gaze, she offered him a faint, rueful smile. "Do you wish you were back in Devon?"

"At the Abbey?"

"You have so much to do there. Mr. Boothroyd must be at sixes and sevens without you."

"He'll manage," Justin said. "Besides, where in King's Abbot could we have had an evening such as this?"

Helena opened the delicate paper fan she wore on a silken cord at her wrist. Its leaves were painted with an elaborately detailed scene of a grand house in the country set in a scenic landscape. Giles had purchased it for her from the celebrated fanmaker M. Duvelleroy when they'd visited the Crystal Palace so many years before.

"It's a terrible play," she said.

"I was speaking of the company."

"Oh." Helena fanned herself.

"You look beautiful this evening. Have I told you?"

He hadn't. When she'd come down the stairs in Half Moon Street, dressed in all her finery, he'd merely looked at her. There had been a brief, unsettling glint in his eyes. Fierce and hungry. Rather like a ravening wolf. It had given her a trembling feeling in her stomach.

"Then again, you always do," he mused. "You would think I'd become used to it by now, but it strikes me anew every time I see you."

"You needn't pay me pretty compliments."

"Ah. That's right. I'd forgotten." His mouth curved in a dry smile. "You'd prefer I refrain from any suggestion of romance."

"I'd prefer you not tease me and put me to the blush."

"I'm not teasing," he said. "But I'll refrain from romancing you in future, if that's what you wish."

"That was the arrangement, wasn't it? No romance. Only friendship."

"And something more than friendship," he reminded her.

Helena searched his face for some sign of what he was thinking. "Is romance the something more?"

His expression was unreadable "You tell me."

It was dim in the theatre, the sound of the play and the audience a steady swell of noise in the background. And yet there was privacy to be found amid so many people. Indeed, at that moment, their box on the second tier felt like a world apart from it all. A gaslit sanctuary in which she could safely give voice to the innermost yearnings of her heart. "No," she said. "The something more isn't romance. It's love."

Justin stared at her, his stern visage half shadowed in the gaslight. "Love," he repeated. His deep voice was as expressionless as his face.

Embarrassment swiftly extinguished the brief flare of hope in Helena's breast. "Speaking in general terms," she added. "Philosophically, not personally."

"Ah," he said. "I see."

She fixed her attention back on the stage.

Justin sat beside her in grim silence. Once or twice she felt his eyes on her, but she didn't regard it. The curtain would lower momentarily. There'd be plenty to deal with then. She needed to keep her countenance. To refrain from upsetting herself over something so foolish as a perceived rejection of her burgeoning feelings.

If anyone had a right to be upset in this relationship, it was Justin. She'd upended his entire life. First by marrying him under false pretenses, and then by thrusting him into the middle of a scandal. She had no right to ask him for anything more. Not when he'd already given so much of himself to her and her wretched cause.

After several long minutes of staring at the stage, affecting not to care about such trivial concepts as love and affection, the curtain finally lowered and the lights in the theatre went up.

The restless crowd rose to their feet, the sound of voices talking and laughing swelling to a crescendo.

Helena wafted her fan, watching as the boxes across the theatre emptied. Gentlemen left to bring their ladies refreshment, and ladies left to visit their friends. It wouldn't be long now.

"Do you see anyone you know?" Justin asked.

She nodded. "Several people."

A trill of nervous tension quickened her pulse.

Had they adequately prepared to meet the inquiring throng? Moments ago, she'd felt relatively confident. She and Justin planned to say that they'd met while she was on holiday in Devon. That they'd been introduced by a mutual acquaintance. It wasn't too far from the truth. However, considering the collective curiosity of polite society, she suddenly wondered if it would be enough of an explanation.

Perhaps they should have come up with a more compelling tale for how they'd met and married? Something to explain how an earl's daughter would find herself wed to a former soldier. A man with no family or connections to speak of.

But there was no time to formulate a new story. Before she could articulate her concerns, the first visitor made his way into their box.

Peregrine Trowbridge, Viscount Wexford was a fair-haired rake with a penchant for loud waistcoats and fast horses. Helena had been acquainted with his younger sister in the years before Giles left for India.

"Lady Helena," he said, bowing. "I knew I recognized you from across the theatre."

"Lord Wexford, may I present my husband, Captain Justin Thornhill."

Justin had risen when Lord Wexford entered. He stood beside her chair, somewhat protectively, or so she imagined. "Wexford," he said.

"Thornhill." Lord Wexford shook Justin's hand. "Lately of Her Majesty's army in India, is that right? I've been hearing about your marriage to Lady Helena. What a march you've stolen on the rest of us, sir. I daresay it was Giles's doing. He always did like to joke that he'd see his sister married to an officer before he'd consent to giving her to one of us."

Helena's heart contracted at the mention of her brother, but she managed to keep her face impassive. Justin's hand came to rest lightly on her shoulder.

"Where are you residing in London?" Lord Wexford asked. "Not with Castleton, I presume, else you'd be sitting in his box across the way."

"We've taken a house in Half Moon Street," Justin said.

"Fancy that. Lady Poole, the widow of old Lord Eustace Poole, resides in Half Moon Street. I was calling on her only last week." Lord Wexford paused to summon someone else into the box. "Letty? Come and meet Lady Helena's new husband."

Lady Leticia Staverley entered their theatre box in an abundance of lace skirts caught up in a spray of wax roses. "Helena, my darling!" she cried.

Helena stood to greet her, receiving Letty's kiss on the cheek with a smile that was only partially forced. She'd known Letty in her youth, but the two of them had never been particularly close. After Giles's disappearance, Helena had heard from her only once.

"I haven't seen you in ages!" she said, clutching Helena's hand. "You haven't been at a single event I've attended since last autumn."

"Letty, this is Lady Helena's new husband, Captain Justin Thornhill," Lord Wexford said. "He served with Giles in India, don't you know?"

Helena exchanged a fleeting glance with Justin. Neither corrected Lord Wexford's misapprehension and, in seconds, the moment in which they might have done so passed into oblivion.

It was a strange and rather fortuitous thing, she reflected as a procession of old acquaintances entered and exited their box. Soon, everyone assumed she'd met Justin through the auspices of her brother. They believed Giles had encouraged a correspondence between the two of them. After his disappearance the previous year, and following her period of mourning, they seemed to think it only natural that she and Justin would wed.

"Your uncle must have been furious," Lady Elmira Yardley said. She was an elderly woman, thrice widowed, and perpetually garbed in layers of black crepe and jet. Her canny gaze flitted from Justin to Helena and back again. "Is that why you're not wearing your jewels, my dear? Has Castleton kept them from you?"

"Indeed, ma'am," Helena said. "My uncle has behaved rather badly since my brother's disappearance in India."

"Has he?" Lady Elmira edged closer, her eyes glinting and her face flushed with ill-disguised anticipation. She had a notorious thirst for gossip. "In what manner, my dear?"

"In an ungentlemanly manner," Helena replied. "As I'm sure you can imagine."

Lady Elmira brows lowered. "Yes, yes. I know too well of what you speak. Castleton has ever been a villain. Haven't I said so these twenty years and more?"

After she departed from the box, Helena turned to Justin to explain. "My uncle courted Lady Elmira after her first husband died. She thought he would propose, but when the moment arrived, he couldn't be brought to the point. She's never forgiven him for the humiliation."

"What do you suppose she'll tell everyone he's done to you?" Justin asked.

Helena shrugged. "I can't guess. Though I doubt it could be anything worse than the truth."

They didn't stay to finish the play. They'd already achieved their purpose. People had seen Helena and talked to her. They could attest that she both looked and sounded perfectly well. As an added bonus, Justin had somehow managed to find himself elevated to the position of best friend to Helena's late brother. He supposed it was the only way all the toplofty lords and ladies they'd conversed with could reconcile his marriage to her.

It bothered him more than a little. He didn't like to be made to feel as if he were lacking somehow. But after the parade of Lord So-and-Sos and Lady Whatsits, how could he feel anything else?

He was naught but the bastard son of a baronet. And not even a fashionable one. Indeed, next to glittering society figures like Lord Wexford and Lady Staverley, Sir Oswald seemed a veritable country bumpkin.

And if Sir Oswald wasn't good enough, then Justin himself was positively unacceptable. Even owning the Abbey couldn't make him so.

He hailed a hansom for them from one of the many idling about outside the theatre and assisted Helena in. Her skirts filled the cab in a frothy sea of lustrous blue silk and lace. When he climbed in after her, he was obliged to carefully move them out of the way lest he crush them under his legs.

As the hansom sprang into motion, rolling swiftly down the busy West End street, Helena leaned back against the seat with a weary sigh. The curving, creamy expanse of her bosom—the sight of which had rendered him speechless when she'd come down the stairs in Half Moon Street—was now concealed by an opera cloak, an expensive-looking affair of white cashmere trimmed in swansdown. She held it around herself like a warm, luxurious blanket.

"Cold?" he asked.

"Tired," she said. "It's been a long, exhausting day."

"You may avail yourself of my shoulder, if you like."

A smile touched her lips. "Do you know, I believe I shall." She rested her head lightly on his arm. It was a bit awkward given the disparity in their heights.

"Here." Justin shifted position, setting his arm around her and drawing her close against his chest. "This is better."

"Mmm. Much more comfortable."

He held her gently as the hansom cab rolled toward Half Moon Street. They didn't speak. There was nothing to say, really.

But as each minute passed, their mutual silence seemed to gain in significance.

"Helena," he said at last. His voice was rough as gravel. "In the theatre, you said that the something more than friendship we spoke of on the train was love."

She stiffened a little in his arms. "I didn't mean that you… that we—"

"Yes, I know. You were speaking in general terms. Philosophically, not personally." He exhaled heavily. "The thing is…I'm not sure I even know what love is, philosophically *or* personally."

"Haven't you ever been in love before?"

"Not that I'm aware."

"Never?" She sounded incredulous.

"Is it so shocking?"

"A little. You're a man of the world. Handsome and of good character. I'd have thought ladies would have flocked to you."

Handsome? He filed that compliment away for later. "There have been some women in my life, certainly, but I didn't love them. And, er, I wouldn't call them ladies."

"Oh."

He paused. "Have you?"

"Have I what?"

"Ever been in love?"

"No. Not in a romantic way. Though I did once have a tendre for one of my brother's friends. Lord Hartright. He used to tease me and pull my hair. I hoped, when I grew up, he might marry me."

Justin didn't know quite how to reply to that. Was it ridiculous to be jealous of a boy from her childhood? Yes, he decided. Patently absurd. And yet…

"Does this budding lothario currently reside in London?" he asked with studied indifference. "Are we likely to cross paths with him?"

"Lord Hartright? Oh no, he's long since married and retired to his estate in Northumberland. He has six children now, I believe."

"He didn't leave you heartbroken, then."

Helena laughed softly. "No, indeed. He didn't have my heart. I was never in love with him. I've never been in love with anyone."

"No? You must have had an army of suitors."

"Not quite so many as that. In truth, my father didn't think any man was good enough for the daughter of the Earl of Castleton."

"No doubt he was right."

"It mattered little in the end. I soon went into mourning— first for him and then for Giles. Courtship and marriage was the last thing on my mind. As for falling in love...I have no experience at all." She grew serious. "But I know what it is to love a person. It's what I felt for my mother and brother."

He turned his face into her hair. Her coiffure was an intricate arrangement of rolls and plaits, secured at the back with a filigree comb. It smelled of jasmine, sweet and faintly exotic. "Describe it to me," he said.

"It's a special bond. A kinship of shared memories and experience. But it's more than that. Oh, I can't explain it." She struggled for the right words. "It's...It's when you see a person and your spirits lift. When their happiness means more to you than your own. When you'd do anything for them, sacrifice anything, even if the sacrifice would hurt you or make you unhappy."

Justin thought of the hell Helena had been put through in the year since her brother disappeared in India. "If they loved you in return, they wouldn't ask for such a sacrifice."

"They wouldn't have to ask," she said. "You'd give it regardless."

As she had done. As she was still doing. "Do you think your brother would be happy to know what you've endured on his behalf?"

His question seemed to take her aback. When she answered it, her voice was threaded with emotion. "I think he would be sad. He willed me that money to secure my future. He wanted to make certain I'd always be taken care of. That I'd always be safe."

Justin didn't know anything about Giles Reynolds, late Earl of Castleton. He might well have been a good and decent brother. Nevertheless, Justin felt an overpowering anger toward the man. "If he wanted you to be safe, he shouldn't have abandoned you. A man who's just inherited an earldom has no cause to continue soldiering. He could have come home, looked after you."

Helena raised her head from his chest. Her eyes found his in the light of the carriage lamp. "You don't understand. He was going to come home when the rebellion was suppressed. He simply wasn't ready yet. Giles couldn't bear life in England. Not after my mother died. He was restless. He needed a purpose. Something active that would keep him from brooding."

"And what about what you needed?"

"*Me?*"

"He left you to shoulder the burden. And then he went and got himself killed. A course of action any soldier should have known was a distinct possibility."

Helena stared at him. Her mouth trembled. "He's not dead, Justin."

Oh, hell. Justin's heart sank as he looked at her face. He couldn't have chosen a worse thing to say if he'd tried.

Her fingers tightened on the lapel of his evening coat. "Do you think he is?"

"I don't know," he said, his voice gone gruff. "Probably."

Her face crumpled. "I can't—" She stopped and looked away from him in a visible effort to regain her composure. "I can't accept it. I have to believe he's coming back."

Justin wouldn't let her hide from him. He drew her close again, urging her to meet his eyes. "Why, sweetheart?" He scarcely registered the endearment he uttered, only vaguely aware that it was one he'd never used with any woman before.

"Because he's all I have," she said. "All that's left of my family."

Justin held her gaze. "He's not all you have."

She bent her head, resting her cheek back against his chest. "I know that. I do. And I'm trying not to be unreasonable. But if there's a chance, Justin. Even a small chance, that Giles is out there somewhere…"

"What can I do?" he asked. "What is it that will set your mind at ease?"

She made a choking sound. It may have been a laugh. Or a sob. "No one has ever asked me that before."

"I'm asking now. Shall I write a few letters to contacts of mine in India? Or set Finchley and Boothroyd to the task?"

"Would you?"

Justin had no desire to write to anyone in India. Nor did he relish asking Finchley and Boothroyd to investigate the matter. But his feelings didn't matter. Not when it meant so much to her. "Of course." His lips brushed over her hair. "Didn't I tell you I'd go to the ends of the earth for you?"

"You did say that, yes." She fell quiet for a long moment. "Justin…"

A frisson of anxiety sharpened his senses. He raised his head at the same moment the hansom cab rolled to a halt in front of the house in Half Moon Street. The jarvey shouted out to them from his perch.

"What is it?" Justin asked.

Helena sat up. She straightened her opera cloak about her shoulders, slanting him a guarded glance from beneath her lashes as she retied the ribbon at her throat. "It's nothing," she said. "Only that I'm famished. I hope Mrs. Jarrow has left something out for us in the kitchen."

Chapter Eighteen

I think I'm falling in love with you.

Helena had almost said it to him. A stupid school-girl confession, which would have made them both dreadfully uncomfortable. Only the hansom cab's timely arrival in Half Moon Street had stopped her.

She was glad she hadn't told him. She'd much rather cling to the infinitely dear moment when he'd called her sweetheart, or the next when he'd promised once again to go to the ends of the earth for her. Either was preferable to seeing, again, the blank look he'd given her in the theatre box when she'd first mentioned love.

There would be time enough to sort out the complicated tangle of her emotions. For now, she needed to focus on the task at hand.

Mr. Pelham had said his editorial would be published in a week. He'd promised to send word before it went to print. It was little enough comfort. She still woke each morning with her nerves on edge, never knowing from one moment to the next if this would be the day her reputation would be ruined forever.

She expected the time spent waiting on the publication of the editorial to pass at an interminable rate. Instead, the next week flew by in a whirlwind of morning calls, afternoon drives in Hyde Park, and evening visits to theatres, operas, and musicales. With Justin ever at her side, Helena's fears began to gradually abate. Even so, wherever they were, whether shopping for gloves in Bond Street or listening to a recital of Beethoven at the home of their neighbor, Lady Poole, Helena still looked diligently about her for any signs of her uncle or Mr. Glyde.

She never saw either of them.

However, news of her uncle was carried to her door with some regularity. Visitors to Half Moon Street delighted in discussing him over tea. His behavior in regard to the jewelry Helena had inherited from her mother was a particularly popular topic.

"An absolute villain," Lady Leticia Staverley declared as she bit into one of the ginger biscuits Mrs. Jarrow had baked earlier that morning. "How dare he keep your jewels from you? Surely something can be done."

Helena was seated across from Letty in the parlor. Jenny sat nearby, her attention appearing to be solely occupied with the bit of needlework on her lap.

"Why has Captain Thornhill not yet intervened?" Letty asked.

"We haven't seen my uncle since our arrival in London," Helena replied. As she sipped her tea, she wondered if she would ever be able to mention her uncle without the accom-

panying quiver of unease. The feeling was always more pronounced when Justin wasn't nearby.

She wished he would join her when callers came to Half
Moon Street, but he rarely did unless the caller was another
gentleman. She supposed he didn't deem the ladies to be a
big enough threat to warrant his presence.

"You must confront him," Letty said. "And I know just
the place." She pulled her little velvet-trimmed reticule onto
her lap and began to rummage about in it. "My aunt Beatrice
is having a ball on Friday at her house in Belgrave Square.
Perhaps you've heard? Invitations went out long ago. It's guaranteed to be a crush. She claims she can't fit a single additional
person inside her ballroom. But after a little wheedling…"
Letty withdrew a thick, cream-tinted card from her reticule.
"I managed to wrangle this out of her."

Helena took the proffered card, quickly skimming over
the engraved black script. "I'm obliged to you, Letty, but…"
She scrambled for an excuse. "Friday? That's only a few days
from now. It leaves me no time to have a dress made."

"Tosh." Letty waved her hand. "You've lately married,
and not very well, if you don't mind my saying. No one will
expect you to be in the first stare of fashion."

Helena bristled. "Indeed, I do mind you saying so. I believe
myself to have married *very* well."

Letty only laughed. "How ardently you defend him. I
knew it must be a love match. I've made a friendly wager with
Lady Angeline Clement, you see. She said you'd married only
because Captain Thornhill was a friend of Giles's. As if any
intelligent female would wed a stranger purely to honor the
memory of her dead brother. The silly widgeon. I'll call on
her directly I leave here and collect my ten pounds."

After Letty had gone, Jenny laid aside her sewing and rose to summon Mrs. Jarrow to clear away the tea things. "A silly widgeon," she muttered after the housekeeper had exited the room with the tray. She sat down beside Helena on the sofa. "That's the precise term I would use to describe Letty Staverley. And that's only if I was being kind."

"She doesn't realize she's being offensive."

"Undoubtedly. The girl has about as much depth of character as a puddle."

Helena handed Jenny the invitation. "Do you think Justin and I need attend?"

Jenny frowned. "I suppose people will want to see how you interact with your uncle."

"Yes, but is it necessary? By Friday, the editorial will have been published. I know I'm meant to show myself afterward. To prove to the world that I'm not mad. But to attend a ball, where everyone in attendance has read about what's been done to me..." Helena gave Jenny an anguished look. "Must I bear it?"

"I don't rightly know," Jenny said. "Mr. Finchley could better advise you. This is all part of his grand plan, isn't it?" She set aside the invitation and, once more, rose to her feet. "I'll invite him to dinner, if you like." She went to the little walnut secretary in the corner and took out a sheet of paper. "Mr. Thornhill will welcome his presence, I daresay. He doesn't enjoy having odd numbers."

"He doesn't mind it."

"Nonsense. I'm a veritable thorn in his side. He'd much rather dine alone with you each evening."

Helena wasn't so certain. It seemed to her that their evening meals were largely informal affairs. They ate as a matter of course before departing for the opera or the theatre. That

Jenny dined with them made little difference. It wasn't as if she and Justin were sharing confidences at the table. Indeed, conversation was limited to the veriest commonplace.

Not that Justin had been behaving in a cool or indifferent manner toward her. Quite the reverse. He sometimes held her hand during performances. And, in the coach, on the journey home, he always offered her his shoulder.

It was during these short cab rides from the West End to Half Moon Street that the greater part of their intimacy took place. Though *intimacy* was a relative word. They weren't sharing a bed, after all. And he hadn't kissed her again, not since their time at the Stanhope Hotel. But his voice deepened when he spoke to her and his gray eyes regarded her with a possessive warmth that made her stomach quiver with the delicate flutter of butterfly wings.

They talked and laughed softly together. They shared humorous anecdotes about their childhoods, and not-so-humorous ones as well. She felt they were getting to know each other. To trust each other.

Was he beginning to fall in love with her, too?

Helena didn't know. And she was afraid to ask. She felt deep down that to broach the subject again and be rejected would put an abrupt end to their present intimacy. The fragile bond they were forging together would be broken.

She didn't dare risk it. Not yet. But she was trying so desperately to be brave. To push past her fears and regain some semblance of the strength and independence she'd once possessed.

Soon, she told herself. Soon, she'd open her heart to him. She'd offer him her love, freely and without expectation. What he chose to do with it would be entirely up to him.

"A ball?" Finchley asked. "Given by Lady Beatrice Wardlow? Naturally you should attend."

Justin lowered his knife to his plate. "Indeed." He glared across the dining table at Finchley, catching his eyes over the branch of flickering beeswax candles. This was not the answer he'd been expecting when he acquiesced to inviting his friend to dinner. "And how does it serve our cause to come face to face with Castleton in such a public setting?"

Finchley speared a piece of boiled mutton onto his fork. He'd arrived promptly at seven, suit freshly pressed, shoes polished, and hair combed back from his forehead and smoothed into place with Macassar oil. He wasn't dandyish by any means, but he looked far more elegant than the rumpled and unshaven version of Tom Finchley that Justin had grown accustomed to over the years.

"Castleton won't be there," he said, after washing down his mutton with a swallow of wine. "Not if the editorial is out."

Justin exchanged a swift glance with Helena. Her brows were knit in a worried line. "And if it hasn't?"

"He still isn't likely to show his face," Finchley said. "Not if he knows you'll be in attendance."

"How on earth do you know so much about what he may or mayn't do?" Miss Holloway asked.

"I have my methods."

Miss Holloway wouldn't be fobbed off. "Then I beg you would reveal them. I've been wont to think you're a magician, but I know there must be a more rational explanation than that."

Finchley's mouth tilted briefly in a lopsided grin. It was almost boyish. "I have a spy in Castleton's house."

Miss Holloway gaped. "What? Who?"

"A footman. He took the place of a lad named Henry at the end of last month."

"The Henry who went to Bridgehampton to visit his sick mother?"

"The Henry who is cooling his heels at a hotel in Margate, with a great deal of money in his pockets."

Miss Holloway sat back in her seat. "My goodness. How devious you are, sir." She laughed suddenly. "I suppose your spy is eavesdropping on Lord Castleton even as we speak."

"He may be." Finchley looked at Justin and Helena, his expression sobering. "Though it wasn't entirely through his efforts that I learned Castleton would seek to avoid the pair of you."

"How, then?" Helena asked.

"Common sense, mostly, coupled with what I know of human nature." Finchley set down his wineglass. "Lord Castleton only put his hands on you on one occasion. The remainder of the physical harm you suffered was administered through his representatives, whether by Mr. Glyde, the physicians, or people affiliated with the asylum."

"Castleton is a physical coward," Justin said.

Finchley nodded. "Precisely. Add to that, he has an immense aversion to this scandal being publicized. If he were to attend the ball, he's not likely to make a scene there."

"But you said he wouldn't attend," Helena reminded him.

"I don't believe he will. As Justin said, the man's a physical coward. And you, my lady, will be in company with a fellow who's anything but." Finchley gave Justin a stern look. "Which reminds me, if by some small chance Castleton does show his face at the ball, you must make an earnest effort not to smash it in."

"I can't promise anything," Justin said.

Finchley sighed. "At least try not to cause a scene. It won't help, you know. We must persuade people that Castleton is the unreasonable one, not Lady Helena, and certainly not you." He paused. "Which brings me to the subject of Mr. Glyde. The man appears to have gone to ground. Pelham is unable to find him. *I'm* unable to find him. It's made me...uneasy."

"What about your spy?" Justin asked. "Has he heard anything?"

"Not a thing. Which could mean that there's nothing to hear. Or else..."

"Or else what?" Justin's voice was sharp with impatience.

"It's possible that Castleton is being exceedingly careful. He may have a plan hatched with Glyde. Though other than straight out abduction, I can't fathom what that plan might be."

A shadow of worry crossed Helena's face. "Do you think he'll come here?"

"No. Not here. But he must be lurking about somewhere. I advise vigilance."

Miss Holloway laid aside her cutlery. "Does this mean you won't be attending the ball?"

Justin turned to Helena. She was a vision of fashionable elegance in a dark gray dress trimmed in ribbons of bright crimson. The bodice was snug, secured at the front by a row of tiny silk-covered buttons fastened from her waist to her throat.

Since their arrival in London, it seemed to him that every time he blinked, she was in a different dress. There were morning gowns and afternoon gowns, walking dresses, dinner dresses, and evening dresses for the theatre. Each of them was made of rich fabrics and trimmed in luxurious trimmings. He had no doubt but that the cost of even one such dress would have beggared a lesser man.

"It's your decision," he said. "We can go, if you wish. Or stay here, if you wish."

Helena hesitated before answering. And then, "I wish to go," she said quietly.

Miss Holloway didn't appear surprised. "They'll be waltzing there. Helena does so love to waltz. How long has it been, my dear?"

"A year," Helena said. "Since Giles disappeared."

"You'll be dreadfully out of trim." Miss Holloway looked at Mr. Finchley, her cheeks blossoming with color. "I have an idea. Why don't we practice?"

"Here?" Finchley asked.

"We can move the furniture in the parlor. It won't leave us much room to dance, but it should be enough."

"I haven't waltzed in an age," Finchley confessed. "What about you, Thornhill?"

"An age and a half," Justin said grimly. And he wasn't too keen on remedial lessons.

"Well then." Miss Holloway stood, obliging both Justin and Finchley to stand as well. "Shall we repair to the parlor?"

"What shall we do about music?" Helena asked as she rose from her chair.

"Hmm." Jenny slanted a questioning glance at Finchley. "I don't suppose Mrs. Jarrow plays the pianoforte?"

"No," Finchley said with a low chuckle. "Emphatically, no."

"Then I'll play. I don't need to dance, after all. It's not as if I'll be attending the ball."

"Nonsense." Helena placed her hand in the crook of Justin's arm, allowing him to escort her from the dining room.

"We'll take turns at the pianoforte. The gentlemen won't mind practicing the waltz with us both. Monsieur Claude always said you could only become skilled by dancing with multiple partners."

"Monsieur Claude?" Justin almost hated to ask.

Helena smiled up at him. "The dancing master my father employed when I was a girl. He was a French émigré and an absolute tyrant."

"Ah," Justin said. "Of course he was."

Despite Jenny's insistence, it was Helena who took the first shift at the small pianoforte in the parlor. She would have had to be blind not to see how much Jenny wanted to dance with Mr. Finchley, and Helena hadn't the least intention of making her friend wait for a turn in his arms.

Did Mr. Finchley know Jenny fancied him? Helena thought he might. Then again, even the most intelligent gentlemen could be a bit thick when it came to matters of the heart.

"Shall I turn the pages for you?" Justin asked, coming to stand beside her.

"It isn't necessary." Her hands moved deftly over the keys. "I've memorized most of this and can fudge the bits I haven't."

"That accomplished, are you?"

"Hardly. I haven't practiced in a year. My playing is slap-dash at best."

"I'm enjoying it," he said.

Helena smiled. "You'd enjoy it more if it was played by an orchestra. A single instrument can never do it justice. Now this…" She switched to one of her favorite waltzes by Chopin. "This was written for the pianoforte."

"Not that one, Helena," Jenny objected from across the room. She and Mr. Finchley, who'd been twirling rapidly, were now at a standstill. "It's far too slow."

Helena dutifully switched back to something more energetic. As she played, she watched Jenny and Mr. Finchley resume their waltz. Jenny was blushing rosily and Mr. Finchley was looking down at her through his spectacles, a smile lighting his usually serious face.

He was an orphan like Justin. A gentleman with no home and no family. No one to call his own. But if he was discontented with his lot in life, he never showed it. Certainly not now, with Jenny in his arms.

"You're the next victim, Thornhill," Mr. Finchley said when the music stopped. "Come and let Miss Holloway show you how it's done."

Justin crossed the room to dance with Jenny. Helena played another waltz, this time choosing a piece that was slower— and shorter. She had the impression that Justin was dancing with Jenny more as a matter of courtesy than pleasure.

Mr. Finchley came to stand next to her, his attention lingering on Justin and Jenny. "Thornhill is too unsentimental to enjoy dancing."

Helena glanced up at him as she played. "You think him unsentimental?"

"I think he'd rather be risking his neck than confined to a ballroom, forced to engage in social niceties. He's a man of action. Always has been. Even as a child."

"So he's told me."

"He was our fearless leader, you know."

Helena dropped her gaze back to the keys as she flubbed her way through a difficult passage. "He feels responsible for all of you."

Mr. Finchley looked at her in mild surprise. "He said that?"

"Not in so many words," she admitted.

He laughed. "Not in any words, I'll wager. But you're quite right, my lady. Thornhill would bear the weight of the world for us if he could. He takes on everyone's burdens, to his own detriment. It's one of the most irritating things about him."

"I'm quite out of breath," Jenny said, coming to a halt. "Come and changes places with me, Helena."

Helena stood and went to Justin. He watched her intently as she crossed the room. When he held out his hand for her, she took it, feeling his other hand curve firmly about her waist. He drew her much closer than he'd drawn Jenny. The proximity to his body, so big and warm, sent a thrill of excitement through her. She tilted her head back to look up at him.

"Mr. Finchley says you don't enjoy dancing."

Justin gazed down at her, a smile at his lips. "Perhaps I've never had the right partner."

Helena wanted to ask if she was the right partner, but it seemed a foolish question. How could he possibly know when they'd never danced together?

Jenny began to play a popular waltz, the tempo slow and regular as clockwork. It was easy for Helena to catch the rhythm, especially with Justin leading her. "One-two-three," she murmured to him as he waltzed her down the length of the parlor.

Justin chuckled. And then he swept her into an elaborate turn.

She gasped in delight, which only inspired him to turn her again.

Jenny transitioned into a lively, rousing piece on the pianoforte, as Justin waltzed Helena round the room. They spun and swooped and turned. It was effortless. Exhilarating. When the music finally stopped, Helena was breathless with laughter.

"Tsk, tsk," Jenny teased. "What's happened to your expression of fashionable ennui?"

"I've never mastered it," Helena said as she caught her breath. She smiled up at Justin. He was still holding her fast in his arms. "I'll try to appear indifferent to you when we waltz together at the ball."

Justin inclined his head in a mock bow. "I'll look forward to it, my lady."

One of her hands was resting on his shoulder. She should have removed it, thereby signaling that he could let her go. Instead, as Jenny and Mr. Finchley exchanged quiet words by the pianoforte, she lifted it and very softly brushed her fingers against his cheek.

At the brief, intimate gesture, Justin went still. She heard his intake of breath, felt his hand tighten reflexively on her corseted waist. Her smile faded along with his.

I'm falling in love with you.

She didn't say it. She couldn't. It would ruin everything.

But the feeling burned within her nonetheless. A bright, radiant flame that she was sure must be shining in the depths of her eyes, revealing all to him.

I like you. I care for you. I'm falling in love with you.

"My turn," Mr. Finchley called out. "Though I won't promise to be as daring as Thornhill with all those swoops and spins."

Helena swiftly dropped her hand from Justin's face. He stepped away from her with equal swiftness. But he didn't relinquish her to Mr. Finchley.

"No more dancing." His voice sounded strange to her ears. It was deeper, and somewhat uneven. "We're all overheated. Let's go to Gunter's for an ice."

Helena felt flustered and more than a little foolish, but she schooled her features. "Oh yes," she agreed. "That sounds marvelous."

"I'm not sure Gunter's is still serving ices at this time of day," Mr. Finchley said. "Then again, I don't suppose it would hurt to drive over to Berkeley Square and find out."

"All of us?" Jenny asked, rising from behind the piano.

"Indeed," Justin replied. "I'll see about summoning a carriage."

And with that, he strode purposefully from the room.

Chapter Nineteen

There was no time before Lady Wardlow's ball to have a new gown made. Instead, Helena was obliged to settle for wearing one of her ball gowns from the previous season, albeit with significant alterations. Jenny and Mrs. Jarrow spent two straight days sewing and Helena herself helped to stitch new trimmings onto the hem.

The end result was a breathtaking creation of white silk with a plaited bodice and a double skirt, looped up by a cordon of fresh flowers and foliage. The deep V-neckline was set low across her shoulders, the short sleeves ending just above the line of her elbow-length gloves. She paired the whole with a painted fan, embroidered silk dancing slippers, and a wreath of flowers in her upswept hair.

Justin had complimented her when she came downstairs at Half Moon Street, but just as in the preceding days, his silence spoke more than his words.

The editorial had still not been published.

Was that what was inspiring his disquiet? Helena couldn't tell. All she knew was that the growing intimacy between them appeared to have come to a screeching halt. Often, she felt him looking at her, but when she attempted to return his gaze, his eyes slid away.

Had he heard something more about her uncle and Mr. Glyde? Something he was too afraid to tell her? Or was it simply that he'd grown tired of London? Tired of her?

"Have you changed your mind about the ball?" she asked during their drive to Lady Wardlow's townhouse in Belgrave Square. They'd hired a carriage for the evening. It was more comfortable than a Hansom cab, Justin had said. But he didn't look particularly comfortable seated across from her. He was staring out the window, his posture stiff and unyielding—like a soldier on the front lines of a battle.

"Justin," she said.

He flicked her a distracted glance. "What's that?"

"I asked if you've changed your mind about attending the ball. We can turn around if you wish."

"After all the effort you've put in?" His gaze lingered over her ball gown for the barest moment. "I think not."

Helena reflected that Justin had put in no little effort himself. He was clad in a black evening suit complete with a white satin waistcoat and black tails. His hair was pomaded into meticulous order, his hat and his gloves lying beside him on the carriage seat. He looked starkly handsome in a severe, soldierly sort of way.

"I don't care about any of that," she said. "If you don't want to go—"

"I'm not objecting."

She pressed her lips together. Was it his burns? Was he tired of people staring at him and asking questions about India? Not that there had been many. Thus far, most of their outings had been limited to evening entertainments—darkened theatres and the like. To be sure, there had been one or two gawkers during their daytime walks in the park, but nothing too untoward. Indeed, Justin had never seemed to mind it overmuch.

The carriage rattled along over the street, the jingle of the harness breaking the silence between them.

"I daresay you'll be glad to be rid of me for the evening," Helena said.

Justin looked at her again, his expression hard to read. "Rid of you?"

"It's considered bad form for husbands and wives to spend too much time in each other's company at a ball," she explained. "They're meant to dance with other people—even to dine with other people. It would be unseemly otherwise."

"That's the fashion, is it?"

"It is."

"Much that I care. I'm not dancing with anyone else."

A primitive ripple of pleasure swept through her at his sullen declaration. "I'll still be expected to. People would think it odd if I didn't. And isn't that the whole point of this exercise? To behave as normally as possible?"

Justin scowled his disapproval. However, when the first gentleman at the ball inquired after a dance with her, he made no objection when she permitted that gentleman to write his name on the little dance card she wore dangling from her wrist. Within half an hour, all of her dances were taken—and Justin's scowl had transformed into an icy mask of displeasure.

"Have you always been so infernally popular?" he growled as he guided her along the edge of the ballroom.

The orchestra was playing an exuberant polonaise. Lady Wardlow had chosen one to open the ball. She and her partner, a distinguished gentleman of middle age, had linked arms and were leading the other couples in a promenade round the room.

Letty hadn't been exaggerating when she said the ball would be a crush. There was scarcely room to maneuver among all the petticoats and wire crinolines. Even worse, the gaslight which flickered from the gilded wall sconces and trio of majestic crystal chandeliers was slowly sucking all of the oxygen out of the overheated room. One portly lady had already fainted into a heap of starched muslin.

"It's not popularity," Helena said. "It's curiosity. Two of those gentlemen, Sir Bernard and Lord Flood—"

"They bespoke the polka and the reel, I believe."

Had they? She'd already forgotten. "Yes, well…they're two of the men I approached for help with my uncle. Two of the men who refused to intervene on my behalf."

Justin's arm tensed under her hand. He looked down at her in bewilderment. "Why the devil would you agree to dance with them?"

"The same reason I agreed to return to London. Because I'm trying to be brave. To face my fears. And because you and Mr. Finchley insist that we must show them all that there's nothing irregular about my behavior."

A muscle in his jaw twitched. "If they'd agreed to help you, could they have done anything? Could they have prevented all of this?"

"I don't know. I thought so at the time, but in hindsight… they're probably not powerful enough to influence my uncle."

A movement across the ballroom caught her eyes. Her hand tightened on Justin's arm. "But he is."

Justin followed her gaze to the tall silver-haired gentleman who stood near the row of young wallflowers and their chaperones arranged against the farthermost wall.

"The Earl of Wolverton," she said. "My father's oldest friend and one of the most powerful men in London."

"Was he one of the men you went to for help?"

"No. I never called on him." She watched as Lord Wolverton detached himself from the group of wallflowers and began to make his way toward them. "I already knew he wouldn't help me. He views the subject of madness in very severe terms. Indeed, it was he who encouraged my father to have my mother put away."

Introductions were short and rather unnecessary. Lord Wolverton had already heard of her marriage. He asked Justin a few particulars about his regiment in India, questioned Helena about the weather in Devon, and then asked her to dance. A waltz was starting. One of the waltzes she'd particularly reserved for Justin. But there was no polite way to refuse the earl.

Helena took his extended hand and allowed him to lead her onto the polished ballroom floor. Gilt-framed wall mirrors reflected the flickering lights and the whirling dancers, giving the illusion that it was even more crowded than it actually was.

"What's this I hear about a rift with your uncle?" Lord Wolverton demanded as soon as they began to dance. "Lady Yardley claims he's stolen your jewels."

"He's kept them from me, yes."

"For what reason?"

"For the same reason he's endeavored to keep the rest of my inheritance from me: greed."

Lord Wolverton maneuvered her through a sedate turn. "What's that you say about your inheritance?"

"He's been pressing me to sign the whole of it over to him. The methods he's employed to persuade me have become increasingly barbaric."

"That's quite an accusation, madam."

"It's the truth, my lord."

Lord Wolverton's bushy silver brows beetled into a disbelieving frown. "Don't know how Castleton could keep anything from you. You're of age, aren't you? Unless the will was found to be invalid."

"It wasn't."

"Then I don't see what the man's argument is. The law's the law."

Yes, it was, Helena thought bitterly, but only for men, and even then, only for the most powerful. For women, and for the poor, the infirm, and the friendless, the law rarely provided any comfort or protection.

"The law is only as good as the men who enforce it," she said.

Lord Wolverton missed a step, nearly treading on her foot. He muttered an apology. "One doesn't anticipate a legal discussion when waltzing with a handsome young lady."

"No, indeed. Forgive me, my lord." Helena had no idea how she managed to keep her voice so steady. "There will be ample time to discuss these matters in the days to come."

Lord Wolverton's gaze was sharp as a freshly honed razor. "Just what are you up to, madam?"

"Nothing untoward, sir, I assure you." Helena looked him straight in the eye as he turned her again.

Somehow, she managed to keep her countenance through the remainder of the dance, but when Lord Wolverton handed her back to Justin, she could feel herself beginning to tremble.

"Will you take me outside please?" she asked him.

Justin did so without question, only stopping to fetch her evening cloak. He draped it round her shoulders as he escorted her through the doors that led out onto the marble terrace.

It was cold outside, but after the oppressive heat of the ballroom, Helena welcomed it.

"What happened?" Justin asked.

She shook her head. "Nothing, nothing." And then, "Perhaps it's all too much for me. Seeing all of these people. Having to pretend."

He leaned against the marble railing of the terrace, regarding her with the same unreadable expression he'd worn since their arrival. "It's not all pretending, is it?"

She didn't answer. Couldn't answer. "When will Mr. Pelham publish his editorial? He said it would be in a week, but it's been ten days since he came to Half Moon Street. Is there something you're not telling me? Has something gone wrong?"

"If it had, I wouldn't keep it from you." He folded his arms. "Pelham is just being thorough. Finchley says he's even tracked down the antecedents of Mr. Glyde, if you can believe it. Though Glyde himself continues to prove somewhat elusive."

Helena's gaze drifted over the garden below. Oil-burning torches placed along the perimeter illuminated small sections of the fashionable landscaping. The remainder of the garden was cast in shifting shadows and darkness. "He could be here right now."

"I haven't seen him."

"Have you been looking?"

"Naturally," Justin said. "It's what I'm here for."

She sighed. "How much like a duty you make it sound. I wish—" She broke off, listening as the orchestra began the music for the next dance. It was the lancers. She couldn't recall to whom she'd promised it.

Justin stepped forward and took her hand. He flicked open the dance card at her wrist, reading the entry in the light of a nearby torch. "Lord Wexford."

"Oh, yes. I'd forgotten." She looked through the terrace doors. Inside, the ballroom glittered with gaslight and candles. The guests glittered as well, the ladies dripping with jeweled necklaces, bracelets, and earrings. "We'd better go back before he misses me."

Justin kept hold of her hand. He was looking at the signatures in her dance card and frowning. "I thought you'd promised every dance."

"I did."

"Then what are all of these blank spots?"

An embarrassed blush warmed her cheeks. "They're *your* dances. I saved them for you. Unless you'd rather—"

He cleared his throat. "No. It's…I hadn't realized…"

"They're only waltzes. And the supper dance, of course. It's a reel, but I thought—"

"Quite." He relinquished her dance card, but not her hand. He tucked that gently into his arm. "I'll escort you back in."

She tugged at him until he looked down at her. "I'm sorry I ever accepted Lady Wardlow's invitation," she said in a low voice. "I know you're not enjoying any of this."

"Nonsense," he replied. "Who doesn't enjoy a ball?"

It was the last dance of the ball. The final waltz. Justin whirled Helena round in another dramatic turn. After four dances together, they'd developed something of a rhythm. A rather good one, he thought. Who the devil cared if they were unfashionable? In his opinion, all that rot about husbands and wives spending most of the evening apart was damned ridiculous. Obviously such rules were promulgated by people in unhappy marriages.

He looked down into Helena's face. She was flushed and beautiful—and infinitely dear. "Careful," he said. "Your indifference is slipping."

A smile twinkled in her eyes. "Oh, I needn't worry about that anymore. Haven't you heard? Our marriage is a love match. We're expected to act foolish."

Justin's heart clenched painfully. "A love match? Who told you that?"

"Lady Leticia Staverley. It's what everyone is saying, apparently. That, and that you're a friend of my brother's." Her silk skirts swished about her legs as he swirled her round the floor. "It seems more trouble than it's worth to correct them. After all, we won't be here much longer, will we?"

Justin didn't know what to say. The future of their marriage was a subject that had been preying on his mind a great deal of late. Indeed, in the past several days, the entire affair had become far more complicated than it had seemed when first he and Helena had met in Devon.

He still wanted her. Of course he did. He wanted all of her. Her laughter and her smiles. Her soft kisses and the tender caress of her hands. He wanted her heart and her soul—and her body. He wanted her so much that at times it was painful to look at her.

The problem was, their relationship could no longer be reduced to what he wanted.

But he didn't wish to think about any of that. Not now. Not when she was in his arms.

"One-two-three," he murmured in her ear.

She laughed softly. "I fear we passed the remedial long ago."

"Indeed. But one mustn't ever forget the basics." He executed another outrageous turn, taking immense pleasure in the way her eyes brightened and her lips curved into a smile.

When the music came to an end, he led her from the floor. They were briefly caught in a sea of other guests saying their farewells and fetching their coats and wraps. But they didn't linger. After taking leave of their hostess, they proceeded outside to the street. It was lined with gleaming black carriages, many of which had crests lacquered on the doors.

Their own more humble vehicle was at the end of the block. There was no use hailing the coachman. The street was too congested for him to drive any closer. "We'll have to walk to it," Justin said.

Helena tucked her gloved hand more securely in his arm as they started off down the street. They'd gone no more than a few steps when Justin felt the fine hairs on the back of his neck lift in warning. He turned around sharply, a flicker of foreboding bringing him to abrupt attention.

"What's wrong?" Helena asked.

Justin looked up and down the street, but there was no sign of Mr. Glyde—or anyone else who appeared to be a villain. Even so, he had the distinct feeling they were being watched.

"Nothing," he said. But when they reached their carriage, he lost no time in bundling Helena inside. He climbed in after her, sitting beside her on the forward facing seat.

Helena withdrew several pins from her coiffure. "The ballroom was uncommonly hot," she said as she removed the floral wreath from her head. "Look. All of my flowers have wilted."

"I noticed. You were dropping petals from your skirts all through the reel."

"Was I? How embarrassing." She set aside the wreath. "I suppose wax flowers would have been tidier. Then again, they wouldn't have smelled half as well."

He stretched his arm along the back of the seat and, as had become their custom during carriage rides home, she settled closer to him, resting her head against his chest.

"Ah well," she sighed. "It was good while it lasted."

He draped his arm around her shoulders, even as her words sent a pang of despair straight through his vitals. She was speaking of the trimmings on her gown, but to him such sentiments took on a whole other meaning. Yes, it was good. And he fervently hoped it would last a very long while. But one must be realistic.

They were reaching the end of things.

That fact had been hammered home to him with each dance at this evening's ball. In her rose-festooned silk gown, her dark tresses bound up in a wreath of flowers and her creamy skin on elegant display, Helena was as dazzling and unattainable as the Koh-i-Noor diamond. A rare and precious jewel of infinite value. And the fashionable glitter of London high society was her proper setting. Not the rural countryside. And certainly not a remote and dilapidated abbey in coastal Devon.

"Do you know what I'd like to do tomorrow?" she asked.

Justin turned his face into her hair. "What's that, my dear?"

"I'd like to do something—go somewhere—with Jenny and Mr. Finchley. It doesn't seem fair that we should go out every night and Jenny should have to wait up for us, all alone in the parlor with only her needlework for company."

"What did she do to occupy herself before all this unpleasantness started?"

"She wasn't obliged to do anything. I was never out this much before. Certainly not every evening. And if I went to a ball or a supper party, I made certain Jenny was invited as well. She's not a servant, you know."

"You pay her, don't you?"

"Yes, an annual sum, but that's more an allowance than a wage. And it's not nearly enough. When the bank releases my funds, I plan to set up an independence for her."

"You'd send her away from you?"

Helena gave his evening coat a little tug. "Don't be silly. I'd never send Jenny away. But she must be free to go if she wishes. It's dreadful to depend on other people. No matter how kind they are, you always feel beholden. As if you're an object of charity."

"I won't argue with that."

"Is that how you felt? At the orphanage?"

"Beholden? Good God, no. There was nothing to be beholden for. We were treated abominably. The entire establishment was corrupt, the children poorly clothed and barely fed. When I left there for my apprenticeship, I didn't feel beholden to them. I felt as if—"

"What?"

"As if they'd taken something from me. As if they'd incurred a debt. When I left England, I was determined that one day they'd repay it."

"You're speaking of vengeance."

"I'm speaking of justice."

Her fingers moved idly on his coat, smoothing a nonexistent wrinkle. "Was it you who closed down the orphanage?"

"Me?" Justin gave a humorless laugh. "No. My sights were set firmly on Sir Oswald at the time. It was Finchley. And he didn't just close it. He had the building razed to the ground."

Helena digested this bit of information in silence. "He's so kind and good-humored," she said at last. "As if nothing troubles him excepting matters of law."

"Finchley is amiable enough, I'll grant you. But he has a diabolical mind and an unforgiving nature. He can hold onto a grudge longer than anyone I've ever known. It doesn't pay to be on the wrong side of him."

"I'll remember that."

"No need. You're not likely to do anything to incur his wrath."

"Goodness, I should hope not." She settled her cheek more comfortably against his chest. "Do you think he'll agree to accompany us on an outing tomorrow?"

"With Miss Holloway? Undoubtedly. What did you have in mind?"

"An evening entertainment. Something lighthearted. We've accepted no invitations yet. We can do whatever we please."

"On a Saturday evening, you may take your choice of amusements. But if it's to be the four of us…" Justin considered the options. "It's closing day at Cremorne Gardens tomorrow. They'll have jugglers and tightrope walkers and the like. Music and dancing, as well."

"I've never been," Helena said. "My father believed places like Cremorne Gardens and Vauxhall were dens of vice."

"They are," Justin said. "That's half the fun."

Chapter Twenty

Located on the northern bank of the Thames, Cremorne Gardens was comprised of twelve sprawling acres on which all manner of entertainments were made available to the public. There were military exhibitions and feats of dangerous daring, including high-wire acts and balloon ascents. Music and dancing were available on a raised platform, hot food and cold drinks were served in the banqueting hall, and a grand pavilion played host to horticultural exhibitions from all over the world.

They entered the gardens through a pair of majestic black iron gates. Helena held onto Justin's arm and Jenny was escorted by Mr. Finchley. It was a chilly evening and both she and Jenny wore mantles over their gowns.

"What shall we do first?" Mr. Finchley asked.

"Dancing," Jenny said emphatically.

The evening commenced in a whirlwind of activity. They danced and laughed and drank champagne. They watched a tightrope walker teetering across a wire cable strung up sixty feet from the ground—a display which made Helena gasp several times and bury her face in Justin's sleeve. And then, at Mr. Finchley's urging, they sought out one of the garden's most popular attractions: the celebrated whist-playing dog.

"The Learned Dog, Lily," Jenny read aloud from a playbill. "What a hum!"

But when a volunteer was drawn from the audience to act as Lily's opponent at whist, the little brown and white spaniel truly did appear to play a creditable game.

"As canny as a Bath dowager," Mr. Finchley remarked.

"Her owner is giving her cues," Justin said. "Look."

"What cues?" Helena couldn't discern any. Indeed, the mustachioed gentleman standing beside the little dog was hardly moving at all.

"Admit it," Mr. Finchley said when they finally drifted away. "The dog is a genius."

"If I had a genius dog," Jenny retorted, "I'd train it up to do something more useful than play whist and dominoes."

Helena laughed. "We have two dogs at the Abbey. Paul and Jonesy. I can't imagine they'd enjoy a card game. Unless there was a marrow bone involved."

Justin glanced down at her, a strange sort of smile playing at his lips. He didn't say anything.

His mood had been somewhat erratic of late.

Most of the time, he behaved just as he had before. He was kind and protective, sometimes confiding in her, sometimes teasing her and making her laugh. But there were moments where he fell quiet. When his thoughts seemed to turn inward. Even worse, there were moments when he fell into a fit of the sullens. When he was terse and gruff, brooding over some problem, the substance of which he seemed quite unwilling to share.

"Shall we visit the Ashburnham Pavilion?" he asked.

They all agreed that they should and proceeded across the gardens to the immense cathedral-like structure that had lately played host to an exhibition of American plants. It was constructed of wood joined with iron bolts and boasted a roof of watertight canvas. More than two hundred glassless rectangular windows lined the upper part of the walls, leaving the pavilion open to the elements.

"It's so dark and empty," Jenny said. "The exhibition must be closed."

Justin lifted his hand and rubbed the back of his neck. He then looked around them, his gaze drifting over the surrounding landscape. It was dotted with trees and shrubs and crisscrossed with paths on which small groups of people were walking, talking, and laughing.

Helena felt his body go rigid at her side. "What's wrong?" she asked. He'd behaved in just such a way outside Lady Wardlow's house. "Do you see someone?"

Mr. Finchley moved to Justin's side. Helena saw the two of them exchange a weighted look. There was more understanding in that look—more history—than she could presently comprehend.

"Justin?" she prompted.

"Finchley is going to take you and Miss Holloway home," he said abruptly.

A shiver of fear traced its icy cold fingers down Helena's spine. "Why? Is it Mr. Glyde? Is he here?"

Mr. Finchley gently took Helena's arm. "If you will, my lady."

She didn't budge. "Justin, I—"

"We'll talk at the house." He gave her a hard glance. "No questions, Helena. I need you to go with Finchley. Now."

"But—"

"*Now!*" he barked.

It was a battlefield command if she'd ever heard one. It made her jump nearly out of her skin. Drat him and his high-handedness! She lifted her chin a notch, drawing her dignity about herself as securely as she drew her velvet mantle. "As you wish."

Her heart pounded like a triphammer as she took Mr. Finchley's arm.

He offered his other arm to Jenny. "Straight to the carriage, ladies. No dawdling."

Helena glanced back at Justin over her shoulder, but he wasn't looking at her. He was looking out at the darkened landscape again.

"I didn't see anything," Jenny said. "Did you see anything? Did you?"

"Not a thing," Mr. Finchley replied as he hurried them to the garden gates. "But I've known Thornhill too long to ask questions when he gets that look in his eye.

Justin stood, immobile, as Horace Glyde emerged from the stand of trees near Ashburnham Pavilion. He was wearing a dark cloth coat and a low-brimmed felt hat tipped low over his eyes.

"How long have you been following us?" Justin asked. His blood was already boiling, but as he looked at the man who'd hunted Helena and hurt her, a white-hot rage ignited within him. It burned away the raw edges of his reason, leaving nothing behind but a primitive urge for swift and brutal violence.

Glyde regarded him warily. "I'm not following you, guv. It's Castleton's niece I'm after."

Justin advanced on him. "She's my wife. Did you truly think I'd let you take her?"

Glyde showed no sign of retreating. He was an enormous brute. He'd likely never had to run away from a fight in the whole of his miserable life. "It's not up to you, is it? It's the law. Just like the magistrate said in Devon."

"If your actions are lawful, why are you skulking about Mayfair and Cremorne Gardens? Why don't you show yourself in the light of day?"

Glyde came forward. He stopped in front of the entrance to the pavilion, only an arm's length away from Justin. "His lordship don't want a scandal, sir. You know that."

"What I know is that you seem to enjoy terrorizing gently bred ladies."

"It's nothing personal."

"It is to me." Justin's fists clenched reflexively at his sides. The ominous sound of his knuckles cracking made Glyde cast an uneasy glance downward.

"Easy, guv," he said. "No need to come to blows. It's just a job."

"To hurt and abuse women?"

"Not a woman. A lunatic. You've seen the papers. Castleton said—*Oomph!*" Glyde's head snapped back on his thick neck as Justin landed a staggering punch square on his jaw.

After that, Glyde abandoned any pretense of civility.

He swung back at Justin, clipping him on the shoulder. Justin nearly lost his footing. *Bloody hell*. The man had fists the size of boulders. Justin hit him in the face again and then in the stomach. Glyde returned the punches blow for blow.

They grappled with each other, stumbling through the door to the pavilion and clattering past a table of plants.

It wasn't a proper fight with perfectly executed hits. It was violent, disorganized, and bloody. Glyde split Justin's lip and opened a cut above his eye. Justin vaguely registered knocking out a few of Glyde's teeth and nearly strangling the man with his own neckcloth.

But no matter how many punches and blows were exchanged, Glyde kept coming. He was big and brutal and seemingly unstoppable. Facts which only served to further stoke Justin's rage.

"You can't win, guv," Glyde panted, circling around him. "It's not an even match."

Justin spat out a mouthful of blood on the pavilion floor. "The hell it isn't."

"I'm no scrawny lad who's taken the queen's shilling. You can't thrash me for impudence."

"Thrash you?" Justin's voice vibrated with fury. "I'm going to *murder* you."

"You?" Glyde snorted. "Not likely." He lunged forward, seizing Justin in an iron grasp. "I know how you gentlemen fight."

Justin caught hold of Glyde by the shirt. "Whoever said I was a gentleman?" he asked. And then he slammed the top of his forehead down onto the bridge of Glyde's nose, shattering it in an audible crunch of cartilage and bone.

Glyde howled in pain as blood spurted from his nostrils. He clutched his face. "You bastard!" he cried. Or something very like it. Justin couldn't quite make out his words.

He hauled Glyde up by his coat before the man could crumple to the ground. "I have half a mind to find some cold water and force you under it for four or five hours," he growled. "But given our present location, I suppose I'll have to settle for beating you into unconsciousness."

An hour after arriving back at the house in Half Moon Street, a boy came to the door with a message for Mr. Finchley. Helena didn't know what the message said. She only knew it had come from Justin.

"Is he all right?" she asked desperately.

Mr. Finchley thrust the folded note into the pocket of his coat. "Well enough to send for me." He retrieved his hat and overcoat from Mr. Jarrow and went to the door. "I must leave right away."

Helena followed after him, Jenny close behind.

"Lock up the house tight, Jarrow," Mr. Finchley said.

And then he was gone.

"Well!" Jenny exclaimed. "He's been no help at all."

Helena didn't have the heart to be irritated with Mr. Finchley. She was too worried about Justin. He must have seen Mr. Glyde or her uncle. That was the only explanation.

But what had happened next? She didn't like to think. Justin was a big man, leanly muscled and broad of shoulder. Her uncle could never hope to best him if the two of them came to blows. However, Mr. Glyde—though nowhere near as tall as Justin—was the approximate size of a house.

She wrung her hands as she climbed the stairs back up to the parlor. Jenny called for another pot of tea and then the two of them sat down together in front of the coal fire and waited.

And waited.

When the little clock on the mantel chimed two, Helena insisted that Jenny retire to bed. "There's no point in both of us staying up until dawn."

Jenny pursed her lips. "You should retire as well, Helena. You're burnt to the socket."

Helena shook her head. "I couldn't sleep a wink."

"At least change out of your evening dress. You can't spend all night in a corset and crinoline." Jenny caught at her hand. "Come up to your room. I'll unpin your hair and brush it out for you. You'll feel better afterward."

Helena reluctantly did as Jenny bid her. A short while later, she returned to the parlor alone, her flannel dressing gown knotted snugly at her waist and her hair in its evening plait. She curled up on the chintz sofa. The house was quiet, the only sounds the rhythmic ticking of the clock and the rustle of hot coals in the grate. She closed her eyes for a brief moment.

The next thing she knew, the clock was chiming three. Her eyes opened blearily. *Botheration!* She must have fallen asleep. She sat upright on the sofa and listened. There was no sound of anyone else in the house, but outside she could hear the faint rattle and clip-clop of a hansom cab departing.

She ran down the stairs, the voluminous skirts of her robe floating behind her. Mr. Jarrow had been waiting on a straight-backed chair in the hall all night. He was still there, but now he was on his feet, unbolting the front door.

Justin and Mr. Finchley entered. Their hats and coats were gone, their hair disheveled, and their shirts and trousers in a despicable state. Had Helena not known better, she'd have suspected they were intoxicated. But as she swiftly descended the stairs, she saw Justin's face illuminated in the gaslight.

Her hand flew to her mouth, barely stifling her gasp of horror.

Justin's gaze shot to hers. "Ah hell," he muttered.

"What's happened?" she cried. "Who did this to you?"

"It looks worse than it is," Justin said as Mr. Jarrow shut the door behind them.

She crossed the hall, reaching out to him with fluttering hands only to draw back in uncertainty. "You're covered in blood!"

"Head wounds always bleed a great deal," Mr. Finchley said helpfully.

She cast him a quelling glance. "Don't pretend it isn't serious. He's obviously been severely beaten."

"Quite severely," Mr. Finchley agreed. "Only look at the damage Glyde has done to his fists."

The irony in Mr. Finchley's voice escaped her. She caught one of Justin's hands in both of hers. His knuckles were torn and bleeding. "Oh Justin," she breathed. "Did you fight him?"

"My lady?" Mrs. Jarrow appeared in the hall. She was in her nightcap and slippers, clutching her dressing gown up to her chin. "Do you have need of me?"

Helena inhaled a steadying breath. She wasn't going to fall apart. She refused to be that person anymore. "Indeed, Mrs. Jarrow. Will you bring hot water and linens to my bedroom? And a bottle of brandy, as well."

"Right away, ma'am."

Justin scowled down at her. At least, it looked like a scowl. It was hard to tell through all of the blood and swelling. "I thought you'd be asleep by now."

"While you were out in the dark somewhere risking your life?" She took hold of his arm and directed him to the stairs. "If that's what you thought, sir, then you don't know me at all."

Mr. Finchley backed toward the door. "As my presence is no longer required…"

"Wait," Helena commanded. "We may yet need you to summon a doctor."

"No we won't." Justin paused at the foot of the stairs to look back at Mr. Finchley. "Go home, Tom. I'll talk to you tomorrow."

Mr. Finchley flashed him a grin. "It's already tomorrow," he replied before taking his leave.

Mr. Jarrow shut and bolted the door after him. "Will you be needing anything else, my lady?"

"No, thank you, Mr. Jarrow. That will be all."

Mr. Jarrow sketched a tired bow and departed the hall.

And then Helena and Justin were alone.

She looked up at his battered face. "Why did you do it?"

"He deserved it."

"But look at you," she said softly. "Your poor face. He can't have been worth it."

Justin gazed steadily back at her. "No. But you are."

Helena dipped another linen in the basin of bloody water and brought it to Justin's face. She'd rinsed away most of the dried blood from his face and hands, revealing a haphazard collection of jagged cuts and scrapes, none of which appeared to be life threatening.

Justin held himself immobile as she tended him, enduring her attentions in stoic silence. He was seated on the edge of her bed with his booted feet on the floor. She stood between his legs, reaching up to dab at a wound on his temple. She felt his eyes on her as she worked.

"Did you think that's what I wanted? To have you engage in fisticuffs with that great lummox?" She smoothed back a wayward lock of hair from his forehead in order to clean the wound beneath. "I would never have asked you to fight him on my behalf. Never."

Justin allowed her to rail at him, unchecked. He offered not a word of explanation.

"How do you think I felt this evening? Never knowing from one minute to the next if you were safe or if you'd been murdered and thrown in the Thames?" She dropped the linen into the blood-tinged water in the basin and reached to unfasten the buttons at the collar of his shirt.

He caught at her hand. "What are you doing?"

"You must take this off," she said.

"I have no injuries under my shirt."

"I'll be the judge of that. Unless you'd prefer I summon a doctor?"

He set his jaw. And then he released her hand, allowing her to unfasten his collar. When she'd finished, he quickly stripped his shirt off over his head.

Her gaze dropped down. There were abrasions on his chest and what looked to be bruises blooming along his ribs, but that wasn't what made her heart stutter and her mouth go dry. No. It was the sight of him, so shockingly, gloriously masculine.

She'd never seen a gentleman's naked chest before, except in books with pictures from classical antiquity. She remembered one such book with a plate depicting a statue of Prometheus chained to a rock. The Greek Titan had been partially unclothed, the lean muscles of his arms and chest well defined. Justin's bare arms and torso were shaped along the same lines as that statue. Indeed, the hard planes and grooves of his muscles might have been chiseled from stone.

But unlike the marble Prometheus, Justin's chest was lightly covered in a mat of black hair which tapered down in a narrow line, disappearing beneath his woolen trousers.

It was also covered with scars.

Along each of his upper arms and layered on both of his sides were burns. The same size and shape as the burn scars that marred his face and neck. They were puckered red, falling in thick lines one over the other. A hot poker, he'd said. *They held it in the fire and then they held it against me.*

Helena moistened her lips. Justin was looking at her, his expression inscrutable as ever. She was painfully aware of the intensity of his regard. Did he think she'd cringe away from the sight of him? She didn't feel much like cringing. Rather the opposite. She wanted to touch him. To trace her fingers over every hollow and groove of his muscled chest.

She reached for a fresh linen, her hands suddenly unsteady as she soaked it in the water and wrung it out. "Could he have broken your ribs?" She pressed it to a minor cut below his right shoulder.

He sucked in his breath. "No."

"Does that hurt?" She swabbed the wet linen very lightly over his chest.

"No," he rasped again.

"You sound as if it does."

"It doesn't."

Helena frowned at him. Were all gentlemen so difficult when they were injured? Giles hadn't been. Then again, she couldn't remember Giles having ever engaged in a bout of fisticuffs with a man of Mr. Glyde's dimensions.

She tossed the scrap of linen back into the basin and then carried the whole of it to the chiffonier and set it down. Mrs. Jarrow had brought up a jar of salve along with the linens. Helena twisted off the lid and gave it a delicate sniff. Satisfied, she went back to stand between Justin's legs.

"What's that?" he asked gruffly.

"Salve of some kind. It smells of beeswax and honey." She touched her fingers to his chin, tipping his face up so that she could apply a dollop of it to one of his cuts. "Where is Mr. Glyde now? Has he gone back to my uncle?"

"No. He's not with your uncle." Justin closed his eyes as she dabbed salve on the cuts over his brow. "He's at the London docks."

"What in heaven is he doing there?"

"At present? He's trussed up in the bottom of a ship."

"*What?*"

Justin's eyes opened again. For the first time since his return, she saw something like humor in his gaze. "Glyde said that terrorizing you was a job to him, nothing more. So…" He shrugged. "I found him a new position."

Helena stared at him, openmouthed. "A new position?" She was both fascinated and appalled. "Where?"

"In the West Indies. He sails with the morning tide."

"He's gone? He's left London?" She pressed a hand to her midriff. "Is he going to come back?"

"No," Justin said, his voice softening. "He won't come back."

Helena was scarcely able to accept it. Mr. Glyde was gone? He'd never hurt her again?

The jar of salve clattered to the floor as she flung her arms around Justin's neck. She was beyond words. Beyond anything. All she could manage was to hold him tight, hoping against hope that he understood how profoundly grateful she was for what he'd done for her.

Justin brought an arm around her waist. He slowly drew back to look at her. "I don't want your gratitude. I didn't do it for that."

"You have it anyway," she said. "And so much more."

Afterward, she would wonder if he'd moved his head of his own accord or if it was she who'd urged him to her with an insistent press of her hand. She very much feared it was the latter.

Whoever instigated the movement, it led to her mouth finding his in a warm, passionate kiss.

He didn't rebuff her. Not at first. For the briefest moment, he returned her kiss with the same tenderness he'd shown her at the Stanhope Hotel. And then—

"No," he said gently "No." He touched her cheek. "It's not a good idea."

Helena went rigid with embarrassment as he pulled away from her. A swell of overwhelming humiliation tightened her throat. "You're right."

But she didn't know what she was agreeing to. She was too mortified to think. Too ashamed to meet his eyes. If only a hole in the floor would open up, she would gladly leap into it.

Good gracious, she had kissed him. And now—

He was *rejecting* her.

"It will only confuse things," Justin said.

"I see." She backed away from him. "Forgive me, I thought— But you're quite right. I was mistaken."

"Helena—"

She took another backward step toward the door. "It's clear as day. I don't know why I couldn't see it before."

He moved to rise from the bed. "What the devil are you talking about?"

"You can't get past it. The lies I told you. The way I tricked you into marriage."

"Don't be ridiculous. That's not why—" He broke off with a low growl of frustration. "Good God, Helena, we've already been over this. You didn't lie to me. I knew you had secrets. I wanted you anyway."

"You don't want me. You can't." Her cheeks burned. "When someone has wronged you, you're incapable of forgiving them."

A spasm of emotion passed over Justin's face. "Not you. Never you."

"Why not? It would be fair, in my case. What I did is unforgiveable. It was stupid of me to think—to expect—" She swallowed. "After what I kept from you, I don't deserve your forgiveness."

A bleak look of resignation flickered in Justin's eyes. It was there a moment and then gone, snuffed out like a candle flame as his expression hardened into firm resolve. "Would you like to know what's unforgiveable?" he asked. "The things I've kept from you."

"Nothing could be worse than this."

"You think not?" He looked at her. "The day we met at the King's Arm, you asked me which general I served under in Cawnpore. You wanted to know if it was Major General

Hugh Wheeler or if I'd arrived later, as part of the relieving forces under Brigadier General Neill."

Helena stared at him, her embarrassment at his rejection temporarily receding. "You said it wasn't General Neill. That you didn't take part in the…" She couldn't bring herself to mention rape. "In the…pillaging…engaged in by his men."

"I didn't," he said. "But if I'd capably performed my duties, there would have been no need for Neill to ride in with his troops and retake the city."

"I don't understand."

"Because of me, more than two hundred women and children were slaughtered in Cawnpore. British women and children. All captured and killed in the most violent manner. Yet I survived. *I*. Who was supposed to be protecting them. Is that not unforgivable?"

A cold, cloying sense of uneasiness seeped into Helena's blood. More than two hundred British women and children? Good lord. He couldn't mean… "The Cawnpore Massacre," she whispered.

She knew about it. Everyone did. It had only happened two years before and had been in all the papers. Early reports had described the atrocities in graphic detail. It had outraged the British public.

And it had galvanized the relieving forces.

Under the command of Brigadier General Neill, they had exacted a brutal vengeance against those deemed responsible. Many innocent Indians had been casualties of their wrath.

Justin sank back down on the edge of the bed. "The British garrison at Cawnpore was under siege. We couldn't last much longer. We hadn't the resources. After three weeks, General Wheeler had no choice but to negotiate with the rebels. In exchange for his surrender, he made their leader—a rebel rajah called Nana Sahib—promise to grant the women and children safe passage out of the city."

Helena moved closer to him as he spoke, her arms folded across her midsection.

"I was one of the soldiers escorting the women and children to the River Ganges. There were boats there that would have taken them to safety." Justin's throat convulsed in a swallow. "But when we arrived at Sati Chaura Ghat—when we began to board the boats—"

"The sepoys attacked," she said.

"They killed most of the soldiers. My batman, as well. I'll spare you the details. As for the women and children…"

"They captured them and imprisoned them in a little house near a well. I read about it in the newspapers."

"They weren't just imprisoned there, Helena. They were slaughtered."

"I know," she acknowledged softly. The newspapers had printed reports of what British soldiers had found when they'd finally arrived to rescue the women. It had been unspeakable. A gruesome, senseless tragedy the likes of which Helena couldn't even imagine. "Oh, but Justin…that wasn't your fault. How could it have been?"

"Because I sympathized with them," he said with sudden fierceness. "I never thought we should be in India. Who could blame them for hating us? We disrespected them. Treated them like animals." One of his fists clenched. "I had friends among them. Decent men and women. I did business with them. Even invested some of my earnings. When all hell broke loose, my judgment was called into question. And when I was tasked with escorting the women and children prisoners to safety…" His face contorted.

"But that's…" Helena was horrified. "Surely no one could have thought…"

"That I didn't fight as hard as I could have? That I didn't do my utmost to protect them from harm?" He leaned forward, his elbows on his knees and his head in his hands. His fingers raked through his already disheveled hair. "They did more than think it. Some of them said it. Though rarely to my face."

"How could they even suggest such a thing? You were captured and tortured!"

"Yes," he said. "But I wasn't killed." He looked up at her, his mouth twisted into a bitter rictus of a smile. "Unlike the other prisoners, my captors let me live."

Chapter Twenty-One

Justin rose abruptly from the bed and crossed the room to the marble-topped chiffonier. Mrs. Jarrow had brought up a bottle of brandy. There were no glasses. He supposed Helena had meant to pour it on his wounds or some such thing. But he didn't really care what it was meant for. He uncorked it with his teeth and took a long drink directly from the bottle.

He was dreadfully conscious of his half-clothed state. With his scarred chest and arms exposed to Helena's view, he felt oddly vulnerable. Like a raw lad with his first woman. But such feelings paled in comparison to the sense of hopeless despair that had descended over him as he'd recounted what had taken place in Cawnpore.

Helena stood near the bed, watching him as he drank. Her hair was bound up in a long braid, secured over the front of one shoulder with a black silk ribbon. He could see spots of blood on her dressing gown from when she'd cleaned his wounds.

There was something startlingly intimate about the two of them together in her bedroom, each in a state of undress. It's what he'd always imagined married life would be like. A level of comfort with a woman. A sense that she accepted him. *All* of him.

Even so, he hadn't planned to tell her anything about the massacre. Not now. Possibly not ever. It was a source of shame to him. A failure which had resulted in the deaths of countless people.

"You said you were just one of the soldiers tasked with escorting the women and children to the boats," Helena said. "Which means there were others."

"That's right."

"What happened to those soldiers? Were they all killed?"

"Not all." He leaned back against the chiffonier, the bottle of brandy still in his hand. "Some managed to get across the river."

"And where are they now?"

"I haven't the slightest idea." He took another swallow of brandy. He knew what she was getting at and he didn't wish to hear it.

Not that that stopped her.

"I wonder if they take as much responsibility for what happened as you do?" she asked. "I wonder if they're out there, enacting their penance somewhere, garbed in hair shirts and the like."

"Helena…"

She folded her arms "Mr. Finchley told me that you take on everyone else's burdens. That you would bear the weight of the world, if you could."

"Did he." It sounded like something Finchley would say.

"I believe he's right. I've seen it myself. With Neville and the servants at the Abbey. With me. You take care of *everyone*. It's in your nature to protect people. But a single soldier couldn't have saved all of those women and children, Justin. You must know that. Not even if that soldier was you."

He shook his head. "It's not as simple as that."

"Of course it is. You need only forgive yourself." She moved toward him, her eyes searching his. "But you can't, can you? You're as unforgiving of your own failings as you are of those in other people."

He flinched. It was the second time she'd mentioned his inability to forgive. Good God, but it was true. He had no forgiveness in him. He couldn't remember if he ever had.

"I don't count you among that group," he said, his voice gone hoarse. "I never have."

She stopped in front of him. The skirts of her dressing gown pooled about his legs. "Then why…" She hesitated a moment, looking endearingly uncertain. "Why did you stop wanting me?"

Her question rendered Justin temporarily speechless. Indeed, he couldn't have been more surprised if she'd taken out a mallet and struck him over the head with it.

"After the night Mr. Glyde came to the Abbey, you never again attempted to kiss me. Or to try and persuade me to…" A blush suffused her face.

He groaned. "You think I don't *want* you? You think it doesn't kill me every time I see you—wanting to kiss you? To take you in my arms?"

Her blush deepened to scarlet. "Then why?"

Why? He'd asked himself that question hundreds of times in the past weeks. The answer was always the same. "What sort of blackguard would have relations with a woman who hasn't chosen him of her own free will?"

Her brow furrowed. "Hypothetically? Any number of gentlemen."

"No they wouldn't. Not if they were worthy of the name."

"You're wrong. I know countless ladies who married gentlemen chosen by their fathers. Their own preference was never taken into account. And their husbands must have had relations with them because many now have children. Some of them two and three."

"It's not the same thing. When you came to me in Devon, it was out of desperation. If not for your uncle's abuse, you'd never have answered a matrimonial advertisement. You'd have been free. Wealthy, titled, and free. I don't believe you'd have married at all. And if you did, it would have been to a man like Wexford or one of those other lords or sirs."

She gave a dismissive huff. "None of that matters now. The past can't be changed. And the fact is, I did answer your advertisement. I did decide to marry you."

"But you wouldn't have done—"

"What difference does that make? We're not living in the land of would have and should have. We're living in the here and now. And here and now I'm married to *you*."

"I won't have you."

Helena drew back as if he'd slapped her.

"Not physically," he said. "Not until all of this is resolved."

"I see." She was still blushing mightily. Such topics weren't meant to be discussed between men and women. Even if they were married. "Am I to have no say in this at all?"

"When this is over. When you're free to choose what you truly want."

"Very well," she said. "But my feelings on the subject won't change."

Justin didn't like to inquire what those feelings were. She hadn't fully articulated them yet. Clearly, she'd wanted him to kiss her. That was something, wasn't it? A physical attraction could be built upon. And, when coupled with a friendship, he supposed the two of them could be content, at least for a short while. If only…

If only he were a different man and the Abbey a different place. If only he could give her everything she deserved. Restore her life to what it might have been if things hadn't gone so terribly wrong with her uncle and Mr. Glyde.

But he couldn't do any of those things. It wasn't in his power to make her happy. He realized that now. The truth of it had been driven home in the past weeks as he watched her move through fashionable society. She belonged here, with people of her own kind. People with grand titles who rode in lacquered carriages and danced in gilded ballrooms.

When this was all over, he was going to have to let her go. It was the only thing he could do. When you cared for someone, you made the sacrifice. They didn't have to ask for it. You made it regardless. Even if it left you desolate. Even if it broke your heart.

After staying up the better part of the night, Helena slept until noon. The rest of the day, she spent with Jenny. They worked on their needlework in the parlor, sitting side by side on the plump chintz sofa. Helena needed something active to occupy her mind. She wasn't going to force her company on Justin.

Not that he was seeking it out. He'd spent most of the afternoon answering letters from Mr. Boothroyd and other of his business associates. Indeed, he didn't emerge from his room until nearly five o'clock, and only then in response to a note sent round by Mr. Finchley.

Helena looked up at him in nervous expectation as he broke the seal and unfolded the paper. He swiftly skimmed the contents. "Finchley says he's heard from Mr. Pelham. The editorial will be printed on Monday."

"Tomorrow?" Jenny glanced from Helena to Justin. "And what happens then?"

"We act as normal," Justin said.

Helena set aside her needlework. Her hands had begun to tremble. Her stomach was trembling, too. "That might prove difficult."

"Why should it?"

"People will naturally want to know why you look as if you've gone ten rounds with a prizefighter."

Justin grimaced. He raised a hand to his face. "That bad, is it?"

"It's not good," Helena said frankly.

"Indeed," Jenny agreed. She turned to Helena. "Perhaps Mr. Finchley can squire you about?"

Helena's chest tightened in silent protest. She didn't want Mr. Finchley to escort her anywhere. Much as she liked the man, he was a poor substitute for Justin. And, after tomorrow morning, she'd need Justin's presence more than ever. How else, but with him at her side, was she to face the world in the aftermath of the editorial?

She rose and went to him. "Come into the light. Let me see."

Justin obediently walked to the windows and turned to face her. She lifted a hand to his cheek on the pretext of examining his wounds; however, there was nothing clinical about her touch. Her fingertips brushed lightly over his brow and then down along his jaw to the swelling at the side of his mouth. She traced the pad of her thumb over his lower lip. "I suggest ice," she said. "For the swelling."

His eyes held hers, his smoke-gray gaze filled with a bewildering tangle of emotion. There was heat there and tenderness, but there was something else as well. Something which made her brows knit into a puzzled frown. It was sadness. Desolation. It flickered for an instant and then was gone, his expression shuttering.

"Do we have any ice?" Jenny moved to rise. "I'll go down to the kitchen and ask Mrs. Jarrow."

"I'll go," Justin said abruptly.

Helena dropped her hand from his face. She watched him stride from the room. He didn't want to be alone with her. Foolish man. Did he really believe she didn't know her own mind? That when things with her uncle were resolved she'd suddenly decide she no longer cared for him?

She went back to the sofa and resumed her seat beside Jenny.

"He looks an absolute ruffian," Jenny remarked quietly. "Do you suppose Mr. Glyde looks better or worse?"

"Worse," Helena said without hesitation.

"Good. He deserves whatever punishment Mr. Thornhill meted out." Jenny threaded her needle. "I only wish I'd been there to see it."

The following morning, Mr. Finchley arrived at daybreak with a copy of the *London Courant* under his arm. They were at breakfast when he came, the table cluttered with half-filled plates, pots of honey and jam, and cups of still-steaming coffee. He sat down to join them in the empty chair across from Justin and spread the newspaper out on the table.

"Here it is," he said. "On pages 5 and 6."

"Have you read it?" Justin asked.

"I have."

"And?"

"It's compelling." Mr. Finchley folded over the page. He looked at Helena. "Shall I read it aloud?"

She clasped her hands together in her lap. Every muscle in her body had gone tense. "If you please."

He cleared his throat and began:

> *"The position of a lunatic appears to be one of the most terrible in which a human can be placed. There is, however, a still worse condition, which is that of a person of sane mind who is treated by his fellow creatures as though he were mad—of one who, being himself of sane mind, is incarcerated in an asylum intended only for the insane— who is, therefore, subjected to bodily restraint, and, still worse, to the moral and intellectual indignities consequent upon a supposed deprivation of reason."*[1]

Helena stared down at her hands as Mr. Finchley continued. The editorial commenced by discussing the case of a young gentleman, heir to a fortune of thirty thousand

---

1   "The Position of a Lunatic." *The London Times* (London, England), 19 August 1858. See Author Notes.

pounds, who was committed to a private asylum by his greedy relatives. Next were three more cases of ladies and gentlemen whose relatives had likewise had them committed, albeit for much smaller sums. And then—at last—the editorial mentioned Helena by name.

> *"Another case of this kind has very recently been brought to light. Lady Helena Reynolds, sister of the late Giles Reynolds, 6th Earl of Castleton, was left an inheritance by her brother in excess of two hundred thousand pounds. In the course of the past year, her uncle, Edward Francis Reynolds, 7th Earl of Castleton, has attempted to obtain control of this inheritance by threatening his niece with committal in a private asylum."*

She listened, a sick feeling in her stomach, as Mr. Finchley read Mr. Pelham's account of all the indignities she'd suffered at the hands of Mr. Glyde, the doctors, and the matrons at Lowbridge House. His writing was spare and efficient, reducing the particulars of her case to a bare and stark reality.

Her heart thumped forcefully in her chest. She was filled with an impending sense of panic. Never in her life had she felt so exposed, so utterly vulnerable. Everyone she knew was likely reading these very same words over their morning tea and coffee. They would be outraged. Disgusted. Even those who pitied her would have no sympathy for the method she'd employed for redress. No lady, however, desperate, would ever expose herself to the press in such a way.

As of this moment, her reputation was ruined beyond all hope of repair.

Her fingers twisted together as Mr. Finchley read the editorial's conclusion:

> *"Private lunatic asylums are the bane of our system. They are mere commercial speculations run for the benefit of the proprietors. All that is required for admittance are two certificates, signed by two medical men unconnected with each other, and a statement signed by a relative— too often the hungry expectant of an inheritance. Under these arrangements, any sane English man or woman may, without much difficulty, be incarcerated in a private lunatic asylum. These are but five cases following one upon the other in rapid succession. How many remain behind of which we know nothing?"*

The breakfast room fell into silence. They all sat, grim-faced, no one venturing to utter a word.

"Well," Jenny murmured finally. "That was…chilling."

"It was powerful," Mr. Finchley said. "And very persuasive." He folded the newspaper and set it aside. "But you're right, Miss Holloway. It's going to send a chill of fear through anyone with greedy relatives."

Helena unclenched her fingers, flattening her hands onto her lap. Her palms were damp against the white cambric skirts of her morning dress.

"This is all precisely according to plan," Justin assured her. "Nothing at all for you to worry about."

She gave him a bleak look. What could she say? No gentleman could ever understand.

Jenny set her napkin beside her plate. "Is it your reputation that's concerning you? Are you thinking it's beyond repair?"

THE MATRIMONIAL ADVERTISEMENT

Helena's gaze found Jenny's. "I know it's stupid."

"Concerns about one's reputation are never stupid."

Mr. Finchley regarded Helena with concern. "If there had been any other course of action…"

"There wasn't," Justin said.

Helena knew Justin was right. There had been only one course available. "Yes, well…it's too late for second thoughts, in any case. Everyone will have read it by now."

"Don't be silly," Jenny said. "Half the ladies we know are still abed."

"They'll be awake soon enough. By luncheon, all of London will be buzzing about me."

Jenny reached out to cover Helena's hand with hers. "Please don't refine on it, my dear. You know it was the only way. And so what if society shuns you? You never cared for their good opinion."

"No," Helena admitted. "But it's easy not to care when one is in a position of strength."

"You're still in a position of strength," Mr. Finchley said. "You've told the truth. What can be stronger than that?"

Since coming to reside in Half Moon Street, Helena had become accustomed to receiving callers between the hours of one and three o'clock in the afternoon. But on the day the editorial was published, nobody came. She sat in the parlor and waited as the little mantel clock delicately chimed one hour and then the next.

"Not even the shamelessly curious have dared show their faces," she said tightly. "Do they suspect my uncle was right? That I might truly be mad?"

"They're cowards," Justin growled. He paced the room, too restless to sit with Helena and Jenny. "They won't make a move until they see which way the wind is blowing."

"Mr. Thornhill's quite right," Jenny agreed. "They'll wait for someone suitably influential to visit and then they'll follow after like lemmings."

Helena acknowledged the truth of this. It was the way of polite society. There weren't many who'd risk putting a foot wrong. They required a leader. Someone to set the fashion.

At a quarter to three, that someone arrived.

"The Earl of Wolverton," Mrs. Jarrow announced.

Helena scrambled to her feet as Lord Wolverton entered the parlor. His face was set in stern lines, his keen eyes blazing. She crossed the room to greet him. "My lord." She extended her hand.

He took it in his. "What's the meaning of these allegations in the morning paper?" he demanded. His gaze flashed briefly to Justin's face, his brows lowering in disapproval at the sight of all the cuts and bruises. "And what's happened to you, Thornhill?"

Justin came to stand beside her. His posture was unwelcoming. "A minor altercation," he said. "Nothing to speak of."

"Please come and sit down." Helena ushered Lord Wolverton into the parlor. He waited for her to resume her seat before lowering himself into a chair.

At his arrival, Jenny had withdrawn to a button-back chair near the fire with her needlework. She never participated in entertaining guests, preferring to take on the role of humble—and silent—companion.

Justin was equally silent, but he didn't withdraw. He sank down in the chair opposite Lord Wolverton.

His lordship didn't mince words. "Your father would be appalled, madam."

Helena lifted her brows. "Because I have gone to the press?"

"You've exposed yourself. Made yourself an object of ridicule. It was badly done." He frowned at her. "You'd have done better to come to me."

"You? Why on earth would I have done that?"

"You father was my oldest friend. Granted, I've not been a fixture in your life these many years, but you might have sought me out as a courtesy. I flatter myself that I still have some influence."

Helena inclined her head. "A great deal of influence, my lord. But this was an issue of madness."

He gave a disdainful grunt. "An issue of greed, more like. You forget, I knew your uncle when he was a lad. He was a conniving opportunist at the best of times. I wouldn't put anything past him. Had you come to me, I might have intervened."

Was it true? Would he have helped her? Helena tended to doubt it. "How was I to know you wouldn't have adjudged me mad yourself? You advised my father to have my mother committed to a private asylum. There was every chance you would recommend the same fate for me."

"Your mother?" Lord Wolverton scowled. "You were a child. You don't know what you're talking about."

"I know my mother had a sadness in her," Helena said quietly. "But she didn't deserve to be put away because of it."

"It was more than a sadness, madam. It was melancholia of the blackest kind. She wouldn't rise from her bed. She refused to eat or to drink. Neglected to tend to her most basic needs. Your father consulted the best physicians. They advised a warmer climate, but when he took her to the continent, she worsened. The asylum was his last resort."

Helena sat back in her seat, stunned. She'd never heard any of this before. She had no recollection of how her mother had behaved when still living at home. She'd been far too young. Her only memories were of her mother in the asylum, listless and unresponsive, with lank hair and skin the color of parchment. "How do you know I don't suffer the same symptoms?"

"Your mother's condition was evident in her eyes—in the pallor of her skin. Had you the same illness, you couldn't disguise it. Not when you're out every evening at the theatre or a ball. It would be plain for all to see."

"It wasn't evident to Lord Flood or Sir Bernard or to any other of the gentleman I went to for help when my uncle first began to torment me. I told them he was trying to get me to sign over my inheritance—that he was making threats. Not a one of them wished to advocate on my behalf."

"Why would they? Your uncle is in debt to each of them—and God knows how many others. Their only hope of repayment is if he takes control of your fortune. They'd hardly have worked to prevent him doing so."

An embarrassed flush heated her cheeks. She'd approached those men so earnestly. So desperately. They must have thought her an absolute fool. "How was I to know to whom he's in debt?"

"Such information is common knowledge."

"Among gentlemen, perhaps."

"Which is why you should have consulted with me." Lord Wolverton looked at Justin. "You're her husband. Couldn't you have advised her against this course?"

"I encouraged her."

"Did you, by God!" Lord Wolverton's expression turned thunderous. "To what end, sir? Do you seek to isolate her from her friends? To strengthen your hold on her fortune?"

Justin's jaw hardened. "What friends? When she came to me, she was alone and frightened. She had no one to protect her."

"Not from you, certainly. How long before you wed her? A month? A week?"

"My husband didn't know of my fortune when we married," Helena objected.

"He's accounted for it now, I'll wager. Down to the last penny. I'd expect nothing less from a man of his origins." Lord Wolverton's lip curled. "Oh yes, I've investigated that taradiddle about your having served with Lady Helena's brother. A load of rubbish, all of it. I don't know what you're playing at, sir, but I warn you—"

"*You* warn *me*?" Justin repeated. "*You*, a man who hasn't lifted a finger on her behalf?"

"Should I have followed your example and embroiled her in the scandal of the season? Of the decade?"

"At least I've made an effort to free her from this tangle. What have you done, Wolverton? Besides coming here to lecture her after the fact."

"Had I known—"

"You know now," Justin said sharply. "What do you intend to do about it?"

The atmosphere in the small parlor fairly crackled with tension as the two men glared at each other. Helena held her breath.

"The only thing I can do at this juncture," Lord Wolverton answered at last. "I'll lend her my countenance."

"And how exactly do you propose to do that?"

"To start, I'll accompany her to call on Castleton this afternoon."

Helena's mouth fell open in disbelief. "*Now?*"

Lord Wolverton nodded. "The sooner he's dealt with the better."

"I agree," Justin said.

A swell of panic clogged Helena's throat. She couldn't formulate the words to object to their scheme. She'd always known she must eventually confront Uncle Edward, but she'd never thought—never expected—it would be quite so soon.

"My carriage is below," Lord Wolverton said. "We can leave within the half hour."

Justin regarded her in silence for a moment.

Helena met his eyes. She knew then that he was leaving the final decision up to her. He believed she was strong enough to deal with her uncle, but he'd never force her to do anything against her will. He'd stand by her and support her whatever she decided.

It was that support—that unflinching loyalty—that finally loosened her tongue. "Very well, then," she said. "Let's pay a visit to Grosvenor Square."

Chapter Twenty-Two

"I still don't think this is a good idea," Justin said.

Lord Wolverton's black-lacquered carriage stopped in front of the Earl of Castleton's residence in Grosvenor Square. All Helena need do was get out and climb the steps to the door.

She sat beside Justin, temporarily immobilized. "Probably not," she acknowledged. "But I feel I must do it."

"I'll go with you."

"No." She took his gloved hand, pressing it for a moment in both of hers. "I must go in alone."

She'd made the decision immediately after departing Half Moon Street. She wouldn't cower behind Justin or Lord Wolverton like some manner of frightened creature. She'd face her uncle once and for all. She'd show him that he hadn't broken her.

"Foolishness," Lord Wolverton muttered from his seat across from them in the carriage. "You've no need to see him alone. He's your husband's problem now. And mine."

"I must," she said again. "It's a matter of dignity. Of self-respect."

Lord Wolverton harrumphed. He couldn't comprehend why it was so important for her to confront her uncle by herself.

But Justin could. He knew what it meant to face one's fears.

She held tight to his hand as one minute passed. And then another.

"Have you changed your mind?" he asked.

"No, no. I only need a moment to gather my courage." She inhaled a steadying breath. "I'm ready now."

Justin climbed out of the carriage and assisted her down to the curb. "I'll be here. If you're not back within twenty minutes, I'm coming to the door."

She nodded and, at last, released his hand. Their arrival had been remarked. The door to the house was already being opened by the earl's elderly butler, Netherby. At the sight of Helena, his usually bland expression brightened infinitesimally.

"My lady," he said, bowing.

"Netherby." She walked into the front hall, her gaze drifting over the familiar surroundings. "I trust you and the rest of the staff are well?"

Netherby glanced at the carriage before shutting the door. The Earl of Wolverton's crest was easily recognizable. "We have been making do in your absence, my lady. Might I inquire as to whether you will be returning to us?"

A pang of sadness caught her unaware. "No, Netherby. I won't be back. I've only come to see my uncle and then I'll be on my way." She permitted the butler to take her hat and gloves, but she didn't remove her paletot. There was a distinct chill in the air. "Where is he?"

"In his study, ma'am. Shall I announce you?"

"No need." She straightened her skirts and raised a hand to smooth her hair as she walked down the hall to the room that had, in years past, been her father's study and then her brother's. She didn't bother knocking before opening the polished wood-paneled door.

Uncle Edward was sitting behind his desk. He was a portly gentleman, gone fleshy from drink and indulgence. His graying hair was slicked with fragrant pomade, his side-whiskers worn long almost to his chin. A ruby stick-pin glittered in the folds of his cravat, blinking as he turned his head this way and that, removing papers from drawers and shuffling things about atop the desk. As he did so, a sheaf of tradesman's bills toppled over, fluttering to the floor.

He looked up, then, and saw her. His face went hard.

"Uncle," she said.

He stood. "Helena."

The familiar fear trickled through her veins. She reminded herself that Justin was right outside, prepared to come to her aid should it be necessary. The knowledge gave her an extra jolt of courage. Enough that she was able to remain outwardly calm as she walked slowly to the desk.

Uncle Edward's eyes darted to the door. "Where is this husband of yours I've been hearing so much about? Isn't he with you?"

"He's waiting for me in the carriage." she said. "Along with Lord Wolverton."

"Wolverton? The man's an infernal busybody. If I discover he's behind the tripe in this morning's paper—"

"You've read it? I did wonder." A paper wafted down at Helena's feet. She bent to retrieve it. "Your affairs appear to be somewhat in disarray."

He snatched the paper from her hand. "My affairs!" he sputtered. "You've announced to the world that I'm as good as bankrupt. You've libeled me. Slandered my good name. I'm ruined in London because of you. I've no choice now but to retire to the country."

"Permanently?"

"Oh, you'll not be rid of me that easily. I'll be consulting my attorneys in Hampshire, you may depend upon it. They'll bring suit. They'll force a retraction. And they'll shut down that damned fool newspaper. Mark my words."

She lifted her brows. "Will they really? My attorney has informed me that truth is an absolute defense to libel. And everything I told the newspaper was the truth. If you bring suit, you'll only prolong the scandal—and add to your humiliation."

His eyes flared with anger. "You greedy little witch. What need have you of all that money? All you had to do was sign the blasted paper. I'd have taken care of you. You'd have wanted for nothing. But no. You must have it all to yourself. You would not be content until you'd ruined my good name, and yours along with it."

Helena placed her hands on the edge of his desk. "You know all about greed, Uncle. You would have seen me die in an asylum in order to take my brother's fortune."

"Don't be absurd," he scoffed. "You know I'd never have gone through with it in the end. All I wanted was your signature. Had you given it, all that other nonsense would have stopped."

A rush of anger swept through her. "All that other nonsense left me black and blue all over. It left me chilled to the heart from ice baths and burned on my arms and legs from electrical shocks. It wasn't nonsense. It was systematic torture."

"It was legitimate medicine." His expression turned mulish. "But I would have put a stop to it if you'd done as I asked."

She shook her head. "I don't believe you."

"You should have believed me. You should have *trusted* me."

"You gave me no good cause."

"Poppycock! Haven't I always been kind to you? Generous?"

She didn't dispute the fact. Indeed, the generous gifts he'd brought her as a child were the only fond memories she had of her uncle. "Papa never wanted you to bring me gifts. I always thought he was being stern. Unfair. But that wasn't it at all, was it? He knew you had a problem with money. He knew you'd fritter your last penny away if left unchecked. Just as you would have done with Giles' fortune."

Uncle Edward's face reddened. "Giles is dead! He's been dead this year and more. What proof do you need? His rotting bones delivered to you in a velvet-lined box?"

His words flayed her like a whip. For an instant, she was tempted to turn and flee. Instead, she gripped the edge of his desk and leaned closer. "Giles may well be dead. But what right did that give you to do the things you did to me?"

"Every right." Uncle Edward drew himself up tall. "*I* am Castleton now. The family is in *my* charge. It was my duty to seek treatment for you. To see you made well again. And that is what I shall say to anyone who has the temerity to ask."

Her heart thumped wildly. "And *I* shall continue to tell them just what an unscrupulous blackguard you are. I shall keep telling them until you're expelled from your clubs. Until no hostess will receive you anywhere."

"You're a vindictive harpy," he said. "But at what price? You've ruined yourself as well. Or are you too stupid to realize it yet? Marrying some bastard ex-soldier from the back of beyond. Spewing private family business to an infernal newspaperman. If I didn't think you mad before, I know it now beyond all doubt."

Helena's voice lowered with sudden fierceness. "That ex-soldier is the finest gentleman I have ever known. You're not fit to polish his boots. As for myself—you may think of me what you will. You have no power over me any longer."

Uncle Edward eyed her warily as she removed her hands from his desk.

"I shall be going to the bank next," she informed him. "I will direct them to cut off your access to my accounts. Naturally, they may continue to apply to me for funds for the servants' wages and pensions, but from this day forward, the bank shall pay them directly. I no longer trust you to behave as a man with honor and I'll not have any of the Castleton servants suffer for your greed."

Her uncle began to sputter again, but she did not regard him.

"Now," she said briskly, "you may bring me my jewels. And see that you don't dawdle. My husband is not a patient man. It wouldn't take much provocation for him to serve you as he served Mr. Glyde."

Mere minutes later, Helena emerged from the house in Grosvenor Square, a footman at her heels carrying a large inlaid box. The day seemed brighter and the air fresher. The weight that had been on her shoulders these many months was lifted.

Gone. When she saw Justin standing beside the carriage, her face lit with a smile broader than any she'd ever given him.

"It's over," she said breathlessly. "I'm free."

Justin smiled back at her as he handed her up into the carriage. It was a strange, bittersweet smile. It didn't quite reach his eyes. "Are you?"

"Well, I shall be after we visit the bank. Unless... Do you suppose I should take Mr. Finchley along with me for that?"

"You have his letter. I daresay all that legal jargon he uses in it will be enough to make the bankers do your bidding."

Lord Wolverton leaned forward in his seat. "You appear unscathed."

"I'm perfectly well," she assured him.

"And Castleton?"

"He's leaving London. He intends to retire to Hampshire for the foreseeable future."

Lord Wolverton moved to disembark from the carriage. "I'll see that he does so." When she opened her mouth to protest, he forestalled her with an upraised hand. "I'll hear no objections. You've done what your conscience requires and so must I."

"Shall we wait for you?" Justin asked.

"No need. John Coachman will return for me."

Helena watched as Lord Wolverton ascended the steps to the house. Netherby promptly opened the door for him. Try as she might, she could muster no pity for her uncle. He deserved society's censure. And if that censure was to be administered in the form of a rebuke by Lord Wolverton, so much the better.

Justin climbed into the carriage beside her.

The footman followed him to the door, still holding the large box in his arms. "Where shall I put this, my lady?"

"Give it to me," Helena said. It was heavy. Almost too heavy for her to lift. "Thank you, James. Take care of yourself, won't you?"

He bowed, his cheeks reddening. "Yes, my lady."

"Another conquest?" Justin asked as the carriage started forward.

"Hardly. His mother is housekeeper at our estate in Hampshire. I've known him since he was a boy." She positioned the box more comfortably on her lap. "Look, Justin." She opened the lid.

Justin stared at the contents of the box. "Good God," he said under his breath. "I thought you were only collecting *your* jewels, not the entire family collection."

"Don't be silly. The entire collection belongs to the earldom. But these...these are mine." She reached in, withdrawing a sparkling brooch. The diamond at its center was as large as a quail's egg. "Some were presents from my father and brother, but most of them I inherited from my mother. She was an earl's daughter herself, you know."

"Of course she was," Justin said.

Helena glanced up from perusing her jewelry. "Is everything all right?"

"Fine. A slight headache, merely."

She closed the box. "My dear, you might have said something."

Justin turned his face away from her, his gaze fixing out the window. She had the impression she'd upset him, but she couldn't imagine how.

Perhaps he was suffering from more than a slight head-ache? He'd not been given much time to recover after his fight with Mr. Glyde. She would have to insist that he rest.

"Shall we forget the bank and go straight back to Half Moon Street?" She touched his arm only to feel it tense beneath her fingers.

"No," he said. "Let's finish this today. Let's put an end to it."

The rest of the week was spent in very much the same manner as the previous weeks, except now, instead of being on Justin's arm, she was on the arm of Mr. Finchley or Lord Wolverton. On Tuesday evening, Lord Wolverton escorted her to a performance of Shakespeare's *Othello* and on Thursday evening to a supper party at the home of his eldest daughter. During the day, Mr. Finchley accompanied her and Jenny on trips to museums and shopping excursions in Bond Street.

There had been no other invitations. Not to parties or dinners or musicales. Mr. Pelham's editorial was still the talk of London. And, though no one dared give her the cut direct while she was under the patronage of Lord Wolverton, no ladies had the courage to call on her in Half Moon Street. Indeed, she counted herself lucky to receive a subdued greeting from them in the street.

"The scandal will pass," Lord Wolverton promised. "As all scandals do."

In the meanwhile, she had to continue moving about in society with her spine straight and her head held high. Given time, she was confident she could weather the storm.

She'd be even more confident with Justin at her side. Unfortunately, his bruised face was still not fit for public view. While she was out and about in fashionable London, he remained in Half Moon Street, dealing with correspondence and, occasionally, sending and receiving telegrams. Whenever she queried him, he said it was merely business, but Helena had never known him to be so distracted. Indeed, he scarcely looked at her anymore.

Something between them had fundamentally changed. She could feel it as well as see it. The following Friday, she arrived back from a trip to the British Museum determined to confront him.

Mr. Finchley had tried to prolong their outing. He'd kept them busy studying the antiquities in the Egyptian Room and admiring the marbles in the Elgin Saloon. Each time she professed her intention to return home, he'd found another reason to keep them there. And when, at last, she'd insisted they leave, he hadn't appeared at all pleased. As their carriage pulled up in front of the little house in Half Moon Street, she finally understood why.

A hansom cab was parked outside, the jarvey waiting patiently on his perch. Mr. Jarrow was loading Justin's luggage into the cab.

Helena didn't wait for Mr. Finchley to hand her down from the carriage. She opened the door herself and stumbled out, her skirts nearly tangling in her legs. She didn't stop to query Mr. Jarrow. Instead, she ran straight into the house. She was only vaguely aware that Jenny and Mr. Finchley had remained behind. The sound of Jenny's voice—hot and fierce—floated after her.

"How dared you," she was saying to Mr. Finchley. "What sort of man are you?"

Helena didn't look back. Her heart was thumping at an extraordinary rate. The hall was empty of everyone save Mrs. Jarrow. Helena passed her without a word as she swiftly climbed up the stairs.

She found Justin in the parlor. He was standing over the little walnut desk in the corner, applying a red wax seal to a letter. His back was to the door, but she knew that he heard her enter the room. He went still for a moment, his shoulders tensing beneath the lines of his black frock coat.

"Where are you going?" she asked.

He slowly turned to face her. His expression was shuttered, but there was no disguising the hard set of his jaw and the grim resolution lingering at the back of his gaze. "I must return to Devon."

"Did something happen to Neville? Or Mr. Boothroyd?"

"No. They're both well. But I've been away far too long. I must go back."

"Yes, of course. Only allow me two minutes to pack a valise."

"No." There was steel in his voice. It stopped her where she stood.

"It won't take a moment."

"It doesn't matter how long it takes. You're not coming with me."

Helena stared at him in incomprehension. "You wish me to come later? After I've closed up the house?"

"No." A muscle flexed in his jaw. He turned back to the desk. "You're not coming at all. I'm traveling back alone. I was meant to go this morning, while you were at the museum.

Finchley thought it would be best for all concerned. But I couldn't do it. Not without taking proper leave of you."

"I don't understand. Are you returning to London directly? Is that it?" There was hope in her question, but the hope in her heart was rapidly disintegrating to dust. She went to him and touched his arm. "Won't you look at me?"

He grudgingly obliged her. But when his eyes met hers, her stomach sank with realization. His face was harder and more inscrutable than she'd ever seen it. He looked an absolute stranger. Cold and impatient. She knew then—she simply knew—that he was leaving her and never coming back.

"I wrote you a letter," he said. "It's here along with the legal documents he's drawn up."

"What legal documents? Is this about my inheritance?"

"This has nothing to do with money. It has to do with this arrangement between us. This…marriage. It was a mistake. There's a means to annul it. I've signed the necessary papers. Finchley can explain the details."

He offered her the letter and she took it, too numb with shock to do otherwise.

"I won't ask anything from you," he went on in the same businesslike tone. "Indeed, it's better we cease communication from this day forward. It will make it easier for the both of us to move on from all of this."

All of this. He meant their lives together. Their friendship. Their marriage.

She looked up at him, searching his face for some sign of emotion. "Why are you doing this?"

"I would think that's abundantly clear."

"Not to me, it isn't."

Justin gave a low growl of frustration. "Need I lay it out for you? We come from two different worlds. There's no reconciling them. Not now. Not ever."

"What does any of that matter? When we're back in Devon, at the Abbey—"

"You're not listening to me. I don't want you with me at the Abbey. As of this moment, you are no longer part of my life. If ever we meet again—an event which I think highly unlikely—it will be as polite and indifferent strangers. Which is exactly as it should be, my lady."

Helena pressed a hand to her midriff. Her breath hurt. It felt as if he'd struck her. "You said you wanted me." The mortifying words came out in the veriest whisper. Too faint to even inspire a blush in her cheeks.

His gaze slid away from hers. "As any man with blood in his veins would. You're a beautiful woman. There's nothing more to it than that. Had you more experience of men, you'd understand."

"But you and I are friends, aren't we? More than friends." She was beginning to sound desperate. God help her, she *was* desperate. "It was to be my decision. When the danger was past, when I was free to make a choice."

"We have nothing at all in common, my lady. A friendship is no more possible between us than any other sort of relationship." He inclined his head to her. "I wish you happy."

She caught his sleeve as he moved to leave. "You said you'd go to the ends of the earth for me."

"I have done. I went to Abbot's Holcombe. I came to London. Places I had no inclination to visit."

"Then why did you? Why did you do any of this?"

"Duty," he said. "But that's at an end now. Your uncle's gone. Wolverton's your ally. You're safe and free to continue your life as it was before." He gently removed her hand from his coat. "Goodbye, my lady."

Helena watched, eyes blurring with tears, as he crossed the parlor. "Wait!" she cried when he reached the door.

Justin stopped but didn't turn around.

She took a step forward. "What about my brother? Will you still make inquiries?"

He gave a curt nod of acknowledgment. "If I hear any news, I'll convey it through Finchley."

And then he was gone.

Helena sank blindly down into a chair. Her heart and lungs contracted in a misery of erratic beats and tortured breaths. It was a physical pain, unlike anything she'd ever experienced before.

He didn't love her. He didn't care for her at all.

A wrenching sob caught in her throat. She felt hot tears spill from her eyes. She bent her head, letting them fall unchecked. Only when she finally raised her hands to dash them away did she realize she was still clutching his letter. She stared at it, uncomprehending.

After a long moment, she wiped her eyes and opened it, but inside was nothing more than legal papers and a terse note from Justin saying only what he'd already said before.

Our marriage was a mistake.

I won't ask anything from you.

I wish you happy.

"I don't want to stay in that house," Helena said.

"No, indeed," Jenny agreed. "There are too many memories in Half Moon Street. But where shall we go?"

Helena linked her arm more firmly with Jenny's as they walked together along a gravel path in Green Park. It was a bright, clear morning and not as chilly as it had been in the days before. "I shall ask Lady Wolverton," she said. "She may know of a house nearer to Belgrave Square. Failing that…" She sighed, her gaze drifting over the stark, autumn landscape. "Perhaps we might take a long holiday somewhere?"

"Such as?"

"Somewhere warm. Somewhere far from here."

"You want to run away again."

"Nonsense. I simply don't wish to be reminded at every turn what a fool I was over a man."

Jenny gave her a brief look of commiseration. "I perfectly understand, my dear. But if every female in your circumstances was to leave the metropolis there'd scarcely be any women left in London. We all of us have made fools of ourselves over a gentleman at one time or another."

Helena couldn't prevent another sigh from escaping. It had been three weeks since Justin left her and her heart was still as heavy as it had been when she'd watched him walk out of the parlor—and out of her life forever.

"Did you care for him awfully?" Jenny asked.

"Dreadfully."

"I wish there was a magic potion I could brew up to take away the hurt. Something to make you forget him."

"Even if such a thing existed, I'm not certain I'd take it. I don't want to forget him. The pain of it helps me to remember."

"How maudlin!"

"It is rather."

"You're lovelorn, that's the trouble. The only cure for that is time, and lots of it."

Helena kicked at a stray pebble with the toe of her kid-leather half boot. "What do you suppose he's doing now?"

Jenny's lips tightened. "I hope he's wet, muddy, and miserable in that Abbey of his," she replied unkindly. "I hope his roof leaks, his wine turns to vinegar, and his cook boils all of his food to a mush. In short, I hope he rots. And Thomas Finchley may do the same."

"I do wish you'd forgive Mr. Finchley. All he's guilty of is supporting his friend. He and Justin are like brothers, you know."

"Forgive him? Ha!"

"Well, at least don't make a martyr of yourself on my account. I don't expect you to give Mr. Finchley up."

"I never had him," Jenny said. "Which works out very well, since I've lately discovered that I do not want him."

Helena sincerely wished she felt the same way about Justin. Unfortunately, his absence had done nothing to diminish her feelings. She wanted him as much now as she had when she'd first fallen in love with him.

"He knew all the time that Mr. Thornhill wished to dissolve your marriage," Jenny continued in tones of disgust. "He was busily drawing up documents and giving legal advice, all the while he squired us about town." She looked at Helena. "It was his idea that Mr. Thornhill slink away while we were at the museum."

"Yes. Justin said as much."

"I'm glad he didn't heed his advice. Though I don't know what's worse. Receiving a farewell letter or being told to your face that—" Jenny broke off, her attention diverted. "Who is that, I wonder?"

Helena followed her gaze.

In the distance, two fashionably dressed ladies approached on the path, their maids trailing a discreet length behind. Helena didn't recognize them. Not immediately. But as they drew closer, she saw it was the Viscountess Parkhurst and Lady Amelia Witherspoon. They acknowledged Helena with a polite bow.

"Lady Helena," Viscountess Parkhurst said coolly.

Helena inclined her head. "Lady Parkhurst. Lady Amelia."

The two ladies were no more than passing acquaintances. However, it was not lack of familiarity which made their exchange stilted and uncomfortable. The unfortunate fact was that, after three weeks, the scandal surrounding Mr. Pelham's editorial had still not completely abated. Most of the ladies and gentlemen Helena encountered during her outings weren't quite sure how to address her.

"A fine morning for walking, isn't it?" Lady Amelia inquired.

"Yes," Helena replied. "It's quite pleasant."

"A riveting conversation," Jenny remarked when the two ladies had moved on down the path.

Helena smiled slightly. "They haven't the vaguest idea what to say to me."

"They're a pair of ninnies."

"I won't complain. It could be much worse." That it hadn't been was largely due to the influence of Lord Wolverton. Taking their cue from his redoubtable countess, some of the older society ladies had lent Helena support. They'd invited her to tea or included her on their guest lists for dinners or recitals. Even more important, a few had willingly taken up the cause of reforms in private asylums. Nothing had been achieved as yet, but Helena had hopes.

"Yet another reason you shouldn't consider leaving London," Jenny said. "No matter how much your heart is breaking."

Helena wondered what state Justin's heart was in. "Do you know, all the time we were together, I truly thought he was growing to care for me, but the day he left—the things he said. He was so cold and so unfeeling. It was as if he was quite another person. As if he'd never felt any warmth or affection for me at all."

"Thornhill was always gruff and grim. In truth, my dear, I never understood what you saw in him. He was brave, I'll admit, and I quite admire how he dealt with Mr. Glyde, but other than that…" Jenny shook her head. "No. In the long term, Thornhill wouldn't have made a conformable husband. I say you're well rid of him."

"This was different. It wasn't mere gruffness. He was cold and cruel. He was never thus before. Never." Helena's brow furrowed. "Wait. That isn't precisely true."

"See? Just as I told you. An unfeeling brute. Indeed, if he's spoken to you in such a way more than once, you may be assured of his unpleasant disposition."

"Yes, he was cold with me once before, but it was—" Helena stopped suddenly. She dropped Jenny's arm. "Oh, Jenny! Why did I not remember this sooner?"

Jenny looked at her, her dark auburn brows raised in question.

"The day he spoke so coldly to me," Helena explained. "It was the first day we met. At the King's Arms in Devonshire. He said something exceedingly vulgar."

"Did he?" Jenny sunk her voice. "What was it, pray?"

Helena waved her hand. "It doesn't matter. Besides, I'd blush to repeat it." She turned and began walking briskly back the way they'd come. "I've been so blind. So stupid."

Jenny trotted after her. "Where are we going?"

"To Half Moon Street," Helena replied. "And then to Grosvenor Square."

"Grosvenor Square!" Jenny gaped. "Good lord, your uncle hasn't returned from Hampshire already, has he?"

"Not that I'm aware," Helena said. "But it isn't my uncle we're going to see."

Chapter Twenty-Three

North Devon, England
October, 1859

Nobility wasn't all it was cracked up to be. Justin had had ample proof of that in the weeks since he'd left Helena in London. He'd always heard that self-sacrifice was good for the soul. That virtue was its own reward, and so forth. But as he went about the daily business of his life in North Devon, all he felt was a crushing misery.

He could find no pleasure in his business dealings. No satisfaction in repairs to the Abbey. Even his daily gallops on Hiran failed to lift his spirits out of the gloom. He'd come to the grim realization that there was nothing for him without her.

Was this love? This aching desolation? As if an essential part of him had been ripped out, leaving behind a yawning emptiness that no amount of activity—or of drink—could ever hope to fill?

Whatever it was, he had to find a way to master it. To reduce it to more manageable proportions. But there seemed no conceivable method to overcome his loss. He wanted Helena. *Needed* Helena. And if something didn't change soon, there was a good chance he'd cast all his honorable intentions to the wind and make straight for London on the next train.

"I'm contemplating returning to India," he said to Boothroyd one morning as they reviewed his correspondence in the library. He was in his shirtsleeves, his face unshaven and his hair in wild disarray. He both looked and felt like hell.

Boothroyd paused in the act of sharpening his quill. "India, sir? What's brought this on?"

"What do you think?"

"Ah yes. I see. And I quite understand. But…if you'll forgive me, sir…there are simpler solutions than traveling halfway round the world."

"Such as?"

"You could find another wife."

Justin shot his steward a murderous glare.

"Yes, yes," Boothroyd said quickly, holding up his hand. "I meant no offense. But consider. Once your current marriage has been dissolved, we can place another advertisement and this time—"

"Have a care, Boothroyd," Justin said.

"It was merely a suggestion, sir."

"If you knew her as I do, you'd never dare make it."

"As you say. Her ladyship was a singular female. Which brings me to my next suggestion." Boothroyd laid aside his quill. "You could simply return to London, find her ladyship, and bring her back to the Abbey. You're her lawful husband. It's within your rights to do so."

"I've given up my rights over her, legal and otherwise. She's free of me for good. I'll not inflict my presence on her again."

"Might I inquire as to why?"

Justin didn't answer. Not directly. He strolled to the bank of windows and gazed out at the sea. "Are you happy here, Boothroyd?"

"At the Abbey, sir? Why, yes. I'm quite content."

"You don't stay merely out of a sense of responsibility?"

Boothroyd considered for a moment. "I do feel a measure of responsibility, as any good steward would. For the Abbey... and for you."

Justin glanced at Boothroyd over his shoulder. "You don't owe me anything. If you ever did, you've long since repaid it." He resumed staring out the window. "You need only say the word and I'll gladly arrange for your retirement somewhere on a generous pension."

"You've always been good to me, sir. But I'm not yet ready to be put out to pasture."

Justin's mouth tilted briefly in a humorless smile. "I confess I'm relieved to hear it. I'll need you here to see to things while I'm gone. Neville isn't helpless, but he requires looking after. And then there's the matter of the servants."

"Indeed, sir. The loss of Mrs. Standish is regrettable. Though one can't entirely fault her. She took the position believing you would have a wife in residence. Serving in a bachelor household was not at all to her taste."

Justin could muster no sympathy for the woman. She'd left soon after he returned from London. Not that it mattered much anymore. "Find someone else if you can. Someone who doesn't consider a houseful of men to be a threat to her virtue."

"I've begun to make inquiries, but there aren't many who care to live in such a remote location." Boothroyd hesitated before adding, "Now, if you were to reconcile with her ladyship, I daresay we may yet lure Mrs. Standish back to us."

Justin scowled. "Leave off, Boothroyd. I've done something noble. Permit me to suffer for it in my own way."

"By going back to India, of all places? After what happened to you there, I would have thought—"

"Yes, well…perhaps it's time to move on from all of that."

Boothroyd's brows shot up nearly to his hairline.

"We both of us have spent far too many years living in the past," Justin said. "There's been no room for anything else. No hope for something like a future."

"I'm sorry you feel that way, sir."

"Don't be. It's been a situation of my own making. No one forced me to return to Devon. To buy this house. At any time, I could have let the past go. But I wanted justice. There were times it was the only thing that got me through the night."

"You weren't the only one wronged by Sir Oswald. I had reasons to want justice, as well."

"It was a long time ago. Too long. I'm tired of looking backward. As for what happened in Cawnpore… It was a tragedy. I don't know if I can ever forgive myself for failing to protect those women. But I was happy there before the uprising. Or at least as happy as I can remember being before…"

"Before her ladyship's arrival?"

Justin stared out at the sea. He *had* been happy with her. Happier than he'd ever been in his life. He had no expectation he would ever be so again. But perhaps, someday, he might find a small measure of contentment. Until then…

"I need to put a continent between myself and Lady Helena," he said.

"And so, to India."

"There or somewhere else. One place is as good as another. Make the arrangements. I can take passage on the next steamer out of Marseilles, if it comes to that." Justin turned from the window. "And now…" He collected his coat. "I'm going to the Inn in King's Abbot, where I intend to drink myself into oblivion."

Helena stood in the doorway of the King's Arms, feeling the most extraordinary sense of déjà vu. Not long ago she'd stood in this exact same place, wearing this exact same gray striped-silk traveling gown, and gazed out over the crowded taproom. It didn't look so different now. The same men huddled about the tables. The same scent of ale, meat pies, and unwashed male skin lingered in the air. And, across the room, the same tall, brooding gentleman leaned against the counter, nursing his drink.

Justin.

Her heart gave a few hard, hopeful thumps.

She navigated her way through the tables, her skirts brushing the legs of seated gentlemen as she passed them. The innkeeper, Mr. Blevins, was refilling someone's tankard of ale. She caught his eye as she stepped into the empty space beside Justin at the counter. "I beg your pardon, sir. Might I bespeak the private parlor for an hour or two?"

Justin's entire frame went rigid.

"Help yourself, my lady," Mr. Blevins said.

She turned her head to look at Justin and found him staring down at her with a look of such incredulity one might think she was an apparition who'd just materialized next to him out of the ether. His black hair was rumpled, as if he'd been raking his hands through it, and his cheeks were shadowed with stubble. He looked tired and despairing and heartbreakingly dear.

"Hello," she said.

A frown darkened his brow. "What are you doing here?"

"I came to see you, of course."

"All the way from London?" He stood up to his full height. "Has something happened with your uncle?"

"No," she said quickly. "As far as I know, he' still in Hampshire. He's made no attempt to contact me."

The look of worry receded from Justin's face, only to be replaced with the same shuttered expression he'd worn on the day he'd rejected her so cruelly. "How did you know I'd be here?"

Helena refused to be intimidated by the coldness in his voice. "Mr. Boothroyd told me."

"You've been to the Abbey?"

"Naturally. We went there first."

"*We?*"

"I'll explain everything, but I'd rather not do it in full public view. Will you accompany me to the private parlor? We can speak there without an audience. Unless you'd rather—"

"Come." He took her by the arm and escorted her across the taproom. He wasn't rough, but she nevertheless felt like a willful child being hauled back to the schoolroom by a stern tutor.

The private parlor was just as she remembered. The same little table where she'd sat with Mr. Boothroyd and the same chairs round the fire where she'd once served Justin tea.

He let go of her when they crossed the threshold. She heard him shut the door behind her, but she didn't turn to face him until she'd removed her bonnet, gloves, and mantle and disposed of them on an empty chair.

Justin stood by the door, watching her. "Explain yourself."

Helena had a brief moment of doubt. His face was so hard, his posture so unwelcoming. What if she'd been mistaken? What if—

But she refused to believe it. She made herself walk slowly to the wooden table. She stopped behind one of the slatted chairs, her hands coming to rest on its back. "We sat here together that first day. Do you remember?"

He folded his arms. "Helena, I thought I made myself clear in London."

Helena pressed on as if she hadn't heard him. "I told you that I was very sorry you'd been burned. And you said…" She moistened her lips. "Do you remember what you said?"

His jaw tensed. "Something crass. What difference does it make?"

"Yes, it was very crass. Indeed, it was quite the most shocking thing anyone has ever said to me. Had I not been so desperate, I would have fled there and then." Her hands tightened on the back of the chair. "Later, at the hotel, I asked why you'd said such a thing. Do you remember?"

Justin looked away from her. "Helena—"

"You said that you knew I was too good for you. That you were trying to be noble."

"I don't see the point of going over all of this—"

"The point is," she said, "I don't need you to be noble. I only need you to be mine."

His gaze slid back to hers. The cold mask he wore was beginning to crack, deep emotion struggling to break through.

A rush of elation almost stole her breath. She'd been right. He did care for her after all.

She dropped her hands from the chair and took a step toward him. "Your bruises are healing nicely."

"It's been several weeks."

"How well I know it." Another step brought her closer. "Have you been reading the news from London?"

He shook his head.

"Mr. Pelham's editorial has caused a bit of an uproar, just as Mr. Finchley predicted. *The Times* has run a series of their own on private asylums. Parliament has shown no inclination to act, as yet, but I have hopes they will. I've been contributing funds to the cause. It's become a sort of charitable project of mine."

Justin didn't say anything. He merely looked at her, emotion warring in his smoke-gray gaze, as she advanced upon him.

"I've had to keep myself busy, you see. I've been so unhappy. Indeed, the day you left me in London, I wept for the first time in nearly a year. I thought my heart was broken."

At the mention of her tears, Justin's mask cracked a little more.

She stopped in front of him, so close that her skirts bunched against his legs. "I've been fretting about what I would say to you for the entirety of the journey here. But now that I see you—now that I'm standing here, looking at you once more—all I can think to tell you is that you may be as cold and indifferent to me as you please, but I'm not going anywhere."

"Helena…"

"I won't agree to dissolve our marriage, or to live apart from you. If you want to be rid of me, you shall have to sue for divorce. Though I warn you, it would be the scandal of the decade and likely ruin us both."

"You don't know what you're saying."

"I know my own mind, Justin. I'm not the same frightened creature I was when we met."

"I realize that," he said with sudden gruffness. "You're much stronger now. If you weren't, I'd never have—" He broke off abruptly, pushing his fingers through his hair in visible frustration. He turned and went to the fireplace, his back to her. "You shouldn't have come here."

"Nonsense. Greyfriar's Abbey is my home now. Where else in the world should I be?"

He muttered something under his breath. It sounded rather like an oath. She couldn't quite make it out. And then he laughed. A short, bitter laugh. "Greyfriar's Abbey. Do you know how many years I planned and schemed to own that cursed place? I wanted it, beyond all thought. Beyond all reason. I believed I deserved it. And I thought that by taking it, the emptiness within me would be…I don't know. Filled or eradicated. Something."

She came to stand behind him.

"And now it's mine. That magnificent, miserable house, which has never once made me happy." He stared into the cold fireplace for a long moment. "The wanting I felt for the Abbey is but a pale shadow of the wanting I feel for you."

Her pulse beat heavy at her throat. "Then why did you try to drive me away? Are you afraid I won't make you happy either?"

367

"How could I be happy when I know I'd be destroying the one thing—the one person—I care about most in all the world?" He turned to face her. And the mask was gone. Vanished. In its place was stark vulnerability. "I've not been a good man, Helena. I've been selfish in my need. Ruthless and unforgiving. But with you…" He shook his head. "I can't be that man anymore."

"I love whatever kind of man you are."

He gave her an arrested look. "What did you say?"

"I said that I love you, exactly as you are." A warm blush flooded her cheeks. She couldn't tell in what spirit he was receiving her declaration. He appeared dumbstruck, gazing down at her as if she'd just said something to him in an as-yet-undiscovered language. "I realized it in London," she continued determinedly. "Indeed, I almost told you after that dreadful *comedietta*. It's the last secret I've been keeping from you." She set her hands against his chest. "I give it to you now with all my heart."

She loved him.

Justin stared down at Helena's face, his gaze tracing over every contour. The sweep of her mahogany brows, the creamy curve of her cheekbones, and the bow of her rose-colored lips. He must have misheard her. Perhaps he was drunk? Either that or hallucinating. Indeed, her very presence—here at the inn, garbed in the same dress she'd worn the day they'd met—had a dreamlike quality. As if she'd been conjured by his fevered imagination. She didn't seem quite real. And yet…

He could smell the delicate jasmine in her perfume and the light starch in her petticoats. Could feel the weight and warmth of her slim hands as they rested on his chest. He'd thought himself resigned to never seeing her again. To continuing his life without her. But one look—one touch—and the feelings rushed back again, stinging at his eyes and clenching in his chest.

Good God, *she loved him*.

He covered her hands with his own. "Helena...I don't know what to say."

"That's easy. Say that you love me, too."

He bowed his head, his forehead coming to rest against hers. "Of course I love you," he said, his voice a husky growl. "Why in blazes do you think I let you go?"

A choked laugh escaped her. It sounded a little like a sob. "What tortured logic is this?"

"It's your logic."

"Mine?"

He tightened his grip on her hands. "You told me that if you loved someone, you'd sacrifice anything to make them happy."

"Is that what you've done? Made a sacrifice of your love for me?" She returned the warm clasp of his fingers. "My dear, how in the world could you ever think I'd be happy without you?"

My dear. His heart turned over. But he couldn't allow himself to be distracted. Not now. He had to maintain some semblance of control. "I'm no gentleman, Helena, and King's Abbott is a fair way from the glitter of London. You deserve better. You should be with someone of your own kind."

"I'm not an exotic bird, Justin. I'm a woman."

"You're a lady. And I'd be the most self-centered bastard alive to keep you here with me."

Helena drew back from him with a sigh. "I suspected it was something of that nature."

"Then you understand why I had to give you up."

"You're not giving me up," she said. "Or, rather, I'm not giving you up."

He searched her face, his heart thudding with something very like hope. "What are you saying?"

"I'm saying that self-sacrifice is all well and good, but unlike you, when it comes to our marriage, I intend to be selfish." She rose up on the toes of her half boots, reaching to slide her arms around his neck. She looked him very steadily in the eye. "You're mine, Justin Thornhill. It doesn't matter where you came from or who your parents were. All that matters is that you belong to me...and I belong to you."

The last of his resolve crumbled to dust. "Yes," he vowed. "Yes. Always." And then he swept her up in his arms and kissed her.

Helena clung to his neck as his mouth moved on hers, returning his kiss in full measure. She was sweet and soft—and fiercely passionate. She held nothing of herself back.

And neither did he.

He kissed her deeply. Thoroughly. Heedless of all propriety. She arched against him, warm and feminine. Her heavy skirts were crushed out of shape against his legs, the hard bones of her corset stiff and unyielding beneath the spread of his hand at her waist. His other hand cradled the back of her head. He vaguely registered the sound of metal pins pinging on the parlor floor as his fingers speared through her fashionably rolled coiffure.

"You're disarranging me awfully," she breathed.

"Shall I stop?"

"No." She pressed a soft kiss to his mouth. "Don't dare." And then another. "I've missed you so much."

He groaned. "Helena…I want you more than life."

"I'm yours," she promised. "Forever."

He stared down into her eyes. "What a fool I've been."

"You have, rather."

"I never meant to hurt you."

"I know that."

"The day I left London…Those things I said to you…"

"Please don't refine on it. Not now." She tugged at his neck. "I'd much prefer you kiss me again."

He gave a sudden huff of laughter. "You would, would you?" He bent his head and brushed his lips over hers with infinite tenderness. "Like this?"

"*Yes.*"

He put his other arm around her waist and slowly backed toward one of the large chairs near the fireplace. He stopped kissing her only long enough to lower himself into the seat and pull her down onto his lap. "Much better." And then he kissed her again.

When at last they broke apart, they were both flushed and breathless.

"Goodness," she said. "Someone might have walked in on us."

Justin glanced at the door. "They may still. Shall I let you up?"

"No, thank you. I'm quite comfortable here."

He gathered her close. "You fit very well in my arms."

"Naturally. We're perfect for each other."

"Fated to be together, isn't that right? Which reminds me…" He briefly released her waist to fumble at the front of his coat. "I have something for you."

"For me? But how? You didn't know I'd be here…" Her voice trailed away as he withdrew a piece of sea glass from his waistcoat pocket. It was a brilliant shade of glossy blue, shaped more like a precious stone than the remnant of a broken bottle worn down by the sand and the surf.

"I found it on the beach this morning when I was riding Hiran. I've never seen a piece so blue. For a moment, I thought it was a sapphire. A remnant of the monk's buried treasure, perhaps."

"Oh, Justin. It's beautiful."

"It made me think of you. Of the first day we walked together on the beach. Do you remember?"

"How could I forget? I still have the piece of sea glass you gave me then. It's in my jewel case."

"This one is yours, too." He dropped it into the palm of her hand. "To add to your collection."

She examined it closely. "Such a fascinating thing, sea glass. It starts its journey so humbly. And then, with time—"

"A great deal of time."

"How much?"

"A decade or more, I'd guess."

"And then it's transformed into something new. Something extraordinary." She looked at him. "What would you have done with it if I hadn't come back?"

"I don't know. I scarcely knew what I was going to do with myself." He smoothed a stray lock of hair from her face. "Yet another reason I'm so very glad you're here. I'm relying on you to tell me what happens next."

"Am I to decide?"

"I suspect you have a plan."

"It's not a very complicated one." She ran the backs of her fingers along the edge of his jaw. "I didn't come to Devon alone. Jenny is with me. I left her at the Abbey to supervise the servants."

"We haven't many of those at the moment. Mrs. Standish deserted us three weeks ago."

"Mr. Boothroyd said as much. But it doesn't matter. I've brought plenty of servants with me. A butler, three maids, and two footmen, to be precise. There were several more at my uncle's townhouse who were anxious to get away, but I didn't like to deprive him of his entire staff all at once."

Justin's lips twitched. "You took his servants."

"He won't miss them. Besides, we needed them more. We're going to restore the Abbey to its former glory. I'm going to make it into a proper home for us."

"A thankless task."

"Not in the least. We'll be grateful for it and so will Neville and Mr. Boothroyd, and our children, too, whenever they arrive." She curved her hand around his neck. The warmth in her gaze made his stomach tremble. "A home, Justin. Yours and mine."

"Anywhere you are is my home."

Her eyes glistened. "What a perfectly lovely thing to say."

"It's the truth. I've been in hell without you, Helena. Good God, today I actually contemplated returning to India."

She frowned. "Yes, I know. Mr. Boothroyd told me."

Justin's brows lowered. "Did he?"

"You must forgive him divulging your secrets. The poor gentleman. He was terribly worried for you—and ever so happy to see me. Even Jonesy and Paul looked relieved." She twined her fingers through the hair at his nape. "My darling, you've been in a dreadful mood, haven't you? Impossible to live with."

He nuzzled her cheek. "I daresay you'll remedy that."

Helena laughed. "Do you know," she said as she drew his mouth to hers for another soft kiss, "I do believe I shall."

Epilogue

*H*elena teetered precariously on the topmost step of the ladder, reaching to affix the final candle on the Christmas tree. It was an enormous pine, tall and full, with sappy branches that stretched out to tangle in her velvet skirts. A glittering tinsel star crowned its head. "I almost have it," she said. "Almost…"

Neville held the old wooden ladder steady. "Be careful."

"I'm being exceedingly careful. It's this dratted candle that won't cooperate. Do we have any more bits of wire? If you could look in the basket—"

"I leave the hall for five minutes and this is what I find on my return." Justin's voice sounded from the doorway. He'd been helping them decorate, but when the afternoon post had arrived, he'd taken one look at it and abruptly retreated to the library.

She glanced at him over her shoulder. "Is everything all right?"

"No, it's not all right." Justin strode across the hall, taking Neville's place at the base of the ladder. "Come down from there, my dear, before you break your neck."

She grasped her skirts in her hand, holding them out of the way as she began to climb down. She'd descended no more than two steps when Justin's hands closed round her waist and lifted her the rest of the way to the floor.

"I wasn't in any danger," she assured him.

He gave her a stern look. "You should have waited for me."

"It's the last tree candle, Justin," Neville explained. "We're putting it in the empty spot."

"There's an empty spot?" Justin cast a dubious glance around the hall. "Where? We've covered every conceivable surface in the Abbey."

Helena couldn't argue the point. In the past week, she'd become somewhat obsessed with decorating for the upcoming holiday. Every room was adorned with festive greenery, winterberries, and ribbon bows. Justin and Neville had never had a proper Christmas before and she was determined to deliver one to them with all the trimmings.

"What was it that came in the post?" she asked. "Was it bad news?"

"It was a letter from India."

Her pulse quickened. "About Giles?"

"Come into the library with me for a moment. We can discuss things there. And Neville? Don't dare climb up that ladder while we're gone. It's not fit for kindling."

His hand at the small of her back, Justin guided her into the library and shut the door behind them. They went to the window embrasure and sat down.

"The letter was from Simon Harding," he said. "You recall my mentioning him?"

Helena nodded. Mr. Harding and his wife were friends of Justin's from his early days in India. They were fairly well-connected, with contacts in both the British and native communities. At Justin's request, Mr. Harding had agreed to do a little investigating. "Has he found out anything?"

"It may be nothing. Then again…it could be significant. It involves the officer who witnessed your brother's death. The one on whose evidence your uncle inherited the title."

"Colonel Anstruther?"

"Harding says there may have been bad blood between Anstruther and your brother." Justin paused. "It's rather indelicate."

"How do you mean?"

"It involves Anstruther's wife. Apparently, she and your brother were rumored to be lovers."

Helena drew back in surprise. She'd known her brother enjoyed the company of beautiful women. He was a handsome fellow with a disposition to flirt. But adultery was quite something else. And with a fellow officer's wife? "Giles would never have been so stupid. And even if he was, what could it possibly have to do with any of this?"

"Probably nothing," Justin said. "Then again…it may call Anstruther's identification of your brother's body into question."

A miniscule spark of hope kindled in Helena's breast. "Is that what Mr. Harding thinks?"

"He doesn't give an opinion. But he says, if we like, he can arrange to speak with Anstruther. To ask him a few questions."

"I would like that," she said. "Very much."

"In all likelihood it will only confirm what's already been reported. That your brother died during the siege. But there's a very small chance that Harding will learn something new.

He has a sense for people. It's one of the reasons he's been so successful in business."

"How soon can he speak with Colonel Anstruther?"

"Not until early spring. Anstruther's retired to Delhi, and Harding won't be back that way until April. Do you mind waiting?"

"Not at all. I'm grateful he's undertaken so much on my behalf."

"Harding's a good man."

She moved to rise. "I must write him a letter, thanking him."

He caught her hand. "You needn't do it right now. Indeed, you needn't do anything." His fingers twined through hers. "Leave the rest of the decorating to Miss Holloway and Neville. It feels an age since I've been alone with you."

"An age? Since this morning?" She smiled. "My darling, what a novel concept of time you have."

He bent his head and kissed her. Softly, softly. "How I adore your little endearments. They make me want to take you straight back to bed."

She laughed, even as a blush heated her cheeks. In the past two months, they'd spent endless hours in the great Elizabethan bed, learning each other. She knew the shape of him now. The warmth and weight of his body and the texture of his sun-bronzed skin. She knew the very beat of his heart. During their most intimate moments, it thumped in rhythm with her own.

"I do love you," she said.

Justin gazed down at her. Intense emotion glimmered in the depths of his gray eyes. "I love you more."

She stroked his cheek. "Impossible."

His mouth hitched in a sudden half smile. "Shall we argue over it?"

"I haven't the strength. I'm exhausted from all this decorating."

"Didn't I warn you it was too large an undertaking? Even with the servants—"

"It makes no matter now. We're almost finished. And you must admit how well everything looks. The holly and the ivy and the candles on the tree." She scratched her fingertips through his afternoon stubble. "Just you wait, my love. I'm going to give you a Christmas season to remember."

He covered her hand with his. "You already have."

She melted a little at his words. It was all so new to him, being loved and cared for. She felt it every time she kissed or caressed him. Every time she lay tangled in his arms. He was drinking her in. Allowing her love for him to blot out the darkness of his past. "Are you disappointed that Mr. Finchley won't be here for the holidays?"

"He might come next month. After Miss Holloway's left us."

Helena sighed. "I wish she wouldn't go."

"She's a creature of London."

"I suppose. She's never been entirely happy in the country. And now I've settled some money on her, she's anxious to return to London and start her life there."

"Does she know the terms of her independence?"

Helena bit her lip. "No. I haven't explained the details yet."

Justin quite pointedly said nothing. He didn't approve of her meddling, but he loved her too much to forbid it.

"Do you think she'll be terribly unhappy with me?" Helena asked.

"If I said yes, would you leave the pair of them alone?"

"I'm not matchmaking. Truly I'm not. It's only that…if left to her own devices, Jenny would never forgive him. She doesn't tolerate any nonsense."

"There isn't much nonsense about Finchley. But you must have realized by now that he's not a typical attorney. He solves problems for his clients. He fixes things that need fixing."

"He's secretive."

"Necessarily so. He's often employed by powerful people. The actions he takes on their behalf aren't always strictly legal."

Helena considered. "I don't know if he's right for Jenny, or she for him. But I won't have the demise of their friendship on my conscience."

"It shouldn't be. I'm the one who had Finchley draw up those annulment papers. At the time, I thought—"

"I know what you thought."

He grimaced. "It was damned foolish of me."

"Now *that* we can agree on." She stretched up to press a kiss to his mouth. His arms circled around her, drawing her close against his chest.

"Are you happy, sweetheart?"

"Mmm. More than happy. So much more." Helena settled into his embrace. "You make me feel strong, Justin. Indeed, when I'm with you, I feel brave enough to face the world."

His lips brushed over her temple. She felt him smile. "We'll face it together, love," he said.

And so they did.

The End

Author's Notes

The Matrimonial Advertisement was inspired by two real life events from the late 1850s.

The editorial that Mr. Pelham writes for the fictional *London Courant* is a paraphrased version of an actual editorial which ran in *The London Times* on August 19, 1858. It addressed abuses in private asylums and revealed, among other disturbing facts, just how often sane people were committed by greedy relatives who were trying to gain control of their money.

The victims in these cases were generally members of the upper classes. When coupled with fictional accounts, such as the case of wrongful confinement outlined in Wilkie Collins 1859 novel *The Woman in White*, it was enough to send a chill through fashionable society. How often, peopled wondered, were sane men and women locked away and tortured with barbaric treatments until they were, in fact, mad? It was a situation almost too grim to contemplate.

Unfortunately, the editorial in *The Times* (and the newspaper articles that followed) effected no significant change in the management of private asylums. They were the province of the very wealthy and, as such, less subject to reform than public institutions.

The second true-life event referenced in *The Matrimonial Advertisement* is the Cawnpore Massacre. Also known as the Bibighar Massacre, it took place during the Indian Rebellion of 1857. What Justin describes happening as he escorted the women and children to the River Ganges really did occur. The rebel sepoys swept in, set fire to the boats, slaughtered the British soldiers, and took the women and children hostage. The hostages were later killed in a manner which shocked the Victorian public—and provoked a brutal retaliation from the relieving forces.

If you'd like to learn more about the Bibighar Massacre, or any of the other people, places, and events which feature in my novels, please visit the blog portion of my author website at MimiMatthews.com.

*A*cknowledgments

I owe tremendous thanks to those who helped to bring *The Matrimonial Advertisement* to life.

To my wonderful British and American beta readers, Sarah, Flora, and Lauren, thank you for your time, your generosity, and your immensely helpful feedback. I'm so grateful to you all for reading this book in its earliest stages. And so quickly, too!

To my brilliant editor, Deb Nemeth, thank you for all of your thoughtful comments and suggestions. Your advice was, as always, both insightful and invaluable.

To my talented—and very patient—formatter, Colleen Sheehan, thank you for making the interior of my books look so lovely.

To fellow historical romance authors Lena Goldfinch and Jayne Fresina, thank you for being so kind and so very gracious. Your encouragement means the world.

To the amazing team at Smith Publicity, especially Emma and Corinne, thank you for your efforts on behalf of my Victorian romances. Your enthusiasm and professionalism is so very much appreciated.

To my fabulous friends, fans, and followers across social media and print, thank you for your readership. Your messages and reviews inspire me to keep writing, even when things get difficult.

And, finally, to my parents, thank you for absolutely everything—especially for babysitting my noisy dogs so I could finish this book in peace!

About the Author

*U*SA *Today* bestselling author Mimi Matthews writes both historical non-fiction and traditional historical romances set in Victorian England. Her articles on nineteenth century history have been published on various academic and history sites, including the *Victorian Web* and the *Journal of Victorian Culture,* and are also syndicated weekly at *BUST Magazine*. In her other life, Mimi is an attorney. She resides in California with her family, which includes an Andalusian dressage horse, two Shelties, and a Siamese cat.

To learn more, please visit
www.MimiMatthews.com

OTHER TITLES BY
Mimi Matthews